# CURSE OF STRAHD

# CREDITS

**Lead Designer:** Christopher Perkins
**Creative Consultants:** Tracy and Laura Hickman
**Designers:** Adam Lee, Richard Whitters, Jeremy Crawford
**Managing Editor:** Jeremy Crawford
**Editor:** Kim Mohan
**Editorial Assistance:** Scott Fitzgerald Gray
**D&D Lead Designers:** Mike Mearls, Jeremy Crawford

**Art Director:** Kate Irwin
**Additional Art Direction:** Shauna Narciso, Richard Whitters
**Graphic Designer:** Emi Tanji
**Cover Illustrator:** Ben Oliver
**Interior Illustrators:** Dave Allsop, François Beauregard, Mark Behm, Eric Belisle, Zoltan Boros, Jedd Chevrier, Daarken, Lake Hurwitz, Chuck Lukacs, Howard Lyon, Ben Oliver, Adam Paquette, Rob Rey, Chris Seaman, Richard Whitters, Kieran Yanner
**Cartographers:** François Beauregard, Mike Schley, Ben Wootten

**Project Managers:** Neil Shinkle, Heather Fleming
**Product Engineer:** Cynda Callaway
**Imaging Technicians:** Sven Bolen, Carmen Cheung, Kevin Yee
**Prepress Specialist:** Jefferson Dunlap

**Other D&D Team Members:** Greg Bilsland, Chris Dupuis, David Gershman, John Feil, Trevor Kidd, Christopher Lindsay, Shelly Mazzanoble, Ben Petrisor, Hilary Ross, Liz Schuh, Matt Sernett, Nathan Stewart, Greg Tito

*Disclaimer: Wizards of the Coast cannot be held liable for any long-term side effects of venturing into the dread realm of Ravenloft, such as lycanthropy, vampirism, a fear of dead things, a fear of living things, an inability to sleep without a nightlight on and a +5 holy avenger under your pillow, and the unsettling suspicion that Strahd is too clever to be so easily defeated and that this is all just part of some grand scheme of his to extend his power beyond Barovia. You didn't think you could escape unless he wanted you to, did you?*

This book is based on the 32-page D&D adventure *Ravenloft* published in 1983 by TSR, Inc. Here are that book's credits:

**Designers:** Tracy and Laura Hickman
**Editor:** Curtis Smith
**Graphic Designer:** Debra Stubbe
**Illustrator:** Clyde Caldwell
**Cartographer:** David C. Sutherland III

The following D&D books also provided material and inspiration:

Cordell, Bruce R. and James Wyatt. *Expedition to Castle Ravenloft.* 2006.
Elrod, P.N. *I, Strahd: The Memoirs of a Vampire.* 1993.
Hickman, Tracy and Laura. *Rahasia.* 1984.
Nesmith, Bruce with Andria Hayday. *Realm of Terror.* 1990.
Pozas, Claudio. "Fair Barovia." *Dungeon* 207. 2012.
TSR, Inc. *Van Richten's Monster Hunter's Compendium, Volume One.* 1999.
———. *Van Richten's Monster Hunter's Compendium, Volume Three.* 2000.

**Playtesters:** Robert Alaniz,* Mal A'menz,* Glen Ausse, Jerry Behrendt, Teddy Benson, Anthony Caroselli,* Christopher D'Andrea,* Jason Fransella,* Jeff Galper, Elyssa Grant, Steve Heitke, Mary Hershey, Sterling Hershey, Justin Hicks, Shaun Horner, Donald Jacobs, James Krot, Yan Lacharité,* Jonathan Longstaff,* Michael LeClair, Ray Lillard, Eric Lopez, J.M., Matt Maranda,* Cris McDaniel, Randy Merkel, Lou Michelli,* Mike Mihalas,* Daniel Norton,* Lucas Pierce, Claudio Pozas,* John Proudfoot,* Rob Quillen II, Karl Resch,* Jason Riley, Sarah Riley, Arthur Severance,* Sam Sherry,* Zach Sielaff, David "Oak" Stark,* Jayson Thiry, Steve Townshend,* Kyle Turner,* Will Vaughn, Peter Youngs

*This playtester provided feedback for a group.*

## ON THE COVER

The master of Ravenloft is having guests for dinner, and you are invited. Ben Oliver sheds light on the vampire Strahd von Zarovich, whose dark past is a tale to be told, and whose evil knows no bounds.

620B6517001001 EN
ISBN: 978-0-7869-6598-4
First Printing: March 2016

9 8 7 6

$\mathsf{C}\,\mathsf{E}$

# Contents

# FOREWORD: RAVENLOFT REVISITED

E TURNED THE CORNER, AND THERE WAS a vampire.

I groaned and rolled my eyes.

It was 1978, and I was playing in one of my first dungeon adventures. It was being run by a friend I had known in high school, John Scott Clegg, and it was typical of the type of adventure that people played in those days. It was all about exploring a hodgepodge collection of rooms connected by dungeon corridors, beating up the monsters that we encountered, searching for treasure, and gaining experience points.

Now we were face to face with random encounter number thirty-four: a vampire. Not a Vampire with a capital V, but a so-many-Hit-Dice-with-such-and-such-an-Armor-Class lowercase vampire. Just another monster in the dungeon.

I remember thinking at the time, What are *you* doing here? This creature seemed completely out of place with the kobolds, orcs, and gelatinous cubes we had seen thus far. This was a creature who deserved his own setting and to be so much more than just a wandering monster. When I came home from that game, I told all these thoughts to Laura.

That was when Strahd von Zarovich was born.

Strahd would be no afterthought—he demanded his own setting, his own tragic history. Laura and I launched into researching the mythology and folklore surrounding the vampire. We started with the vague, black-and-white image of Bela Lugosi in 1931, but found so much more.

The first "modern" literary foundation of the vampire was penned by John William Polidori based on a fragment of a story by Lord Byron. It was while at the Villa Diodati—a rented house next to Lake Geneva, Switzerland—that Byron and Polidori met Mary Wollstonecraft Godwin and her husband-to-be, Percy Shelley. One night in June, Byron suggested that they each write a ghost story. Mary Shelley's contribution to the effort would later become *Frankenstein*. The short story "The Vampyre," published in 1819, was Polidori's contribution. He was Byron's personal physician, and the first of the so-called "romantic" vampires under Polidori's hand was actually modeled after Lord Byron.

Byron—like the fictional vampires that he inspired, from Polidori's Lord Ruthven down through the penultimate work of Bram Stoker—was a decadent predator, an abuser hidden behind a romantic veil. He was a comely and alluring monster—but a monster nevertheless. The romantic vampire of the earliest years of the genre was not just a spouse abuser but a spouse killer, the archetype of abuse in the worst kind of destructive codependency.

For Laura and me, those were the elements that truly defined Strahd von Zarovich—a selfish beast forever lurking behind a mask of tragic romance, the illusion of redemption that was ever only camouflage for his prey.

Initially we were going to title the adventure *Vampyr*—one of a series of games we called Nightventure that Laura and I were self-publishing back in 1978. The castle was called Ravenloft, and when Halloween came around each year, our friends asked us if we could play "that Ravenloft game" again ... and so the better title won out. It was, in part, because of this design that I was hired by TSR, Inc., to write DUNGEONS & DRAGONS adventures in 1982. Soon thereafter, I6 *Ravenloft* was published.

Since then, fans of *Ravenloft* have seen many different creative perspectives on Barovia (a country which, by absolute coincidence, is featured in a 1947 Bob Hope movie called *Where There's Life*). It continues to be one of the most popular DUNGEONS & DRAGONS adventures of all time. In its various incarnations, each designer has endeavored to bring something new to the ancient legend of Strahd, and to each of them we are grateful.

But the vampire genre has taken a turn from its roots in recent years. The vampire we so often see today exemplifies the polar opposite of the original archetype: the lie that it's okay to enter into a romance with an abusive monster because if you love it enough, it will change.

When Laura and I got a call from Christopher Perkins about revisiting *Ravenloft*, we hoped we could bring the message of the vampire folktale back to its original cautionary roots. The talented team at Wizards of the Coast not only graciously took our suggestions but engaged us in a dialogue that delivered new insights on the nightmare beyond the gates of Barovia.

Now we invite you again as our guests to pass through the Svalich Woods if you dare. For here the romance is tragically dangerous ... and a true monster smiles at your approach.

Tracy Hickman
May 2015

# Introduction

**U**NDER RAGING STORM CLOUDS, A LONE figure stands silhouetted against the ancient walls of Castle Ravenloft. The vampire Count Strahd von Zarovich stares down a sheer cliff at the village below. A cold, bitter wind spins dead leaves about him, billowing his cape in the darkness.

Lightning splits the clouds overhead, casting stark white light across him. Strahd turns to the sky, revealing the angular muscles of his face and hands. He has a look of power—and of madness. His once handsome face is contorted by a tragedy darker than the night itself.

Rumbling thunder pounds the castle spires. The wind's howling increases as Strahd turns his gaze back to the village. Far below, yet not beyond his ken, a party of adventurers has just entered his domain. Strahd's face forms a twisted smile as his dark plan unfolds. He knew they were coming, and he knows why they have come—all according to his plan. He, the master of Ravenloft, will attend to them.

Another lightning flash rips through the darkness, its thunder echoing through the castle's towers. But Strahd is gone. Only the howling of the wind—or perhaps a lone wolf—fills the midnight air. The master of Ravenloft is having guests for dinner. And you are invited.

## Running the Adventure

*Curse of Strahd* is a story of gothic horror, presented here as a Dungeons & Dragons roleplaying game adventure for a party of four to six adventurers of levels 1–10. A balance of character classes is helpful, since the adventurers will face a variety of challenges. Each character class will certainly have its moment to shine.

---

### A Classic Retold

This adventure is a retelling of the original *Ravenloft* adventure, which was published in 1983 by TSR, Inc. In the years since, the original has gained a reputation as one of the greatest Dungeons & Dragons adventures ever, and it went on to inspire the creation of a campaign setting of the same name in 1990: Ravenloft, home of the Domains of Dread.

Module 16: *Ravenloft*, written by Tracy and Laura Hickman, broke new ground by presenting a D&D adventure that was as much story-driven as location-based, featuring a villain who was complex and terrifying. Castle Ravenloft, with its amazing three-dimensional maps, remains to this day one of the most iconic and memorable of all D&D dungeons.

This book includes the original adventure, as well as expanded material developed in consultation with Tracy and Laura Hickman. It expands what we know about the lands around Castle Ravenloft and sheds new light on the dark past of the castle's lord. The lands of Barovia are from a forgotten world in the D&D multiverse, and this adventure gives glimpses into that world. In time, cursed Barovia was torn from its home world by the Dark Powers and bound in mist as one of the Domains of Dread in the Shadowfell.

---

This book is meant for you, the Dungeon Master, alone. We recommend you read all of it before you run it. It assumes you have the fifth edition *Player's Handbook, Dungeon Master's Guide,* and *Monster Manual.*

The *Monster Manual* contains stat blocks for most of the monsters and nonplayer characters (NPCs) found in this adventure. Descriptions and stat blocks for new monsters and NPCs are provided in appendix D. When a creature's name appears in **bold** type, that's a visual cue pointing you to the creature's stat block in the *Monster Manual.* If the stat block is in appendix D, the adventure's text tells you so.

Spells and nonmagical equipment mentioned in the adventure are described in the *Player's Handbook.* Magic items are described in the *Dungeon Master's Guide,* unless the adventure's text directs you to an item's description in appendix C.

---

Text that appears in a box like this is meant to be read aloud or paraphrased for players when their characters first arrive at a location or under a specific circumstance, as described in the text. Indoor and nighttime descriptions are written with the assumption that the adventurers are using a torch or other light source to see by.

---

## Story Overview

Adventurers from a foreign land find themselves in Barovia, a mysterious realm surrounded by deadly fog and ruled by Strahd von Zarovich, a vampire and wizard. Using a deck of tarokka cards to predict their future, a fortune-teller named Madam Eva sets them on a dark course that takes them to many corners of Barovia, culminating with a vampire hunt in Castle Ravenloft.

Madam Eva's people are called the Vistani. They travel in covered wagons from world to world, luring strangers into Strahd's domain.

Barovia is a land of ghosts, werewolves, and other fell creatures. The wilderness hides many secrets, including forgotten ruins and battlefields that tell the story of Strahd's life as a conqueror. Adventurers who explore the wilderness find the remnants of Strahd's ancient enemies, not all of them as dead as one might expect.

For the people of Barovia, there is no escape from this harsh land. The town of Vallaki stands ready to defend itself against the servants of Strahd, but it's far from the sanctuary it purports to be. The village of Krezk lies near the edge of Strahd's domain, its abbey now in the clutches of evil, misguided creatures.

Of all the settlements in Strahd's domain, the village of Barovia is by far the most oppressed. Many of its shops are closed, and the locals have succumbed to despair. It is well known that Strahd desires the burgomaster's adopted daughter, Ireena Kolyana. The villagers neither protect nor harm her, lest they incur the vampire's wrath. Few know that Ireena bears an uncanny resemblance to Tatyana, Strahd's dead beloved.

The village of Barovia cowers in the shadow of Castle Ravenloft, Strahd's home and fortress. The castle stands atop a great spire of rock, invincible and ever watchful. Every night, thousands of bats fly out of the castle to feed. It is said that Strahd sometimes flies with them. Barovia will never be safe until the evil in his castle is destroyed.

Once Strahd becomes aware of the adventurers, he and his spies watch them closely. When the time is right, Strahd invites his "guests" to Castle Ravenloft. He aims to turn them against one another, torment them, and kill them, as he has done with so many other visitors. Some will become undead thralls. Others will never rise again.

The adventurers' best hope of defeating Strahd is to learn his secrets, for he is no ordinary vampire. Guided by Madam Eva's card reading, they must scour his domain and his castle for magic items that might weaken or slay him, all the while trying to stay alive.

Although the adventurers can escape by slaying Strahd, he can't be truly destroyed. Barovia is his prison, and not even death can free him from his curse.

The adventure ends when either Strahd von Zarovich or the characters are defeated. Your goal is to keep Strahd in play for as long as possible, using all the abilities and resources at his disposal.

## ADVENTURE STRUCTURE

Much of the adventure's action is driven by the clash between the adventurers' decisions and Strahd's goals, and the adventurers and the vampire are all caught in strands of fate that are represented by a special card reading detailed in chapter 1, "Into the Mists." Before you run the adventure, you need to conduct that reading to determine the location of several items that are key to the story, as well as one of the locations where Strahd can be found.

Chapter 1 also outlines Strahd's goals, and it suggests adventure hooks to draw the player characters into the cursed realm of Barovia. If the characters are 1st level, the character background in appendix A is available to them, and consider starting their time in Barovia with the mini-adventure "Death House" in appendix B.

Chapter 2, "The Lands of Barovia," provides an overview of the realm and includes special rules for it and its people, including the mysterious Vistani. Chapters 3–15 detail areas that correspond to places on the map of Barovia in chapter 2.

The epilogue offers ways for you to end the adventure. Appendix C details the special items—magical or otherwise—introduced in the adventure, and appendix D provides stat blocks for Strahd and various NPCs and monsters that can be met in Barovia. Appendix E shows the tarokka cards that the Vistani use for their fortune telling, and appendix F contains handouts for you to show the players.

## CHARACTER LEVELS

The adventure is meant for characters of levels 1–10 and includes threats for those levels and beyond. Strahd can be an especially deadly challenge at these levels. It is assumed that the characters will gain levels over the course of the adventure, as well as acquire allies and powerful magic items that can tip the scales in their favor. Characters who head directly to Castle Ravenloft without first increasing their power will likely die.

You can award experience points for the defeat of foes, use milestone awards, or a mixture of both. Given the fact that much of the adventure involves social interaction and exploration, rather than combat, your work will probably be easier if you use milestone awards. Appropriate milestone awards include the following:

**Finding Artifacts.** The characters gain a level when they obtain the *Tome of Strahd*, the *Sunsword*, or the *Holy Symbol of Ravenkind*.

**Defeating Villains.** The characters gain a level when they defeat the featured antagonist(s) in a location, such as the hags in Old Bonegrinder (chapter 6).

**Accomplishing Story Goals.** The characters gain a level when they accomplish something significant, such lighting the beacon of Argynvostholt (chapter 7), thwarting the druids' ritual atop Yester Hill (chapter 14), or forging an alliance with Ezmerelda d'Avenir (appendix D).

Appendix B, "Death House," uses milestone awards by way of example.

Be prepared for the fact that the adventure is exceedingly open-ended—one of the hallmarks of the original *Ravenloft*. The card reading in chapter 1 and the adventurers' choices can lead them all over the map, and a party can easily wander into an area well beyond their power. If you'd like to steer them toward places that correspond to their level, consult the Areas by Level table, but beware of undermining the sense that the characters' choices matter. Sometimes the adventurers will simply need to flee or hide when they are out of their depth.

If an area of the adventure ends up feeling free of mystery or danger, consider using tips from the "Marks of Horror" section to increase the ominousness. If a combat encounter feels too easy, either (a) guide it to its end as quickly as possible or (b) increase the threat by raising a foe's hit point maximum to the upper end of its hit point range, by adding monsters/traps, or both.

## AREAS BY LEVEL

| Avg. Level | Area | Chapter |
|---|---|---|
| 1st–3rd | Village of Barovia | 3 |
| 4th | Town of Vallaki | 5 |
| 4th | Old Bonegrinder | 6 |
| 5th | Village of Krezk | 8 |
| 5th | Wizard of Wines Winery | 12 |
| 6th | Van Richten's Tower | 11 |
| 6th | Yester Hill | 14 |
| 7th | Argynvostholt | 7 |
| 7th | Werewolf Den | 15 |
| 8th | Tsolenka Pass | 9 |
| 8th | The Ruins of Berez | 10 |
| 9th | Castle Ravenloft | 4 |
| 9th | The Amber Temple | 13 |

# Marks of Horror

A gust of air like the foul-smelling breath of some horrible monster greets the adventurers as they climb the steps of a tower in Castle Ravenloft. Nearing the top, they begin to hear the beating of a heart in the darkness above. Not a human heart, but the heart of something monstrous and horrible. Such is the nature of gothic horror: fear bred by anticipation and the dark realization that all will be truly and horribly revealed in time.

The following tips can help you make this adventure a chilling experience for you and your players.

## The Unknown

Horror is born out of fear of the unknown. Our fear is heightened when the darkness engulfs us and we can't see, or when the truth is behind a locked door, covered by a sheet, or buried in the soft earth. It's not the monster, but its shadow, that breeds horror. The more we know about a monster, the less we fear it, so the trick is to keep it out of the light for as long as possible. Here are two tricks to heighten fear of the unknown:

- When it seems as though the characters have everything under control, you can have a gust of wind suddenly blow out their torches, plunging them into darkness.
- Before a monster appears, take a moment to describe the odor that precedes it, the eerie sound it makes, or the weird shadow it casts.

## Foreshadowing

Foreshadowing is about finding clues to a horrible truth yet to be revealed. Consider the following examples:

- Before characters encounter a monster, hint at the monster's presence with clues such as claw marks, gnawed bones, and bloodstains.
- Whenever characters take a long rest, give one character a prophetic dream in which he or she glimpses something yet to be found or encountered.

## Age

Barovia is the grim reflection of its undead master. Almost everything here is old and timeworn. Everywhere the adventurers go, they should be reminded of death, decay, and their own mortality. Here are a couple of ways to reinforce these pervasive themes:

- Take time to describe the rotting timbers of buildings, the faded and moth-eaten clothing of the Barovian peasantry, the worm-ridden pages of old books, and the rust on iron fences and gates.
- A character gazing into a mirror, a pool, or other reflective surface might glimpse an older, more decrepit version of himself or herself.

## Light

A tale that is perpetually dark in tone becomes tiresome very quickly. It needs to feature the occasional ray of light for contrast and to create a sense of hope. Monsters and other terrors must be offset with creatures that are kind and lovable, giving the characters even more reasons to stand against the darkness. Here are a couple of ways to add glimmers of light to a tragic tale:

- In a land as dreary as Barovia, take the time to describe the occasional scene of beauty, such as a pretty flower growing atop a grave.
- Make sure that the heroes have contact with NPCs who are honest, friendly, and helpful, such as the Martikovs in Vallaki or the Krezkovs in Krezk.

## Personification

Ascribing human characteristics to an inanimate thing is one way to turn something ordinary into something malevolent. A groaning house, the wailing wind, grasping mud, and a squatting chest aren't just mundane things—they're characters in your story, made all the creepier thanks to their humanlike traits. Torches sputter nervously, rusty hinges shatter silence with their sudden cries of anguish, and cobwebs quietly beckon us to our doom. Here are more examples:

- Imagine darkness as a silent crowd that follows the characters everywhere and stares at them while they sleep.
- Imagine trees as towering giants that stand idle yet ever watchful as characters face the perils of the Svalich Woods alone.

## Details

In a horror story, there's no telling where danger might be lurking. A leering gargoyle might be a monster in disguise, or merely a fiendish sculpture. A mirror hanging on a wall might have the power to transfix all who gaze into it, or it might be nothing out of the ordinary. In a horror story, taking the time to describe an object in detail draws attention to it, makes one suspicious of it, and might distract from the real danger. Here are a couple of tricks you can use:

- In a given encounter area, choose one object or feature to describe in some detail. It need not be important to the story.
- Allow the character who has the highest passive Wisdom (Perception) score to see, hear, or smell something that no one else can perceive.

## Humor

There are no stranger bedfellows than horror and humor. Tension can't be sustained indefinitely, so a dash of humor provides a respite, giving horror a chance to sneak up on us later and catch us off guard. While humorous situations will occur naturally in the course of running the adventure, here are some tips for creating humor when needed:

- Allow NPCs (even evil ones) to tell jokes, speak in a funny voice, or behave idiotically. Even morbid humor is better than none.
- When a hero, villain, or monster rolls a natural 1 on an attack roll, ability check, or saving throw, describe a humorous mishap that occurs as a result of the low roll, such as a character accidentally knocking over a lamp and setting some drapes on fire while trying to hide or move silently.

# Chapter 1: Into the Mists

ERIE MISTS SURROUND BAROVIA AND bind its inhabitants there. This chapter gives you the information you need to prepare for the adventurers' journey into those mists. The chapter first outlines the history and goals of Count Strahd von Zarovich so that you are prepared for what awaits the characters. In the "Fortunes of Ravenloft" section, the chapter walks you through the tarokka card reading that helps set the stage for the adventure's action, and the chapter closes with adventure hooks that you can use to draw the characters into the horror of Barovia.

## Strahd von Zarovich

Strahd von Zarovich, a vampire and wizard, has the statistics presented in appendix D. Although he can be encountered almost anywhere in his domain, the vampire is always encountered in the place indicated by the card reading later in this chapter, unless he has been forced into his tomb in the catacombs of Castle Ravenloft.

### The Vampire's History

In life, Strahd von Zarovich was a count, a prince, a soldier, and a conqueror. After the death of his father, King Barov, Strahd waged long, bloody wars against his family's enemies. He and his army cornered the last of these enemies in a remote mountain valley before slaying them all. Strahd named the valley Barovia, after his deceased father, and was so struck by its scenic beauty that he decided to settle there.

Queen Ravenovia lamented the death of Barov and was fearful of Strahd. War had made him cold and arrogant. She kept her younger son, Sergei, away from the battlefield. Strahd envied the love and attention his mother visited upon his brother, so in Barovia he remained. Peace made Strahd restless, and he began to feel like his best years were behind him. Unwilling to go the way of his father, Strahd studied magic and forged a pact with the Dark Powers of the Shadowfell in return for the promise of immortality.

Strahd scoured his conquered lands for wizards and artisans, brought them to the valley of Barovia, and commanded them to raise a castle to rival the magnificent fortresses of his ancestral homeland. Strahd named the castle Ravenloft, after his mother, to demonstrate his love for her. When it was complete, Strahd commanded his mother and brother to come to Barovia and stay with him. Sergei eventually took up residence at Ravenloft, but Ravenovia passed away while traveling to her namesake. In sorrowful disappointment, Strahd sealed his mother's body in a crypt beneath the castle.

Strahd's attention soon turned to Tatyana, a young Barovian woman of fine lineage and remarkable beauty. Strahd believed her to be a worthy bride, and he lavished Tatyana with gifts and attention. Despite Strahd's efforts, she instead fell in love with the younger, warmer Sergei. Strahd's pride prevented him from standing in the way of the young couple's love until the day of Sergei and Tatyana's wedding, when Strahd gazed into a mirror and realized he had been a fool. Strahd murdered Sergei and drank his blood, sealing the evil pact between Strahd and the Dark Powers. He then chased Sergei's bride-to-be through the gardens, determined to make her accept and love him. Tatyana hurled herself off a castle balcony to escape Strahd's pursuit, plunging to her death. Treacherous castle guards, seizing the opportunity to rid the world of Strahd forever, shot their master with arrows.

But Strahd did not die. The Dark Powers honored the pact they had made. The sky went black as Strahd turned on the guards, his eyes blazing red. He had become a vampire.

After slaughtering the guards, Strahd saw the faces of his father and mother in the thunderclouds, looking down upon him and judging him. He had destroyed the family bloodline and doomed all of Barovia. The castle and the valley were spirited away, locked in a demiplane surrounded on all sides by deadly fog. For Strahd and his people, there would be no escape.

---

I AM THE ANCIENT. I AM THE LAND.
*My beginnings are lost in the darkness of the past. I am not dead. Nor am I alive. I am undead, forever.*
—Tome of Strahd

---

CONJURER

9

DARKLORD

9

Strahd has been the master of Ravenloft for centuries now. Since becoming a vampire, he has taken several consorts—none as beloved as Tatyana, but each a person of beauty. All of them he turned into vampire spawn. Although he feeds on the hapless souls of Barovia, they provide little nourishment and no comfort. From time to time, strangers from faraway lands are brought to his domain, to play the vampire's game of cat-and-mouse. Strahd savors these moments, for though these strangers offer him no lands to conquer, they aren't so easily destroyed and therefore provide a welcome diversion.

Strahd believes that the key to his escaping Barovia lies in finding someone worthy to rule in his stead, but his arrogance are so indomitable that no one is ever good enough in his eyes. He believes in his cold heart that only a von Zarovich as great as he or his father could sway the Dark Powers to release him.

## STRAHD'S GOALS

Strahd has the following goals in the adventure.

### TURN IREENA KOLYANA

Strahd's unrequited love for Tatyana drove him to slay his brother, Sergei. Some time ago, Strahd glimpsed the young woman Ireena Kolyana in the village of Barovia and felt extreme déjà vu. Ireena looked exactly like Tatyana! Strahd now believes that Ireena is the latest reincarnation of Tatyana, and thus he seeks to claim her.

Strahd's evil courtship has led him to visit Ireena twice. On both occasions, he charmed his way into her home—the house of her adopted father, the burgomaster of the village of Barovia—and drank her blood. He intends to kill Ireena during their next meeting and turn her into his vampire spawn consort.

Chapter 3 gives details about Ireena and where to find her in the village of Barovia.

### FIND RUDOLPH VAN RICHTEN

Although he is usually focused on making Ireena Kolyana his bride, Strahd has been distracted by reports that a legendary vampire hunter named Rudolph van Richten has come to Barovia. It takes more than one old man with a death wish to frighten Strahd; nevertheless, the vampire has his spies searching Barovia for van Richten. Strahd would like very much to meet the old vampire hunter, lock him in the dungeons of Castle Ravenloft, and slowly break his spirit.

Chapter 5 describes the town of Vallaki, where van Richten currently resides incognito.

### SEARCH FOR A SUCCESSOR OR CONSORT

Strahd can sense the arrival of new blood in his domain. When newcomers enter Barovia, he shifts his attention from Ireena Kolyana and van Richten to his new guests so that he can determine whether any of them is worthy to be his successor or consort. (Eventually, he decides that none of them can replace him as master of Barovia, but he doesn't arrive at this conclusion immediately.)

Strahd pays close attention to adventurers who are charismatic and arrogant, like himself. He focuses his attacks on them, to see how much they can withstand. If they crumble easily, he loses interest in them. If they exhibit great fortitude and defiance, his interest is piqued—even more so if the character displays uncommon knowledge or beauty. Such a person might not be worthy to succeed him, but the man or woman might provide amusement to Strahd as a new possession.

## ROLEPLAYING STRAHD

Strahd believes his soul is lost to evil. He feels neither pity nor remorse, neither love nor hate. He doesn't suffer anguish or wallow in indignation. He believes, and has always believed, that he is the master of his own fate.

When he was alive, Strahd could admit to letting his emotions get the better of him from time to time. Now, as a vampire, he is more monster than man, with barely a hint of emotion left. He is above the concerns of the living. The only event that occasionally haunts him is the death of Tatyana, but his view of the past is bereft of romance or regret. In his mind, her death couldn't have been prevented, and what is done cannot be undone.

In life, Strahd lived to conquer. In undeath, he conquers still—not realms, but people, driving good souls to become corrupt and destroying those who won't yield. Characters who try to appeal to Strahd's humanity will be gravely disappointed, because there is little humanity left in him. If they ask Strahd why he's preying on Ireena Kolyana, he tells them that Ireena's body is the host for Tatyana's soul, and Tatyana's soul belongs to him.

Strahd can be seductive and subtle when he chooses to be, especially if a person is clever or attractive. Men and women of beauty and cunning amuse Strahd for a time—playthings to possess or discard as he desires.

If he senses a lack of cohesion in a party of adventurers, he preys on that weakness and tries to drive a wedge between the characters by promising to help one at the expense of another. If Strahd senses evil in a person, he cultivates that tendency by offering to turn that character into a full-fledged vampire after helping Strahd destroy the rest of the party. Ultimately, Strahd doesn't honor his promise, instead turning the character into a vampire spawn under his control.

## WHEN STRAHD ATTACKS

Strahd isn't a villain who remains out of sight until the final scene. Far from it—he travels as he desires to any place in his realm or his castle, and (from his perspective) the more often he encounters the characters, the better. The characters can and should meet him multiple times before the final encounter, which most likely takes place in the location determined by the card reading. His combat details are available in appendix D.

When Strahd wants to terrorize the characters, he pays them a visit, either under the cloak of night or beneath overcast skies during the day. If they're indoors, he tries to charm or goad a character into inviting him inside (along with his vampire spawn, if they are present). Strahd and his minions never attack Ireena.

These encounters are meant to test the characters, not kill them. After a few rounds of toying with them, Strahd and his creatures withdraw. If the characters retreat, Strahd is likely to allow them to flee, savoring their fear and believing he has broken them.

# FORTUNES OF RAVENLOFT

The events of this adventure are part of dark twists of fate that a fortuneteller can discern with the cards of a tarokka deck. Before you run this adventure, you must draw cards from a deck to determine the following elements of the adventure:

- Strahd's location inside Castle Ravenloft
- The placement of three important treasures that can be used against Strahd—the *Tome of Strahd*, the *Holy Symbol of Ravenkind*, and the *Sunsword*
- The identity of a powerful ally in the fight against Strahd

This card reading can make the adventure different each time you play it.

At some point during the adventure, the characters are likely to meet Madam Eva, the old Vistani seer (see chapter 2, area G), who can perform the same card reading for them. Characters can also have Ezmerelda d'Avenir perform a card reading for them, provided she has her deck of tarokka cards. Ezmerelda's cards are hidden in her wagon (chapter 11, area V1).

Appendix E shows all the cards of the tarokka deck and summarizes their symbolic meanings.

## USING REGULAR PLAYING CARDS

If you like, you can use a regular deck of playing cards in place of the tarokka deck. To do so, separate the numbered cards from the face cards and jokers, and treat them as two separate decks: the common deck (the numbered cards) and the high deck (the face cards and jokers).

**Common Deck.** Each suit in a regular deck of playing cards corresponds to a suit in the tarokka deck. The ace cards represent the "1" cards in the tarokka deck, and the "10" cards represent the "master" cards in the tarokka deck.

Hearts = Glyphs  
Spades = Swords

Diamonds = Coins  
Clubs = Stars

**High Deck.** Each jack, queen, king, and joker corresponds to a card in the tarokka high deck.

| Playing Card | Tarokka Card |
| --- | --- |
| King of hearts | Ghost |
| Queen of hearts | Innocent |
| Jack of hearts | Marionette |
| King of spades | Darklord |
| Queen of spades | Mists |
| Jack of spades | Executioner |
| King of diamonds | Broken One |
| Queen of diamonds | Tempter |
| Jack of diamonds | Beast |
| King of clubs | Donjon |
| Queen of clubs | Raven |
| Jack of clubs | Seer |
| Joker 1 | Artifact |
| Joker 2 | Horseman |

# CARD READING

When you perform a card reading before running the adventure, write down the results for reference later. If the characters have their fortunes read in the adventures, do the card reading again, out loud for the players' benefit. Substitute the new results for the old ones.

When you're ready to begin the card reading, remove the fourteen cards with the crown icon (the high deck) and shuffle them. Then shuffle the remaining cards (the common deck), keeping the two decks separate. Draw the top three cards from the common deck and lay them face down in the 1, 2, and 3 positions. Then draw the top two cards from the high deck and lay them face down in the 4 and 5 positions, as shown below:

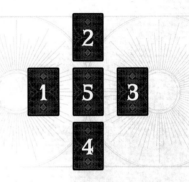

Once all five cards are drawn and placed face down, follow the instructions below for each card in order.

## 1. THE TOME OF STRAHD
Flip over card 1, and read:

> This card tells of history. Knowledge of the ancient will help you better understand your enemy.

This card determines the location of the *Tome of Strahd* (described in appendix C). Read the boxed text for the appropriate card, as given in the "Treasure Locations" section that follows.

## 2. THE HOLY SYMBOL OF RAVENKIND
Flip over card 2, and read:

> This card tells of a powerful force for good and protection, a holy symbol of great hope.

This card determines the location of the *Holy Symbol of Ravenkind* (described in appendix C). Read the boxed text for the appropriate card, as given in the "Treasure Locations" section that follows.

## 3. THE SUNSWORD
Flip over card 3, and read:

> This is a card of power and strength. It tells of a weapon of vengeance: a sword of sunlight.

This card determines the location of the *Sunsword* (described in appendix C). Read the boxed text for the appropriate card, as given in the "Treasure Locations" section that follows.

## 4. Strahd's Enemy

Flip over card 4, and read:

> This card sheds light on one who will help you greatly in the battle against darkness.

This card determines where the characters can find a powerful ally. Read the boxed text for the appropriate card, as given in the "Strahd's Enemy" section later in the chapter.

## 5. Strahd

Flip over card 5, and read:

> Your enemy is a creature of darkness, whose powers are beyond mortality. This card will lead you to him!

The revealed card determines where Strahd can always be found. Read the boxed text for the appropriate card, as given in the "Strahd's Location in Castle Ravenloft" section later in the chapter.

## Treasure Locations

The cards of the common deck determine the locations of the *Tome of Strahd* (card 1), the *Holy Symbol of Ravenkind* (card 2), and the *Sunsword* (card 3).

### Swords (Spades)

> **1 of Swords — Avenger**
> The treasure lies in a dragon's house, in hands once clean and now corrupted.

The treasure is in the possession of Vladimir Horngaard in Argynvostholt (chapter 7, area Q36).

> **2 of Swords — Paladin**
> I see a sleeping prince, a servant of light and the brother of darkness. The treasure lies with him.

The treasure lies in Sergei's tomb (chapter 4, area K85).

> **3 of Swords — Soldier**
> Go to the mountains. Climb the white tower guarded by golden knights.

The treasure lies on the rooftop of the Tsolenka Pass guard tower (chapter 9, area T6).

> **4 of Swords — Mercenary**
> The thing you seek lies with the dead, under mountains of gold coins.

The treasure lies in a crypt in Castle Ravenloft (chapter 4, area K84, crypt 31).

> **5 of Swords — Myrmidon**
> Look for a den of wolves in the hills overlooking a mountain lake. The treasure belongs to Mother Night.

The treasure lies in the shrine of Mother Night in the werewolf den (chapter 15, area Z7).

> **6 of Swords — Berserker**
> Find the Mad Dog's crypt. The treasure lies within, beneath blackened bones.

The treasure lies in the crypt of General Kroval "Mad Dog" Grislek (chapter 4, area K84, crypt 38).

> **7 of Swords — Hooded One**
> I see a faceless god. He awaits you at the end of a long and winding road, deep in the mountains.

The treasure is inside the head of the giant statue in the Amber Temple (chapter 13, area X5a).

> **8 of Swords — Dictator**
> I see a throne fit for a king.

The treasure lies in Castle Ravenloft's audience hall (chapter 4, area K25).

> **9 of Swords — Torturer**
> There is a town where all is not well. There you will find a house of corruption, and within, a dark room full of still ghosts.

The treasure is hidden in the attic of the burgomaster's mansion in Vallaki (chapter 5, area N3s).

> **Master of Swords — Warrior**
> That which you seek lies in the womb of darkness, the devil's lair: the one place to which he must return.

The treasure lies in Strahd's tomb (chapter 4, area K86).

## Stars (Clubs)

### 1 of Stars — Transmuter
Go to a place of dizzying heights, where the stone itself is alive!

The treasure lies in Castle Ravenloft's north tower peak (chapter 4, area K60).

### 2 of Stars — Diviner
Look to the one who sees all. The treasure is hidden in her camp.

The treasure lies in Madam Eva's encampment (chapter 2, area G). If she is the one performing the card reading, she says, "I think the treasure is under my very nose!"

### 3 of Stars — Enchanter
I see a kneeling woman—a rose of great beauty plucked too soon. The master of the marsh knows of whom I speak.

The treasure lies under Marina's monument in Berez (chapter 10, area U5). "The master of the marsh" refers to Burgomaster Lazlo Ulrich (area U2), whose ghost can point characters toward the monument.

### 4 of Stars — Abjurer
I see a fallen house guarded by a great stone dragon. Look to the highest peak.

The treasure lies in the beacon of Argynvostholt (chapter 7, area Q53). "Great stone dragon" refers to the statue in area Q1.

### 5 of Stars — Elementalist
The treasure is hidden in a small castle beneath a mountain, guarded by amber giants.

The treasure is inside a model of Castle Ravenloft in the Amber Temple (chapter 13, area X20).

### 6 of Stars — Evoker
Search for the crypt of a wizard ordinaire. His staff is the key.

The treasure is hidden in the crypt of Gralmore Nimblenobs (chapter 4, area K84, crypt 37).

### 7 of Stars — Illusionist
A man is not what he seems. He comes here in a carnival wagon. Therein lies what you seek.

The treasure lies in Rictavio's carnival wagon (chapter 5, area N5).

### 8 of Stars — Necromancer
A woman hangs above a roaring fire. Find her, and you will find the treasure.

The treasure lies in Castle Ravenloft's study (chapter 4, area K37).

### 9 of Stars — Conjurer
I see a dead village, drowned by a river, ruled by one who has brought great evil into the world.

The treasure is in Baba Lysaga's hut (chapter 10, area U3).

### Master of Stars — Wizard
Look for a wizard's tower on a lake. Let the wizard's name and servant guide you to that which you seek.

The treasure lies on the top floor of Van Richten's Tower (chapter 11, area V7).

## Coins (Diamonds)

### 1 of Coins — Swashbuckler
I see the skeleton of a deadly warrior, lying on a bed of stone flanked by gargoyles.

The treasure lies in the crypt of Endorovich (chapter 4, area K84, crypt 7).

### 2 of Coins — Philanthropist
Look to a place where sickness and madness are bred. Where children once cried, the treasure lies still.

The treasure is in the nursery of the Abbey of Saint Markovia (chapter 8, area S23).

### 3 of Coins — Trader
Look to the wizard of wines! In wood and sand the treasure hides.

The treasure lies in the glassblower's workshop in the Wizard of Wines winery (chapter 12, area W10).

### 4 OF COINS — MERCHANT

Seek a cask that once contained the finest wine, of which not a drop remains.

The treasure lies in Castle Ravenloft's wine cellar (chapter 4, area K63).

### 5 OF COINS — GUILD MEMBER

I see a dark room full of bottles. It is the tomb of a guild member.

The treasure lies in the crypt of Artank Swilovich (chapter 4, area K84, crypt 5).

### 6 OF COINS — BEGGAR

A wounded elf has what you seek. He will part with the treasure to see his dark dreams fulfilled.

The treasure is hidden in Kasimir's hovel (chapter 5, area N9a).

### 7 OF COINS — THIEF

What you seek lies at the crossroads of life and death, among the buried dead.

The treasure is buried in the graveyard at the River Ivlis crossroads (chapter 2, area F).

### 8 OF COINS — TAX COLLECTOR

The Vistani have what you seek. A missing child holds the key to the treasure's release.

The treasure is hidden in the Vistani treasure wagon (chapter 5, area N9i). "A missing child" refers to Arabelle (see chapter 2, area L).

### 9 OF COINS — MISER

Look for a fortress inside a fortress, in a place hidden behind fire.

The treasure lies in Castle Ravenloft's treasury (chapter 4, area K41).

### MASTER OF COINS — ROGUE

I see a nest of ravens. There you will find the prize.

The treasure is hidden in the attic of the Blue Water Inn (chapter 5, area N2q).

## GLYPHS (HEARTS)

### 1 OF GLYPHS — MONK

The treasure you seek is hidden behind the sun, in the house of a saint.

The treasure lies in the main hall of the Abbey of Saint Markovia (chapter 8, area S13).

### 2 OF GLYPHS — MISSIONARY

I see a garden dusted with snow, watched over by a scarecrow with a sackcloth grin. Look not to the garden but to the guardian.

The treasure is hidden inside one of the scarecrows in the garden of the Abbey of Saint Markovia (chapter 8, area S9).

### 3 OF GLYPHS — HEALER

Look to the west. Find a pool blessed by the light of the white sun.

The treasure lies beneath the gazebo in the Shrine of the White Sun (chapter 8, area S4).

### 4 OF GLYPHS — SHEPHERD

Find the mother—she who gave birth to evil.

The treasure lies in the tomb of King Barov and Queen Ravenovia (chapter 4, area K88).

### 5 OF GLYPHS — DRUID

An evil tree grows atop a hill of graves where the ancient dead sleep. The ravens can help you find it. Look for the treasure there.

The treasure lies at the base of the Gulthias tree (chapter 14, area Y4). Any wereraven encountered in the wilderness can lead the characters to the location.

### 6 OF GLYPHS — ANARCHIST

I see walls of bones, a chandelier of bones, and a table of bones—all that remains of enemies long forgotten.

The treasure lies in Castle Ravenloft's hall of bones (chapter 4, area K67).

### 7 OF GLYPHS — CHARLATAN

I see a lonely mill on a precipice. The treasure lies within.

The treasure lies in the attic of Old Bonegrinder (chapter 6, area O4).

### 8 OF GLYPHS — BISHOP

What you seek lies in a pile of treasure, beyond a set of amber doors.

The treasure lies in the sealed treasury of the Amber Temple (chapter 13, area X40).

### 9 OF GLYPHS — TRAITOR

Look for a wealthy woman. A staunch ally of the devil, she keeps the treasure under lock and key, with the bones of an ancient enemy.

The treasure is hidden in the master bedroom of Wachterhaus (chapter 5, area N4o).

### MASTER OF GLYPHS — PRIEST

You will find what you seek in the castle, amid the ruins of a place of supplication.

The treasure lies in Castle Ravenloft's chapel (chapter 4, area K15).

## STRAHD'S ENEMY

Drawn from the high deck, the fourth card in the card reading determines the location of an NPC who can improve the characters' chances of defeating Strahd. (Some cards offer two possible results, A and B; in such a case, you can pick the one you prefer or that better suits the circumstances of the adventure.)

Strahd senses that this NPC is a danger to him and tries to eliminate the threat as quickly as possible. This NPC, whoever it ends up being, gains the following additional action:

*Inspire.* While within sight of Strahd, this character grants inspiration to one player character he or she can see.

Each of the NPCs described in this section has a role to play in the adventure, even if that individual isn't indicated in the card reading. For the one so designated, however, the information in this section regarding the NPC's behavior takes precedence over whatever is said elsewhere in these pages; that NPC is extraordinary.

### ARTIFACT (JOKER 1)

Look for an entertaining man with a monkey. This man is more than he seems.

This card refers to Rictavio (see appendix D), who can be found at the Blue Water Inn in Vallaki (chapter 5, area N2). Normally reluctant to accompany the characters, Rictavio changes his tune if the characters tell him about the card reading. He sheds his disguise and introduces himself as Dr. Rudolph van Richten.

The characters might think that Gadof Blinsky, the toymaker of Vallaki (area N7), is the figure they seek, because he has a pet monkey. If they speak to him about this possibility, Blinsky jokes that he and the monkey are "old friends," but if the characters ask him to come with them to fight Strahd, he politely declines. If the characters tell him about the tarokka reading, Blinsky admits that he acquired the monkey from a half-elf carnival ringmaster named Rictavio.

### BEAST (JACK OF DIAMONDS)

A werewolf holds a secret hatred for your enemy. Use her hatred to your advantage.

This card refers to the werewolf Zuleika Toranescu (see chapter 15, area Z7). She will accompany the characters if they promise to avenge her mate, Emil, by killing the leader of her pack, Kiril Stoyanovich.

### A. BROKEN ONE (KING OF DIAMONDS)

Your greatest ally will be a wizard. His mind is broken, but his spells are strong.

This card refers to the Mad Mage of Mount Baratok (see chapter 2, area M).

### B. BROKEN ONE (KING OF DIAMONDS)

I see a man of faith whose sanity hangs by a thread. He has lost someone close to him.

This card refers to Donavich, the priest in the village of Barovia (see chapter 3, area E5). He will not accompany the characters until his son, Doru, is dead and buried.

### DARKLORD (KING OF SPADES)

Ah, the worst of all truths: You must face the evil of this land alone!

There is no NPC who can inspire the characters.

### A. DONJON (KING OF CLUBS)

Search for a troubled young man surrounded by wealth and madness. His home is his prison.

This card refers to Victor Vallakovich (see chapter 5, area N3t). Realizing that the characters are the key to his salvation, he enthusiastically leaves home and accompanies them to Castle Ravenloft.

## B. Donjon (King of Clubs)

Find a girl driven to insanity, locked in the heart of her dead father's house. Curing her madness is key to your success.

This card refers to Stella Wachter (see chapter 5, area N4n). She grants the party no benefit unless her madness is cured. With her wits restored, Stella is happy to join the party and leave her rotten family behind.

## Seer (Jack of Clubs)

Look for a dusk elf living among the Vistani. He has suffered a great loss and is haunted by dark dreams. Help him, and he will help you in return.

This card refers to Kasimir Velikov (see chapter 5, area N9a). The dusk elf accompanies the characters to Castle Ravenloft only after they lead him to the Amber Temple and help him find the means to resurrect his dead sister, Patrina Velikovna.

## A. Ghost (King of Hearts)

I see a fallen paladin of a fallen order of knights. He lingers like a ghost in a dead dragon's lair.

This card refers to the revenant Sir Godfrey Gwilym (see chapter 7, area Q37). Although initially unwilling to accompany the characters, he will do so if the characters convince him that the honor of the Order of the Silver Dragon can be restored with his help. Doing this requires a successful DC 15 Charisma (Persuasion) check.

## B. Ghost (King of Hearts)

Stir the spirit of the clumsy knight whose crypt lies deep within the castle.

This card refers to Sir Klutz the phantom warrior (see chapter 4, area K84, crypt 33). If Sir Klutz is Strahd's enemy, then the phantom warrior disappears not after seven days, but only after he or Strahd is reduced to 0 hit points.

## Executioner (Jack of Spades)

Seek out the brother of the devil's bride. They call him "the lesser," but he has a powerful soul.

This card refers to Ismark Kolyanovich (see chapter 3, area E2). Ismark won't accompany the characters to Castle Ravenloft until he knows that his sister, Ireena Kolyana, is safe.

## A. Horseman (Joker 2)

I see a dead man of noble birth, guarded by his widow. Return life to the dead man's corpse, and he will be your staunch ally.

This card refers to Nikolai Wachter the elder, who is dead (see chapter 5, area N4o). If the characters cast a *raise dead* spell or a *resurrection* spell on his preserved corpse, Nikolai (LN male human **noble**) agrees to help the characters once he feels well enough, despite his wife's protests. Although his family has long supported Strahd, Nikolai came to realize toward the end of his life that Strahd must be destroyed to save Barovia.

If the characters don't have the means to raise Nikolai from the dead, Rictavio (see appendix D) gives them a *spell scroll* of *raise dead* if he learns of their need. If they're staying at the Blue Water Inn, he leaves the scroll in one of their rooms.

## B. Horseman (Joker 2)

A man of death named Arrigal will forsake his dark lord to serve your cause. Beware! He has a rotten soul.

This card refers to the Vistani assassin Arrigal (see chapter 5, area N9c). If the characters mention this card reading to him, he accepts his fate and accompanies them. If the characters succeed in defeating Strahd, Arrigal betrays and attacks them, believing that he is destined to become Barovia's new lord.

## A. Innocent (Queen of Hearts)

I see a young man with a kind heart. A mother's boy! He is strong in body but weak of mind. Seek him out in the village of Barovia.

This card refers to Parriwimple (see chapter 3, area E1). Although he's a simpleton, he won't travel to Castle Ravenloft without good cause. Characters can manipulate him into going by preying on his good heart. For instance, he might go there to help rescue missing Barovians, or to save the life of Ireena Kolyana, who is very beautiful. The characters must somehow deal with Bildrath, Parriwimple's employer, who won't let the foolish boy go to the castle for any reason.

## B. Innocent (Queen of Hearts)

Evil's bride is the one you seek!

This card refers to Ireena Kolyana (see chapter 3, area E4). Her brother, Ismark, opposes the idea of Ireena's being taken to Castle Ravenloft, but she insists on going there once the characters tell her about the card reading. Ireena won't accompany the characters, however, until Kolyan Indirovich's body is laid to rest in the cemetery.

### A. Marionette (Jack of Hearts)

What horror is this? I see a man made by a man. Ageless and alone, it haunts the towers of the castle.

This card refers to Pidlwick II (see chapter 4, area K59, as well as appendix D).

### B. Marionette (Jack of Hearts)

Look for a man of music, a man with two heads. He lives in a place of great hunger and sorrow.

This card refers to Clovin Belview (see chapter 8, area S17), the two-headed mongrelfolk. Clovin serves the Abbot out of fear and a perverse sense of loyalty. His job is to deliver food to the other mongrelfolk, whom he abhors. If the Abbot still lives, Clovin doesn't want to earn his master's ire by attempting to leave, and he refuses to accompany the characters. But if the Abbot dies, Clovin doesn't have any reason to remain in the abbey, so he's willing to come along if he is bribed with wine. Clovin provides no benefit to the party without his viol.

### Mists (Queen of Spades)

A Vistana wanders this land alone, searching for her mentor. She does not stay in one place for long. Seek her out at Saint Markovia's abbey, near the mists.

This card refers to Ezmerelda d'Avenir (see appendix D). She can be found in the Abbey of Saint Markovia (see chapter 8, area S19), as well as several other locations throughout Barovia.

### Raven (Queen of Clubs)

Find the leader of the feathered ones who live among the vines. Though old, he has one more fight left in him.

This card refers to Davian Martikov (see chapter 12, "The Wizard of Wines"). The old wereraven, realizing that he has a chance to end Strahd's tyranny, leaves his vineyard and winery in the capable hands of his sons, Adrian and Elvir. But before he travels to Castle Ravenloft to face Strahd, Davian insists on reconciling with his third son, Urwin Martikov (see chapter 5, area N2).

### A. Tempter (Queen of Diamonds)

I see a child—a Vistana. You must hurry, for her fate hangs in the balance. Find her at the lake!

This card refers to Arabelle (see chapter 2, area L). She gladly joins the party. But if she returns to her camp (chapter 5, area N9), her father, Luvash, refuses to let her leave.

### B. Tempter (Queen of Diamonds)

I hear a wedding bell, or perhaps a death knell. It calls thee to a mountainside abbey, wherein you will find a woman who is more than the sum of her parts.

This card refers to Vasilka the flesh golem (see chapter 8, area S13).

## Strahd's Location in the Castle

Drawn from the high deck, the fifth card in the card reading determines the location of the final showdown with Strahd—the place in Castle Ravenloft where the characters are sure to find him. The first time the characters arrive at the foretold location, Strahd is there, provided he hasn't been forced back into his coffin.

### Artifact (Joker 1)

He lurks in the darkness where the morning light once shone—a sacred place.

Strahd faces the characters in the chapel (area K15).

### Beast (Jack of Diamonds)

The beast sits on his dark throne.

Strahd faces the characters in the audience hall (area K25).

### Broken One (King of Diamonds)

He haunts the tomb of the man he envied above all.

Strahd faces the characters in Sergei's tomb (area K85).

### Darklord (King of Spades)

He lurks in the depths of darkness, in the one place to which he must return.

Strahd faces the characters in his tomb (area K86).

### Donjon (King of Clubs)

He lurks in a hall of bones, in the dark pits of his castle.

Strahd faces the characters in the hall of bones (area K67).

### Seer (Jack of Clubs)

He waits for you in a place of wisdom, warmth, and despair. Great secrets are there.

Strahd faces the characters in the study (area K37).

## Ghost (King of Hearts)

Look to the father's tomb.

Strahd faces the characters in the tomb of King Barov and Queen Ravenovia (area K88).

## Executioner (Jack of Spades)

I see a dark figure on a balcony, looking down upon this tortured land with a twisted smile.

Strahd faces the characters at the overlook (area K6).

## Horseman (Joker 2)

He lurks in the one place to which he must return—a place of death.

Strahd faces the characters in his tomb (area K86).

## Innocent (Queen of Hearts)

He dwells with the one whose blood sealed his doom, a brother of light snuffed out too soon.

Strahd faces the characters in Sergei's tomb (area K85).

## Marionette (Jack of Hearts)

Look to great heights. Find the beating heart of the castle. He waits nearby.

Strahd faces the characters in the north tower peak (area K60).

## Mists (Queen of Spades)

The cards can't see where the evil lurks. The mists obscure all!

The card offers no clue about where the final showdown with Strahd will occur. It can happen anywhere you like in Castle Ravenloft. Alternatively, Madam Eva tells the characters to return to her after at least three days, and she will consult the cards again for them, but only to discern the location of their enemy.

## Raven (Queen of Clubs)

Look to the mother's tomb.

Strahd faces the characters in the tomb of King Barov and Queen Ravenovia (area K88).

## Tempter (Queen of Diamonds)

I see a secret place—a vault of temptation hidden behind a woman of great beauty. The evil waits atop his tower of treasure.

Strahd confronts the characters in the treasury (area K41). "A woman of great beauty" refers to the portrait of Tatyana hanging in the castle's study (area K37), which contains a secret door that leads to the treasury.

# Adventure Hooks

In the event that begins the adventure, the fates of Strahd and the adventurers are entwined as the characters are invited or forced into his domain. Different ways to get the adventurers to Barovia are described in the sections that follow. Use whichever one you favor.

In "Plea for Help," a colorfully dressed stranger approaches the characters while they are staying at a tavern. The stranger delivers a letter from his master, inviting them to the village of Barovia with an urgent request for their assistance. If the characters take the bait, the fog engulfs them as they cross into Strahd's domain.

In "Mysterious Visitors," the characters are asked to scare off a band of rowdy travelers who are camped outside the town of Daggerford, on the Sword Coast in the Forgotten Realms campaign setting. The travelers welcome the characters to their camp and invite them to sit by their fire while their elder recounts a tragic tale of a cursed yet noble prince. The characters, lulled into a trance by the fire, awaken to find themselves on a foggy road, delivered to Barovia by their Vistani hosts.

In "Werewolves in the Mist," the characters are drawn together by a series of werewolf attacks. The hunt for this pack of lycanthropes leads the characters into a forest, where they are swept into the land of Barovia. This hook assumes the use of the five factions featured in the Adventurers League.

In "Creeping Fog," the characters are traveling a lonely road through the woods when the fog engulfs them, spiriting them away to the land of Barovia.

## Plea for Help

The characters start their adventure in an old tavern, the details of which are for you to decide.

To a party of seasoned adventurers such as yourselves, what you see is but another dull tavern in another dull town in some nameless province. It is but another span of time between the challenges of true adventuring.

Outside the tavern, a fog lies over the town this evening. The damp, cobbled pavement glistens as the lights of street lanterns dance across the slick stones. The fog chills the bones and shivers the soul of anyone outside.

Yet inside these tavern walls the food is hearty, and the ale is warm and frothy. A fire blazes in the hearth, and the tavern is alive with the tumbling voices of country folk.

Suddenly, the tavern door swings open, and a hush falls over the room. Framed by the lamp-lit fog, a form strides through the doorway. His heavy, booted footfalls and the jingle of his coins shatter the silence. His brightly colored clothes are draped in loose folds about him, and his hat hangs askew, hiding his eyes in shadows. Without hesitation, he walks up to your table and stands proudly in a wide stance with folded arms.

In an accented voice he says, "I have been sent to you to deliver this message. If you be creatures of honor, you will come to my master's aid at first light. It is not advisable to travel the Svalich Woods at night!" He pulls from his tunic a sealed letter, addressed to all of you in beautiful flowing script. He drops the letter on the table. "Take the west road from here some five hours march down through the Svalich Woods. There you will find my master in Barovia."

Amid the silent stares of the patronage, the gypsy strides to the bar and says to the wary barkeep, "Fill the glasses, one and all. Their throats are obviously parched." He drops a purse heavy with gold on the bar. With that, he leaves.

The babble of tavern voices resumes, although somewhat subdued. The letter is lying before you. The seal is in the shape of a crest you don't recognize.

The characters can interrupt the messenger at any time. His name is Arrigal (NE male human **assassin**), and he is a Vistani. The other tavern patrons regard his people as friendly folk who travel about in covered wagons and usually keep to themselves.

Arrigal describes Barovia as a valley of great beauty and his master as a remarkable man. If the characters question Arrigal about the identity of his master, he claims to serve Burgomaster Kolyan Indirovich, but in truth he serves Strahd. After delivering the letter, Arrigal mounts his horse and rides off. He doesn't wait for the characters to follow him.

The crest depicted on the letter's seal belongs to Strahd, though the characters have never seen it before. Show the players Strahd's crest on page 239.

The letter, which seems to have been written by the burgomaster, was actually penned by Strahd. If the characters read the letter, show the players "Kolyan Indirovich's Letter (Version 1)" in appendix F. The letter is bait to lure the adventurers to Barovia. If the characters take the bait, they arrive at area A (see chapter 2, "The Lands of Barovia").

## Mysterious Visitors

The details of this adventure hook assume that your D&D campaign is based in or near Daggerford, a town on the Sword Coast in the Forgotten Realms, but you can change the location to suit your campaign.

Duchess Morwen of Daggerford is having guests for dinner—and you are invited. No strangers to Daggerford, you have come to the town's defense on more than one occasion, and you count Lady Morwen as a friend and a benefactor.

A cool autumn breeze blows through the streets as you make your way to the keep. As you dine on hot, spicy soup and tenderly cooked pheasant, you can tell that the duchess seems more out of sorts than usual. Then a pall comes over the occasion as she voices her concern about a band of wayward travelers camped outside the town's walls. They seemed harmless at first, but Morwen has received reports that they have begun harassing townsfolk and other visitors as they come and go, demanding money and wine, and threatening to put hexes on anyone who doesn't pay up.

Yesterday, the duchess ordered several guards to scare away the mysterious visitors, but they couldn't get the job done. When the guards returned, they spoke sympathetically about the visitors. It seemed as if the guards had been magically charmed.

Morwen doesn't want an armed conflict, but she aims to send a stern message to the visitors and asks you to deliver it on her behalf. "If they don't leave before dawn," she says, "I'll burn their wagons to the ground."

The characters are asked to deliver Duchess Morwen's message immediately after dinner.

The travelers are camped on the hill outside the gates of Daggerford, near the road. Guards atop the walls watch the camp closely at all hours.

When the characters approach the camp, read:

> As the evening grows dark, you see a dozen men and women gathered around a crackling bonfire. The folk are in good spirits. A few of them sing and dance around the fire while others find happiness in their flasks and wineskins. Three barrel-topped wagons are parked at odd angles. Tied to a nearby tree, grazing, are half a dozen draft horses wearing bright coats with bangles and tassels.

The men and women are Vistani. They have no interest in Daggerford. Their orders are to deliver the characters safely to Barovia.

The leader of this group is Stanimir (CN male human), an old man with the statistics of a **mage** who has the following spells prepared:

Cantrips (at will): *friends, light, mage hand, prestidigitation*
1st level (4 slots): *charm person, mage armor, shield, sleep*
2nd level (3 slots): *misty step, suggestion*
3rd level (3 slots): *bestow curse, phantom steed, vampiric touch*
4th level (3 slots): *greater invisibility, stoneskin*
5th level (1 slot): *dominate person*

Stanimir is joined by his daughter, Damia (CN female human **spy**), and his son, Ratka (CN male human **bandit captain**). Nine other Vistani (male and female **bandits**) heed Ratka's commands. The six **draft horses** are used to pull the Vistani wagons, which contain their belongings but nothing of value.

## The Dancing Fire

Stanimir introduces himself and welcomes the characters to his camp. If they deliver Duchess Morwen's warning, read:

> Stanimir laughs. "Don't worry. We have no wish to make enemies of Lady Morwen. I have a story to tell all of you. First you listen, then we go."

If the characters agree to hear Stanimir's story, he invites them to gather around the fire and hear his tale:

> Stanimir fills his mouth with wine, then spits into the fire. The flames turn from orange to green. As they dance and sway, a dark shape appears in the bonfire's core.
>
> "We come from an ancient land whose name is long forgotten—a land of kings. Our enemies forced us from our homes, and now we wander the lost roads."
>
> The dark shape in the fire takes the form of a man being knocked from his horse, a spear piercing his side.
>
> Stanimir continues. "One night, a wounded soldier staggered into our camp and collapsed. We nursed his terrible injury and quenched his thirst with wine. He survived. When we asked him who he was, he wouldn't say. All he wanted was to return home, but we were deep in the land of his enemies. We took him as one of our own and followed him back toward his homeland. His enemies hunted him. They said he was a prince, yet we didn't give him up, even when their assassins fell upon us like wolves."
>
> Deep in the bonfire, you see the dark figure standing with sword drawn, fighting off a host of shadowy shapes.
>
> "This man of royal blood fought to protect us, as we protected him. We bore him safely to his home, and he thanked us. He said, 'I owe you my life. Stay as long as you wish, leave when you choose, and know that you will always be safe here.'"
>
> The figure in the dancing fire vanquishes its final foe, then disperses in a cloud of smoke and embers.
>
> Stanimir's face becomes a somber mask. "A curse has befallen our noble prince, turning him into a tyrant. We alone have the power to leave his domain. We've traveled far and wide to find heroes such as yourselves to end our dread lord's curse and put his troubled soul to rest. Our leader, Madam Eva, knows all. Will you return to Barovia with us and speak with her?"

These Vistani refuse to speak the name of their "dread lord" and provide no additional information. If the characters press them for details, the Vistani reply, "Madam Eva has the answers you seek."

If the characters agree to accompany the Vistani, the Vistani lead them south along the Trade Way. After several days of uneventful travel, the mists of Ravenloft engulf the caravan, transporting the characters and the Vistani to Barovia. The Vistani then lead the party safely to their leader, Madam Eva, at area G (see chapter 2). The characters arrive at area A and are taken through areas B, E, and F on the way to Madam Eva's camp. If the characters rid themselves of their Vistani hosts before reaching Madam Eva's camp, they're on the own.

If the characters decline Stanimir's invitation, the Vistani are disappointed but leave as promised. A day or two later, use the "Creeping Fog" adventure hook or some variation of it to draw the characters into Barovia.

## WEREWOLVES IN THE MIST

This adventure hook assumes you're running a campaign in or near Daggerford (see "Mysterious Visitors" for more information). It also assumes you're using the five player factions featured in the Adventurers League.

> "Werewolves in the mist!" You've heard these dreaded words spoken again and again by farmers, merchants, and adventurers alike. The hamlets east of Daggerford have fallen prey to a pack of werewolves that spills out of the Misty Forest on nights of the full moon, cloaked in crawling mist that seems to follow them wherever they go. The beasts spread death and mayhem, slaughtering adults and stealing children before retreating back into the woods. Others have tried to combat the werewolf menace, with little success.

The Misty Forest lies thirty miles east of Daggerford. Before the characters embark on their quest, those who have faction allegiances receive additional information described in the sections that follow. Take the players aside, and read them the boxed text for their faction.

### HARPERS

> A Harper named Zelraun Roaringhorn knows a metalsmith who will silver your weapons for free. He also provides some helpful magic.
>
> "We strive to protect the powerless," he says. "If the children kidnapped by the werewolves are still alive, I would see them safely returned."

Zelraun Roaringhorn (LN male human **mage**) has come to Daggerford to meet with its ruler, Duchess Morwen, and offer the Harpers' support.

Zelraun gives each Harper character a *spell scroll* of *remove curse*. He has also made arrangements with a metalsmith in Waterdeep to sheathe the characters'

weapons in silver. The party can have up to six weapons silvered in this manner. Twenty pieces of ammunition count as one weapon for this purpose.

***About the Harpers.*** The Harpers is a network of spellcasters and spies who advocate equality and who covertly oppose the abuse of power. The organization's longevity is largely due to its decentralized, grassroots, secretive nature, and the autonomy of its members. The Harpers have small cells and lone operatives throughout the Forgotten Realms. They share information with one another from time to time as needs warrant. The Harpers' ideology is noble, and its members pride themselves on their ingenuity and incorruptibility.

### ORDER OF THE GAUNTLET

> You met with the heads of the Order of the Gauntlet chapter house in Waterdeep. They've stationed members of the order at various inns and homesteads east of Daggerford, so that locals need not fear the night. Now they're counting on you to find the werewolves' lair in the Misty Forest. Only then can the order mount an organized assault. As you prepare to depart, a knight of the order named Lanniver Strayl offers you his blessing.

Lanniver Strayl (LG male human **knight**), a devout follower of Tyr recently arrived in Daggerford, gives a *potion of heroism* to each member of the order in the party.

***About the Order of the Gauntlet.*** Founded by paladins and clerics of Helm, Torm, and Tyr, the order is a dedicated group of like-minded individuals driven by religious zeal or a finely honed sense of justice and honor. The order is ready to lash out the moment evil acts, and not a moment before. The order strikes hard and fast, without waiting for the blessings of temples or the permission of rulers. The order believes that evil must be smashed, or it will swiftly overcome all.

### EMERALD ENCLAVE

> You don't need to consult with others in the Emerald Enclave to know that the werewolves are upsetting the natural order. For balance to be restored, they must be eradicated. It seems the gods of nature agree, for they've sent good weather and preserved the monsters' tracks.

Members of the Emerald Enclave in the party gain inspiration whenever the party kills a werewolf.

***About the Emerald Enclave.*** This widespread group of wilderness survivalists preserves the natural order while rooting out unnatural threats. Druids, rangers, and barbarians make up most of its membership.

Branches of the organization can be found wherever untamed wilderness exists. Members of the Emerald Enclave know how to survive, and more important, they want to help others do the same. They aren't opposed to civilization or progress, but they strive to prevent civilization and the wilderness from destroying one another.

## LORDS' ALLIANCE

> A Lords' Alliance operative from Waterdeep named Eravien Haund comes to Daggerford bearing news that alliance agents have not only captured one of the werewolves but also conducted a thorough interrogation before putting the creature out of its misery.

Eravien Haund (LN male half-elf **noble**) imparts the following information to fellow Lords' Alliance members and tells them not to share it:

- The werewolf pack has almost a dozen members. The leader of the pack is a man named Kiril.
- The werewolves come from a distant land called Barovia. The Lords' Alliance has no information about it.
- The werewolves worship a deity called Mother Night.
- The werewolves leave and return to Barovia through some kind of ancient portal. (This is a deduction on Eravien's part, based on the werewolf prisoner's vague description of how the pack gets to and from Barovia.)

Eravien believes that he can gain prestige within the Lords' Alliance if he learns the whereabouts of the "ancient portal" that the werewolves are using and destroys it. He is convinced that the portal represents a danger not only to Daggerford but also to Waterdeep. Any Lords' Alliance character who agrees to destroy it is given a *spell scroll* of *magic weapon*. Eravien also promises to furnish the character with a letter of recommendation (see "Marks of Prestige" in chapter 7 of the *Dungeon Master's Guide*) once the portal is destroyed.

**About the Lords' Alliance.** The Lords' Alliance is a coalition of political powers concerned with their mutual security and prosperity. Heading the coalition are rulers in the North and along the Sword Coast.

Although alliance members have pledged to join forces against common threats, every lord in it places the fate and fortune of his or her settlement above all others. Agents of the alliance are chosen primarily for their loyalty, and are trained in observation, stealth, innuendo, and combat. Backed by the wealthy, they carry well-made equipment (often disguised to appear common). Alliance operatives are often glory hounds.

## ZHENTARIM

> The Black Network sees the werewolf menace as an opportunity to provide lords and nervous landowners with mercenaries to protect their holdings. But at least one of your fellow members has a grudge against the lycanthropes. Davra Jassur, a member of the Zhentarim based in Waterdeep, arranges a private meeting with you.

Davra Jassur (LE female human **assassin**) poses as a recruiter for the Black Network but is, in fact, a cutthroat who quietly disposes of competitors. Her husband, Yarak, was also a member of the Black Network. He was escorting a caravan traveling from Daggerford to the Way Inn (about sixty miles southeast of Daggerford, along the Trade Way) when the werewolves attacked. Yarak was slain, and Davra wants revenge; she wants the head of the werewolf pack leader. She is too tied up with "business" to engage in a personal vendetta, but if another member of the Black Network were to help, she would owe that individual a special favor (see "Marks of Prestige" in chapter 7 of the *Dungeon Master's Guide*).

**About the Zhentarim.** The Zhentarim is an unscrupulous shadow network that seeks to expand its influence throughout the Forgotten Realms. The public face of the Black Network appears relatively benign. It offers the best and cheapest goods and services, both legal and illicit, hoping to undercut its competitors.

Members of the Zhentarim think of themselves as members of an extended family and rely on it for resources and security. At the same time, members are granted the autonomy to increase their own wealth and influence. As a whole, the Zhentarim promises "the best for the best," although in truth the organization is more interested in spreading its own propaganda and influence than investing in the improvement of its members.

## WELCOME TO BAROVIA

Strahd is using the werewolves to lure adventurers to his domain. Characters can follow the werewolves' tracks into the Misty Forest. After hours of fruitless searching, the characters are engulfed by thick fog:

> The woods darken as the trees begin to close ranks, their needle-covered arms interlocking to blot out the sun. The shroud of mist that covers the ground turns into creeping walls of gray fog that silently envelop you until you can't see more than a few feet in any direction. Soon, even the werewolf tracks disappear.

No matter which direction they go, the characters come to a lonely dirt road that cuts through the woods, leading to area A (see chapter 2). As an alternative, you can have them enter Barovia near Krezk (see chapter 8).

## CREEPING FOG

This scenario assumes that the characters are camping in a forest when the fog engulfs them. They are quietly borne to the edge of Barovia.

> The woods are quiet this night, and the air grows chill. Your fire sputters as a low mist gathers around the edges of your camp, growing closer as the night wears on. By morning, the fog hangs thick in the air, turning the trees around you into gray ghosts. Then you notice these aren't the same trees that surrounded you the night before.

No matter which direction they go, the characters come to a lonely dirt road that cuts through the woods, leading to area A (see chapter 2). As an alternative, you can have them enter Barovia near Krezk (see chapter 8).

# CHAPTER 2: THE LANDS OF BAROVIA

THE IDYLLIC VALLEY NESTLED IN THE Balinok Mountains was a slice of heaven to those who knew of its existence before Strahd's arrival. The serenity of the place was forever shattered when Strahd led a bloody crusade against the enemies of his family that ended here with the slaughter of hundreds. Struck by the scenic beauty of his most recent conquest and eager to escape the shadow of his father's legacy, Strahd made the valley his home and named it Barovia after the late King Barov, his father.

The land now called Barovia is no longer part of the world that Strahd once tried to conquer. It now exists within a demiplane formed by Strahd's consciousness and surrounded by a deadly fog. No creature can leave without Strahd's permission, and those that try become lost in the mist.

Strahd allows the Vistani to come and go as they please because he admires their lust for life and their willingness to serve him when he needs them. He also owes an ancient debt to the Vistani people. As a soldier centuries ago, he suffered a grievous injury in battle, and the Vistani tended his wounds and returned him safely to his family without making any demand for payment. The Vistani claim to possess potions that allow them to leave Strahd's domain, but the potions are false concoctions with no magical power. Nevertheless, the Vistani are willing to sell them for a hefty price.

Native Barovians have been terrorized for centuries by the one they call "the devil Strahd." Only a handful of them have the will to oppose him. Barovians congregate in the valley's three main settlements—the villages of Barovia and Krezk and the town of Vallaki—for fear of falling prey to wolves and other beasts that prowl the woods. Among these people are the Keepers of the Feather, a secret society of wereravens. Not powerful enough to defeat Strahd on their own, the Keepers readily assist adventurers who find themselves drawn into Strahd's domain.

## LAY OF THE LAND

Rolling thunderclouds cast a gray pall over the land of Barovia. A deathly stillness hangs over the dark woods, which are patrolled constantly by Strahd's wolves and other servitors.

The evergreen trees of the Svalich Woods climb the sides of the mountains that enclose the valley. The largest of these peaks is Mount Baratok, with its snow-covered cap and rugged slopes. Baratok's slightly smaller twin, Mount Ghakis, is mostly bald with tufts of trees here and there. Between these two mountains stands Lake Zarovich, which is fed by streams of ice-cold water pouring down the face of Mount Baratok. On the south side of the lake rests the town of Vallaki, enclosed by a palisade. West of the two mountains, atop a hill, stands the Abbey of Saint Markovia, around which the Barovians built a walled village named Krezk. Between Vallaki and Krezk lie the ruins of Argynvostholt, the fallen bastion of a knightly order called the Order of the Silver Dragon, wiped out by Strahd and his army. East of the mountains lies the village of Barovia, shrouded in mist and bereft of walls and defenses. The dark silhouette of Castle Ravenloft looks down on this village from its perch atop a 1,000-foot-high column of rock known as the Pillarstone of Ravenloft.

## MISTS OF RAVENLOFT

A deadly fog surrounds the land of Barovia and engulfs any creature that tries to leave. Even flying creatures are subject to the fog's effects, which are as follows:

- A creature that starts its turn in the fog must succeed on a DC 20 Constitution saving throw or gain one level of exhaustion (see appendix A in the *Player's Handbook*). This exhaustion can't be removed while the creature is in the fog.

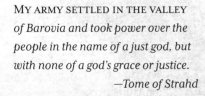

MY ARMY SETTLED IN THE VALLEY *of Barovia and took power over the people in the name of a just god, but with none of a god's grace or justice.*
—Tome of Strahd

- No matter how far a creature travels in the fog, or in which direction it goes, it gets turned around so that it eventually finds itself back in Barovia.
- The area within the fog is heavily obscured (see "Vision and Light" in chapter 8 of the *Player's Handbook*).

## Sunlight in Barovia

By the will of the Dark Powers, the sun never fully shines in the lands of Barovia. Even during the day, the sky is dimmed by fog or storm clouds, or the light is strangely muted. Barovian daylight is bright light, yet it isn't considered sunlight for the purpose of effects and vulnerabilities, such as a vampire's, tied to sunlight.

Nevertheless, Strahd and his vampire spawn tend to stay indoors most of the day and venture out at night, and they are subject to sunlight created by magic.

# Alterations to Magic

The land of Barovia resides in its own demiplane, isolated from all other planes, including the Material Plane. No spell—not even *wish*—allows one to escape from Strahd's domain. *Astral projection*, *teleport*, *plane shift*, and similar spells cast for the purpose of leaving Barovia simply fail, as do effects that banish a creature to another plane of existence. These restrictions apply to magic items and artifacts that have properties that transport or banish creatures to other planes. Magic that allows transit to the Border Ethereal, such as the *etherealness* spell and the Etherealness feature of incorporeal undead, is the exception to this rule. A creature that enters the Border Ethereal from Strahd's domain is pulled back into Barovia upon leaving that plane.

For the purpose of spells whose effects change across or are blocked by planar boundaries (such as *sending*), Strahd's domain is considered its own plane. Magic that summons creatures or objects from other planes functions normally in Barovia, as does magic that involves an extradimensional space. Any spells cast within such an extradimensional space (such as that created by *Mordenkainen's magnificent mansion*) are subject to the same restrictions as magic cast in Barovia.

While in Barovia, characters who receive spells from deities or otherworldly patrons continue to do so. In addition, spells that allow contact with beings from other planes function normally—with one proviso: Strahd can sense when someone in his domain is casting such a spell and can choose to make himself the spell's recipient, so that he becomes the one who is contacted.

## Cosmetic Spell Modifications

At your discretion, a spell can be modified cosmetically to enhance the horrific atmosphere. Here are examples:

**Alarm:** Instead of hearing a mental ping when the alarm is triggered, the caster hears a scream.
**Bigby's hand:** The conjured hand is skeletal.
**Find familiar:** The familiar is undead—not a celestial, fey, or fiend—and is immune to features that turn undead.
**Find steed:** The summoned steed is undead—not a celestial, fey, or fiend—and is immune to features that turn undead.

**Find the path:** A child's spirit appears and guides the caster to the desired location. The spirit can't be harmed and doesn't speak.
**Fog cloud:** Misty, harmless claws form in the fog.
**Gust of wind:** A ghastly moan accompanies the summoned wind.
**Mage hand:** The summoned hand is skeletal.
**Maze:** The surfaces of the demiplane's maze are made of mortared skulls and bones.
**Phantom steed:** The steed resembles a skeletal horse.
**Rary's telepathic bond:** Characters linked together by the spell can't shake the feeling that something vile is telepathically eavesdropping on them.
**Revivify:** A creature restored to life by a *revivify* spell screams upon regaining consciousness, as though waking from some horrible nightmare.
**Spirit guardians:** The spirits appear as ghostly, skeletal warriors.
**Wall of stone:** A wall created by the spell has ghastly faces sculpted into it, as though tortured spirits were somehow trapped within the stone.

## Resurrection Madness

In Barovia, the souls of the dead are as trapped as the souls of the living. They become caught in the mists and can't travel to the afterlife.

When a humanoid who has been dead for at least 24 hours returns to life, either by way of a spell or some supernatural means, it gains a random form of indefinite madness brought on by the realization that its spirit is trapped in Barovia, likely forever. To determine how this madness is expressed, roll on the Indefinite Madness table in chapter 8 of the *Dungeon Master's Guide*.

# Barovians

After his armies occupied the valley and slew its inhabitants, Strahd repopulated the area with human subjects drawn from his other conquered lands. As a result, Barovians have a wide variety of ethnic backgrounds.

Barovians are deeply invested in their homes and their traditions. They are wary of strange peoples and customs. The way Barovians deal with strangers can be unsettling to those newcomers. Barovians have a tendency to stare openly, in silence, thereby expressing their disapproval of anything that isn't familiar to them. Barovians aren't talkative with strangers, to the extent of being pointedly rude. Most Barovians have violent tempers that boil up through their customary silence when they are provoked. They also have a social cohesiveness (thrust upon them by their weird circumstances) that can make them act together against outsiders if a Barovian is mistreated.

Barovians were a happy people once, but their history and current conditions aren't pleasant. If one manages to win the trust of a Barovian, one has a friend for life and a stalwart ally.

Barovian children aren't happy children. They are raised in a culture of fear and told time and again not to wander too far from their homes or enter the woods. They experience little hope or joy, and they are taught to fear the devil Strahd above all.

Barovian adults eke out modest livings. With no new wealth pouring into the valley, they trade in old coins that bear the profile of their dark lord, Strahd, as he looked when he was alive. They hide their precious baubles in their houses and dress plainly outdoors, so as not to attract the attention of Strahd or his spies.

Barovians live within a closed ecosystem. Every Barovian adult is expected to learn a trade or serve a function. Barovians stitch their own clothing, craft their own furniture, grow their own food, and make their own wine. With fewer than three thousand people living in the entire valley, finding the perfect mate isn't easy, so Barovians have learned to settle for what they can get.

## Souls and Shells

Barovians are made of flesh and blood. They are born, they live, they age, and they die. But not all of them—only about one in every ten—have souls.

When a being with a soul dies in Barovia, that soul remains trapped in Strahd's domain until it is reincarnated in a newborn. It can take decades for a bodiless soul to find a host, and Barovians who share the same soul over generations tend to look alike. That is why Ireena Kolyana looks exactly like Strahd's beloved Tatyana—both women were born with the same soul.

Strahd needs loyal subjects to feed his ego. Barovians without souls are empty shells created by his consciousness to fill out the local population. Although they are physically indistinguishable from Barovians with souls, they tend to be bereft of charm and imagination and to be more compliant and depressed than the others. They dress in drab clothing, whereas Barovians who have souls wear clothes with a splash of color or individuality.

A Barovian woman, soulless or not, can give birth. A child born in Barovia might have a soul even if one or both parents do not. Conversely, the child of two parents with souls isn't certain to have a soul of its own. Barovians without souls are maudlin folk who experience fear but neither laugh nor cry.

Ireena Kolyana and her brother Ismark both have souls, as do all Vistani. Which Barovians have souls and which don't is left up to you.

Strahd periodically feeds on the blood of Barovians who have souls, but he can't draw nourishment from the blood of the soulless. He can tell at a glance whether a Barovian has a soul or is merely a shell.

### Barovian Names

You can use the following lists to create Barovian NPC names on the fly.

**Male Names:** Alek, Andrej, Anton, Balthazar, Bogan, Boris, Dargos, Darzin, Dragomir, Emeric, Falkon, Frederich, Franz, Gargosh, Gorek, Grygori, Hans, Harkus, Ivan, Jirko, Kobal, Korga, Krystofor, Lazlo, Livius, Marek, Miroslav, Nikolaj, Nimir, Oleg, Radovan, Radu, Seraz, Sergei, Stefan, Tural, Valentin, Vasily, Vladislav, Waltar, Yesper, Zsolt

**Female Names:** Alana, Clavdia, Danya, Dezdrelda, Diavola, Dorina, Drasha, Drilvia, Elisabeta, Fatima, Grilsha, Isabella, Ivana, Jarzinka, Kala, Katerina, Kereza, Korina, Lavinia, Magda, Marta, Mathilda, Minodora, Mirabel, Miruna, Nimira, Nyanka, Olivenka, Ruxandra, Sorina, Tereska, Valentina, Vasha, Victoria, Wensencia, Zondra

**Family Names:** Alastroi, Antonovich/Antonova, Barthos, Belasco, Cantemir, Dargovich/Dargova, Diavolov, Diminski, Dilisnya, Drazkoi, Garvinski, Grejenko, Groza, Grygorovich/Grygorova, Ivanovich/Ivanova, Janek, Karushkin, Konstantinovich/Konstantinova, Krezkov/Krezkova, Krykski, Lansten, Lazarescu, Lukresh, Lipsiege, Martikov/Martikova, Mironovich/Mironovna, Moldovar, Nikolovich/Nikolova, Nimirovich/Nimirova, Oronovich/Oronova, Petrovich/Petrovna, Polensky, Radovich/Radova, Rilsky, Stefanovich/Stefanova, Strazni, Swilovich/Swilova, Taltos, Targolov/Targolova, Tyminski, Ulbrek, Ulrich, Vadu, Voltanescu, Zalenski, Zalken

If Strahd is defeated, the fog that surrounds Barovia fades away, allowing the inhabitants of the valley to leave if they wish. Only those who have souls, however, can truly leave this place. Soulless Barovians cease to exist as soon as they exit the valley.

## BAROVIANS AND NONHUMANS

Barovians are human. Although they know that dwarves, elves, halflings and other civilized races exist, few living Barovians have seen such "creatures," let alone interacted with them.

Aside from the secretive dusk elves of Vallaki (see chapter 5), the only nonhumans most Barovians are familiar with are the adventurers that Strahd has lured to his dark realm. Barovians thus react to nonhuman characters the same way most humans in the real world would react to elf, dwarf, or half-orc adventurers suddenly walking the streets. Most such outsiders are scorned, feared, or shunned.

## BAROVIAN LORE

Typical Barovians know certain facts, or have certain beliefs, about their existence and their surroundings. This common lore is summarized here. Characters can learn this information after earning a Barovian's trust.

### THE DEVIL STRAHD

About Strahd and vampires, the Barovians believe the following:

- Strahd von Zarovich is a vampire, and he dwells in Castle Ravenloft. No one is welcome at the castle.
- The devil Strahd is a curse placed on the land because of a forgotten sin of the Barovians' ancestors. (This is untrue, but Barovians believe it nonetheless.)
- A vampire must rest in its coffin during the day. At night, it can summon wolves and vermin to do its bidding. A vampire can transform into a bat, a wolf, or a cloud of mist. In its humanoid form, it can dominate you with its powerful gaze.
- A vampire can't enter a residence without an invitation from one of the occupants.
- Running water burns a vampire like acid, and sunlight causes a vampire to burst into flame.

### THE LAND OF BAROVIA

Barovians know the following facts about their homeland:

- Anyone who attempts to leave the land of Barovia begins to choke on the fog. Those who don't turn back perish.
- Many strangers have been drawn to Barovia over the years, but they all die or disappear before long.
- Wolves, dire wolves, and werewolves prowl the Svalich Woods, and hungry bats fill the skies at night.
- The village of Barovia sits at the east end of the valley. Its burgomaster is named Kolyan Indirovich.
- The town of Vallaki lies in the heart of the valley. Its burgomaster is named Baron Vargas Vallakovich.
- The fortified village of Krezk lies at the west end of the valley and is built around an old abbey. The village burgomaster is named Dmitri Krezkov.

### BAROVIAN CALENDAR

Barovia has its own calendar, and Barovians are accustomed to measuring the passage of time in "moons" instead of months. As a measurement of time, each moon begins on the first night of a full moon and lasts a full lunar cycle. A year consists of twelve moons, or twelve lunar cycles.

Strahd was born in 306. In 346, he inherited his father's crown, lands, and army. Strahd conquered the valley in 347, finished construction of Castle Ravenloft in 350, and died and became a vampire in 351. The current year is 735.

- Wine is the lifeblood of Barovia—for some, it is the only reason to keep living. Barovian taverns get their wine from the Wizard of Wines winery near Krezk.
- A mad wizard of great power haunts the foothills of Mount Baratok. He is an outsider and no friend of the vampire's.

### BELIEFS AND SUPERSTITIONS

Barovians have deep-rooted religious beliefs and superstitions that they pass down from one generation to the next:

- Two divine forces watch over the Barovian people: the Morninglord and Mother Night.
- Before the curse of Strahd befell the land, the Morninglord watched over the Barovian people from sunrise until sundown. Now, the sun has not shone unobscured for centuries, and the Morninglord no longer answers their prayers.
- The presence of Mother Night is felt most strongly between dusk and dawn, although nighttime prayers to her go unanswered. It is widely believed that she has forsaken the Barovian people and sent the devil Strahd to punish them for their ancestors' offenses.
- Spirits drift along the Old Svalich Road toward Castle Ravenloft in the dead of night. These phantoms are all that remain of Strahd's enemies, and this damnable fate awaits anyone who opposes him.
- The Vistani serve the devil Strahd. They alone are allowed to leave Barovia.
- Never harm a raven, lest ill fortune befall you!

## VISTANI

The Vistani (singular: Vistana) are wanderers, traveling about in horse-drawn, barrel-topped wagons, which they build themselves. Compared to Barovians, they are flamboyant, dressing in bright clothes and laughing often. As much as they feel at home in Strahd's dreary land, they know they can leave it whenever they please and aren't damned to spend eternity there.

Vistani are silversmiths, coppersmiths, haberdashers, cooks, weavers, musicians, entertainers, storytellers, toolmakers, and horse traders. They also earn money by telling fortunes and selling information. They spend whatever they earn to support a lavish lifestyle, display their wealth openly as a sign of prosperity, and share their good fortune with family and friends.

Each family or clan of Vistani is its own little gerontocracy, with the oldest member ruling the roost. This elder carries the bulk of the responsibility for enforcing traditions, settling disputes, setting the course for the group's travels, and preserving the Vistani way of life. Vistani elders make all the important decisions, but whether by choice or because of their age, tend to speak in cryptic, flowing riddles.

Vistani families and clans are closely knit. They resolve disagreements through contests that end with reconciliatory singing, dancing, and storytelling. The Vistani are quick to act when their lives or traditions are threatened and are merciless when they believe they must be. Vistani who knowingly bring harm or misfortune to others of their kind are banished—the worst punishment a Vistana can imagine, even worse than death.

## STRAHD'S VISTANI SERVANTS

During one of Strahd's military campaigns, years before he became a vampire, a group of Vistani rescued him after he was wounded in battle. These Vistani not only nursed Strahd back to health but also delivered him safely home. As a reward for their generosity, Strahd declared that all Vistani had the right to come and go from his land as they please, and this privilege extends to the present day. Thus, Vistani can travel freely through the fog that surrounds Barovia, without fear of harm or entrapment.

Strahd honors his debt to the Vistani in part because he envies the Vistani way of life—the freedom they have to go where they please, their devotion to family, and their festive spirit. The courtesy he shows them is not simply a matter of honor but is also born from his admiration of them.

In the centuries since Strahd became a vampire, many Vistani have allowed themselves to be corrupted by Strahd, to the extent that they consider him their king. Vistani who serve Strahd are less lively and friendly than normal Vistani, and their hearts are poisoned with dark intentions. Strahd uses them to lure adventurers into his domain and keep him informed about the events occurring in lands beyond his reach. These Vistani will lie to protect the vampire, and they fear the consequences of disobeying him.

When it comes to sharing information about their dark master, Strahd's Vistani pretend to be helpful, but the information they impart is misleading at best and often deceptive. They readily tell adventurers that they have a potion that protects them from the deadly fog that surrounds Barovia. Although this is a lie, they attempt to sell their fake potion for as much money as they can get.

## VISTANI LORE

Vistani know or believe certain facts about their people and their surroundings. This common lore is summarized here. Characters can learn this information after earning a Vistana's trust.

### STRAHD VON ZAROVICH

About Strahd, the Vistani believe the following:

- Strahd comes from a royal bloodline. He died centuries ago yet endures as one of the undead, feasting on the blood of the living. Barovians refer to him as "the devil Strahd."
- Strahd has taken many consorts, but he has known only one true love: a Barovian peasant girl named Tatyana. (The Vistani don't know what happened to her.)
- Strahd named his castle, Ravenloft, after his beloved mother, Queen Ravenovia. Strangers aren't welcome at the castle without an invitation.

### THE LAND OF BAROVIA

Vistani know the following facts about Barovia and Barovians:

- Strahd conquered this land centuries ago and named it after his father, King Barov. Strahd uses wolves, bats, and other creatures to spy on all of his realm.
- Barovians are simple, frightened people. Some have old souls, but many do not. The soulless ones are easy to spot, for they know nothing but fear. They have no charm, hope, or spark, and they don't cry.
- The Old Svalich Road passes through Strahd's domain. Three settlements lie on the road like beads on a string: Krezk to the west, Vallaki in the heart of the valley, and Barovia to the east. Strahd has spies in each settlement.
- There's an old windmill on the road between the village of Barovia and the town of Vallaki. It should be avoided at all costs! (The Vistani refuse to say more.)
- It is wise to stick to the road. Wild druids, wayward ghosts, and packs of wolves and werewolves haunt the Svalich Woods.

### BELIEFS AND SUPERSTITIONS

The Vistani have deep-rooted beliefs and superstitions that they pass down from one generation to the next:

- The souls of those who die in Barovia can't escape to the afterlife. They are prisoners in Strahd's domain.
- Some Vistani women are blessed with prescience. Of all the great Vistani fortune-tellers, none compares to Madam Eva. If knowledge of the future is what you seek, Madam Eva will tell you your fate.
- A prescient Vistana can't see her own future or the future of another Vistana. It is the burden of the Vistani's great gift that their own fates can't be divined.
- Vistani curses are potent, but they are invoked with great caution. Vistani know that to curse one who is undeserving of such punishment can have grave consequences for the one who utters such a curse.
- Ravens carry lost souls within them, so killing one is bad luck. (The ravens don't carry souls within.)

## VISTANI CURSES

A Vistana, regardless of age, can use an action to utter a curse. The curse targets another creature within 30 feet that the Vistana can see. The Vistana can't utter another such curse before finishing a long rest.

The curse is a repayment for an injustice or a slight. The target must succeed on a Wisdom saving throw to avoid the curse. The saving throw DC is 8 + the Vistana's proficiency bonus + the Vistana's Charisma modifier. The curse lasts until ended with a *remove curse* spell, a *greater restoration* spell, or similar magic. It doesn't end when the target dies. If a cursed target is returned to life, the curse remains in effect.

When the curse ends, the Vistana suffers a harmful psychic backlash. The amount of this psychic damage depends on the severity of the curse that was invoked.

The Vistana chooses the curse's effect from the options that follow; other Vistani curses are possible. All such effects deal psychic damage to the Vistani who uttered them when they end:

- The target is unable to perform a certain kind of act involving fine motor control, such as tying knots, writing, playing an instrument, sewing, or casting spells that have somatic components. When this curse ends, the Vistana takes 1d6 psychic damage.
- The target's appearance changes in a sinister yet purely cosmetic way. For example, the curse can place a scar on the target's face, turn the target's teeth into yellow fangs, or give the target bad breath. When this curse ends, the Vistana it takes 1d6 psychic damage.
- A nonmagical item in the target's possession (chosen by the DM) disappears and can't be found until the curse ends. The lost item can weigh no more than 1 pound. When this curse ends, the Vistana takes 1d6 psychic damage.
- The target gains vulnerability to a damage type of the Vistana's choice. When this curse ends, the Vistana takes 3d6 psychic damage.
- The target has disadvantage on ability checks and saving throws tied to one ability score of the Vistana's choice. When this curse ends, the Vistana takes 3d6 psychic damage.
- The target's attunement to one magic item (chosen by the DM) ends, and the target can't attune to the chosen item until the curse ends. When this curse ends, the Vistana takes 5d6 psychic damage.
- The target is blinded, deafened, or both. When this curse ends, the Vistana takes 5d6 psychic damage.

## EVIL EYE

As an action, a Vistana can target a creature within 10 feet that the Vistana can see. This magical ability, which the Vistani call the Evil Eye, duplicates the duration and effect of the *animal friendship*, *charm person*, or *hold person* spell (Vistana's choice), but requires neither somatic nor material components. The spell save DC is 8 + the caster's proficiency bonus + the caster's Charisma modifier. If the target succeeds on the save, the Vistana is blinded until the end of the Vistana's next turn.

A Vistana who uses Evil Eye can't use it again before finishing a short or long rest. Once a target succeeds on a saving throw against a Vistana's Evil Eye, it is immune to the Evil Eye of all Vistani for 24 hours.

## RANDOM ENCOUNTERS

Dangers abound in the land of Barovia. Check for a random encounter after every 30 minutes that the adventurers spend on the roads or in the wilderness (don't check if they have already had two random encounters outdoors in the past 12 hours):

- If the characters are on a road, an encounter occurs on a roll of 18 or higher on a d20.
- If the characters are in the wilderness, an encounter occurs on a roll of 15 or higher on a d20.

If an encounter occurs, roll on the daytime or the nighttime encounter table, depending on the time, or have Strahd's spies appear (see the "Strahd's Spies" sidebar).

## DAYTIME RANDOM ENCOUNTERS IN BAROVIA

| d12 + d8 | Encounter |
|---|---|
| 2 | 3d6 Barovian **commoners** |
| 3 | 1d6 Barovian **scouts** |
| 4 | Hunting trap |
| 5 | Grave |
| 6 | False trail |
| 7 | 1d4 + 1 Vistani **bandits** |
| 8 | Skeletal rider |
| 9 | Trinket |
| 10 | Hidden bundle |
| 11 | 1d4 **swarms of ravens** (50%) or 1 **wereraven** (see appendix D) in raven form (50%) |
| 12 | 1d6 **dire wolves** |
| 13 | 3d6 **wolves** |
| 14 | 1d4 **berserkers** |
| 15 | Corpse |
| 16 | 1d6 **werewolves** in human form |
| 17 | 1 **druid** with 2d6 **twig blights** |
| 18 | 2d4 **needle blights** |
| 19 | 1d6 **scarecrows** |
| 20 | 1 **revenant** |

## NIGHTTIME RANDOM ENCOUNTERS IN BAROVIA

| d12 + d8 | Encounter |
|---|---|
| 2 | 1 **ghost** |
| 3 | Hunting trap |
| 4 | Grave |
| 5 | Trinket |
| 6 | Corpse |
| 7 | Hidden bundle |
| 8 | Skeletal rider |
| 9 | 1d8 **swarms of bats** |
| 10 | 1d6 **dire wolves** |
| 11 | 3d6 **wolves** |
| 12 | 1d4 **berserkers** |
| 13 | 1 **druid** and 2d6 **twig blights** |
| 14 | 2d4 **needle blights** |
| 15 | 1d6 **werewolves** in wolf form |
| 16 | 3d6 **zombies** |
| 17 | 1d6 **scarecrows** |
| 18 | 1d8 **Strahd zombies** (see appendix D) |
| 19 | 1 **will-o'-wisp** |
| 20 | 1 **revenant** |

Use the descriptions that follow to help run each random encounter. The table entries are presented in alphabetical order.

## BAROVIAN COMMONERS

> The sound of snapping twigs draws your attention to several dark shapes in the fog. They carry torches and pitchforks.

If the characters are moving quietly and not carrying light sources, they can try to hide from these Barovians, who carry pitchforks (+2 to hit) instead of clubs, dealing 3 (1d6) piercing damage on a hit.

Barovian commoners rarely leave their settlements. This group might be a family looking for a safer place to live, or an angry mob searching for the characters or heading toward Castle Ravenloft to confront Strahd.

## BAROVIAN SCOUTS

If at least one character has a passive Wisdom (Perception) score of 16 or higher, read:

> You see a dark figure crouched low and perfectly still, aiming a crossbow in your direction.

If more than one scout is present, the others are spread out over a 100-foot-square area.

These scouts are Barovian hunters or trappers searching for a missing villager or townsperson. Once they realize the characters aren't out to kill them, they lower their weapons and request help in finding their missing person. If the characters decline, the scouts point them in the direction of the nearest settlement and depart without so much as a farewell. They wield light crossbows (+4 to hit, range 80/320 ft.) instead of longbows, dealing 6 (1d8 + 2) piercing damage on a hit.

## BERSERKERS

These wild mountain folk are covered head to toe in thick gray mud, which makes them hard to see in the fog and well hidden in the mountains they call home. While so camouflaged, they have advantage on Dexterity (Stealth) checks made to hide. Characters whose passive Wisdom (Perception) scores are higher than the berserker's Dexterity (Stealth) check can spot the nearest berserker.

### STRAHD'S SPIES

As the undisputed master of Barovia, Strahd has many spies, from swarms of bats to wandering Vistani, who report to him at dawn and dusk each day. These agents constantly patrol the land of Barovia and report everything they see to him.

Every day and night that the characters remain in Barovia, one or more of the vampire's spies check on them and attempt to return to Strahd with a report. When a spy appears, characters who have a passive Wisdom (Perception) score equal to or greater than the spy's Dexterity (Stealth) check notice it. A spy does not constitute an encounter if the characters are unaware of its presence. If they do notice it, the spy's goal is usually escape, not combat. A secondary goal for a spy might be to acquire some physical object—a possession, an article of clothing, or even some part of a character's body such as a lock of hair—that Strahd can use to improve the efficacy of his *scrying* spell. If one of Strahd's spies is confronted by the party, the spy attempts to grab some accessible item from a character before fleeing. If Strahd acquires such an item, he uses his *scrying* spell to learn as much as he can about the party before planning his next attack, and to verify what his spies have already told him.

If someone spots the berserker, read:

> You startle a wild-looking figure caked in gray mud and clutching a crude stone axe. Whether it's a man or a woman, you can't tell.

The berserkers shun civilized folk. They try to remain hidden and withdraw if they are spotted, attacking only if trapped or threatened.

## CORPSE

This encounter occurs only if the characters are traveling; otherwise, treat the result as no encounter.

> You find a corpse.

Roll a d6 to determine the nature of the corpse:

**1–2.** The corpse belonged to a wolf killed by spears and crossbow bolts.

**3–5.** The corpse belongs to a Barovian man, woman, or child who was clearly torn to pieces by dire wolves. If the party is accompanied by Barovian scouts (see above), the scouts recognize the corpse as the person they were searching for.

**6.** The corpse looks like one of the characters (determined randomly) but has been stripped of armor, weapons, and valuables. If moved, its flesh melts away until only the skeleton remains.

## DIRE WOLVES

> A snarling wolf the size of a grizzly bear steps out of the fog.

The area is lightly obscured by fog. If more than one dire wolf is present, the others aren't far behind and can be seen as dark shadows in the fog. The dire wolves of Barovia are cruel, overgrown wolves and Strahd's loyal servants. They can't be charmed or frightened.

## DRUID AND TWIG BLIGHTS

> A gaunt figure with wild hair and bare feet bounds toward you on all fours, wearing a tattered gown of stitched animal skins. You can't tell whether it's a man or a woman. It stops, sniffs the air, and laughs like a lunatic. The ground nearby is crawling with tiny twig monsters.

The Barovian wilderness is home to druids who worship Strahd because of his ability to control the weather and the beasts of Barovia. The druids are savage and violent, and each controls a host of twig blights, which fights until destroyed. If all the twig blights are destroyed or the druid loses more than half of its hit points, the druid flees, heading toward Yester Hill (area Y).

## FALSE TRAIL

This encounter occurs only if the characters are traveling; otherwise, treat the result as no encounter.

> You discover a foot trail that cuts through the wilderness.

Evil druids left this trail. Following it in either direction leads to a spiked pit (see "Sample Traps" in chapter 5 of the *Dungeon Master's Guide*). A thin tarp made of twigs and pine needles conceals the pit, the bottom of which is lined with sharpened wooden stakes.

## GHOST

> A baleful apparition appears before you, its hollow eyes dark with anger.

Many ghosts haunt this land. This particular ghost is all that remains of a person drained of life by Strahd (decide whether it's a man or a woman). It appears and hisses, "No one will ever know you died here." It then attacks. If the ghost succeeds in possessing a character, it leads its host to the gates of Ravenloft (area J) and hurls the host's body into the chasm.

## GRAVE

This encounter occurs only if the characters are traveling; otherwise, treat the result as no encounter.

> You stumble upon an old grave.

There is a 25 percent chance that the grave is intact, appearing as an elongated earthen mound or a rocky cairn. Characters who dig up the grave find the skeletal remains of a human clad in rusted chain mail (a soldier). Among the bones lie corroded weapons.

If the grave isn't intact, it has been violated. The characters find a shallow, mud-filled hole with dirt or rocks strewn around it and a few scattered bones within.

## HIDDEN BUNDLE

This encounter occurs only if the characters are traveling; otherwise, treat the result as no encounter.

The characters find a leather-wrapped bundle hidden in the underbrush, stuffed inside a hollow log, or nestled in the boughs of a tree. If they open the bundle, read:

> The bundle contains one set of common clothes sized for a human adult.

The clothes have a drab Barovian style to them. They belong to a wereraven or werewolf.

## HUNTING TRAP

This encounter occurs only if the characters are traveling; otherwise, treat the result as no encounter.

Have each of the characters in the front rank of the party's marching order make a DC 15 Wisdom (Survival) check. If one or more of them succeeds, read:

> You spot a wolf trap, its steel jaws caked with rust. Someone has carefully hidden the trap under a thin layer of pine needles and detritus.

Barovian hunters and trappers set these traps hoping to thin out the wolf population, but Strahd's wolves are too clever to be caught in them. If none of the characters in the front rank spots the hidden trap, one random party member steps on it. Rules for the hunting trap are presented in chapter 5, "Equipment," of the *Player's Handbook*.

## NEEDLE BLIGHTS

> Hunched figures lurch through the mist, their gaunt bodies covered in needles.

The woods crawl with needle blights that serve the evil druids of Barovia. If the characters are moving quietly and not carrying light sources, they can try to hide from these blights.

## REVENANT

> A figure walks alone with the stride and bearing of one who knows no fear. Clad in rusty armor, it clutches a gleaming longsword in its pale hand and looks ready for a fight.

From a distance, the revenant looks like a zombie and might be mistaken for such. A character within 30 feet of the revenant who succeeds on a DC 10 Wisdom (Insight) check can see the intelligence and hate in its sunken eyes. The revenant is clad in tattered chain mail that affords the same protection as leather armor.

The revenant was a knight of the Order of the Silver Dragon, which was annihilated defending the valley against Strahd's armies more than four centuries ago. The revenant no longer remembers its name and wanders the land in search of Strahd's wolves and other minions, slaying them on sight. If the characters attack it, the revenant assumes they are in league with Strahd and fights them until destroyed.

As an action, the revenant can attack twice with its longsword, wielding the weapon with both hands and dealing 15 (2d10 + 4) slashing damage on each hit.

If the characters present themselves as enemies of Strahd, the revenant urges them to travel to Argynvostholt (chapter 7) and convince Vladimir Horngaard, the leader of the Order of the Silver Dragon, to help

them. The revenant would like nothing more than to kill Strahd, but it will not venture to Castle Ravenloft unless it receives orders to do so from Vladimir. If the characters ask the revenant to lead them to Horngaard in Argynvostholt, it does so while avoiding contact with Barovian settlements.

## SCARECROWS

If at least one character has a passive Wisdom (Perception) score of 11 or higher, read:

> A scarecrow lurches into view. Its sackcloth eyes and rictus are ripe with malevolence, and its gut is stuffed with dead ravens. It has long, rusted knives for claws.

If more than one scarecrow is present, the others are close by. If none of the characters has a passive Wisdom (Perception) score of 11 or higher, the scarecrows catch the party by surprise.

Baba Lysaga (see chapter 10, area U3) crafted these scarecrows to hunt down and kill ravens and wereravens. The scarecrows are imbued with evil spirits and delight in murdering anyone they encounter.

## SKELETAL RIDER

> Through the mist comes a skeletal warhorse and rider, both clad in ruined chainmail. The skeletal rider holds up a rusted lantern that sheds no light.

The human **skeleton** and **warhorse skeleton** are all that remain of a rider and mount, both of whom perished trying to escape through the fog that surrounds Barovia. They are doomed to ride through the valley in search of another way out, without hope of salvation. The skeletons ignore the characters unless attacked.

If both the rider and its mount are destroyed, this encounter can't occur again. The destruction of one skeleton doesn't prevent future encounters with the other.

## STRAHD ZOMBIES

> Not even the cloying fog can hide the stench of death that descends upon you. Something evil approaches, its footsteps betrayed by snapping twigs.

If the characters are moving quietly and not carrying light sources, they can try to hide from the Strahd zombies. These undead soldiers once served as guards in Castle Ravenloft. They fled the castle after Strahd became a vampire but couldn't avoid their master's wrath. They still wear bits of tattered livery, and they attack the living on sight.

## Swarms of Bats

> The stillness of the night is shattered by the shriek of bats and the flapping of tiny black wings.

These bats are the servants of Strahd. They attack the characters without provocation.

## Swarms of Ravens

> Your presence in this dreary land has not gone unnoticed. A raven follows you for several minutes while keeping a respectful distance.

The raven doesn't caw or try to communicate with the characters. If they leave it alone, read:

> More ravens begin to take an interest in you. Before long, their numbers swell, and soon hundreds of them are watching you.

The ravens fly away if attacked. If they are left alone, they watch over the party, remaining with the characters until they reach Castle Ravenloft or a settlement. If the characters have a random encounter with hostile creatures, the raven swarms aid the characters by attacking and distracting their enemies.

## Trinket

> You find something on the ground.

A random character finds a lost trinket. Roll on the Trinkets table in appendix A, select a specific trinket from the table, or create one on the fly.

## Vistani Bandits

> You catch a whiff of pipe smoke in the cold air and hear laughter through the fog.

These Vistani servants of Strahd march through the Barovian wilderness, laughing and telling ghost stories. They are searching for graves to plunder or hunting small game. For a price of 100 gp, they offer to serve as guides. As long as these Vistani are with the party, roll a d12 instead of a d12 + d8 when determining random encounters in the wilderness. In addition, wolves and dire wolves don't threaten the characters as long as the Vistani are traveling with them and aren't their prisoners.

***Treasure.*** One Vistani bandit carries a pouch that holds 2d4 small gemstones (worth 50 gp each).

## Wereraven

This wereraven in raven form watches the characters from a distance. Compare its Dexterity (Stealth) check result to the characters' passive Wisdom (Perception) scores to see whether it remains hidden from the party. If one or more characters spot the creature, read:

> Through the mist, you see a black bird circling overhead. When it feels your eyes upon it, the raven flies away, but it's back before long, keeping its distance.

The wereraven belongs to a secret order called the Keepers of the Feather. If the characters don't spot it, the wereraven shadows them for 1d4 hours. At the end of that time, or anytime sooner if the characters attack it, the creature flies home to report what it has seen.

If the party has a second random encounter with a wereraven, this one presents itself to the characters as an ally and requests that they travel to the Blue Water Inn in Vallaki to meet "some new friends." It then flies off in the direction of the town.

## Werewolves

If the werewolves are in human form, read:

> A deep voice calls out, "Who goes there?" Through the chill mist you see a large man in drab clothing wearing a tattered gray cloak. He has shaggy, black hair and thick muttonchops. He leans heavily on a spear and has a small bundle of animal pelts slung over his shoulder.

If the werewolves are in wolf form, read:

> You hear the howl of a wolf some distance away.

How the werewolves act depends on the form they have taken.

***Human Form.*** Werewolves in human form pretend to be trappers. If more than one is present, the others are within whistling distance.

They try to befriend the characters to see if they are carrying silvered weapons. If the characters appear to have no such weapons, the werewolves assume hybrid form and attack. Otherwise, they part company with the characters and leave well enough alone.

***Wolf Form.*** Werewolves in wolf form follow the party from a safe distance for several hours. If their Dexterity (Stealth) checks exceed the characters' passive Wisdom (Perception) scores, the werewolves attack with surprise when the characters decide to take a short or long rest. Otherwise, they wait until the characters are weakened by another random encounter before moving in for the easy kill.

The werewolves' lair is a cave complex that overlooks Lake Baratok (area Z). If you used the "Werewolves in the Mist" adventure hook to lure the characters to Barovia, captured werewolves can be forced to divulge the location of their den, where they keep their prisoners.

### WILL-O'-WISP

This random encounter occurs only once. If it comes up again, treat the result as no encounter.

> Several hundred yards away, through the fog, you see a flickering torchlight.

If the characters follow the flickering light, read:

> The torchlight flutters as it moves away from you, but you never lose sight of it. You make your way quickly yet cautiously through the fog until you come upon the shell of a ruined tower. The upper floors of the structure have collapsed, leaving heaps of rubble and shattered timber around the tower's base. The feeble light moves through an open doorway on the ground floor, then flickers and goes out.

The light is a will-o'-wisp that enters the ruined tower and becomes invisible, hoping to lure the characters inside to their doom.

The floor of the tower is made of packed earth. Its interior is desecrated ground (see "Wilderness Hazards" in chapter 5 of the *Dungeon Master's Guide*). Against the inside wall of the tower, across from the open doorway, is a closed, empty wooden chest.

If the characters disturb the chest, 3d6 **zombies** erupt from the earthen floor and attack. Once the zombies appear, the will-o'-wisp becomes visible and joins the fray.

### WOLVES

> This land is home to many wolves, their howls at the moment too close for comfort.

Characters have a few minutes to steel themselves before these wolves attack. They heed the will of Strahd and can't be charmed or frightened.

### ZOMBIES

> The ungodly stench of rotting flesh hangs in the air. Up ahead, the walking, moaning corpses of dead men and women lumber about.

These unfortunate Barovians fell prey to the evils of the land and now shamble from place to place as a ravenous mob.

# AREAS OF BAROVIA

The following areas correspond to labels on the map of Barovia on page 35 and on the poster map.

## A. OLD SVALICH ROAD

> Black pools of water stand like dark mirrors in and around the muddy roadway. Giant trees loom on both sides of the road, their branches clawing at the mist.

If the characters are walking along the road, they arrive at area B after 5 hours. If the characters are traveling in Vistani wagons, the travel time is halved.

## B. GATES OF BAROVIA

Two sets of these gates exist: one west of the village of Barovia and one east of the village.

> The fog spills out of the forest to swallow up the road behind you. Ahead, jutting from the impenetrable woods on both sides of the road, are high stone buttresses looming gray in the fog. Huge iron gates hang on the stonework. Dew clings with cold tenacity to the rusted bars. Two headless statues of armed guardians flank the gate, their heads now lying among the weeds at their feet. They greet you only with silence.

If the characters are traveling on foot, the gates swing open as they approach, screeching as the hinges move.

---

**THE LANDS OF BAROVIA: COMMON FEATURES**

Unless the text says otherwise, the following rules apply to doors, secret doors, locks, and webs in these lands.

*Doors.* A wooden door can be forced open with a successful DC 10 Strength check, or DC 15 if the door is barred or reinforced in some other manner. Increase the DC by 5 if the door is made of stone, or by 10 if it is made of iron. Decrease the DC by 5 if the door is made of glass or amber, or if the door is weakened in some manner (such as by rot or corrosion).

*Secret Doors.* If there are obvious clues to a secret door's presence, such as scratch marks on a nearby wall or footprints leading to it, a character with a passive Wisdom (Perception) score of 15 or higher notices the secret door. Otherwise, finding a secret door requires a search of the area and a successful DC 15 Wisdom (Perception) check.

*Locks.* A creature proficient with thieves' tools can use them to pick a typical lock with a successful DC 15 Dexterity check. A typical padlock can be broken by smashing it with a bludgeoning or slashing weapon and succeeding on a DC 20 Strength check.

*Webs.* Characters can pass through ordinary webs, including thick cobwebs, without fear of being restrained or slowed down. A character can clear away the cobwebs from a 10-foot square as an action. Webs woven by giant spiders are a different matter; see "Dungeon Hazards" in chapter 5 in the *Dungeon Master's Guide* for rules on giant spider webs.

---

The gates close behind the characters after they pass through. If the characters are riding in Vistani wagons, the gates open in front of the lead wagon and close when the rear one has entered.

The eastern gates don't open for people trying to leave Strahd's domain unless they are accompanied by Vistani. The fog chokes any non-Vistani that passes through the gates or skirts around them when they are closed (see "Mists of Ravenloft" earlier in this chapter).

If Strahd is defeated, the gates of Barovia swing open, and the road east becomes clear of fog.

## C. Svalich Woods

> Towering trees, whose tops are lost in heavy gray mist, block out all but a death-gray light. The tree trunks are unnaturally close to one another, and the woods have the silence of a forgotten grave, yet exude the feeling of an unvoiced scream.

If the characters are traveling in Vistani wagons, they can continue on to the village of Barovia (area E) without incident.

If the characters are following the road on foot, the party member who has the highest passive Wisdom (Perception) score notices something:

> You catch the scent of death on the air.

The character can follow the stench to its source:

> The foul scent leads you to a human corpse half-buried in the underbrush about fifteen feet from the road. The young man appears to be a commoner. His muddy clothes are torn and raked with claw marks. Crows have been at the body, which is surrounded by the paw prints. The man has obviously been dead for several days. He holds a crumpled envelope in one hand.

The dead man, Dalvan Olensky, was trying to escape from Barovia with a letter from his master when he was killed on the road by Strahd's dire wolves. Wanting to return at once to Strahd, the wolves left the body in the woods but have not yet returned to feast.

The letter in Dalvan's hand has a large "B" set into its wax seal. The parchment is worn and flimsy. If the characters open and read the letter, show the players "Kolyan Indirovich's Letter (Version 2)" in appendix F. The letter is dated one week ago.

Dalvan was instructed to place the letter at the gates, in the hope that visitors would find it and turn back.

If the characters linger in the woods, they hear a lone wolf howl far off in the forest. Each round, one more wolf adds its voice to the howling, with the sound getting progressively closer to the party. If the characters are still in the woods after 5 rounds of howling, five **dire wolves** arrive and attack. If the characters are trying to leave Barovia, these dire wolves are joined by a pack of twenty **wolves**. The wolves and the dire wolves stop their attack if the characters return to the road and head toward the village of Barovia (area E).

One square = 1/4 mile

## D. River Ivlis

When the characters come within sight of this river for the first time, read:

> This river flows as clear as a blue winter sky through the valley.

The river is roughly 50 feet wide, with a depth ranging from 5 to 10 feet. Arching stone bridges span the river at two points, one near the village of Barovia (area E) and the other near Tser Falls (area H).

## E. Village of Barovia

Chapter 3 describes the village of Barovia and the gloomy folk who reside there.

## F. River Ivlis Crossroads

Check for a random encounter whenever the characters reach area F, unless they are accompanied by Vistani.

> An old wooden gallows creaks in a chill wind that blows down from the high ground to the west. A frayed length of rope dances from its beam. The well-worn road splits here, and a signpost opposite the gallows points off in three directions: Barovia Village to the east, Tser Pool to the northwest, and Ravenloft/Vallaki to the southwest.

The northwest fork slants down and disappears into the trees, while the southwest fork clings to an upward slope. Across from the gallows, a low wall, crumbling in places, partially encloses a small plot of graves shrouded in fog.

The northwest fork leads down to the river and area G. The road southwest leads to area H. The east road leads to an arching stone bridge and continues on to the village of Barovia (area E). If the characters are traveling with Vistani, the Vistani lead them along the northwest road to the Vistani encampment.

The gallows stand atop a rotting platform 5 feet high, with wooden stairs leading up to it.

Eleven graves are here with blank gravestones. The forgotten people buried here were hanged from the gallows. Characters who dig up the graves find rotted coffins containing moldy bones.

### The Hanged One

As the characters leave the area, read:

> You hear a creaking noise behind you, coming from the gallows. Where there was nothing before now hangs a lifeless, gray body. The breeze turns the hanged figure slowly, so that it can fix its dead eyes upon you.

One random character sees him- or herself hanging from the gallows. The other characters see an unfamiliar Barovian. The corpse looks and smells real, and it rapidly melts away into nothing if touched or moved.

### FORTUNES OF RAVENLOFT

If your card reading reveals that a treasure is here, it is buried in one of the graves. For each grave the characters dig up, there's a cumulative 10 percent chance of finding the treasure.

## G. TSER POOL ENCAMPMENT

> The road gradually disappears and is replaced by a twisted, muddy path through the trees. Deep ruts in the earth are evidence of the comings and goings of wagons.
>
> The canopy of mist and branches suddenly gives way to black clouds boiling far above. There is a clearing here, next to a river that widens to form a small lake several hundred feet across. Five colorful round tents, each ten feet in diameter, are pitched outside a ring of four barrel-topped wagons. A much larger tent stands near the shore of the lake, its sagging form lit from within. Near this tent, eight unbridled horses drink from the river.
>
> The mournful strains of an accordion clash with the singing of several brightly clad figures around a bonfire. A footpath continues beyond this encampment, meandering north between the river and the forest's edge.

The eight **draft horses** drinking from the river are used to pull the Vistani wagons and aren't easily startled.

If the characters are brought to this camp by the Vistani, their escorts remain at the camp and don't accompany the adventuring party any farther.

Twelve Vistani (male and female human **bandits**) are standing and sitting around the fire, telling stories and guzzling wine. They are intoxicated and have disadvantage on attack rolls and ability checks. Three sober Vistani (male and female human **bandit captains**) are resting in three of the four wagons but leap quickly into action if an alarm is raised.

Although the Vistani in this camp are in league with Strahd, they attack only if the characters provoke them with threats or insults. Otherwise, the characters are offered flasks of wine and invited to join the reverie.

If the characters linger at the camp, continue with "A Vistana's Tale" below. If they seem in a hurry to leave, one of the Vistani tells them, "It was fated that you would visit our humble camp. Madam Eva foretold your coming. She awaits you." The Vistana then points to the largest tent. If the characters head that way, continue with "Madam Eva's Tent."

### A VISTANA'S TALE

If the characters linger by the fire, one of the Vistani recounts the following tale:

> "A mighty wizard came to this land over a year ago. I remember him like it was yesterday. He stood exactly where you're standing. A very charismatic man, he was. He thought he could rally the people of Barovia against the devil Strahd. He stirred them with thoughts of revolt and bore them to the castle en masse.

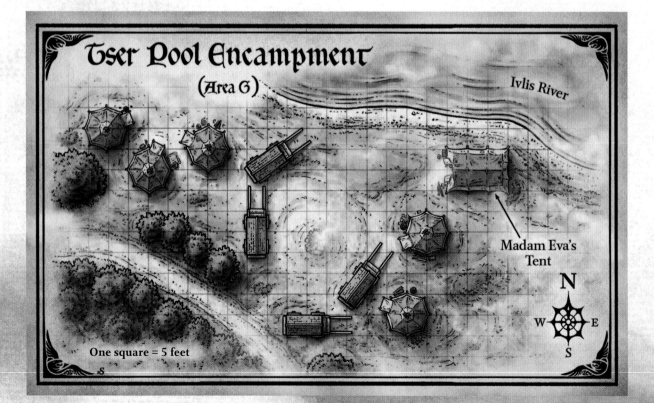

"When the vampire appeared, the wizard's peasant army fled in terror. A few stood their ground and were never seen again.

"The wizard and the vampire cast spells at each other. Their battle flew from the courtyards of Ravenloft to a precipice overlooking the falls. I saw the battle with my own eyes. Thunder shook the mountainside, and great rocks tumbled down upon the wizard, yet by his magic he survived. Lightning from the heavens struck the wizard, and again he stood his ground. But when the devil Strahd fell upon him, the wizard's magic couldn't save him. I saw him thrown a thousand feet to his death. I climbed down to the river to search for the wizard's body, to see if, you know, he had anything of value, but the River Ivlis had already spirited him away."

The Vistana storyteller doesn't remember the wizard's name, but recalls that it sounded important. If the characters haven't spoken with Madam Eva, the storyteller urges them to do so.

### Madam Eva's Tent

If the characters decide to see Madam Eva, read:

Magic flames cast a reddish glow over the interior of this tent, revealing a low table covered in a black velvet cloth. Glints of light seem to flash from a crystal ball on the table as a hunched figure peers into its depths. As the crone speaks, her voice crackles like dry weeds. "At last you have arrived!" Cackling laughter bursts like mad lightning from her withered lips.

**Madam Eva** (see appendix D) speaks the name of each party member and makes some reference to that individual's past deeds. She then asks the characters if they want their fortunes read. If they say yes, Madam Eva produces a worn deck of cards and proceeds with the sequence outlined in chapter 1. (If the characters don't want a reading of their fates, continue play using the card reading you performed before starting the adventure.)

Madam Eva might seem mad, but she is, in fact, cunning and sharp of mind. She has met a good many adventurers in her time and knows they can't be fully trusted. She wants to free the land of Barovia from its curse, and her fate is interwoven with Strahd's (see appendix D for details). She does the vampire's bidding when called upon and does nothing to anger Strahd or bring harm to the Vistani. She never gives aid and never asks for any.

### Treasure

For each Vistani tent or wagon that the characters search, roll once on the following table to determine what treasure is found:

| d20 | Treasure |
| --- | --- |
| 1–10 | None |
| 11–13 | Sack of 100 ep (each coin stamped with Strahd's visage in profile) |
| 14–16 | Pouch containing 4d6 gemstones worth 100 gp each |
| 17–19 | Sack containing 3d6 pieces of cheap jewelry worth 25 gp total and 1d6 pieces of fine jewelry worth 250 gp each |
| 20 | One magic item (roll once on Magic Item Table B in the *Dungeon Master's Guide*) |

#### Fortunes of Ravenloft

If your card reading reveals that a treasure is here, it is hidden in one of the Vistani wagons. Madam Eva grants the characters permission to search the wagons if they ask, and any such search yields the treasure.

## H. Tser Falls

If the characters reach area H by following the footpath from the Vistani encampment (area G), read:

You follow the river to the base of a canyon, at the far end of which a great waterfall spills into a pool, billowing forth clouds of cold mist. A great stone bridge spans the canyon nearly one thousand feet overhead.

If the characters are on the high road instead, read:

You follow the dirt road as it clings to the side of a mountain and ends before an arching bridge of mold-encrusted stone that spans a natural chasm. Gargoyles cloaked in black moss perch on the corners of the bridge, their frowns weatherworn. On the mountainous side of the bridge, a waterfall spills into a misty pool nearly a thousand feet below. The pool feeds a river that meanders into the fog-shrouded pines that blanket the valley.

The chasm's walls are slippery and sheer, and can't be scaled without the aid of magic or a climber's kit.

The bridge is slick with moisture but safe to cross. The road south of the bridge leads down the mountainside to area F; the road north cuts through the mountains to area I.

The gargoyles on the bridge are harmless sculptures.

## I. Black Carriage

Even here, in the mountains, the forest and the fog are inescapable. Ahead, the dirt road splits in two, widening toward the east. There you see patches of cobblestone, suggesting that the eastern branch was once an important thoroughfare.

If Strahd has invited the characters to Castle Ravenloft or otherwise wants to steer them in his direction, add:

> Parked at the fork in the road, pointed east, is a large black carriage drawn by two black horses. The horses snort puffs of steamy breath into the chill mountain air. The side door of the carriage swings open silently.

The two black **draft horses** are under Strahd's control. The horses wait for the characters to pile into the carriage if they so desire. There is room inside for eight of them. If they get into the carriage, the horses draw it down the road to area J. The horses can't be discouraged from their course, not even by a skilled teamster.

Characters who don't want to travel east in the carriage can follow the road northwest through a set of iron gates (area B) that open as they approach and close behind them, or the characters can travel south along the winding road to the bridge at Tser Falls (area H).

## J. GATES OF RAVENLOFT

The following text assumes that the characters arrive here in the carriage from area I. Modify the text as needed if the characters arrive by another means.

> After winding through the forest and craggy mountain peaks, the road takes a sudden turn to the east, and the startling, awesome presence of Castle Ravenloft towers before you. The carriage comes to a dead stop before twin turrets of stone, broken from years of exposure. Beyond these guard towers is the precipice of a fifty-foot-wide, fog-filled chasm that disappears into unknown depths.
>
> A lowered drawbridge of old, shored-up wooden beams stretches across the chasm, between you and the archway to the courtyard. The chains of the drawbridge creak in the wind, their rust-eaten iron straining under the weight. From atop the high walls, stone gargoyles stare at you out of their hollow eye sockets and grin hideously. A rotting wooden portcullis, green with growth, hangs above the entry tunnel. Beyond this location, the main doors of Ravenloft stand open. A rich, warm light spills from within, flooding the courtyard. Torches flutter sadly in sconces on both sides of the open doors.

The drawbridge appears sturdy, but a few of its boards are missing and it creaks and groans under any weight. Each time a creature other than Strahd or a horse that draws his carriage crosses the drawbridge, there is a 5 percent chance of one of its boards breaking under the creature. If a board breaks, the creature must succeed on a DC 10 Dexterity saving throw or fall to the bottom of the cliffs, 1,000 feet below. If a companion is within 5 feet of the creature and reaches out to grab it, the creature has advantage on the save.

### GREEN SLIME

A patch of green slime (see "Dungeon Hazards" in chapter 5 of the *Dungeon Master's Guide*) clings to the portcullis in the entry tunnel, and can be spotted with a successful DC 20 Wisdom (Perception) check. The slime will not fall on characters entering the castle, but it does fall on the first character who leaves by this route.

## K. CASTLE RAVENLOFT

Chapter 4 explores Castle Ravenloft, lair of the vampire Strahd von Zarovich.

## L. LAKE ZAROVICH

> At the foot of a mountain, nestled in the misty forest, is a large lake. The water is perfectly still and dark, reflecting the black clouds overhead like a monstrous mirror.

If the characters arrive along the shore north of Vallaki in the daytime, add:

> Pulled up along the south shore are three small rowboats. A fourth boat can be seen in the middle of the lake, with a lone figure sitting in it, fishing pole in hand.

Each rowboat can safely hold five people. The person fishing on the lake is Bluto Krogarov (NE male human **commoner**), a resident of Vallaki. He is in a trance and doesn't respond to anything or anyone unless attacked. His boat is 400 feet from the nearest shore. Tied up in the boat is a seven-year-old Vistana named Arabelle (LN female human **commoner** with 2 hit points and no effective attacks). She is bound with hempen rope, wrapped in a burlap sack, and lying prone so that she can't be seen or heard from the shore.

### ROLEPLAYING BLUTO

Bluto Krogarov is a destitute drunkard. He's desperate to catch some fish and trade them for wine at the Blue Water Inn. After he was unable to catch a single fish for a week, he kidnapped Arabelle, believing that Vistani are lucky. He intends to sacrifice her to the lake, hoping it will give up some of its fish in return.

If the characters watch Bluto from the shore for several minutes, or if they row out into the lake to greet him, he tosses the burlap sack into the water, watches it sink, and waits with fishing pole in hand for his reward.

Bluto is a hollow shell of a man, barely able to understand his own actions. He is unarmed and does nothing to aid or thwart the characters.

### ROLEPLAYING ARABELLE

Characters who act quickly can save Arabelle before she drowns. A character on the shore must succeed on a DC 15 Strength (Athletics) check to reach her in time. The DC is 10 for characters who took a rowboat out onto the lake.

Arabelle has alabaster-white skin and raven-black hair. If rescued, she demands to be returned to her family's camp outside Vallaki (chapter 5, area N9). She is certain that her father, Luvash, will give the characters a reward for doing so.

A descendant of Madam Eva with the blood of Barovian royalty in her veins, Arabelle is unaware of her connection to Strahd. She acts more like an adult than a child. Despite her recent misadventure, she believes that a great destiny awaits her.

# M. Mad Mage of Mount Baratok

This encounter can occur anywhere along the base of Mount Baratok.

North of the mountain lake, the trees begin their steady climb up the slopes of Mount Baratok, its monolithic presence oppressive at this distance. The ground here is rocky, uneven, and tiring to navigate. Even the wolves avoid this neck of the woods. Soon, you climb above the blanket of fog that engulfs the valley. Dark thunderclouds roll overhead.

You see an elk standing on a rocky spur about sixty feet away. Suddenly, it assumes the form of a man in tattered black robes. His hair and beard are long, black, and streaked with gray, and his eyes crackle with eldritch power.

The Mad Mage of Mount Baratok (CN male human **archmage**) came to Barovia more than a year ago to free its people from Strahd's tyranny, but he underestimated Strahd's hold over the land and the creatures in it. After a battle between the two in Castle Ravenloft, Strahd drove the Mad Mage to the mountains and sent the wizard hurling over Tser Falls (area H). The wizard, his staff and spellbook lost, survived the fall and retreated into the mountains, hoping to regain his power, only to be driven mad by the realization that he no longer has any hope of defeating Strahd or freeing the people of the vampire's damned realm.

The Mad Mage has forgotten his name and the world whence he came. In fact, he doesn't remember anything that happened before the madness. He suffers from the paranoia that powerful enemies are hunting him, and that their evil agents are everywhere and watching him.

Believing that the characters aim to kill him, the Mad Mage unleashes his destructive magic. As he tears into them, he shouts, "You think my magic has grown weak? Think again!" If he is reduced to 50 hit points or fewer, he shouts, "Tell your dark masters they can break my body, but never my spirit!" He then tries to escape.

Under normal circumstances, a *greater restoration* spell cast on the Mad Mage would restore his wits and ends the madness, allowing him to remember that he is none other than Mordenkainen, an archmage of Oerth and the leader of a powerful group of adventurers called the Circle of Eight. But in this case, the Mad Mage has cast a *mind blank* spell on himself. As long as that spell

remains in effect, his sanity can't be restored by any spell. If the characters surmise that powerful magic is preventing them from restoring the Mad Mage's wits, they can, with a successful DC 15 Charisma (Persuasion) check, convince the Mad Mage to divulge the reason why their spell failed. A character can also ascertain the cause of the spell's failure with a successful DC 18 Intelligence (Arcana) check. The Mad Mage's *mind blank* spell has a remaining duration of 3d6 hours, after which his madness can be cured normally.

The Mad Mage has a different spell list from that of the archmage in the *Monster Manual*, and he has already used one 1st-level spell slot to cast *mage armor* on himself, one 4th-level spell slot to cast *polymorph* on himself, one 7th-level spell slot to cast *Mordenkainen's magnificent mansion* (see "The Mad Mage's Mansion"), and one 8th-level spell slot to cast *mind blank* on himself.

Cantrips (at will): *fire bolt, light, mage hand, prestidigitation, shocking grasp*
1st level (4 slots): *detect magic, mage armor, magic missile, shield*
2nd level (3 slots): *mirror image, misty step, web*
3rd level (3 slots): *counterspell, fly, lightning bolt*
4th level (3 slots): *Mordenkainen's faithful hound, polymorph, stoneskin*
5th level (3 slots): *Bigby's hand, cone of cold, scrying*
6th level (1 slot): *true seeing*
7th level (1 slot): *Mordenkainen's magnificent mansion*
8th level (1 slot): *mind blank*
9th level (1 slot): *time stop*

## The Mad Mage's Mansion

If the characters rescue the archmage from his madness, he invites them to his "mansion." He leads them up the mountain to an invisible doorway that serves as the entrance to his extradimensional lair, created using the *Mordenkainen's magnificent mansion* spell. There, he provides them with food and sanctuary away from the prying eyes of Strahd and his spies. Characters are free to take a short or long rest, during which time they aren't disturbed.

Mordenkainen is familiar with worlds beyond his own. For example, if the characters come from the Forgotten Realms and mention this fact to Mordenkainen, he asks them if they know his old friend Elminster of Shadowdale.

If Mordenkainen isn't the party's ally as foretold in Madam Eva's card reading (see chapter 1), he declines to join them if asked. With his wits restored, he sets out to find his missing staff and spellbook, leaving the characters on their own. He doesn't allow them to help him, for he fears they might be tempted to steal either his staff or his spellbook. (Being an adventurer himself, he knows how the lure of powerful magic can bring out the worst in adventurers.) Before he leaves, as a parting gift, the archmage imbues each character with a *charm of heroism* (see "Supernatural Gifts" in chapter 7 of the *Dungeon Master's Guide*).

## Fortunes of Ravenloft

If your card reading reveals that the Mad Mage is the party's ally in the battle against Strahd, Mordenkainen can be persuaded to help them once his sanity is restored. He won't join them on their travels, but he will help them in a fight with Strahd if they have discovered where to find the vampire and how to destroy him.

With his sanity restored, Mordenkainen can be stubborn and difficult even with his friends, and doesn't suffer fools. He normally spends more time listening than talking, but when he does speak, his pronouncements are authoritative and not to be questioned.

The archmage has never had his fortune read by Madam Eva and doesn't care to, but if he is told about the *Holy Symbol of Ravenkind*, the *Tome of Strahd*, and the *Sunsword*, he insists that these items be recovered before he and the party confront Strahd. If Strahd is defeated and Mordenkainen survives, the archmage gladly accompanies the characters back to their world if they invite him, if only not to disappoint them.

## N. Town of Vallaki

Chapter 5 describes the town of Vallaki.

## O. Old Bonegrinder

Chapter 6 details Old Bonegrinder, a decrepit windmill occupied by hags.

## P. Luna River Crossroads

Always check for a random encounter when the characters reach area P in their travels.

> The road comes to an X intersection, with branches to the northwest, northeast, southwest, and southeast. The lower half of a snapped wooden signpost thrusts upward at an angle near the eastern elbow of the intersection. The top half of the sign, featuring arms pointing in four directions, lies in the weeds nearby.

The characters can easily figure out how the top half of the signpost connects to the lower half. When the two parts of the sign are aligned and rejoined, the arms indicate Krezk and Tsolenka Pass to the southwest, Lake Baratok to the northwest, Vallaki and Ravenloft to the northeast, and Berez to the southeast.

The Old Svalich Road, which runs northeast to southwest between Vallaki (area N) and Krezk (area S), is generally level. About a quarter mile along the northeast branch, an arching stone bridge crosses the Luna River.

The northwest branch of the crossroads climbs gently, becoming a dirt trail through the woods within half a mile. It merges with the Old Svalich Road again after a couple of miles, but not before sprouting a branch that leads to Van Richten's Tower on Lake Baratok (area V). The southeast branch wends gently downward as it follows the river into a valley. This trail eventually ends at the mostly abandoned riverside burg of Berez (area U).

## Q. Argynvostholt

Chapter 7 details the ruined mansion Argynvostholt, once a refuge of the Order of the Silver Dragon, which opposed Strahd and failed.

## R. Raven River Crossroads

Always check for a random encounter whenever the characters reach area R.

This stretch of the Old Svalich Road has multiple branches. One branch heads north, quickly turning into a dirt path that leads to Van Richten's Tower on Lake Baratok (area V). One branch heads south, becoming Tsolenka Pass (area T) as it winds through the lower mountains and clings to the side of Mount Ghakis. A third branch heads west toward the Wizard of Wines winery and vineyard (area W), dipping south as it changes from a road into a gravel trail.

Standing at the intersection of the Old Svalich Road and the road to the winery is a signpost:

> You see a weatherworn signpost next to the road. The three arms of the sign point along the three branches of the road. The arm pointing north reads Krezk, and through the woods you can see an arching stone bridge spanning a river. The arm pointing east reads Vallaki, and the road slopes up gradually in that direction. The arm pointing southwest reads The Wizard of Wines. The road slopes gently downward in that direction.

## S. Village of Krezk

Chapter 8 visits the village of Krezk and the nearby Abbey of Saint Markovia.

## T. Tsolenka Pass

Chapter 9 explores the Tsolenka Pass, which hugs the side of Mount Ghakis.

## U. Ruins of Berez

Chapter 10 describes the ruins of Berez, a riverside village that is now home to the hag Baba Lysaga.

## V. Van Richten's Tower

Chapter 11 details Van Richten's Tower, a dilapidated structure that originally belonged to the wizard Khazan.

## W. The Wizard of Wines

Chapter 12 visits the Wizard of Wines, the vineyard and winery that provides Barovia much of its wine.

## X. The Amber Temple

Chapter 13 delves into the Amber Temple, the dungeon complex where Strahd gave himself to the Dark Powers.

## Y. Yester Hill

Chapter 14 describes Yester Hill, a remote hilltop that belongs to druids who venerate Strahd as lord of the land.

## Z. Werewolf Den

Chapter 15 delves into the cave complex that is the main den of Barovia's werewolves.

# CHAPTER 3: THE VILLAGE OF BAROVIA

 HE VILLAGE OF BAROVIA IS THE SADDEST place in the land, its residents so terrified of Strahd that they rarely venture from their homes. The village lies in the shadow of Castle Ravenloft, buried under fog but still unable to hide from the vampire's sight.

Until recently, Strahd had been paying nightly visits to Ireena Kolyana, the adopted daughter of the village burgomaster. Ireena carries the soul of Strahd's beloved Tatyana and looks exactly like her. Strahd intends to make Ireena his bride, turn her into a vampire, and lock her away in the castle crypts for all time.

## APPROACHING THE VILLAGE

When the characters first approach the village, read:

> Tall shapes loom out of the dense fog that surrounds everything. The muddy ground underfoot gives way to slick, wet cobblestones. The tall shapes become recognizable as village dwellings. The windows of each house stare out from pools of blackness. No sound cuts the silence except for mournful sobbing that echoes through the streets from a distance.

The sobbing comes from Mad Mary's townhouse (area E3). With the exception of areas E1 and E2, all the shops in the village are permanently closed, and the unoccupied shops have been looted of anything valuable. Claw marks cover most of the walls.

When the fog eventually burns off, Castle Ravenloft looms over the village, like a lance piercing the sky.

## HOUSE OCCUPANTS

If the characters explore a residence other than Mad Mary's townhouse (area E3) or the burgomaster's mansion (area E4), roll a d20 and consult the following table to determine the house's occupants.

*SAME VOICE, SAME FACE, SAME graceful body, she was Tatyana come back to life again. I was absolutely witless from astonishment.*

*—Strahd von Zarovich in I, Strahd: The Memoirs of a Vampire*

## OCCUPANTS OF HOUSES IN BAROVIA

| d20 | Occupants |
| --- | --- |
| 1–3 | None |
| 4–8 | 2d4 **swarms of rats** |
| 9–16 | Barovian villagers |
| 17–20 | 2d4 **Strahd zombies** (see appendix D) |

### RATS

A house infested with rats looks abandoned. The rats are servants of Strahd and attack if the characters explore the interior of the house.

### BAROVIAN VILLAGERS

A house of Barovian villagers is home to 1d4 adults (male and female human **commoners**) and 1d8 − 1 children (male and female noncombatants). Characters who listen at the door hear low, muffled whispers from within. These villagers aren't interested in speaking with strangers and never attack first, always fleeing from danger if possible. At night they cower by candlelight and keep makeshift holy symbols close at hand.

### STRAHD ZOMBIES

When the characters open a door or a shuttered window of a house infested with Strahd zombies, they are assailed by the stench of death. If the characters dare to enter, the zombies converge on their location.

# Village of Barovia
## (Area E)

E6

E5

E7

E2

E1

E3

E4

N
W · E
S

One square = 40 feet

# Areas of the Village

The following areas correspond to labels on the map of the village of Barovia on page 42.

## E1. Bildrath's Mercantile

> The sparse light from this building spills out from behind drawn heavy curtains. A sign over the door, creaking on its hinges, reads "Bildrath's Mercantile."

The establishment is 70 feet long by 40 feet wide. The owner, Bildrath Cantemir (LN male human **commoner**), sells items from the Adventuring Gear table in the *Player's Handbook*, but only items with a price lower than 25 gp in the table, and he sells them for ten times the price.

Bildrath trades with the Vistani when they pass through. He is also happy to make a profit from any strangers unlucky enough to find themselves here. He serves his own interests and offers no sanctuary. He never bargains since, as he says, "If you want it badly enough, you'll pay for it." He has no competition in the village.

If the characters give Bildrath a hard time, he calls Parriwimple (LG male human), his nephew and stockboy, to help him out. Parriwimple has the statistics of a **gladiator**, except that he has an Intelligence of 6 and doesn't carry a shield (AC 14). Parriwimple's real name is Parpol Cantemir, but no one in the village calls him that. His muscles rippling beneath his leather tunic should give ample notice of his strength. At the same time, Parriwimple is simple-minded. He is devoted to his uncle and will not follow the characters as long as Bildrath has something to say about it.

## E2. Blood of the Vine Tavern

> A single shaft of light thrusts illumination into the main square, its brightness looking like a solid pillar in the heavy fog. Above the gaping doorway, a sign hangs precariously askew, proclaiming this to be the Blood on the Vine tavern.

The tavern building is about 60 feet square. Close inspection of the sign reveals that it originally read "Blood of the Vine." (An "n" has been scratched over with the "f.") This once finely appointed tavern has grown shoddy over the years. A blazing fire in the hearth gives scant warmth to the few huddled souls within. They include the barkeep, three Vistani sitting together, and a man named Ismark Kolyanovich—who happens to be the son of the village burgomaster, Kolyan Indirovich.

### Roleplaying Ismark

Ismark (LG male human **veteran**) is a young man who sits by himself at a corner table, sipping his wine. Other villagers call him "Ismark the Lesser" because he has lived in the shadow of his father for most of his life.

Ismark isn't a typically dour Barovian. He invites the characters to join him, offers to pay for their wine, and asks for their aid in protecting his adopted sister, Ireena Kolyana. If they agree to help, he takes them to the burgomaster's residence (area E4). He wants the characters to help him escort Ireena to Vallaki, a settlement in the heart of the valley, beyond the view of Castle Ravenloft and (he hopes) beyond the reach of Strahd. Ismark knows that moving Ireena is a gamble, since she's vulnerable to Strahd when she is outside their home, but he has heard assertions that Vallaki is well defended.

Ismark is as tight-lipped as any of the other Barovian villagers, unless the talk deals with Ireena or Strahd. Ismark knows everything the other villagers know. He also knows that, for some unknown reason, Strahd is attracted to Ireena and desires her above all others.

If you used the "Plea for Help" adventure hook and the characters show Ismark the letter they received, he knows the burgomaster's handwriting well enough to confirm that the letter was not written by his father.

Ismark has spent most of his adult life training with weapons in the hope of one day confronting and killing the Strahd. If the characters suggest that he accompany them, Ismark agrees provided that Ireena is first taken to a place of safety. As long as Ismark accompanies the characters, he acts as a party member for the purpose of determining each character's share of experience points (though he gains no experience points himself).

### Roleplaying the Other NPCs

Use the following information to roleplay the other NPCs in the tavern.

**Arik the Barkeep.** A pudgy little man named Arik Lorensk (CN male human **commoner**) tends bar.

Mindlessly, he cleans glasses, one after another. When they're all clean, he starts over. If he is spoken to, he takes orders for drinks in a dull, hollow voice. A small glass of wine costs 1 cp. A pitcher of wine costs 1 sp. After serving drinks, Arik returns to cleaning glasses. He ignores all attempts to question him.

**Vistani Owners.** Three Vistani **spies** (N female humans) named Alenka, Mirabel, and Sorvia sit at a table near the front door. They own the tavern and see to it that all customers pay their tabs. They otherwise show little interest in the characters.

If the characters arrive in the company of other Vistani, the owners are much more likely to engage them in conversation and provide useful information. They suggest that the characters visit Madam Eva (see chapter 2, area G) to have their fortunes read.

## E3. MAD MARY'S TOWNHOUSE

> A moaning sob floats through the still, gray streets, coloring your thoughts with sadness. The sounds flow from a dark, two-story townhouse.

The house, which is about 40 feet square, is boarded up and barricaded from the inside. Mad Mary (CN female human **commoner**) sits in the center of the floor in an upstairs bedroom, clutching a malformed doll. She is lost in her sorrow and despondency. She barely rec-

ognizes the presence of anyone in the room. She says nothing in the presence of anger, but she will talk, albeit haltingly, to someone who talks with her gently.

Mary hid her beloved daughter, Gertruda, in this house for the girl's entire life. Gertruda, now a teenager, broke out of the house a week ago and has not been seen since. Her mother fears the worst—and is justified in doing so. See area K42 in chapter 4 for more information on Gertruda's fate.

The malformed doll has a strange leer and wears a sackcloth dress. It belonged to Mary in her youth and was passed down to Gertruda. Gadof Blinsky, the toymaker of Vallaki (see chapter 5, area N7), made the doll. Stitched into the hem of its dress is a frayed tag bearing the words "Is No Fun, Is No Blinsky!"

## E4. BURGOMASTER'S MANSION

> A weary-looking mansion squats behind a rusting iron fence. The iron gates are twisted and torn. The right gate lies cast aside, while the left swings lazily in the wind. The stuttering squeal and clang of the gate repeats with mindless precision. Weeds choke the grounds and press with menace upon the house itself. Yet, against the walls, the growth has been tramped down to create a path all about the domain. Heavy claw markings have stripped the once-beautiful finish of the walls. Great black marks tell of the fires that have assailed the mansion. Not a pane nor a shard of glass stands in any window. All the windows are barred with planks, each one marked with stains of evil omen.

Characters who survey the grounds can, with a successful DC 11 Wisdom (Perception) check, discern trampled weeds all around the mansion as well as scores of wolf paw prints and human footprints. The footprints were made by zombies and ghouls under Strahd's control.

Ireena Kolyana (LG female human **noble** with 14 hit points), the adopted daughter of the burgomaster, is inside the mansion and won't open the heavily barred door to anyone unless she is convinced that those outside her door have no allegiance to Strahd. If the characters convince her, either with good roleplaying or a successful DC 15 Charisma (Deception or Persuasion) check, or if Ismark is with them, she opens the door and invites them in.

If the characters enter the mansion, read:

> The interior of the mansion is well furnished, yet the fixtures show signs of great wear. Noticeable oddities are the boarded-up windows and the presence of holy symbols in every room. The burgomaster is in a side drawing room on the floor—lying in a simple wooden coffin surrounded by wilting flowers and a faint odor of decay.

Ismark and Ireena made the coffin themselves.

MAD MARY

## ROLEPLAYING IREENA

Ireena, a striking young woman with auburn hair, has been bitten twice by Strahd. The villagers are afraid of her and avoid her. The characters are Ireena's best hope for protection, so she is willing to accompany them under certain conditions. Although she appears mild, she has a strong will, and she aids the party as best she can in saving herself. She doesn't remember her early past. She doesn't know how she came to Barovia or where she came from. Moreover, her encounters with Strahd are fuzzy memories, thanks to his vampiric charm, but she can recall clearly the blazing hunger in his eyes.

She tells the characters that wolves and other terrible creatures attacked the house night after night for weeks. The burgomaster's heart couldn't stand the constant assault, and he died three days ago. Strangely, since his death, the house has not come under attack.

She says that no one from the village has been brave enough to help Ismark take Kolyan Indirovich to the cemetery for proper burial. Ireena asks the characters if they would be so kind as to help Ismark deliver her father's body safely to Donavich, the local priest (area E5). She refuses to be taken to Vallaki or anywhere else while the burgomaster lies dead on the mansion floor.

# E5. CHURCH

> Atop a slight rise, against the roots of the pillar stone that supports Castle Ravenloft, stands a gray, sagging edifice of stone and wood. This church has obviously weathered the assaults of evil for centuries on end and is worn and weary. A bell tower rises toward the back, and flickering light shines through holes in the shingled roof. The rafters strain feebly against their load.

IREENA KOLYANA

If the characters approach the church doors, add:

> The heavy wooden doors of the church are covered with claw marks and scarred by fire.

The village priest, Donavich, lives here. Other Barovians shun the church for reasons that will quickly become obvious.

The following areas correspond to labels on the map of the church on page 46.

## E5A. HALL

> The doors open to reveal a ten-foot-wide, twenty-foot-long hall leading to a brightly lit chapel. The hall is unlit and reeks of mildew. Four doors, two on each side of the hall, lead to adjacent chambers.
>
> You can see that the chapel is strewn with debris, and you hear a soft voice from within reciting a prayer. Suddenly, the prayer is blotted out by an inhuman scream that rises up from beneath the wooden floor.

The scream comes from the church's undercroft (area E5g). The soft voice uttering the prayer belongs to Donavich, the priest (see area E5f).

## E5B. DORU'S BEDROOM

> This dirty, lightless room contains a wooden bed with a straw-filled mattress. Mounted above the bed's headboard is a wooden holy symbol.

This room once belonged to Doru, Donavich's son, who is trapped in the undercroft (area E5g). It hasn't been used in more than a year and contains nothing of value.

## E5C. DONAVICH'S BEDROOM

> This dirty room contains a wooden bed with a straw-filled mattress, next to which rests a small table with an oil lamp burning brightly on it. Mounted above the bed's headboard is a wooden sun-shaped holy symbol.

This is Donavich's room and contains nothing of value.

## E5D. TRAPDOOR

> Time and neglect have punched holes in the ceiling of this moldy room, which contains a few broken roof shingles amid puddles of water. In one corner, set into the floor, is a heavy wooden trapdoor held shut with a chain and a padlock. A young man's screams of anguish can be heard through the door.

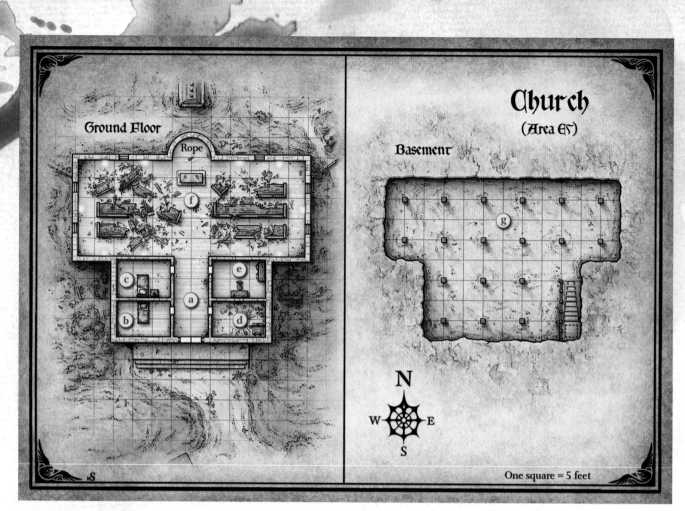

**Ground Floor**

Rope

f

c

a

e

b

d

**Church**

(Area E5)

**Basement**

g

N
W E
S

One square = 5 feet

Donavich lost the key to the iron padlock. If the chain is removed and the trapdoor is opened, the screaming in the undercroft stops. The trapdoor is swollen and stuck in its frame, so that a successful DC 12 Strength check is required to pull it open. Below it is a wooden staircase that descends 15 feet into the undercroft (area E5g).

### E5E. OFFICE

An old desk and chair stand against the south wall, a wooden holy symbol mounted above them—a sunburst. A ten-foot-long iron rod attached to the north wall stands bare, suggesting a tapestry once hung there. Against the far wall stands a wooden cabinet with four tall doors.

An empty wooden poor box rests on the seat of the chair. The desk drawers contain a few sheets of blank parchment, along with a couple of quill pens and dried-up jars of ink.

For its size, the wooden cabinet contains very little. Inside are a tinderbox, a few wooden boxes full of candles, and two well-used books: *Hymns to the Dawn*, a volume of chants to the Morninglord, and *The Blade of Truth: The Uses of Logic in the War Against Diabolist Heresies, as Fought by the Ulmist Inquisition*, a strange book that mixes logic exercises with lurid descriptions of fiend-worshiping cults.

### E5F. CHAPEL

The chapel is a shambles, with overturned and broken pews littering the dusty floor. Dozens of candles mounted in candlesticks and candelabras light every dusty corner in a fervent attempt to rid the chapel of shadows. At the far end of the church sits a claw-scarred altar, behind which kneels a priest in soiled vestments. Next to him hangs a long, thick rope that stretches up into the bell tower.

If the characters have not already entered the undercroft, add:

From beneath the chapel floor, you hear a young man's voice cry out, "Father! I'm starving!"

Donavich (LG male human **acolyte**) has been praying throughout the night. His voice is hoarse and weak. He is, in a word, insane. A little more than a year ago, his twenty-year-old son Doru and several other villagers stormed Castle Ravenloft in revolt, having been lured there by a wizard in black robes who came to Barovia from a faraway land (see chapter 2, area M, for more information on the wizard). By all accounts, the wizard died by Strahd's hand, and so too did Doru, who re-

DONAVICH

DORU

turned to his father as a vampire spawn. Donavich was able to trap his son in the church's undercroft, where he remains to this day.

Doru hasn't fed since he was imprisoned, and he cries out to his father at all hours. Meanwhile, Donavich prays day and night, hoping that the gods will tell him how to save Doru without destroying him. If the characters seem intent on slaying Doru, Donavich does his best to stop them. If Doru dies, Donavich falls to the floor and weeps inconsolably, overcome with despair.

In addition to the lore known to all Barovians (see "Barovian Lore" in chapter 2), Donavich knows the following useful information:

- Ireena Kolyana isn't the natural daughter of Kolyan Indirovich. Although Ireena never knew, Kolyan found her at the edge of the Svalich Woods near the Pillarstone of Ravenloft. She was but a girl then and seemed to have no memory of her past. Kolyan adopted her and loved her dearly.
- Every night at midnight, the spirits of dead adventurers rise up out of the church graveyard, forming a silent procession as they walk the road toward Castle Ravenloft. (See "March of the Dead" in the "Special Events" section at the chapter's end.)

***Funeral for the Burgomaster.*** If the characters bring Kolyan Indirovich's body to the church, Donavich presses the characters into helping him bury the burgomaster in the cemetery (area E6) at dawn. During the burial, Donavich offers prayers to the Morninglord in exchange for Kolyan Indirovich's deliverance from Barovia.

Once Kolyan is put in the ground, Donavich suggests that Ireena be taken as far from Castle Ravenloft as possible. He proposes that the characters take her to the Abbey of Saint Markovia in Krezk (chapter 8) or, failing that, the fortified town of Vallaki (chapter 5). Donavich is unaware that the abbey, once a bastion of good, has become a den of evil.

## E5G. UNDERCROFT

> The church's undercroft has rough-hewn walls and a floor made of damp clay and earth. Rotting wooden pillars strain under the weight of the wooden ceiling. Candlelight from the chapel above slips though the cracks, allowing you to glimpse a gaunt shape in the far corner.

The shape is Doru, a **vampire spawn** sent by Strahd to torment Donavich and cast down the church. Doru is starved for blood and brave enough to attack a lone character. If the characters approach as a group, he does his best to avoid them while hissing, "I can smell your blood!" If they cut off his escape, he lunges forth and attacks.

If the characters restrain Doru and either promise him blood or threaten to destroy him, or if they kill him and then raise him from the dead, he recounts the events that led to his downfall (see area E5f).

### FORTUNES OF RAVENLOFT

If your card reading reveals that a treasure is in the undercroft, it's contained in a moldy, old chest in the southwest corner of the room. The chest is unlocked and not trapped.

## E6. Cemetery

> A fence of wrought iron with a rusty gate encloses a rectangular plot of land behind the dilapidated church. Tightly packed gravestones shrouded by fog bear the names of souls long passed. All seems quiet.

During daytime, the cemetery is a still and peaceful place. Every night at midnight, however, a ghostly procession takes place (see "March of the Dead" below).

## E7. Haunted House

This haunted house is described in appendix B, "Death House."

# Special Events

You can use one or both of the following special events while the characters explore the village.

## March of the Dead

Every night at midnight, one hundred spirits rise from the cemetery (area E6) and march up the Old Svalich Road to Castle Ravenloft.

> An eerie green light suffuses the graveyard. From this light emerges a ghostly procession. Wavering images of doughty women toting greatswords, woodwise men with slender bows, dwarves with glittering axes, and archaically dressed mages with beards and strange, pointed hats—all these and more march forth from the graveyard, their numbers growing by the second.

These aren't the spirits of the people buried here, but of previous adventurers who died trying to destroy Strahd. Every night, the ghostly adventurers attempt to complete their quest, and each night they fail. They have no interest in the living and can't be hit, damaged, or turned. They will not communicate with the characters.

Once they reach the castle, the spirits march straight to the chapel (area K15) and up the high tower stair (area K18) to the top of the tower (area K59). There, they throw themselves down the shaft toward the crypts (area K84), where they disappear.

## Dream Pastries

This event occurs as the characters make their way through the village.

> You hear the sound of small, wooden wheels rolling across damp cobbles. You trace the lonely sound to a hunched figure bundled in rags, pushing a rickety wooden cart through the fog.

Morgantha, a **night hag** in the guise of an old woman, has come to the village from Old Bonegrinder to sell her dream pastries for 1 gp apiece (see chapter 6 for a description of the pastries). She goes from house to house, knocking on doors. Most of the time, no one answers. When someone does, Morgantha tries to peddle her wares, offering customers an escape from the misery and despair of everyday Barovian life. If the characters shadow her for a while, she collects payment from one household in the form of a seven-year-old boy named Lucian Jarov (LG male human noncombatant). Lucian's parents plead with Morgantha not to take their boy, but she snatches the crying child from their grasp, stuffs him in a sack, straps him down to her peddler's cart, and casually makes her way back to Old Bonegrinder.

Morgantha recognizes that the characters are strangers and does her best to avoid them. If the characters demand the release of the child, she grudgingly complies, knowing that she can always come back for the boy later. She fights only in self-defense and offers the following information in exchange for her life:

- Strahd has mastery over the land and the weather, and his spies include the Vistani.
- There's a Vistani camp to the west, on the shores of Tser Pool (chapter 2, area G), and another on the outskirts of Vallaki (chapter 5, area N9).
- Strahd has undead enemies in Barovia, namely the fallen knights of the Order of the Silver Dragon. These revenants can be found in a ruined mansion west of Vallaki (see chapter 7, "Argynvostholt").
- Strahd's most carefully guarded secret is a temple of forbidden lore hidden in the mountains (see chapter 13, "The Amber Temple"). The temple can be reached by following the long and winding Tsolenka Pass (see chapter 9).

# Chapter 4: Castle Ravenloft

ASTLE RAVENLOFT WAS BUILT ATOP THE RUIN of an older fortress by artisans, wizards, and workers loyal to Strahd's family. Strahd rewarded the castle's genius architect, Artimus, with a crypt in the castle's catacombs. The castle was named after Strahd's mother, Ravenovia, who also lies entombed below.

The poster map that accompanies this book displays the castle in its entirety. Map 1 on the poster shows a diagram of the castle's face, and the other maps show the castle's interior and exterior areas. All those locations are described in this chapter, starting in the "Walls of Ravenloft" section on page 52.

## Random Encounters

The first time the characters enter a castle area that isn't otherwise occupied, check for a random encounter. Also check for a random encounter every 10 minutes the characters spend resting in the castle.

In most circumstances, a random encounter occurs on a roll of 18 or higher on a d20. To determine what the characters encounter, consult the table below.

### Random Encounters in Castle Ravenloft

| d12 + d8 | Encounter |
|---|---|
| 2 | **Ezmerelda d'Avenir** (see appendix D) |
| 3 | **Rahadin** (see appendix D) |
| 4 | 1 black **cat** |
| 5 | 1 **broom of animated attack** (see appendix D) |
| 6 | 1d4 + 1 **flying swords** |
| 7 | Blinsky toy |
| 8 | Unseen servant |
| 9 | 1d4 Barovian **commoners** |
| 10 | 2d6 **crawling claws** |
| 11 | 1d6 **shadows** |
| 12 | 1d6 **swarms of bats** |
| 13 | 1 crawling **Strahd zombie** (see appendix D) |
| 14 | 1d4 + 1 Vistani **thugs** |
| 15 | 1d4 **wights** |
| 16 | Trinket |
| 17 | Giant spider cocoon |
| 18 | 1 **Barovian witch** (see appendix D) |
| 19 | 1d4 + 1 **vampire spawn** |
| 20 | **Strahd von Zarovich** (see appendix D) |

*I CALLED FOR MY FAMILY, LONG unseated from their ancient thrones, and brought them here to settle in the castle Ravenloft.*

—Tome of Strahd

Use the descriptions that follow to run each encounter.

### Barovian Commoners

> A loud clamor fills the unhallowed halls of Ravenloft. Cries of "Kill the vampire!" are mixed with bold voices shouting, "Never again!" and "To the crypts!"

Angry villagers who have entered the castle brandish torches and pitchforks in a ridiculous display of force. Everywhere they go, they shout for justice. They follow the characters unless prevented from doing so. As long as these Barovians are with the adventurers, random encounters occur on a roll of 9 or higher.

### Barovian Witch

> You hear a woman's scratchy voice calling out a name. "Grizzlegut! Grizzlegut, where are you? A pox on you, you mangy cat!"
>
> Through the darkness comes a crone wearing a pointed black hat and a burlap gown stained with soot.

Characters can try to hide from the witch (who has darkvision) or catch her by surprise. This Barovian witch is one of the servants of Strahd dwelling in area K56. She is calling out the name of her black cat familiar, which has gone missing. If the characters confront her, the old bat spits at them and begins casting a spell.

This encounter happens only once. If this result comes up again, treat it as no encounter.

## Black Cat

> The darkness lets out a demonic hiss as a black cat darts out of the shadows, trying its best to avoid you.

This familiar is searching for its mistress (a Barovian witch). It wants nothing to do with the characters but attacks if cornered.

If the characters capture or kill the cat, this encounter doesn't occur again. If this result comes up again, treat it as no encounter.

## Blinsky Toy

A Blinsky toy is encountered only if the characters are moving about the castle (not resting); otherwise, treat this result as no encounter.

> You find a discarded toy—something no child could love.

The toy has a slogan stitched or printed on it in tiny letters: "Is No Fun, Is No Blinsky!" Roll a d6 to determine the specific toy:

| d6 | Toy |
|----|-----|
| 1 | A plush werewolf stuffed with sawdust and tiny wood-carved babies. It has dull knife blades for claws and retractable teeth. |
| 2 | A smiling jester marionette with tangled strings and tiny copper bells sewn into its cap. |
| 3 | A wooden puzzle box, 6 inches on a side, carved with silhouettes of leering clown faces. The box rattles when shaken. A character who spends a short rest fiddling with the box can figure out how to open it with a successful DC 20 Intelligence check. The box is empty, with nothing inside to explain the rattling. |
| 4 | A faceless doll in a wedding dress that has yellowed and frayed with age. |
| 5 | A vaguely coffin-shaped jack-in-the-box containing a pop-up Strahd puppet. |
| 6 | A spring-loaded set of wooden teeth with fangs, all painted white. The teeth gnash and chatter for 1 minute when the spring is wound tight (requiring an action) and released. |

## Broom of Animated Attack

> You hear a scratching noise. Out of the shadows comes a broom, sweeping its way toward you as though held by invisible hands.

When it gets within 5 feet of a party member, the broom attacks.

## Crawling Claws

> A mob of severed hands, their mummified flesh black with soot, skitters out of the darkness across the dusty floor.

The crawling claws gang up on one party member. During the confusion, one of the claws tries to crawl into the character's backpack and hide there. It makes a Dexterity (Stealth) check contested by the character's passive Wisdom (Perception) score. If the claw loses the contest, the character sees the claw enter the backpack. If the claw wins the contest, it waits until the character takes a long rest before scuttling out to attack.

## Crawling Strahd Zombie

> You hear the deathly groans of something vile.

The groans are coming from a Strahd zombie that is missing both of its legs, so that only its head, torso, and arms remain. It uses its arms to drag itself across the floor. The crawling zombie has 15 hit points remaining.

If the characters are moving quietly and not using light sources, they can try to hide from the crawling zombie.

## Ezmerelda d'Avenir

Ezmerelda has cast a *greater invisibility* spell on herself and is stealthily exploring the castle. Choose one character in the back rank of the party's marching order, and read the following text to that character's player:

> You feel a gentle tap on your shoulder but see nothing behind you.

If the character who is touched by Ezmerelda reacts in an alarming or threatening manner, she hastily whispers, "Don't be frightened. We're on the same side."

Ezmerelda is hunting Strahd, but her efforts to corner the vampire have so far been thwarted, and she fears that she might be in over her head. If the characters don't ask her to join the party, she wishes them well and goes on her way (perhaps to be encountered again later). If they invite her to accompany them, Ezmerelda tests the characters' knowledge about vampires by asking them questions such as "Have you ever seen a vampire change its form?" and "Do you know how to counteract a vampire's regenerative ability?" Whatever their answers, she ultimately agrees to come along.

This random encounter happens only once. If this result comes up again, treat it as no encounter.

## Flying Swords

> Out of the gloom flies a rusty blade, followed by another!

If more than two flying swords are encountered, the others aren't far behind. These weapons drift about the castle and attack intruders within range of their blindsight.

## GIANT SPIDER COCOON

A giant spider cocoon is encountered only if the characters are moving about the castle (not resting); otherwise, reroll.

> A white cocoon is suspended from the ceiling amid thick webs and appears to hold something human-like.

A giant spider made this cocoon. Characters who can reach it can cut it open to free whatever is inside. Roll a d6 to determine the cocoon's contents:

| d6 | Cocoon's Contents |
|----|----|
| 1 | A wooden mannequin wearing a gown. |
| 2 | A **Barovian witch** (see appendix D). She screams like a wild animal and begins casting spells. |
| 3 | A **Strahd zombie** (see appendix D). It fights until killed. |
| 4 | A Barovian lunatic (CN male **commoner**). If freed, he cackles until silenced or until a *calm emotions* spell is cast on him. A *lesser restoration* spell cures his madness, at which point he tries to flee the castle. |
| 5 | A dead Barovian that serves as host to a **swarm of insects** (spiders). The baby giant spiders (each one the size of a tarantula) crawl out of the Barovian's gaping mouth or burst forth from its distended belly. |
| 6 | A Vistana **bandit** (CN male or female). The Vistana knows the castle's layout and helps the characters until Strahd or more Vistani appear, at which point the treacherous Vistana turns on the characters. |

## RAHADIN

If Rahadin was killed or captured in a previous encounter, this encounter doesn't occur. Otherwise, Strahd's mysterious chamberlain approaches quietly. A character whose passive Wisdom (Perception) score meets or exceeds Rahadin's Dexterity (Stealth) check hear him.

> "The master wishes to see you," intones a grim voice in the darkness.

Rahadin directs the characters to a random location in the castle, determined by rolling a d6:

| d6 | Location |
|----|----|
| 1 | Chapel (area K15) |
| 2 | Audience hall (area K25) |
| 3 | Study (area K37) |
| 4 | Tower roof (area K57) |
| 5 | Wine cellar (area K63) |
| 6 | Torture chamber (area K76) |

Strahd isn't actually at that location unless the card reading (see chapter 1) indicates that he is.

If the characters ask Rahadin to lead the way, he declines. If the characters ask for directions, he tells them whether they need to ascend, descend, or remain on the level they're at. If they attack him, he fights to the death. Otherwise, he doesn't leave until after they do.

## SHADOWS

If one or more characters have a passive Wisdom (Perception) score of 16 or higher, read:

> You can't shake the feeling that something is behind you. When you look back, you see a shadow, tall and still, but nothing of its dimensions that could cast it.

If more than one shadow is present, the others are close by but hidden in the darkness. These undead shadows follow the characters but do not attack unless attacked first. They otherwise obey Strahd's commands.

## STRAHD VON ZAROVICH

Strahd makes a surprise appearance.

> A crack of thunder shakes the castle, stirring the dust and cobwebs. You hear a voice: "Good evening."

Any character who has a passive Wisdom (Perception) score lower than 19 is surprised as Strahd appears seemingly out of nowhere. The vampire prefers to attack a surprised character, choosing the one closest to him. Otherwise, see appendix D for the vampire's tactics.

## SWARMS OF BATS

> You hear a peal of thunder, followed by the flapping of tiny black wings. Suddenly, a dark cloud of bats descends upon you!

These bats are the servants of Strahd. They attack the characters without provocation.

## TRINKET

One random character finds a lost trinket. Read the following text to the player of that character:

> You kick something—a trinket buried in the dust.

To determine what the character finds, roll on the Trinkets table in appendix A.

## UNSEEN SERVANT

> A curious object drifts into view, as though held aloft by an invisible force.

This unseen servant was created by Strahd and is permanent until destroyed (see the *unseen servant* spell in the *Player's Handbook*). Roll a d6 to determine what the servant is carrying, or choose one of the options below.

| d6 | Items |
|---|---|
| 1 | A tarnished silver platter with a lid (worth 25 gp). If a character comes within 5 feet of the servant, it lifts the lid, revealing a bunch of moldy scones. The first character to eat a scone gains inspiration. On later occurrences of this encounter, the platter holds a **crawling claw** that attacks the nearest character. |
| 2 | A silver goblet (worth 50 gp) filled to the brim with wine. A character who drinks the wine must make a DC 15 Constitution saving throw, taking 44 (8d10) poison damage on a failed save, or half as much damage on a successful one. On future occurrences of this encounter, the wine acts as a *potion of healing*. |
| 3 | A gold candelabrum (worth 150 gp) with three branches, each one holding an unlit candle. |
| 4 | A purple silk handkerchief with white ruffled edges (worth 1 gp). On future occurrences of this encounter, the handkerchief is smeared with fresh blood. |
| 5 | A crystal dinner bell (worth 25 gp). The unseen servant rings the bell if the characters come within 10 feet of it. The sound attracts 1d4 hungry **vampire spawn** (see below), which arrive in 1d4 + 1 rounds. |
| 6 | A wizard's spellbook with a black velvet dust jacket over its stitched leather cover. The book contains all the spells Strahd has prepared (see appendix D). On subsequent occurrences of this encounter, the tome is a nonmagical leather-bound storybook worth 25 gp. |

### VAMPIRE SPAWN

If any character has a passive Wisdom (Perception) score of 16 or higher, the party isn't surprised. In that case, read:

> Creatures with pale flesh scuttle across the ceiling like spiders, their red eyes glowing in the dark. As they draw near, their cracked and bloodstained lips open wide, revealing sharp fangs.

These minions of Strahd—former adventurers all—creep along ceilings and drop down on unsuspecting prey. The vampire spawn fight until destroyed.

### VISTANI THUGS

> You hear voices with thick accents.

A small group of Vistani (NE male and female human **thugs**) claim that they were the vampire's captives, only recently escaped from the castle's dungeon, and they offer to help the party. In truth, they are loyal to Strahd and betray the characters as soon as he appears. If the characters accept their offer, the Vistani pretend to be the party's allies for as long as they remain with the party, or until Strahd appears. If the characters leave the castle, the Vistani accompany them, since choosing to remain in the castle would likely arouse the characters' suspicion.

***Treasure.*** One Vistani thug carries a pouch that holds 2d8 small gemstones (50 gp each).

### WIGHTS

> The air grows much colder, and you can hear the march of footsteps drawing near.

If the characters are moving quietly and not carrying light sources, they can try to hide from the wights. These undead soldiers once served as guard captains in Castle Ravenloft. They still wear bits of tattered livery, and they attack the living on sight.

***Treasure.*** The wights carry longswords that have the crest of Barovia worked into their cross guards. Each wight also carries a pouch holding 2d20 ep, each coin of Barovian mintage and featuring the profiled visage of Strahd von Zarovich.

# WALLS OF RAVENLOFT

Refer to map 2 of the castle for areas K1 through K6.

## K1. FRONT COURTYARD

As the characters enter the castle, the weather worsens. Dismal rain starts to fall, becoming a torrent within the hour. Lightning routinely lights the sky, followed by peals of thunder that make the castle shudder.

> Thick, cold fog swirls in this courtyard. Sporadic flashes of lightning lance the weeping clouds overhead as thunder shakes the ground. Through the drizzle, you see torch flames fluttering on each side of the keep's open main doors. Warm light spills out of the entrance, flooding the courtyard. High above the entrance is a round window with shards of broken glass lodged in its iron frame.

The walls that enclose the courtyard are 90 feet high. The dark towers of the castle rise even higher. Doors in the gate towers on each side of the tunnel entrance are shut against the rain, and a howling wind rushes through the courtyard.

The open main doors to the keep lead to area K7. The large, shattered window overlooking the main entrance is 50 feet above the courtyard and leads to area K25. No light can be seen through the great window.

### GATE TOWERS

Each outer gate tower has an ironbound door with a built-in lock.

Characters who enter a gate tower find themselves on a flagstone floor with a hollow tower stretching high above them. The mechanisms for raising and lowering

**MAP 2**
**Walls of Ravenloft**

J

K2

K1

K4

K3

K2

K5

K6

N
W — E
S

the drawbridge and portcullis fill both gate towers. The latch mechanism in each tower is magically activated by a word that only Strahd knows. It can also be activated with a successful casting of *dispel magic* (DC 14). Neither the drawbridge nor the portcullis will move until both latches are activated.

## K2. CENTER COURT GATE

Two gates, one north of the keep and one to the south, prevent easy access to what lies beyond them.

> A massive wall juts out to connect the outer walls of the castle with the keep. A twenty-foot-wide, twenty-foot-tall archway offers passage through the connecting wall but is blocked by a rusting iron portcullis.

The portcullis is unlocked and can be lifted with a successful DC 15 Strength check. It can also be opened with a command word that only Strahd and Cyrus Belview (area K62) know. Unless the portcullis is wedged or propped open, it falls back into place once it is let go.

## K3. SERVANTS' COURTYARD

> This courtyard northeast of the keep is enclosed by towering walls. A stone carriage house with hinged wooden doors stands silent in the corner where the outer walls meet. Across from the carriage house, a slender wooden door reinforced with iron bands leads into the keep.

The carriage house is described in area K4. The wooden door, which leads to area K23, is swollen and stuck in its frame. A character can shoulder open the stuck door with a successful DC 10 Strength check.

## K4. CARRIAGE HOUSE

Read the following text if the characters open the carriage house doors:

> The double doors swing open to reveal a sleek, black carriage fitted with glass windows and brass lanterns.

## K5. CHAPEL GARDEN

> At the back of the keep, behind towering buttresses and tall, boarded-up stained-glass windows, a small garden struggles to survive. Small flowers press skyward against the gloom. A pair of large iron gates blocks the way to some kind of overlook.

The large iron gates squeal loudly on rusted hinges when opened. Beyond them lies area K6.

## K6. OVERLOOK

> Dark clouds overhead drizzle constantly. A flagstone avenue passes between empty outbuildings, leading to a stone-paved overlook. The overlook has a low stone wall adorned with outward-facing gargoyle carvings.

If a character peers over the balcony, read:

> A flash of lightning illuminates the dismal village of Barovia, its rooftops visible above a smothering blanket of fog one thousand feet below.

If a character who has a passive Wisdom (Perception) score of 15 or higher peers over the wall, add:

> Underneath the platform on which you stand, about one hundred feet down, a stone construction protrudes from the cliff face. Three dirt-caked windows are set into it.

The windows are so dirty as to be opaque, although a character within reach of one can scrape the dirt away and see a dusty tomb beyond (area K88). Characters who try to reach the windows from the overlook must descend 110 feet and move 20 feet back under the platform. This descent can't be accomplished without the aid of magic or the use of a climber's kit.

Anyone who falls from the overlook plummets 1,000 feet.

### FORTUNES OF RAVENLOFT

If your card reading indicates an encounter with Strahd in this area, he is looking out over the balcony.

# MAIN FLOOR

Refer to map 3 of the castle for areas K7 through K24.

## K7. ENTRY

Read the following text if the characters approach from the courtyard (area K1):

> The ornate outer doors of the castle hang open, flanked by fluttering torches in iron sconces. Twenty feet inside the castle is a second set of doors.

If one or more characters approach from area K1 and come within 10 feet of the double doors, read:

> The doors in front of you suddenly swing open, revealing a grand hall filled with the sound of organ music.

If the characters approach from area K8 and have not yet visited this area, read:

> A set of double doors to the west appears to be, or to lead to, an exit from the castle.

If the characters enter from either direction, read:

> Overhead, in the vaulted entry foyer, four statues of dragons glare down, their eyes flickering in the torchlight.

If anyone except Strahd enters this area through the doors that adjoin area K8, the dragons come alive, drop to the floor hissing and spitting, and attack. The dragons don't attack characters who enter this area from area K1, heading east. The dragons are four **red dragon wyrmlings**, and they have instructions to allow guests to enter the castle, but not to leave it. If intruders vacate this area, the dragons fly up to their perches and revert to stone. In their stone forms, they are impervious to weapon damage. The dragons never leave the room.

## K8. GREAT ENTRY

> Cobwebs stretch between the columns that support the vaulted ceiling of a great, dusty hall dimly lit by sputtering torches in iron sconces. The torches cast odd shadows across the faces of eight stone gargoyles squatting motionlessly on the rim of the domed ceiling. Cracked and faded ceiling frescoes are covered by decay.

> Double doors of bronze stand closed to the east. To the north, a wide staircase climbs into darkness. A lit hallway to the south contains another set of bronze doors, through which you hear sad and majestic organ tones.

The southern hallway is described in area K9. The wide staircase leads up to area K19.

If the characters are here by invitation, add the following:

> An elf with brown skin and long black hair descends the wide staircase, quiet as a cat. He wears a gray cloak over black studded leather armor and has a polished scimitar hanging from his belt. "My master is expecting you," he says.

The elf is **Rahadin**, the castle chamberlain (see appendix D). He fights only if attacked. Otherwise, he leads the characters to the dining hall (area K10), points them inside, pulls the doors shut behind them, and withdraws to area K72 by way of the South Tower Stair (area K21).

### DEVELOPMENT

After all the characters leave this room, the eight **gargoyles** attack any character who dares to return. The gargoyles also swoop down to fight if they are attacked. When the gargoyles attack, the turbulence in the air from their wings extinguishes the feeble torches in the sconces, plunging the hall into darkness unless the characters have light sources.

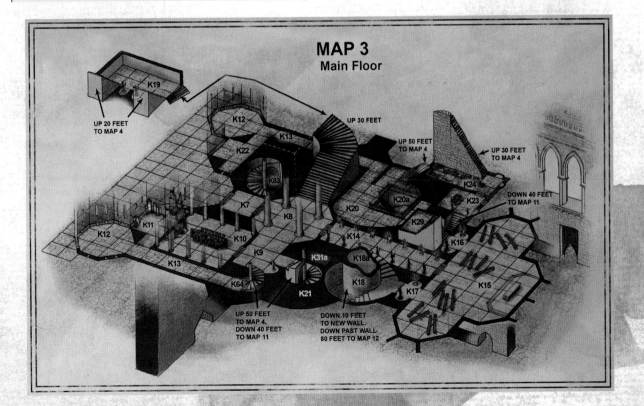

MAP 3
Main Floor

UP 20 FEET
TO MAP 4

UP 30 FEET

UP 50 FEET
TO MAP 4

UP 30 FEET
TO MAP 4

DOWN 40 FEET
TO MAP 11

K19
K12
K13
K22
K83
K7
K11
K12
K10
K20
K20a
K24
K23
K29
K14
K16
K9
K31a
K18a
K64
K13
K21
K18
K15
K17

UP 50 FEET
TO MAP 4,
DOWN 40 FEET
TO MAP 11

DOWN 10 FEET
TO NEW WALL.
DOWN PAST WALL
80 FEET TO MAP 12

## K9. GUESTS' HALL

> Torchlight flutters against the walls of this vaulted hall. To the east, an arched hallway stretches for twenty feet, ending at a spiral staircase that goes up and down. Next to the hallway, a suit of armor, oiled and glistening, stands at attention in a shallow alcove. To the west, large double doors hang slightly open, and a steady bright light escapes through the opening. Swells of organ music come from behind the doors, spilling their melody of power and defeat into the hall.

The suit of armor standing in the alcove is merely a normal suit of plate armor that is well cared for.

The staircase leads down to area K61 and up to area K30. The double doors provide access to area K10.

## K10. DINING HALL

The first time the characters enter this room, read:

> Three enormous crystal chandeliers brilliantly illuminate this magnificent chamber. Pillars of stone stand against dull white marble walls, supporting the ceiling. In the center of the room, a long, heavy table is covered with a fine white satin cloth. The table is laden with many delectable foods: roasted beast basted in a savory sauce, roots and herbs of every taste, and sweet fruits and vegetables. Places are set for each of you with fine, delicate china and silver. At each place is a crystal goblet filled with an amber liquid with a delicate, tantalizing fragrance.
>
> At the center of the far west wall, between floor-to-ceiling mirrors, stands a massive organ. Its pipes blare out a thunderous melody that speaks in its tone of greatness and despair. Seated at the organ, facing away from you, a single caped figure pounds the keys in raptured ecstasy. The figure suddenly stops, and as a deep silence falls over the dining hall, it slowly turns toward you.

The figure is an illusion of Strahd. It welcomes the characters and invites them to dine. The illusion acts like Strahd and plays the part of the gracious host, speaking kindly and telling the characters that they're free to explore the castle. "Strahd" might talk about his family or shed light on the castle's history, but the illusion provides no useful information about the castle's inhabitants, treasures, or dangers other than to say that the castle doesn't receive many guests. The illusory vampire converses with the characters for no more than

3 rounds, never moving from the organ bench. When the time is up, or if the illusion is attacked, it simply disappears with a mocking laugh.

The moment the figure disappears, a fierce, bone-chilling wind rises up and roars through the hall, putting out all open flames. The characters hear the screech of ancient hinges and the solid thud of many heavy doors slamming shut, one after another, into the distance. They also hear the portcullis clang shut and the tired groan of the aged drawbridge pulling up. Finally, unless the doors to this room are being held open, they slam shut (but do not lock). If the characters open the doors, they see that all the torches in areas K7, K8, and K9 have gone out.

The organ appears locked in place and immovable, but a character who makes a successful DC 20 Wisdom (Perception) check notices scratch marks on the floor that suggest that the organ can be slid outward. A character who tries pushing various keys and pedals discovers that one of the pedals, when depressed, causes the organ to slide outward about 2 feet, allowing access to a secret door in the back wall that swings open into area K11. Because this secret door is hidden behind the organ, it can't be found and opened until the organ is moved out of the way.

The food on the table is tasty, the wine delicious.

## K11. SOUTH ARCHERS' POST

> The castle courtyard is visible through arrow slits in the north and west walls. Leaning against the walls are mirrors of various sizes, some as tall as a human and others small enough to fit in a backpack.

Each arrow slit is 2½ feet tall and 4 inches wide. The framed mirrors (seventeen in all) used to hang on various walls of the castle. Strahd had them taken down and stored here.

A secret door in the east wall can be pulled open to reveal the back of the pipe organ in area K10. Characters can't pass through the secret door while the organ is blocking it, and the organ can't be moved from this side.

## K12. TURRET POST

> A high, domed ceiling caps the thirty-foot-wide octagonal room before you. Frescoes faded with age adorn the ceiling, but their images are impossible to make out. Tall, thin arrow slits look out over the courtyard.

Each arrow slit is 2½ feet tall and 4 inches wide.

## K13. TURRET POST ACCESS HALL

> This long, narrow corridor runs east to west. Cobwebs fill the hall, obstructing sight beyond a few feet.

## K14. HALL OF FAITH

> This grand hall is choked with dust and stretches into darkness ahead. Webs hang from the arched ceiling like drapes, and life-sized statues of knights line the hallway on both sides, their eyes seeming to watch you.

The statues are harmless. Their moving eyes are a simple optical illusion.

Double doors stand at both ends of the hall. Above the doors leading to area K15 hangs a symbol of beaten bronze that looks like a rising or setting sun.

## K15. CHAPEL

> Dim, colored light filters through tall, broken, and boarded-up windows of stained glass, illuminating the ancient chapel of Ravenloft. A few bats flutter about near the top of the ninety-foot-high domed ceiling. A balcony runs the length of the west wall, fifty feet above the floor. In the center of the balcony, two dark shapes are slumped in tall chairs.
>
> Benches coated with centuries of dust lie about the floor in jumbled disarray. Beyond this debris, lit by a piercing shaft of light, an altar stands upon a stone platform. The sides of the altar are carved with bas-reliefs of angelic figures entwined with grape vines. The light from above falls directly on a silver statuette. A cloaked figure is draped over the altar, and a black mace lies on the floor near its feet.

The figure slumped on the altar is all that remains of Gustav Herrenghast, a lawful evil human cleric who tried to obtain the *Icon of Ravenloft* and did not survive the attempt. See "Treasure" below for more information on the icon and Gustav's possessions.

A sculpted stone railing cordons off the upstairs balcony, which is described in area K28.

### TREASURE
The statuette on the altar is an artifact called the *Icon of Ravenloft* (see appendix C). Any evil creature that touches the statuette must make a DC 17 Constitution saving throw, taking 88 (16d10) radiant damage on a failed save, or half as much damage on a successful one. The statuette is safe for all creatures to handle once it is no longer in contact with the altar.

Gustav's corpse wears a handsome, fur-lined black cloak embroidered with golden thread (worth 250 gp) and a suit of chain mail, both nonmagical. Gustav's black mace is a *mace of terror*.

### FORTUNES OF RAVENLOFT
If your card reading reveals that a treasure is here, it lies on the floor behind the altar.

If your card reading indicates an encounter with Strahd in this area, he is among the bats fluttering below the ceiling or he is standing at one end of the chapel—a dark shape in the vast hall.

# K16. NORTH CHAPEL ACCESS

This arched room connects a vast chamber to the east and a staircase that rises to the west. Alcoves in the north and south walls hold eight-foot-tall sculptures of helmed knights with muscular builds. Black shadows fall across their faces.

The statues are harmless. The vast chamber to the east is the chapel (area K15). The staircase to the west is described in area K29.

# K17. SOUTH CHAPEL ACCESS

This arched room connects a vast chamber to the east and the landing of a staircase to the west. To the left of the landing, the stairs curl down into darkness. To the right, the stairs climb into thick drapes of cobwebs. Alcoves in the north and south walls hold eight-foot-tall sculptures of helmed knights with bright blades. Black shadows obscure their faces.

The statues are harmless. The vast chamber to the east is the chapel (area K15). The staircase to the west is described in area K18.

# K18. HIGH TOWER STAIRCASE

The large flagstones of this spiraling staircase lead up and down around a twenty-foot-wide stone core. Cobwebs fill the staircase, making it difficult to see even the ceiling. Heavy beams sag overhead from centuries of supporting weight.

The staircase starts at area K84 and spirals upward around a central shaft (area K18a), climbing 300 feet to the top of the high tower (area K59).

A recently constructed masonry wall blocks the staircase 10 feet below the landing west of area K17. A chink in this wall allows gas (or a vampire in gaseous form) to pass from one side of the wall to the other. A character who inspects the wall closely can spot the chink with a successful DC 10 Wisdom (Perception) check. The wall is too sturdy for characters to knock down, but they can create a hole wide enough to crawl through in 1 hour, or reduce the entire wall to a pile of masonry bricks and rubble in 2 hours.

Thirty feet below the masonry wall and 50 feet above the foot of the steps, a small crack has formed in the outer wall of the stairwell. The crack is 1/2 inch wide,

5 inches tall, and 12 inches deep; it leads to the castle's wine cellar (area K63). Characters can notice the crack automatically as they climb or descend the stairs. Widening the crack enough to squeeze through the wall requires major excavation and would take several days.

The shaft that these stairs wrap around (area K18a) runs vertically from area K59 to area K84 without any holes or obstructions. The inner wall of the stairwell, between the staircase and the shaft, is solid.

# K18A. HIGH TOWER SHAFT

Characters can access this 10-foot-diameter, 390-foot-tall stone shaft from the top or the bottom of the high tower (areas K59 and K84, respectively).

The shaft is dark and choked with cobwebs. A rushing wind causes the webs to stir. Climbing the shaft is impossible without the aid of magic or the use of a climber's kit, since there are few handholds.

The bats in the catacombs (area K84) fly up the shaft at night, exiting Castle Ravenloft through various arrow slits and holes in the tower's peak (area K59). After feeding, they return by the same route.

# K19. GRAND LANDING

Massive stairs rise to a landing twenty feet wide by forty feet long. Stone arches support a ceiling covered with frescoes twenty feet overhead. The frescoes depict armored knights on horseback, their finer features faded beyond recognition.

Dust floats in the air here. At each end of the south wall, a staircase rises into darkness. Between the staircases are twin alcoves, each one containing a standing suit of armor covered with dark stains. Each suit of armor clutches a mace, the "business end" of which is shaped like a dragon's head. Words engraved on the arches above the suits of armor have been scratched out.

Both staircases on the south wall climb to area K25. The massive stairs lead down to area K8. Anyone who crosses in front of the alcoves along the south wall activates the suits of armor.

Both suits of armor are mechanical traps, each one activated by a pressure plate hidden in the floor in front of its alcove. A character who searches for traps in one of these locations notices both pressure plates with a successful DC 15 Wisdom (Perception) check.

When 40 or more pounds of weight are placed on a pressure plate, the suit of armor nearest to that plate springs forward, flailing its arms and wielding its mace. Any creature standing on a pressure plate when its trap triggers must succeed on a DC 14 Dexterity saving throw or take 7 (2d6) bludgeoning damage from the flailing armor. After leaping out and attacking, the armor retracts. The pressure plate resets after 1 minute, after which its armor trap can be triggered again.

The suits of armor act much like metal puppets—a little joke intended to spook visitors more than damage them. A pressure plate can be disabled by a character who uses thieves' tools and makes a successful DC 15 Dexterity check. A trap can also be disabled by destroying its suit of armor, which has AC 18, 5 hit points, and immunity to psychic and poison damage.

## K20. Heart of Sorrow

A mosaic floor adds a touch of color to the otherwise dark, cold, empty tower that rises above you. A spiral staircase rises slowly into darkness, hugging the outer wall. In the center of the room, another set of stairs leads down.

The staircase in the center of the floor (area K20a) leads down to area K71.

The spiral staircase has no railing and connects the main floor of the castle with each level above it. First, the staircase climbs 50 feet to a landing (shown on map 4), from which an open archway leads to area K13. East of that opening is a secret door that conceals a ladder leading down to area K34.

The stairs ascend another 40 feet to another landing (shown on map 5), with archways that lead to areas K45 and K46, and then climb another 100 feet to a landing beneath the tower's heart (shown on map 8). The staircase wraps around the heart, ending at the top of the tower (area K60).

### The Heart

The tower, including the spiral staircase, is alive. When the characters set foot on the staircase for the first time, read:

As you step onto the spiral staircase, a reddish light flares high overhead, then settles into a dull, pulsing red glow. You now see the full immensity of this tower. The spiral staircase circles up the tower's full height. The tower, sixty feet wide at its base, becomes narrower as it climbs. At the pinnacle of the hollow tower, a large crystal heart pulsates with red light. Above the heart, the stairs continue upward.

Have the characters and the Heart of Sorrow roll initiative. If the characters leave the tower and later return, they can reroll initiative, but the heart's initiative count doesn't change.

The awakened tower shakes and pitches on the Heart of Sorrow's initiative count. Any creature on the stairs or hanging on a tower wall at the start of the heart's turn must succeed on a DC 10 Dexterity saving throw or fall to the base of the tower. Characters who are crawling on the staircase or who lie prone on the stairs succeed automatically.

The Heart of Sorrow is a 10-foot-diameter red crystal heart that floats near the top of the tower. Characters standing on the nearby stairs can make melee attacks against the heart, provided their weapons have a reach of at least 10 feet. The glass heart has AC 15 and 50 hit points. If the heart is reduced to 0 hit points, it shatters, and its crystal shards transform into blood, which rains down on the tower interior and staircase. The destruction of the Heart of Sorrow causes the tower to stop shuddering, and the interior of the tower becomes dark. Destroying the heart earns the characters 1,500 XP.

Strahd and the Heart of Sorrow are connected, such that any damage Strahd takes is transferred to the heart. If the heart absorbs damage that drops it to 0 hit points, it is destroyed, and Strahd takes any leftover damage. The Heart of Sorrow regains all its hit points at dawn if it has at least 1 hit point remaining.

The Heart of Sorrow is held aloft by the will of Strahd. Casting *dispel magic* on it has no effect.

**Animated Halberds.** Mounted on the walls along the section of staircase nearest the heart are ten animated halberds; use the stat block for the **flying sword** in the *Monster Manual*, but increase each halberd's damage to 1d10 + 1 and reduce its AC to 15. The halberds attack any creature that threatens the Heart of Sorrow.

**Vampire Spawn.** Strahd senses if any damage is done to the Heart of Sorrow and sends four **vampire spawn** to destroy those responsible. These vampire spawn are former adventurers whom Strahd defeated long ago. They use their Spider Climb feature to scuttle along the tower walls and arrive in 3 rounds.

## K20a. Tower Hall Stair

This stairway connects areas K20 and K71.

## K21. South Tower Stair

Fluttering torches in iron sconces illuminate this spiral staircase. A chill wind rushes down the circling stairway, seeming to kill the very heat of the torches.

These stairs start at area K73 and go up through areas K61, K9, K30, and K35 before ending at area K47.

## K22. North Archers' Post

The castle courtyard is visible through arrow slits in the walls.

Each arrow slit is 2½ feet tall and 4 inches wide.

## K23. Servants' Entrance

Dim light filters in through a dust-caked window in the east wall. A door next to the window leads to the castle's northeast courtyard.

> Everything in this room is coated with dust, including a large, heavy table in the center of the floor. A thick book lies open on a desk, with an inkwell and a quill next to it. There is a broken door in the north wall, and a staircase in the south wall plunges into darkness. On each side of the staircase, a skeletal figure draped in gleaming chain mail stands sagging at attention, holding a rusty halberd.

The skeletons, which were assembled by Cyrus Belview (see area K62), are held together with wire frames and hung on pegs. They pose no threat.

The staircase descends to area K62. The east door leading to the courtyard is swollen in its frame and requires a successful DC 10 Strength check to force open. The north door is cracked and hangs loose on its hinges; beyond it lies another dust-filled chamber (area K24).

The ancient book is weathered and brittle, but the ink in the well is fresh. At the top of each page is scribed the message "Please register for your own convenience and that of your next of kin." The book is more than half-filled with names, all of them illegible.

## K24. Servants' Quarters

> Broken furniture and torn cloth are strewn about this twenty-by-forty-foot room. Dim light comes from a pair of dirt-caked windows in the northeast corner. A narrow staircase with no railing ascends along the north wall.

The stairs lead to area K34.

# Court of the Count

Refer to map 4 of the castle for areas K25 through K34.

## K25. Audience Hall

> Dim light from the courtyard falls into this great hall through the broken glass and iron latticework of a large window in the west wall. This immense room is a place of chilly, brooding darkness. Empty iron sconces dot the walls. Hundreds of dust-laden cobwebs drape the hall, hiding the ceiling from view. Directly across from the window stand a set of double doors in the east wall. Farther south, a single door also leads from the east wall. Staircases at both ends of the north wall lead down.
>
> At the far southern end of the hall, a large wooden throne stands atop a marble dais. The high-backed throne faces south, away from most of the room.

A secret door in the south wall leads to area K13. It is hidden by dust and cobwebs, and requires a successful DC 16 Wisdom (Perception) check to find.

Both staircases in the north wall lead down to area K19. The eastern double doors can be pulled open to reveal area K26 beyond. The single door in the east wall opens into area K30.

### Fortunes of Ravenloft

If your card reading reveals that a treasure is here, it lies on the marble dais, just behind the throne.

If your card reading indicates an encounter with Strahd in this area, he is sitting on the wooden throne.

## K26. Guards' Post

If the characters enter this hall through either set of double doors, read:

> The doors open to reveal another set of double doors ten feet ahead. Between these doors, a ten-foot-wide corridor stretches north to south. At each end of the hall, floating in the darkness, is a human skeleton clad in the rusted armor and tattered livery of a castle guard.

The "floating" skeletons hang from pegs on the north and south walls. The skeletons, which were assembled by Cyrus Belview (see area K62), are held together with wire and are harmless. Behind the skeleton on the north wall is a secret door that can be pushed open into area K33.

If the characters enter this hall by way of the secret door that adjoins area K33, they see the skeleton hanging on the inside of the secret door as soon as they pull it open, and, with a light source or darkvision, can see the skeleton at the south end of the hall as well.

## K27. King's Hall

> This twenty-foot-high hall has a dark, vaulted ceiling draped with cobwebs. A low moan seems to travel the length of the corridor as it rises and falls, intoning sadness and despair.

The moaning is only the wind.

Characters who examine the ceiling can, with a successful DC 20 Wisdom (Perception) check, spot pulleys and a rope that run the full length of the corridor along the ceiling, well hidden by the cobwebs. These items are explained in "Flight of the Vampire" below.

Halfway down the hall on the south side is a narrow secret door that can be pulled open to reveal area K31.

### Flight of the Vampire

Hidden in a compartment above the western set of double doors is a dressed wooden mannequin that looks exactly like Strahd. It wears a black cloak, its fangs are bared, and its arms and clawed fingers are outstretched in a threatening manner. The mannequin is attached to a rope that runs through pulleys fastened along the length of the hallway ceiling.

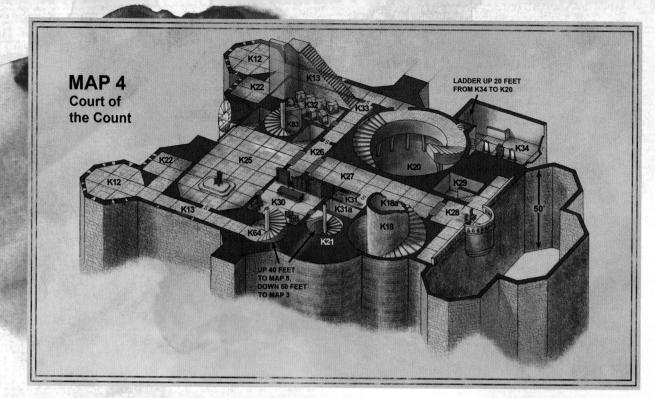

**MAP 4
Court of
the Count**

LADDER UP 20 FEET
FROM K34 TO K20

UP 40 FEET
TO MAP 5,
DOWN 50 FEET
TO MAP 3

When one or more characters reach the midpoint of the hall from either direction, read:

> You hear a scraping sound of stone against stone, followed by the squeaking of a bat. In the direction of the noise, you see the fanged visage, outstretched claws, and flapping black cape of a vampire bearing down on you from above! A deep, throaty chuckle fills the hall.

The scraping noise is the sound of the hidden compartment opening, and the squeaking is the sound of the pulleys supporting the weight of the mannequin as it glides through the air. The chuckling is a harmless magical effect similar to that created by a *prestidigitation* cantrip.

Have the players roll initiative, and run this as a combat encounter with the "vampire" acting on initiative count 5. On its turn, the mannequin flies over the characters, 10 feet above the floor, and doesn't stop until it reaches the east end of the hall. On its next turn, it reverses direction and flies back to its compartment. The trap resets after 1 minute.

A character who attacks the mannequin from the floor needs a range of at least 10 feet. The mannequin has AC 15 and 10 hit points, and it is immune to poison and psychic damage. If the mannequin is reduced to 0 hit points while in the air, it falls to the floor.

## K28. KING'S BALCONY

> A sculpted stone railing encloses this long balcony, which overlooks Ravenloft's chapel. Two ornate thrones stand side by side in the center of the balcony, covered with dust and strung with cobwebs. The thrones face away from the double doors that give access to the balcony.

Two **Strahd zombies** (see appendix D) are slouched on the thrones. They remain motionless until one of them is disturbed or another creature comes within a zombie's reach, whereupon they attack.

The balcony is 50 feet above the floor of the chapel (area K15). A staircase north of the double doors leads down to area K29.

## K29. CREAKY LANDING

> This staircase is made of old wood that strains underfoot, creaking and groaning.

The staircase climbs from area K16 to area K28. It seems unstable but is sturdy. The creatures in area K28 can't be surprised by anyone climbing the creaky steps.

## K30. KING'S ACCOUNTANT

> Dusty scrolls and tomes line the walls of this room. More scrolls and books lie scattered on the floor, around four heavy wooden chests fitted with study iron locks. The only unobstructed floor space is directly in front of the doors on the east and west walls.
>
> In the center of this clutter stands a great black desk. A figure crouches atop a tall stool, scratching on a seemingly endless scroll of paper with a dry quill pen. Nearby a tasseled rope hangs from a hole in the ceiling.

The figure is Lief Lipsiege (CE male human **commoner**), an accountant. He is chained to the heavy wooden desk and has no interest in the characters or their concerns. Under no circumstances does he voluntarily leave the room. Lief pulls the rope the instant he feels threatened.

Pulling the rope requires an action. When the rope is pulled, a tremendously loud gong sounds. One or more creatures arrive 1d6 rounds later, attacking any characters still in the room. Determine the creatures randomly by rolling a d4:

| d4 | Creature |
| --- | --- |
| 1 | 1d6 shadows |
| 2 | 1d4 vampire spawn |
| 3 | 1d4 wights |
| 4 | 1 wraith and 1d4 + 1 specters |

Lief was pressed into service by Strahd many years ago. He keeps all the books for Strahd, recording the vampire's riches and conquests. Lief has been here longer than he can remember. He is grumpy because Strahd doesn't allow him to know about all his treasures. Even so, Lief has found out where one of Strahd's secret treasures lies. If he is treated with kindness, Lief will divulge the hiding place of the *Holy Symbol of Ravenkind* (see appendix C), as indicated by your card reading. Lief can draw a crude map showing a route to that location. His map is geographically accurate, but he admits that it doesn't acknowledge or avoid any dangers that might lie along the way. Lief doesn't necessarily know the most direct path to the symbol's location.

Lief knows that there's a key that unlocks all four chests, but he can't remember where he hid it. See "Treasure" below for more information.

The western door leads to area K25. The eastern door provides access to a staircase (area K21) that leads down to area K9 and up to a landing outside area K35, continuing upward from there to area K47.

### Treasure

The room contains hundreds of worthless books and scrolls describing accounting procedures. The first character who spends at least 10 minutes searching the room and succeeds on a DC 15 Intelligence (Investigation) check finds a book with a bloodstained leather cover. The pages of this book have been hollowed out, creating a hole in which Lief has hidden the iron key that unlocks the four wooden chests in this room.

Two of the locked chests contain 10,000 cp each. A third chest contains 1,000 gp. The fourth chest holds 500 pp, hidden under which is a *manual of bodily health*.

## K31. Trapworks

> The aromas of grease and well-oiled wood hit your nostrils as you pull open the door. This ten-by-twenty-foot room is filled with intricate machinery, except for small spaces between the stone gears and the iron chains and pulleys. On the other side of the machinery, to the south, is a rectangular shaft that rises up from the darkness and continues past this room. Attached to the west wall is a steel plate that has an iron lever protruding downward.

See the diagram on page 76. The shaft (area K31a) descends 90 feet from here to area K61, and ascends 40 feet to area K31b. Another 40 feet above that is a stone trapdoor in the ceiling that opens into area K47.

Operating the machinery in this room raises a stone elevator compartment from the bottom of the shaft, lifting it past this room to the top of the shaft. See area K61 for more information on the elevator trap.

A character can spend 1 minute disabling the machinery in this room. The elevator trap won't function until the machinery is repaired.

The iron lever set into the western wall is normally in the "down" position. Moving it to the "up" position activates the trap and raises the elevator. Sliding it back down lowers the elevator and resets the trap.

When the elevator trap in area K61 is activated, all the chains, pulleys, and gears in this room move at once. It takes 10 seconds (1 round) for the elevator to reach the top of the shaft, and the machinery doesn't stop until the elevator completes its journey.

A secret door in the north wall is easy to spot from this side (no ability check required) and opens into area K27.

## K31A. Elevator Shaft

> Cold air fills this rectangular shaft, the walls of which are coated with mildew and worn smooth. Taut iron chains extend up and down the shaft. The links of the chains are thick and covered with grease.

The shaft is 170 feet tall. It starts at area K61, climbs 90 feet to area K31, another 40 feet to area K31b, and another 40 feet to area K47. When the elevator trap

LIEF LIPSIEGE

is activated (see area K61 for details), a stone elevator compartment measuring 10 feet on a side rises up the western half of the shaft. At the same time, a solid block of stone, also 10 feet on a side, descends in the eastern half of the shaft, acting as a counterweight. Both stone blocks have thick iron chains bolted to them, by which they are hoisted and lowered them as needed.

Scaling the shaft is impossible without the aid of magic or the use of a climber's kit, because the walls are smooth and slick with mildew, and the greasy iron chains are too thick and slippery to grasp.

Set into the roof of the shaft is a 5-foot-square stone trapdoor that can be pushed open to reveal area K47.

## K31B. SHAFT ACCESS

This ten-foot-square room overlooks a vertical shaft to the south that plunges into darkness and continues upward.

This vantage point is 130 feet from the bottom of the shaft (area K31a). Forty feet down is area K31, and 40 feet up is a stone trapdoor in the ceiling that opens into area K47.

A door in the north wall is easy to spot from this side (no ability check required) and opens into area K39.

## K32. MAID IN HELL

Oil lamps illuminate this long, rectangular chamber with oak-paneled walls. Stained, yellowed lace hangs neatly from eight canopied beds. The figure of a woman moves lithely about the room, dusting furniture and humming quietly. Around her pale, slender neck is a gold necklace with a ruby pendant.

The maid, Helga Ruvak, is a **vampire spawn** who claims to be the daughter of the village bootmaker, kidnapped and forced into service by Strahd. She pleads, on her hands and knees if necessary, to be saved from this awful place.

Helga will join the party if the characters ask her along. She intends to attack the characters but does so only if she senses an opportunity that doesn't involve having to fight the entire party. She also attacks if commanded to do so by Strahd.

Helga plays the part of the innocent damsel in distress to the last, revealing her ferocity only when she attacks. She is, in fact, the bootmaker's daughter she claims to be, but she chose a life of evil with Strahd.

### TREASURE

Helga's gold necklace with its ruby pendant is a gift from Strahd. The necklace is almost five centuries old and is worth 750 gp.

## K33. KING'S APARTMENT STAIR

This dark hall is concealed behind two secret doors.

This arched corridor has been swept clean. Oak paneling decorates the walls to a height of four feet. Mounted on the east wall above the wood paneling are three unlit oil lamps spaced ten feet apart. A plain wooden door is set into the west wall, and light seeps through its cracks. A staircase at the north end of the west wall ascends into darkness.

The staircase climbs 40 feet to area K45. The door in the west wall opens into area K32.

## K34. SERVANTS' UPPER FLOOR

Dirt-caked windows allow little light to enter this upstairs room. Broken bed frames and torn bits of mattress litter the floors. A tall, dusty wardrobe roughly shaped like a coffin, its black doors painted with fey creatures, stands between two cracked, full-length mirrors hanging on the south wall. A staircase descends along the north wall.

If someone opens the wardrobe, read:

A plain white dress yellowed with age flies out of the wardrobe and begins to dance in the middle of the room. The dress flaps around to the music of the storm.

If anyone touches the dancing dress, it collapses in a lifeless heap on the floor. Otherwise, it dances forever. Hanging in the wardrobe are a few rotted servant's uniforms, none of which are animate or valuable.

Set into the south wall, behind the hanging mirror west of the wardrobe, is a secret door. It can be pulled open to reveal a closet choked with dust and cobwebs and that contains a wooden ladder that leads up 20 feet to another secret door in the tower stairway (area K20).

The staircase leads down to area K24.

# ROOMS OF WEEPING

Refer to map 5 of the castle for areas K35 through K46.

## K35. GUARDIAN VERMIN

A door of delicately engraved steel stands at the west end of this short, dark hallway. Intricate details stand out clearly on the door's surface. The door seems to shine with a light of its own, untouched by time. Flanking the door are two alcoves in shadow. A dark, vaguely man-shaped figure stands in each alcove.

The dark figures are four **swarms of rats** piled atop one another to form manlike shapes (two swarms per alcove). These rats are under Strahd's control and attack anyone that tries to move through this area.

The steel door is engraved with images of a human king in armor astride a horse, a majestic range of mountains and shooting stars in the background. Tiny figures of people and wolves frame the image.

## K36. Dining Hall of the Count

> Dust assaults your lungs. A sweet yet pungent smell of decay fills this room, in the center of which stands a long oak table. A blanket of dust covers the tabletop and its fine china and silverware. In the center of the table, a large, tiered cake leans heavily to one side. The once white frosting has turned green with age. Cobwebs hang like dusty lace down every side of the cake. A single doll figure of a well-dressed woman adorns the crest of the cake. Suspended above is a web-shrouded chandelier of forged iron. An arched window in the south wall is draped with heavy curtains. Resting in a wooden stand by the window is a dusty lute, and standing quietly in the southwest corner is a tall harp shrouded in cobwebs.

The wedding cake is over four centuries old, kept in its current rotten state by the will of Strahd. The toy figure of the groom from the top of the cake was cast on the floor long ago. A character who searches the dusty floor finds the figurine with a successful DC 10 Wisdom (Perception) check.

If the characters take the groom figurine out of the room, read the following if they return to the room at a later time:

> Billowing drapes draw your eye to the window, which has been broken outward. Scattered about the floor are chunks of the moldy cake, as if something had burst out of it.

There are two explanations for the burst cake and broken window. Choose the one you think is creepier:

- Strahd smashes the cake and breaks the window to make the characters think something terrible has escaped and is now stalking them.
- Strahd's hate assumes a corporeal form, bursts out of the cake (the symbol of Sergei and Tatyana's love), and escapes through the window. "Strahd's hate" has the statistics of an **invisible stalker** and tries to kill whichever character is carrying the groom figurine.

The room has wooden doors in the north and west walls, and an ornate steel door in the east wall (see area K35 for details).

The harp stands 6½ feet tall, weighs close to 300 pounds, and is fashioned of dark, stained wood carved with images of harts and roses. Its taut strings are made of gut.

A character who plays the harp and succeeds on a DC 15 Charisma (Performance) check does well enough to summon the ghost of Pidlwick, a short little man dressed as a fool, with a tiny jingling bell at the end of his pointy dunce cap. He asks, "Why have you summoned me from beyond the grave?" Regardless of the answer, he commends the character for playing well and says, "In my crypt below the castle, thou shalt find

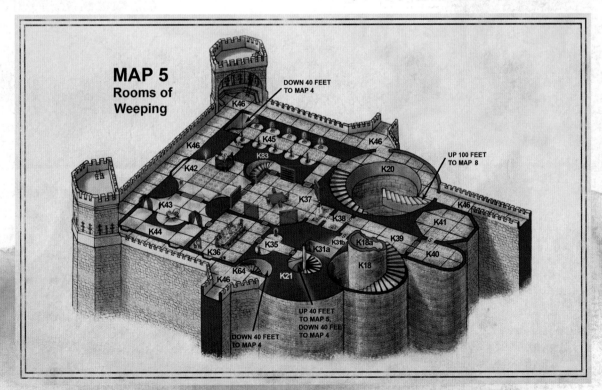

a treasure worthy of one so talented as thee! May it help thee set this troubled place to rest." If the characters think to ask him who he is, the fool replies, "Pidlwick." If asked how he died, he replies humorlessly, "I fell down the stairs." If Pidlwick II (see area K59) is with the party, the ghost points at the clockwork effigy and says, "He pushed me down the stairs."

With nothing more to add, the ghost of Pidlwick fades away and doesn't appear again. If the characters attack the ghost, it attacks them in turn.

### TREASURE

The lute, though old and covered in dust, has survived the passage of time. It is a magic *instrument of the bards* called a *Doss lute*.

## K37. STUDY

> A blazing hearth fire fills this room with rolling waves of red and amber light. The walls are lined with ancient books and tomes, their leather covers well oiled and preserved through careful use. All is in order here. The stone floor is concealed beneath a thick, luxurious rug. In the center of the room is a large, low table, waxed and polished to a mirrored finish. Even the poker in its stand next to the blazing fireplace is polished. Large, overstuffed divans and couches are arranged about the room. Two chairs of burgundy-colored wood with padded leather seats and back cushions face the hearth. A huge painting hangs over the mantelpiece in a heavy, gilded frame. The rolling firelight illuminates the carefully rendered portrait. It is an exact likeness of Ireena Kolyana.

This chamber has several exits, including a large set of double doors in the west wall, a door at each end of the north wall, and a door to the south.

The painting above the fireplace depicts Tatyana, a beautiful young woman with auburn hair. Strahd commissioned the painting over four centuries ago to impress his beloved. The fact that Ireena Kolyana looks exactly like Tatyana is proof to Strahd that both women were born with the same soul.

The back wall of the fireplace contains a secret door, which is opened by lifting the poker from its stand. The fire must be extinguished in order for anyone to reach the secret door safely. Otherwise, a creature that enters the fireplace for the first time on a turn or starts its turn there takes 5 (1d10) fire damage and catches fire. Until someone takes an action to douse the flames on the creature, it takes 5 (1d10) fire damage at the start of each of its turns. (This fire damage is cumulative with the damage from standing in the fireplace.)

The secret door provides access to area K38.

### TREASURE

The real treasure here is Strahd's collection of books—over one thousand unique tomes in all. The collection is worth 80,000 gp. Transporting it would be a challenge.

Roll a d12 and consult the following table to determine the subject matter of a randomly chosen book.

| d12 | Book |
| --- | --- |
| 1 | Alchemist's tome |
| 2 | Bestiary of strange beasts |
| 3 | Biography of a forgotten king or queen |
| 4 | Book of exotic recipes |
| 5 | Book of heraldry |
| 6 | Book of military strategy |
| 7 | Epic novel |
| 8 | Guide to fine wines |
| 9 | Heretical text |
| 10 | Historical text |
| 11 | Poetry anthology |
| 12 | Theological text |

### TELEPORT DESTINATION

Characters who teleport to this location from area K78 arrive in front of the painting of Tatyana.

### FORTUNES OF RAVENLOFT

If your card reading reveals that a treasure is here, it is resting on the mantelpiece under the portrait of Tatyana.

If your card reading indicates an encounter with Strahd in this area, he is sitting back in one of the overstuffed chairs, staring into the fire.

## K38. FALSE TREASURY

> Resting on the floor of this smoke-filled room is a closed chest surrounded by piles of gold, silver, and copper coins. The fittings and clawed feet on the chest are evidence of great workmanship.
>
> Attached to the east wall are two torch sconces. The southernmost one holds a torch with an intricate metal base. The other is empty. A skeleton in broken plate armor lies against the wall. The skeleton's right hand is on its throat, and its left hand holds the matching torch from the empty sconce.

The coins scattered around the trapped chest total 50 gp, 100 sp, and 2,000 cp. The chest weighs 40 pounds and is unlocked. When opened, it releases a cloud of sleeping gas that fills the room. Any creature in the room must succeed on a DC 18 Constitution saving throw or be paralyzed for 4 hours. If all the characters succumb to the gas, they are found by the witches who lair in area K56 and dragged to area K50, then left there unharmed. If even one character resists the effect of the gas, the witches do not appear.

The armored skeleton on the floor is all that remains of an adventurer. His corpse has nothing of value.

### SECRET DOORS

This room is concealed behind two secret doors.

The secret door to the west is set into the back wall of the fireplace (area K37) and can be pulled open from

TATYANA

The hall has an arched ceiling 20 feet overhead, hidden behind thick webbing. At the eastern end are a pair of arched bronze doors of ornate design. These doors can be pulled open to reveal area K40 beyond.

Most of the hall is full of giant spider webs (see "Dungeon Hazards" in chapter 5, "Adventure Environments," of the *Dungeon Master's Guide*). Characters who stray from the unobstructed path through the webs risk becoming stuck.

### Secret Doors

At the west end of the hall are two secret doors.

The secret door on the west wall can't be opened from this side, except by magic (such as a *knock* spell). See area K38 for more information on this secret door. If the characters pass through this door coming from area K38, it closes and locks behind them if they don't take measures to prop it open.

A narrow secret door at the western end of the south wall is hidden behind a mass of webs. If these webs are cleared away, characters can search for the secret door, finding it with a successful DC 15 Wisdom (Perception) check. The door can be pulled open to reveal area K31b.

## K40. Belfry

> You can hear the rain and thunder outside, and the air here is cold and damp. Veils and curtains of webbing fill the room, making it hard to gauge its width and depth. A single, narrow path leads to the dark center of the room, where a rope dangles from high above.

The rope is attached to a great bell mounted in a wooden framework 50 feet overhead. Pulling the rope or attempting to climb it brings forth a loud, long "GONG." That sound causes five **giant spiders** to drop from their webs and attack. The spiders attack only if they are attacked or if the bell is sounded.

Most of the belfry is filled with giant spider webs (see "Dungeon Hazards" in chapter 5, "Adventure Environments," of the *Dungeon Master's Guide*). Characters who blunder into them risk becoming stuck.

At the west end of the north wall, behind thick webs, is a secret door that opens into area K41.

## K41. Treasury

> This octagonal vault is free of dust and cobwebs. The domed ceiling forty feet above is painted black and sparkles with a display of stars in unfamiliar constellations. Barely contained within this vault is a square tower, twenty feet on a side and thirty feet high, with arrow slits on all sides and a battlemented roof.

The domed ceiling is coated with dry pitch. The "stars" are shards of glowing crystal embedded in the pitch,

within this room by lifting a simple locking mechanism (which is connected to the poker in the study). It's possible that a character might open this secret door inadvertently by lifting the poker in area K37. Characters can otherwise locate the secret door normally, but a successful check doesn't reveal the mechanism to open it. That can be found only through trial and error, or the characters can bypass the mechanism with a *knock* spell or similar magic.

The secret door at the northern end of the east wall is sealed shut. If the torch is taken from the skeleton's hand and placed back in the empty sconce, the secret door swings inward, revealing area K39 beyond. Removing the torch from its sconce at any time causes the secret door to close and lock shut, becoming sealed as before. Characters can locate this secret door normally, but a successful check doesn't reveal the mechanism to open it. That can be found only through trial and error, or the characters can bypass the mechanism with a *knock* spell or similar magic.

## K39. Hall of Webs

> This ancient hall is choked with spider webs broken by a single clear path down its center.

each one as bright as a candle flame. Thanks to the starry "night sky," the vault is dimly lit.

The plundered riches of Strahd's secret hoard lie within this adamantine tower, which is actually a *Daern's instant fortress* (see chapter 7, "Treasure," of the *Dungeon Master's Guide*). Only Strahd knows the command word to alter its shape and size, which can't be done until every bit of treasure inside it is removed. Only Strahd can open the two means of entry: a sealed adamantine door set into the base of the tower on the north side, and an adamantine trapdoor on the roof.

The arrow slits of the tower are 4 inches wide and 2 feet tall, and the walls of the fortress are 3 inches thick. Characters who are able to reduce their size or assume gaseous form can enter the tower through these slits.

### Treasure

The ground floor of the *Daern's instant fortress* contains 50,000 cp, 10,000 sp, 10,000 gp, 1,000 pp, 15 assorted gems (100 gp each), and a *+2 shield* emblazoned with a stylized silver dragon that is the emblem of the Order of the Silver Dragon (see chapter 7). The shield whispers warnings to its bearer, granting a +2 bonus to initiative if the bearer isn't incapacitated.

The upper floor of the tower contains 10 pieces of jewelry (250 gp each) in a red velvet sack, an *alchemy jug*, a *helm of brilliance*, a *+1 rod of the pact keeper*, and an unlocked wooden coffer with four compartments, each one containing a *potion of greater healing*.

### Fortunes of Ravenloft

If your card reading reveals that a treasure is here, it is lying atop the coins on the ground floor inside the tower.

If your card reading indicates an encounter with Strahd in this area, he is perched atop the tower.

## K42. King's Bedchamber

> Sweet smells waft from this delicately lit room. A great arched window along the west wall is covered by heavy red draperies, their golden tassels glinting in the light of three candelabras sitting atop small tables about the room. Tall white candles burn with bright, steady light.
>
> A large bed, canopied by silk curtains, sits with its headboard against the north wall. Carved into the headboard with great skill is a large "Z." Lying amid the velvet and satin sheets and bedclothes is a young woman in a nightgown. One of her dainty slippers has fallen to the floor at the bed's foot.

Arched double doors lead from this room to the south and east.

The window is divided into four tall panes of glass, each enclosed by a lead framework. The two outermost sections have small iron hinges built into them so that they can be opened, as well as iron latches to lock them in place when they're closed. The window looks out onto the parapet (area K46).

GERTRUDA

The figure on the bed is Gertruda (NG female human **commoner**), the daughter of Mad Mary (see chapter 3, area E3). Gertruda is oblivious to any danger to herself—especially from Strahd, who has charmed her. Sheltered by her mother, she was never allowed to leave home as a child. She finally slipped away and made her way to the castle, drawn by its majesty.

Gertruda is innocent, and years spent as a shut-in have twisted her sense of reality. Consequently, she maintains a fairy-tale view of life. When faced with a decision, she almost always makes the most simplistic choice. She is naive to the point of being a danger to herself and others. Fortunately for her, Strahd has not yet bitten her, though he intends to. (If he can do so while the characters look on helplessly, so much the better.)

Next to the bed, set into the north wall, is a secret door. It can be pushed open to reveal a dusty hall that ends at a similar secret door in the back of an alcove (see area K45 for details). Gertruda doesn't know that this secret door exists.

## K43. Bath Chamber

> Red satin curtains hang in archways at both ends of the south wall in this dark room. Between them, in the center of the chamber, stands a large, ornate iron tub with clawed feet. The tub is full of blood.

Both curtained archways lead to area K44.

TORMENTED SPIRIT

The spirit of Varushka, a maid, haunts this chamber. She took her own life when Strahd began feeding on her, denying him the chance to turn her into a vampire spawn.

The blood in the tub isn't real, but rather a manifestation of Varushka's tormented spirit. If the blood is disturbed in any way, read:

> A blood-drenched creature explodes out of the tub and attaches to the ceiling, cackling maniacally. Blood pours off its pale flesh, bony limbs, and stringy hair as it scuttles away.

The creature that erupts from the tub is no more real than the blood. It can't be harmed and doesn't attack. It scuttles across the ceiling, disappearing into area K44 through one of the archways. Once there, it disappears.

## K44. CLOSET

> The walls here are lined with iron hooks, upon which hang black capes and formal wear. Two arched windows in the south wall are covered by heavy curtains.

Twenty-eight capes and sixteen sets of fine clothes are stored here. Red satin drapes hang in the archways that connect this closet to the adjoining bath chamber (area K43).

## K45. HALL OF HEROES

> Dark alcoves line the walls of this long hall. The ceiling has fallen here, leaving rubble strewn across the floor. Overhead, the beams of Ravenloft's roof are exposed. Lightning from the dark clouds above sporadically illuminates the hall, lighting the faces of life-sized human statues in the alcoves. Each visage is frozen in terror.

The ten statues that line this corridor depict ancient heroes. In actuality, the faces of the statues are stoic and expressionless, but whenever the lightning flashes, their expressions change to utter horror until the hall goes dark again.

The statues are imbued with the spirits of Strahd's ancestors, all of which grieve over the termination of their bloodline. Each spirit will answer one question if addressed directly. The spirits' answers are always short and vague, and there is a 20 percent chance that a spirit's answer is wrong.

The stairs at the west end of the hall descend 40 feet to area K33. An open archway to the east reveals a tower landing beyond (part of area K20).

## K46. PARAPETS

> You stand on a ten-foot-wide walkway that encircles most of the keep. The drizzle of rain continues, punctuated by the occasional clap of thunder or stroke of lightning. Far below these parapets are the shining wet cobblestones of the courtyard.

The walkway runs around the front of the upper portion of the keep. Battlemented walkways extend from the keep north, south, and east to the outer walls of the castle as well. (See map 2 for the length and location of the castle walls.) All the windows leading from this area into the keep are shut and locked, but can easily be broken.

If the characters loiter on the parapets or atop the castle walls for more than 5 minutes, they encounter **Strahd's animated armor** (see appendix D) making the rounds. It patrols the parapets and the outer walls of Ravenloft day and night. Under a darkened sky, characters without darkvision are more likely to hear the clatter of the armor approaching before they can see it.

The armor can't be salvaged if it is reduced to 0 hit points.

# SPIRES OF RAVENLOFT

Refer to maps 6 through 10 of Castle Ravenloft for areas K47 through K60.

## K47. PORTRAIT OF STRAHD

> You come to a dark landing ten feet wide and twenty feet long. A cold draft of wind rushes down the spiral staircase at the north end of the east wall and whistles mournfully through the room before streaming down the stairs to the south.
>
> An ornate, square rug covers the floor to the south. Set into the west wall is an ironbound wooden door with a wooden trapdoor set into the floor in front of it. Hanging on the north wall above the trapdoor is a framed portrait of a handsome, well-dressed man with a serene yet penetrating gaze.

The ornate rug is actually a **rug of smothering**. It attacks creatures, other than undead, that move across it or anyone who tries to move it or otherwise disturb it. Underneath the rug is a bare stone floor.

The wooden, square trapdoor is 4 feet on a side and as thick as the floor, with recessed iron hinges and an iron ring built into the side opposite the hinges. Pulling up on the ring opens the door. Below the trapdoor, characters see one of two things: either a 170-foot-deep shaft (area K31a) or, if the elevator trap has been activated (see area K61), a stone elevator compartment with a secret hatch in its top.

The portrait on the wall depicts Strahd von Zarovich before he became a vampire. Even in life, he was pale. The eyes of the portrait seem to watch and follow the characters as they explore the area. The picture frame is bolted to the wall and can't be removed without destroying it.

If the characters attack the rug or the picture, or if they attempt to remove either item, the **guardian portrait** (see appendix D) attacks.

## K48. OFFSTAIR

> This spiraling staircase is dark and dusty.

This stairway rises from area K47, past area K54, to area K57.

## K49. LOUNGE

> As thunder shakes the tower, heavy beams groan under the weight of the ceiling. Three ornate lanterns hang by chains from these beams, each casting a dim glow. The curved west wall is fitted with three windows of leaded glass in steel latticework. A bookcase sits on the east wall between two doors. Plush, overstuffed chairs and couches are placed about the room. The fabric has faded with age, and the patterns it depicts are nearly gone. Lounging on one couch is a handsome young man whose attire, while elegant, is worn and faded.

The youthful man on the couch is Escher, a dashing **vampire spawn** to whom Strahd has shown favor in the past. Escher is feeling somewhat neglected of late and has retreated here until Strahd's mood improves. If attacked, he hurls himself out the window and lands like a cat on the roof of the keep (area K53). He leads pursuers right to Strahd, wherever the lord of the castle happens to be (and regardless of whether the characters are ready to face Strahd).

In conversation, Escher displays wit with a hint of melancholy. Beneath his arch mood is a dread that Strahd is growing bored of him and will lock him in the catacombs (area K84) with Strahd's other castoff consorts.

The leaded windows are fitted with iron hinges and can be opened. They can be locked from the inside, though they are currently unlocked. The leaded glass doesn't allow for much of a view. If a character opens a window and leaves it open, there's a 50 percent chance that a **vampire spawn** crawling around the outside wall of the tower notices the open window and investigates.

The books in the bookcase have no value and aren't much help to the characters. Some of the titles found on the bookshelf include *Embalming: The Lost Art*, *Life Among the Undead: Learning to Cope*, *Castle Building 101*, and *Goats of the Balinok Mountains*.

### TREASURE
On the third finger of his left hand, Escher wears a platinum ring engraved with tiny roses and thorns (worth 150 gp). Around his neck, he wears a gold and ruby pendant (worth 750 gp).

## K50. GUEST ROOM

> A large bed sits in the center of this room, its four corner posts supporting a black canopy trimmed with gold tassels. Several comfortable divans are placed about the room. There is a banded door in the west wall and a smaller unbanded door in the east wall.

There is no danger in this area during the day. But if the characters try to take a short rest here during the night, the rest is interrupted by the arrival of 1d4 Barovian witches from area K56. They try to subdue the party with *sleep* spells. A witch retreats to area K56 if wounded.

## K51. CLOSET

> This small, wood-paneled room reeks of mildew and has a ten-foot-high ceiling. Iron hooks line the walls, and a dusty black cloak hangs from one hook in the center of the south wall.

The cloak is ordinary. The witches in area K56 placed it here to help them remember which hook opens the secret trapdoor in the ceiling.

**MAP 6**
**Spires of Ravenloft**

K52

K53

K53

K20

K49

K47

K21

K50

K51

K18a

K18

DOWN 40 FEET
TO MAP 5

The trapdoor can be found after a search of the room and a successful DC 13 Wisdom (Perception) check. Locating the trapdoor doesn't enable someone to discover its opening mechanism. The door has a hidden lock and can be opened by pulling down on the hook from which the black cloak hangs. Once it has been found, the trapdoor can be opened by pulling on the hook, or it can be unlocked by someone using thieves' tools, a *knock* spell, or similar magic. It swings down when unlocked.

## K52. Smokestack

> Jutting from the steeply sloping rooftop of the castle, a spindly smokestack, five feet in diameter at the top, rises thirty feet above the roof's peak. Smoke belches from its iron-pronged capstone.

The chimney leads down 60 feet to the blazing fireplace in area K37. A creature that starts its turn in the chimney takes 3 (1d6) fire damage.

## K53. Rooftop

> Rain splashes against the sagging, sloping rooftop. Flashes of lightning illuminate gargoyles perched on the roof's end peaks, their hideous stares forever fixed on the courtyard some one hundred thirty feet below.

If a character tries to traverse the rooftop, read:

> Some of the ancient roof tiles slide easily underfoot, easily dropping into the fog-shrouded darkness. Each falling tile resounds with a hollow click as it hits the flagstones of the parapet or courtyard below.

A character must succeed on a DC 15 Dexterity (Acrobatics) check to traverse the roof. The check succeeds automatically if the character crawls. If the check fails by 5 or more, the character slides off the edge of the roof ans falls 40 feet to the castle parapet (area K46).

## K54. Familiar Room

> The low ceiling of this twenty-foot-square room presses down on you. Torn and broken couches lie in heaps, haphazardly strewn about. Deep claw marks cover the hardwood furniture, and the once lush upholstery has been sliced to shreds. From the dark shadows amid the rubble, three pairs of green eyes stare back at you.

The three **cats** are familiars of the witches in area K56. If the familiars see the characters here, the witches are alerted to their presence.

# K55. Element Room

> Heavy beams support the ceiling of this large room, the outer wall of which curves to follow the shape of the tower. Dim light filters into the room through the steel lattice squares of two leaded glass windows. Several tables stand throughout the room, weighed down by stacks of glass jars and bottles, all of them bearing labels.

The labeled glass containers hold various elements that the witches use in their fell concoctions and rituals. The labels identify such items as "Eye of Newt," "Hair of Bat," "Snail Hearts," and "Frog's Breath." There are no magic potions among the bottles and jars.

The leaded windows are fitted with iron hinges and can be opened. They are currently locked from the inside. If a character opens a window and leaves it open, there's a 50 percent chance that a **vampire spawn** crawling around the outside wall of the tower notices the open window and investigates.

Characters who search the room spot numerous boot prints in the dust, as well as a short trail in the dust on the floor, leading from the northeast corner of the room to the easternmost door. It looks like something heavy was dragged across the floor toward the doorway.

There is a secret trapdoor in the northeast corner of the floor. Because of the trail through the dust, the trapdoor can be found without an ability check. Tapping or knocking on the trapdoor three times releases a hidden latch, causing the trapdoor to swing down. Area K51 lies below. (There's no ability check that will let the characters figure out the trick to opening the door. They can get that information from the witches, or perhaps by using a *divination* spell or similar magic.)

# K56. Cauldron

Characters who stand outside the door to this room can smell a pungent odor coming from within.

If the witches in this room have not been warned that the characters are coming, the characters can hear their horrid cackling. If the characters open the door slightly, they witness the scene described below:

> Green-glowing wisps of steam bubble up from a fat, black cauldron in the center of this dark, oppressive room. Surrounding the cauldron are several gaunt women in soiled black robes. These witches sit hunched on tall wooden stools, their tangled hair tucked under black, pointed hats. They take turns tossing ingredients into the cauldron, uttering fell incantations, and cackling maniacally.

If the witches know the characters are coming, read the following text instead:

> Green-glowing wisps of steam bubble up from a fat, black cauldron in the center of this dark, oppressive room. Surrounding the cauldron are seven tall wooden stools.

The **Barovian witches** (see appendix D) that dwell in this area have sworn themselves to Strahd's service in exchange for arcane power. Seven witches are present when the characters arrive, minus any that might have been encountered and defeated in area K50. If the witches are expecting the characters, they cast *invisibility* spells and stand quietly in the corners of the room, hoping that the cauldron draws their prey inside. Although they prefer to attack at range with their spells, they can grow magic claws using *alter self*.

When the cauldron is touched by someone who also speaks the proper command word ("Gorah!"), it magically heats any liquid placed inside it and remains hot for 3 hours, or until the command word is spoken again by someone within 5 feet of the cauldron. Once the cauldron's property has been used, the cauldron can't be activated again until the next dawn.

Captured witches will trade information in exchange for their lives and freedom, and can be forced to divulge the command word for activating and deactivating the cauldron. They also know how to open the trapdoor in area K55.

## Treasure

Each witch carries a *potion of healing* that she made herself. There is a 30 percent chance that a potion has "gone bad," in which case it's actually a *potion of poison*.

Not visible from the entrance is a small table behind the cauldron on which sits an opened spellbook, seemingly on the verge of falling apart. The book is evil. Any non-evil creature that touches it or starts its turn with the book in its possession takes 5 (1d10) psychic damage. The book contains the following spells:

1st level: *burning hands, charm person, detect magic, find familiar, fog cloud, mage armor, protection from evil and good, ray of sickness, sleep, Tasha's hideous laughter, unseen servant, witch bolt*

2nd level: *alter self, arcane lock, cloud of daggers, darkness, enlarge/reduce, invisibility, knock, misty step*

# K57. Tower Roof

> The sixty-foot-diameter tower roof is rimmed with battlements. A slender stone bridge with no railing spans the gap between this tower and the slightly taller tower to the north. To the east, the high tower of Ravenloft thrusts skyward with no apparent opening at this level. Black, boiling clouds hurl rain down from above.

The courtyard is 190 feet below, the roof of the keep 80 feet below. A stone railing encloses a stone spiral staircase that descends into the tower.

## K58. Bridge

> A strong wind blows across this slender bridge of stone and masonry. The bridge's old iron railings have rusted away years ago, leaving the bridge without handholds.

The bridge connects areas K20 and K57. The wind isn't strong enough to knock creatures off the bridge, but a creature that takes damage while standing on the bridge must succeed on a DC 10 Dexterity saving throw or fall 60 feet onto the roof of the keep.

## K59. High Tower Peak

If the characters climb the stairs to reach the tower peak, read:

> The spiral staircase finally ends at a five-foot-wide stone walkway that circles the shaft. In the center of the tower's highest floor, a fifteen-foot-diameter hole drops into the cold heart of Ravenloft itself. Cold air rushes up out of the shaft, sending a chill through you. Arrow slits line the walls, and aging beams support a steep, cone-shaped roof. One beam and part of the roof have fallen away, leaving a gaping hole open to the stormy sky.

The hole in the floor forms the mouth of an enclosed shaft (area K18a) that descends 450 feet to the castle catacombs (area K84).

### Pidlwick II

Hiding in the rafters is **Pidlwick II** (see appendix D). A character spots Pidlwick II with a passive Wisdom (Perception) score that meets or exceeds its Dexterity (Stealth) check. If Pidlwick II is spotted, read:

> Something lurks among the rafters—a small, spindly man not much larger than a child. A flash of lightning illuminates his face, which is painted like a grinning jack-o'-lantern.

Although he appears to be a petite man wearing face paint and a fool's costume, Pidlwick II is actually a clockwork effigy of the real-life Pidlwick, who lies entombed in the catacombs. The dark paint on his face is soot.

If the characters see Pidlwick II in bright light, read:

> It's obvious that you're looking not at a small man, but a mockery of one. This thing is not a creature of flesh and bone, but a construct made of dyed leather stitched and tightly wrapped over an articulated frame. You hear the soft tumbling and clicking of gears.

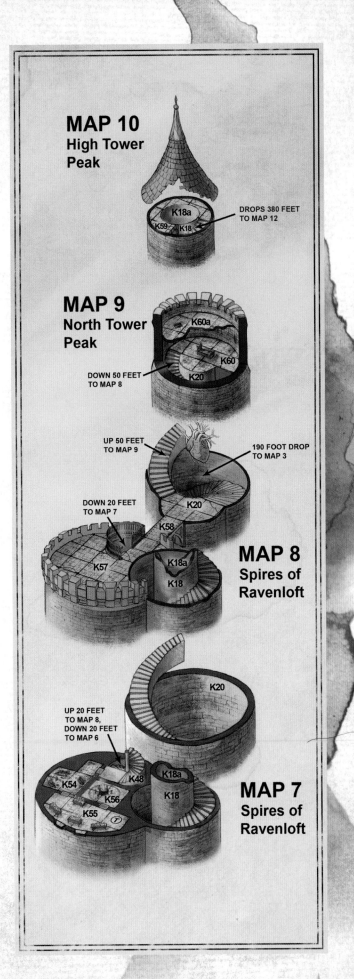

Pidlwick II can't speak and doesn't have an expressive face, so he relies mostly on hand gestures and simple diagrams to communicate. He understands Common but can't read or write.

If the characters show kindness to the clockwork effigy, it accompanies them and tries its best to be helpful and entertaining. It knows its way around the castle and can serve as a silent guide.

If one or more characters are mean toward Pidlwick II, its quiet resentment of them grows, and at some point when the group is at the top of a staircase, it pushes one of the offending party members down the stairs. The target must succeed on a DC 10 Dexterity saving throw or tumble to the bottom of the staircase, taking 1d6 bludgeoning damage per 10 feet fallen.

## K60. North Tower Peak

If the characters climb the stairs to this area, read:

> The stairs end at a dark and dreary room with manacles attached to the walls. In the middle of the room is a wood-framed bed fitted with leather restraints. At the foot of the bed rests a closed iron chest, is lid sculpted with an emblem.
>
> A wooden ladder leads up to a trapdoor in the ceiling. Thin streams of water drip through the trapdoor's rotting wood, forming a puddle around the base of the ladder.

The ceiling here is 9 feet high. The manacles are rusted and can be easily torn from the walls. The trapdoor in the ceiling leads to the tower rooftop (area K60a).

The emblem worked into the lid of the iron chest is Strahd's family crest. (Show the players Strahd's crest on page 239.) Cyrus Belview (see area K62) stashed the chest here for safekeeping.

### Treasure

The iron chest is locked, and its key is with Cyrus Belview in area K62.

The chest contains a bejeweled gold crown (worth 2,500 gp) resting on a silk pillow.

### Teleport Destination

Characters who teleport to this location from area K78 arrive in the middle of the room.

### Fortunes of Ravenloft

If your card reading reveals that a treasure is here, it is inside the iron chest.

If your card reading indicates an encounter with Strahd in this area, he is standing next to the iron chest.

## K60a. North Tower Rooftop

> A cold wind greets you atop the tower roof, its rain-slicked flagstones surrounded by a twenty-foot-diameter ring of stone battlements. The thunderclouds above suddenly coalesce into the terrible visage of Strahd. The face utters a ghastly moan as thousands of bats fly out of its gaping maw and descend upon the tower.

Characters who remain on the roof are accosted by ten **swarms of bats**, which arrive in 3 rounds. If the characters descend into the tower, the bats don't follow and instead fly into the high tower (area K59), descend its central shaft (area K18a), and roost in the catacombs (area K84).

The courtyard lies 260 feet below, and the roof of the keep is 130 feet below.

# Larders of Ill Omen

Refer to map 11 of the castle for areas K61 through K72.

## K61. Elevator Trap

See area K31 and the accompanying Elevator Trap diagram before running this encounter.

> This dusty, ten-foot-wide, thirty-foot-long corridor has a flat ceiling ten feet overhead. To the south, a web-filled stairway spirals down into darkness. The north end of the hall ends at a wooden door.

This hallway contains an elevator trap, triggered when at least 400 pounds of pressure is applied to the 10-foot-square section of floor in the center of the hall (marked T on the map), or when the lever in area K31 is raised. A party of adventurers moving in close formation down the hall is certainly heavy enough to trigger the trap.

A character who searches for traps while crossing the hall and succeeds on a DC 15 Wisdom (Perception) check detects seams in the floor, walls, and ceiling that suggest that the middle section isn't attached to the rest of the hall. A character who makes a successful DC 15 Intelligence (Investigation) check discerns that the trap can't be disarmed from this location.

The middle 10-foot section of the hall is a cleverly hidden elevator compartment, open to the north and south so that it appears to be part of the passageway. When the trap is sprung, two steel portcullises drop from the ceiling at lightning speed to seal off the compartment, trapping within those creatures that triggered the trap. An instant later, the closed-off elevator is propelled up the western half of a 20-foot-wide, 170-foot-tall shaft (area K31a) to the sounds of turning gears and rattling chains. Magic sleep gas fills the compartment as it rises,

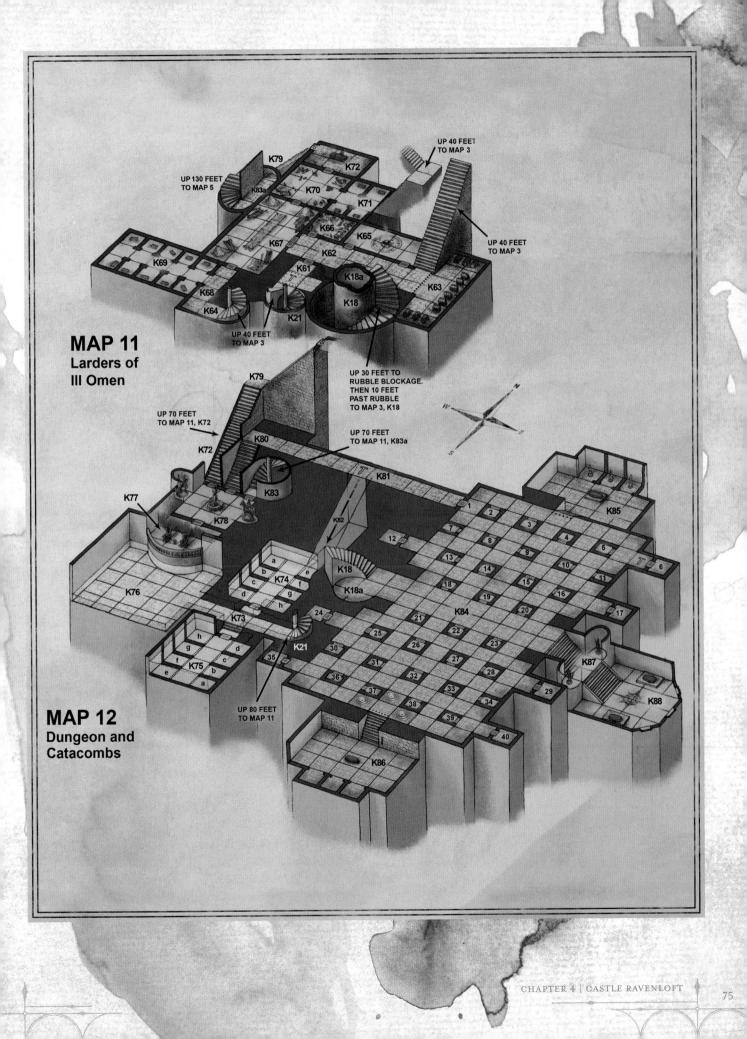

MAP 11
Larders of
Ill Omen

MAP 12
Dungeon and
Catacombs

UP 130 FEET
TO MAP 5

UP 40 FEET
TO MAP 3

UP 40 FEET
TO MAP 3

UP 40 FEET
TO MAP 3

UP 30 FEET TO
RUBBLE BLOCKAGE.
THEN 10 FEET
PAST RUBBLE
TO MAP 3, K18

UP 70 FEET
TO MAP 11, K72

UP 70 FEET
TO MAP 11, K83a

UP 80 FEET
TO MAP 11

K79
K72
K83a
K70
K71
K66
K67
K65
K62
K69
K61
K68
K18a
K64
K18
K21
K63

K79
K80
K72
K83
K77
K78
K81
K82
K76
K74
K18
K18a
K73
K75
K21
K84
K85
K86
K87
K88

N
W        E
S

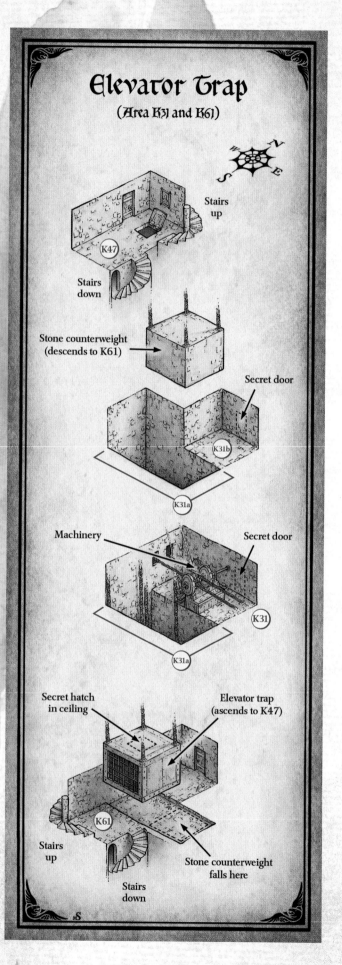

# Elevator Trap
## (Area K31 and K61)

Stairs up

K47

Stairs down

Stone counterweight (descends to K61)

Secret door

K31b

K31a

Machinery

Secret door

K31

K31a

Secret hatch in ceiling

Elevator trap (ascends to K47)

K61

Stairs up

Stairs down

Stone counterweight falls here

and a creature trapped inside must succeed on a DC 15 Constitution saving throw or fall unconscious as though affected by a *sleep* spell.

At the same time the elevator rises, a 10-foot cube of granite suspended from heavy chains descends in the eastern half of the shaft, acting as a counterweight. The massive block lands gently at the bottom of the shaft, filling the previously open 10-foot-by-10-foot space adjacent to where the elevator stood. The block weighs thousands of tons and pulverizes anything in the space where it comes to rest.

Once the elevator starts rising, its portcullises are locked in place and can't be lifted. The walls of the shaft are nearly flush with the elevator compartment; only a few inches of space exist between the portcullises and the shaft walls.

All creatures trapped inside the elevator (including unconscious ones) must roll initiative. The compartment takes 1 round to reach the top of the shaft, stopping just beneath area K47. Each creature inside has one turn to act before the compartment comes to a dead stop. Their initiative rolls determine the order in which the occupants act. Conscious party members can take whatever actions they like. They might search for a way out, wake sleeping party members, cast spells, or take other actions. Unconscious ones can do nothing.

A character who uses an action to search the ceiling of the elevator finds a secret trapdoor with a successful DC 10 Wisdom (Perception) check. The trapdoor opens downward.

Any creature on top of the elevator when it reaches the top of the shaft must make a successful DC 15 Dexterity saving throw to avoid being crushed against the ceiling of the shaft. The character takes 44 (8d10) bludgeoning damage on a failed save, or half as much damage on a successful one. When the elevator comes to a stop, its portcullises retract.

The elevator remains at the top of the shaft until the lever in area K31 is moved to the "down" position. When that happens, the trap resets in 1 round: the portcullises come down, and the elevator compartment descends to its place in the hallway at the bottom of the shaft as the stone block rises to the top of the shaft. When the elevator reaches the bottom, its portcullises rise again.

## DEVELOPMENT

The sound of the elevator moving can be heard throughout the castle. Characters who are trapped or asleep in the elevator compartment are easy prey for Strahd, who can reach them by way of the trapdoor in area K47.

# K62. SERVANTS' HALL

> This hall stands in deadly silence. Heavy beams support a sagging, ten-foot-high ceiling. Fog clings to the floor, obscuring everything that lies less than three feet above it. A giant shadow lurches across the ceiling as a dark figure shuffles purposefully down the corridor toward you.

The figure approaching is Cyrus Belview, a **mongrel-folk** (see appendix D) and Strahd's faithful servant. He stands 4 feet, 9 inches tall but appears shorter because of his hunched posture. He has the Keen Hearing and Smell feature. The left side his face is covered with lizard scales, and he has the ears of a panther. His left foot looks like a duck's webbed foot, and his arms have patches of black dog fur.

The light in the hall comes from a lantern on the floor behind Cyrus. If the characters have their own light sources, Cyrus sees them, but he will not attack first. He wears a loop of twine around his neck, hanging from which is an iron key and a decorative wooden pendant fitted with a varnished human eyeball. The key unlocks the iron chest in area K60. The wooden pendant is a *hag eye* given to Cyrus by the night hag Morgantha (see chapter 6), so that she could spy on Strahd. Cyrus doesn't know that the necklace is magical. See the "Hag Covens" sidebar in the hags entry in the *Monster Manual* for information about the *hag eye*.

Poor old Cyrus is obviously crazy. He has served the master for uncounted years and is devoted to him. Cyrus tries to get the characters to retire to their "room in the tower" (area K49). If the characters aren't sure what room he is talking about, he offers to lead them there.

If the characters follow Cyrus, he tells them to stay close to him as he leads them through the south door to area K61 and deliberately sets off the elevator trap there. Cyrus tries his best not to succumb to the sleeping gas as the elevator compartment climbs the shaft (area K31), and he has advantage on the saving throw. Assuming he's still conscious when the elevator compartment reaches the top of the shaft, Cyrus opens the trapdoor to area K47 and either leads the characters to area K49 or, if they're unconscious, drags them there. After assuring characters who are conscious that "the master will be along shortly," Cyrus then makes his way back downstairs to the kitchen (area K65).

If the characters don't go to their room, Cyrus shakes his head and returns to the work of preparing his dinner in area K65. If the characters take his key, he screams, "The master will not be pleased!" and begins to moan and slap his head, obviously upset. A successful DC 10 Charisma (Intimidation) check is enough to make him divulge the key's purpose, the location of the iron chest, and the chest's contents.

When he isn't being threatened, Cyrus giggles to himself from time to time for no clear reason. He also likes to tell poor jokes at the most inopportune moments.

Stairs at the east end of the north wall lead up to area K23.

Along the east wall is a rusted but sturdy iron portcullis that bars the way to area K63. (If the characters peer through the portcullis, read the boxed text for area K63.) The portcullis bars are 1 inch thick and spaced 4 inches apart. The portcullis can be lifted with a successful DC 20 Strength check.

The double doors at the west end of the hall are made of heavy planks banded with steel. They open into area K67.

## K63. WINE CELLAR

> Arched frames of stone form a low, wet ceiling over this wine cellar. Great casks line the walls, their bands rusting and their contents long since spilled onto the floor. A few hungry rats make their home here, but upon your sudden arrival, they retreat to the shadows.

The rats are harmless. Cyrus Belview (see area K62) treats them like pets.

Characters who search the room find a crack at the southern end of the west wall. The crack is half an inch wide, 5 inches tall, and 12 inches deep; it leads to area K18.

### WINE CASKS

Each of the twelve large casks here rests on its side in a heavy wooden brace. Three casks stand against the north wall, six against the east wall, and three against the south wall. Decorative lettering is burned into the top of each cask, showing the winery name—the Wizard of Wines—and the name of the wine in the cask.

**Northern Casks.** All three of these casks are rotted and empty. The wine's name is Champagne du le Stomp.

**Eastern Casks.** Five of these casks are rotted and empty. The wine name burned on each is Red Dragon

CYRUS BELVIEW

Crush. Lining the interior of the sixth one is a patch of yellow mold (see "Dungeon Hazards" in chapter 5, "Adventure Environments," of the *Dungeon Master's Guide*). A character who inspects the cask closely and succeeds on a DC 13 Wisdom (Perception) check sees yellow mold in the cracks between the planks of the cask. If this cask is smashed open, the yellow mold releases a cloud of spores.

**Southern Casks.** Two of these casks are rotted and empty. The wine name burned on each is Purple Grapemash No. 3. The middle one is home to a purplish **black pudding** that bursts forth if the cask is broken open.

### FORTUNES OF RAVENLOFT
If your card reading reveals that a treasure is here, it is inside one of the empty casks along the north wall, hidden there by Cyrus Belview.

## K64. GUARDS' STAIR

The long, hollow sigh of the wind breathes a semblance of life into this otherwise featureless staircase.

The stairway starts at area K68 and goes up past area K13 to area K46.

## K65. KITCHEN

A horrible odor of decay fills this steaming hot room. A huge pot bubbles over a blazing fire pit in the center of the room, its green, muddy contents churning. The far wall is lined with pegs, hanging from which are numerous large cooking implements—some of which could easily double as implements of torture.

If a character looks into the pot, three human **zombies** rise up from the bubbling depths and attack. The zombies are slowly being boiled to death, and each has only 13 hit points remaining. If Cyrus Belview (see area K62) is present when the zombies attack, he grabs a heavy club and tries to beat them back into the pot. Cyrus explains that he just isn't the cook he used to be, and his meals tend to get out of hand these days.

## K66. BUTLER'S QUARTERS

This twenty-foot-square room is filled wall to wall with clutter. A long, sagging bed sits to one side under a huge faded tapestry that depicts Castle Ravenloft. Dusty lanterns sit in various places, and bright curtains are draped haphazardly about the room. Thousands of pieces of junk cover the floor. Broken swords, crumpled shields, and helmets lie in piles all about.

Cyrus Belview (see area K62) uses this room as his lair. There is nothing of value here.

If Cyrus is with the party, the characters notice that he is caressing their equipment and chuckling to himself. Cyrus has been salvaging equipment from dead adventurers for years. He looks forward to adding to his collection after Strahd gets through with the characters.

## K67. HALL OF BONES

Once a mess hall for the castle guards, this room is now desecrated ground (see "Wilderness Hazards" in chapter 5, "Adventure Environments," of the *Dungeon Master's Guide*).

Dark stains cover the floor of this area. Large oak tables, scarred and beaten, lay scattered like toys about the room, their wood crushed and splintered. Replacing them are furnishings made entirely of human bones.

The walls and the twenty-foot-high vaulted ceiling are a sickly yellow color, not because of faded or timeworn plaster but because they are adorned with bones and skulls arranged in a morbidly decorative fashion, giving the room a cathedral-like quality. Four enormous mounds of bones occupy the corners of this ossuary, and garlands of skulls extend from these mounds to a chandelier of bones that hangs from the ceiling above a long table constructed of bones in the center of the room. Ten chairs made of bones and festooned with decorative skulls surround the table, resting atop which is an ornate, bowl-shaped vessel made of yet more bones.

The doors to the north and south are sheathed in bone, but the steel-banded double doors in the center of the east wall are not. Above these eastern doors is mounted the skull of a dragon.

Cyrus Belview (see area K62) created this enormous work of art out of the bones of dead servants and slain adventurers. It has taken him many years to complete it. The bones and skulls are held together with gray mortar and white paste. The dark stains on the floor are old bloodstains, caused here when Strahd hunted down and killed the remainder of his castle guards.

The dragon skull mounted above the eastern doors belonged to Argynvost (see chapter 7), a silver dragon that was killed in the valley by Strahd and his army before the founding of Castle Ravenloft. The skull weighs 250 pounds.

### FORTUNES OF RAVENLOFT
If your card reading reveals that a treasure is here, it is lying on the bone table.

If your card reading indicates an encounter with Strahd in this area, he is sitting comfortably at one end of the table, holding the skull of a long-dead foe.

## K68. Guards' Run

> This ten-foot-wide arched corridor is cold and moist. The cold seems to emanate from an open archway in the west wall.

The archway leads to area K69. A door at the north end of the hall opens into area K67. To the south, the hallway ends at the foot of a staircase (area K64) that spirals upward.

## K69. Guards' Quarters

> Sickly, yellow lichen covers the ceiling of this cold, damp, ten-foot-wide passage running east and west. Opening off both sides of this passage are ten-foot-square alcoves that contain rotting cots, rags, and the skeletal remains of castle guards. A deathly silence fills the hall.

The yellow lichen is harmless. When one or more characters reach the midpoint of the hall, ten human **skeletons** leap from the alcoves and attack.

## K70. Kingsmen Hall

> This thirty-foot-square room is a shambles. Scattered furniture lies in heaps near the walls. Broken bones lie scattered amid crumpled and crushed plate armor. Shields and swords jut from the walls as if driven into them by some tremendous force.
>
> Two doors stand opposite one another in the center of the north wall and the south wall. A dark archway leads out through the east wall.

After Strahd was transformed into a vampire, several of the castle guards retreated to this room, but Strahd caught them and slaughtered them in a brutal show of violence. Removing one of the shields or swords from the wall requires a successful DC 10 Strength check. None of the items found here are valuable.

## K71. Kingsmen Quarters

> This dark passage runs for twenty feet, connecting an archway to the west with an ascending stone staircase to the east. To the north and south are four ten-foot-square alcoves cluttered with rotting cots and dirty rags. The ceilings here are covered with yellow lichen.

The yellow lichen is harmless. Beyond the archway to the west is area K70. The staircase (area K20a) that goes up along the east wall leads to area K20.

### Treasure

Three of the alcoves contain nothing of value. A loose flagstone in the southeast alcove covers a hidden cubbyhole in the floor, in which is hidden a moldy sack containing 150 ep. The coins have the profiled visage of Strahd von Zarovich stamped on them. A character who searches the alcove can find the loose flagstone with a successful DC 10 Wisdom (Perception) check.

## K72. Chamberlain's Office

> This shadowy room is in perfect order. A great table stands here with its chair, inkwell, and quill set carefully in place. Lances, swords, and shields that bear the Barovian crest are hung neatly on the dark, oak-paneled walls.

If he has not been defeated elsewhere, **Rahadin** (see appendix D) is here, waiting for the characters to arrive so he can kill them.

A **shadow demon** also haunts this room. In the round after the characters engage Rahadin, the demon leaps out and attacks the nearest character from behind. The character doesn't notice the demon, unless the character's passive Wisdom (Perception) score meets or exceeds the demon's Dexterity (Stealth) check. Both Rahadin and the shadow demon fight until slain.

A secret door is set into the north end of the west wall. It can be pulled open to reveal a dusty, web-choked staircase of ancient, worn stone (area K79) that descends into darkness.

# Dungeon and Catacombs

Refer to map 12 of the castle for areas K73 through K88.

## K73. Dungeon Hall

The following boxed text assumes that the characters arrive by way of the staircase to the east (area K21). Adjust as needed if the characters enter this hall from another direction.

> The stairs descend into black, still water that fills an arched hallway before you. The water's surface is like dark, mirrored glass, disturbed only occasionally by the "thwick" of a drop falling from the ceiling. Twenty feet ahead, arched doorways lead downward from each side of the hallway. In each arched doorway, an iron door stands closed and partially submerged. You hear a weak cry for help from beyond the south door.

The water is 3 feet deep in the hallway and opaque. The steps on both sides of the hallway descend another 2 feet before ending at the iron doors to the north and south.

The floor beneath the water isn't as solid as one might expect. There is a safe path around several weight-sensitive trapdoors (see the Traps in Area K73 diagram), but the water makes it impossible to see where the trapdoors are. For every 10 pounds of weight on a trapdoor, there is a 5 percent chance that the trapdoor will open. The 10-foot-deep pit under each trapdoor contains a magic teleport trap that activates as soon as the trapdoor opens. Any Medium or smaller creature on a trapdoor when it opens plunges into the pit and is teleported to a cell in either area K74 or K75, as the diagram indicates.

When a character sets off a trap, other characters in the hall see an explosion of air and water fly up around the triggering character (air that was trapped in the pit is released suddenly when the trapdoor opens). The triggering character suddenly falls from sight. An instant later, the trapdoor closes, leaving only a slowly dissipating swirl in the water. It doesn't open again until 24 hours have passed, at which point its teleport trap is recharged.

Characters who fall victim to the teleport traps are transported to dungeon cells closed with iron bars and under 5 feet of brackish water (areas K74 and K75).

## K74. North Dungeon

The rusty iron door connecting this hall to area K73 is submerged in 5 feet of water and requires a successful DC 10 Strength (Athletics) check to open.

> A mold-covered ceiling hangs three feet above the still, black water that fills this dungeon corridor. The water is five feet deep. Ten-foot-square cells, their entrances blocked by iron bars, line both sides of the hall. One of the cells is dimly lit.

The corridor is 40 feet long. Branching off it are eight cells, four along each wall. Light spills out of cell K74h.

A hinged door made up of 1-inch-thick rusted iron bars spaced 4 inches apart, with horizontal crossbars spaced 6 inches apart, closes off each cell. Each door is fitted with an iron lock. A character using thieves' tools can try to pick a lock, which requires 1 minute and a successful DC 20 Dexterity check. The check is made with disadvantage if the character is trying to pick the lock from inside the cell. If the check fails, the character can try again.

A character can force open a barred door by using an action and succeeding on a DC 25 Strength check.

Strahd visits the dungeon occasionally to see whether any characters have become trapped here. He can enter a cell by assuming mist form.

### K74a. Forgotten Treasure

This cell is linked to a teleport trap in area K73. Characters who enter the cell can feel coins shifting beneath their feet.

**Treasure.** Scattered across the floor of this cell are 3,000 ep. The coins have the profiled visage of Strahd von Zarovich stamped on them. A character can scoop up one hundred coins every minute.

### K74b. Forgotten Treasure

> The rusted door to this cell hangs open slightly.

Characters who enter the cell can feel coins shifting beneath their feet.

**Treasure.** Scattered across the floor of this cell are 300 pp. The coins have the profiled visage of Strahd von Zarovich stamped on them. A character can scoop up one hundred coins every minute.

### K74c. Rotting Corpse

> Clinging to the bars of this otherwise empty cell is the rotting corpse of a male half-elf dressed in leather armor.

This cell is linked to a teleport trap in area K73.

**Treasure.** A search of the corpse yields a sheathed longsword and two belt pouches, one containing five gemstones (50 gp each) and the other containing a *potion of heroism*.

### K74d. Empty Cell
This cell contains nothing of interest.

### K74e. End of the Ride
This cell is linked to a teleport trap in area K73.

**Secret Door.** A secret door is 5 feet up from the floor on the north wall of this cell. The secret door can't be opened from this side without the use of a *knock* spell or similar magic. Behind the secret door is a chute of polished black marble that slants upward (area K82).

### K74f. Empty Cell
This cell contains nothing of interest.

## K74g. Gray Ooze

Clinging to the floor of this cell is a **gray ooze** that attacks anything that enters. While underwater, the ooze is effectively invisible.

## K74h. Lost Sword

> A glowing blade can be seen beneath the water near the back of the cell.

This cell is linked to a teleport trap in area K73.

**Treasure.** The source of the underwater glow is a sentient lawful good *+1 shortsword* (Intelligence 11, Wisdom 13, Charisma 13). It has hearing and normal vision out to a range of 120 feet. It communicates by transmitting emotion to the creature carrying or wielding it.

The sword's purpose is to fight evil. The sword has the following additional properties:

- The sword continually sheds bright light in a 15-foot radius and dim light for an additional 15 feet. Only by destroying the sword can this light be extinguished.
- A lawful good creature can attune itself to the sword in 1 minute.
- While attuned to the weapon, the sword's wielder can use the sword to cast the *crusader's mantle* spell. Once used, this property of the sword can't be used again until the next dawn.

# K75. South Dungeon

The rusty iron door connecting this hall to area K73 is submerged in 5 feet of water and requires a successful DC 10 Strength (Athletics) check to open.

> A mold-covered ceiling hangs three feet above the still, black water that fills this dungeon corridor. The water is five feet deep. Ten-foot-square cells, their entrances blocked by iron bars, line both sides of the hall. From one of the cells, you hear a gruff voice ask, "Who's there?"

The corridor is 40 feet long. Branching off it are eight cells, four along each wall. The voice comes from one of the southernmost cells (area K75a).

## K75a. Prisoner

> A strong young man clutches the bars of his cell while struggling to keep his teeth from chattering. His clothes are shredded, and he is soaked from head to toe.

The man is Emil Toranescu, a **werewolf** with 72 hit points. He claims to be a resident of Vallaki who was chased by dire wolves to the castle. He begs the characters to rescue him, offering to help them in exchange.

In truth, Strahd locked Emil here as punishment for causing a schism in his werewolf pack (see chapter 15). Anxious to prove his worth to Strahd, Emil rewards the characters for freeing him by attacking them when a good opportunity arises. Emil doesn't turn against the characters if they claim to be allies of his wife, Zuleika (see chapter 15, area Z7). In that case, he tries to leave the castle and reunite with her, staying with the characters only until an opportunity to leave presents itself.

EMIL TORANESCU

## K75b. Forgotten Treasure

Characters who enter the cell can feel coins shifting beneath their feet.

**Treasure.** Scattered across the floor of this cell are 2,100 ep. The coins have the profiled visage of Strahd von Zarovich stamped on them. A character can scoop up one hundred coins every minute.

## K75c. Empty Cell

This cell contains nothing of interest.

## K75d. Dead Dwarf

This cell is linked to a teleport trap in area K73. The skeletal remains of a dwarf fighter lie at the bottom of the cell, enclosed in rusted plate armor. The dwarf's nonmagical but usable battleaxe lies nearby.

## K75e. Empty Cell

This cell contains nothing of interest.

### K75f. Dead Wizard

> Shackled to the back wall of this cell is an emaciated figure in a blue robe, its spindly arms spread wide and its head tilted forward. Long, gray hair hangs down in front of the dead man's face.

The skeletal figure is all that remains of a human wizard whom Strahd captured and slowly bled to death. Flesh still clings to the wizard's bones, and puncture marks from the vampire's fangs are visible on the wizard's neck.

### K75g. Hanging Bard

> Pounded into the roof of this cell is a rusted iron pulley, strung through which is a rope that is tied to one of the crossbeams of the barred door. Dangling upside down from the pulley is a man, flabby and stout of build, in tight-fitting leather armor. His boots are bound with rope just below the pulley, his fleshy hands are tied behind his back, and his head is underwater. He isn't moving.

Strahd had this human bard suspended from the ceiling as a test to see how long he could keep his head above water. The man weakened and drowned. On the floor of the cell, below the hanging corpse, is a smashed lyre.

### K75h. Empty Cell
This cell contains nothing of interest.

## K76. Torture Chamber

> Dark, low shapes thrust up out of the still, brackish water that fills this fifty-foot-square room, the ceiling of which is festooned with hanging chains that look like thick, black web strands. A balcony set into the north wall overlooks the room and has two large thrones atop it, with a red velvet curtain behind them.

The ceiling is 17 feet above the surface of the water, which is 3 feet deep. The balcony to the north stands 7 feet above the water's surface, 10 feet above the floor.

If the characters approach the "dark, low shapes" in the water, read:

> The dark shapes in the water are racks, iron maidens, stocks, and other instruments of torture. The skeletons of their last victims lie within them, their jaws seemingly frozen open in silent screams.

As soon as one or more characters move more than 10 feet into the room, six **Strahd zombies** rise slowly

out of the water, their slime-gray arms clawing upward through the water as they attack.

## K77. Observation Balcony

> Two large, wooden thrones rest on this balcony. Behind the thrones hangs a red velvet curtain thirty feet long. The ceiling here is ten feet high.

The room continues behind the curtain an additional 10 feet to a wall that has a door in its center.

## K78. Brazier Room

> This room is thirty feet square, rising to a twenty-foot-tall flat ceiling. A stone brazier burns fiercely in the center of the room, but its tall white flame produces no heat. The rim of the brazier is carved with seven cup-shaped indentations spaced evenly around the circumference. Within each indentation is a spherical stone, twice the diameter of a human eyeball and made of a colored crystal. No two stones are the same color.
>
> Overhead, a wood-framed hourglass as tall and wide as a dwarf hangs ten feet above the brazier, suspended from the ceiling by thick iron chains. All the sand is stuck in the upper portion of the hourglass, seemingly unable to run down into the bottom. Written in glowing script on the base of the hourglass is a verse in Common.
>
> Two nine-foot-tall iron statues of knights on horseback, poised to charge with swords drawn, stand in deep alcoves facing each other. The brazier sits between them.

The two statues are **iron golems**. Each horse and rider is considered one creature, and they are inseparable. The golems will not leave the room under any circumstances, and they attack only under specific conditions (see the "Development" section that follows).

The hourglass has AC 12, 20 hit points, immunity to poison and psychic damage, and vulnerability to thunder damage. If the hourglass is reduced to 0 hit points, its glass shatters, causing the sand within it to fall to the floor. The magic writing on the base of the hourglass reads as follows:

*Cast a stone into the fire:*
*Violet leads to the mountain spire*
*Orange to the castle's peak*
*Red if lore is what you seek*
*Green to where the coffins hide*
*Indigo to the master's bride*
*Blue to ancient magic's womb*
*Yellow to the master's tomb*

The brazier's flame is magical and sheds no warmth. A successful casting of *dispel magic* (DC 16) extinguishes the flame for 1 hour. The fire is permanently extinguished if the brazier is destroyed. The brazier has AC

17, 25 hit points, immunity to poison and psychic damage, and resistance to all other damage.

The stones set into the brazier's rim are colored red, orange, yellow, green, blue, indigo, and violet, respectively. Tossing one into the brazier causes its flame to change from white to the color of the stone, and the sand begins falling through the hourglass. Any creature that touches the colored flame is teleported to a location within Strahd's domain, as determined by the color:

| Flame Color | Teleports to ... |
|---|---|
| Red | Study (area K37) |
| Orange | North tower peak (area K60) |
| Yellow | Strahd's tomb (area K86) |
| Green | Coffin maker's shop (chapter 5, area N6f) |
| Blue | Amber Temple (chapter 13, area X42) |
| Indigo | Abbey of Saint Markovia (chapter 8, area S17) |
| Violet | Tsolenka Pass (chapter 9, area T4) |

After 5 rounds, the sand runs out, and the color of the flame returns to white. When the flame does so, the sand instantly reappears in the top part of the hourglass (provided the hourglass is intact), and the stone that was cast into the fire reappears in the brazier's rim.

### Development

If the brazier, the hourglass, or either golem is attacked, the doors of the room magically slam shut and lock (unless they are being held or wedged open), and the golems animate and attack. On the first round, the golems fill the room with their poison breath, which issues from the horses' mouths. (Each creature in the room must make two saving throws, one for each breath weapon.) On subsequent rounds, each golem makes one attack with its sword and one slam attack with its hoof. When there are no creatures left to fight in the room, the golems return to their alcoves, and the doors unlock. Forcing open a locked door requires a successful DC 25 Strength (Athletics) check. Each door has AC 15, 25 hit points, and immunity to poison and psychic damage.

## K79. Western Stair

> This staircase of ancient stone is worn smooth. Thick dust covers its steps, and cobwebs choke the passage.

The stairs rise at a 45-degree angle for a distance of 40 feet horizontally, leading to a 10-foot-square landing (see below). A second set of stairs continues upward to the east at a similar angle for a distance of 30 feet horizontally, ending at a secret door that opens into area K72.

### Landing

Inscribed on the landing, hidden under years of dust, is a *glyph of warding*. If the characters brush away the dust, someone can spot the glyph with a successful DC 15 Intelligence (Investigation) check.

The glyph triggers the first time a living creature passes over it. Triggering it activates a *major image* spell, conjuring an illusion of Strahd von Zarovich that appears either halfway up the stairs leading to area K72 or halfway down the stairs leading to area K78, so that the vampire appears in front of the triggering character. When "Strahd" appears, read:

> A sickly mist fills the stairway ahead, then coalesces into the form of the vampire Strahd, his eyes burning red with anger. "You have worn out your welcome," he says. "Whatever gods you believe in cannot save you now!"

Have the characters roll initiative. Any attack or spell that hits "Strahd" passes through, revealing that he is an illusion. On initiative count 0, the illusory vampire chuckles and melts away like a wax doll in a bonfire, leaving no trace behind, and the glyph disappears.

## K80. Center Stair

If the characters enter this area through the door at the bottom of the stairs, read:

> The door creaks open to reveal a stone staircase between rough masonry walls. There is little dust on the steps, but light fog tumbles down the steps from above.

If the characters enter this area at the top of the staircase, read:

> The rough-hewn corridor ends at a stone staircase that descends to the south. Flanked by walls of rough masonry and relatively free of dust, these stairs descend before ending at a lonely door.

The stairs slope at a 45-degree angle for a distance of 20 feet horizontally, connecting areas K78 and K81.

## K81. Tunnel

> This tunnel is cut into the Pillarstone of Ravenloft itself. Its surface is slick, and its ceiling is barely 6 feet high. A lingering fog limits visibility to a few feet.

Characters who have knowledge of stonecutting can tell that this passage is a relatively new construction compared to other areas of Ravenloft. The tunnel is 120 feet long, with a stone door at its eastern end.

Near the midpoint of the tunnel is a trapdoor hidden under a layer of fog. Characters can't spot the trapdoor passively, but an active search accompanied by a successful DC 20 Wisdom (Perception) check locates it. Unless the trapdoor is fastened shut with an iron spike or by some other means, it opens when 100 pounds of weight or more is placed on it. When the trapdoor opens, everyone who is standing on it slides into the marble chute below (area K82). The trapdoor then resets.

## K82. MARBLE SLIDE

If one or more characters fall through the trapdoor in area K81, read:

> You fall into a chute of polished black marble and slide into the darkness.

The chute plunges from the trapdoor in area K81 through a one-way secret door into a flooded cell (area K74e). Characters who slide all the way to the bottom are deposited in the cell, but take no damage. The slide contains no handholds and is too slippery to ascend without the aid of magic.

## K83. SPIRAL STAIR

> Behind the door lies a dark spiral staircase.

The staircase starts at area K78, climbs to a landing at area K83a, and continues upward to area K37.

## K83A. SPIRAL STAIR LANDING

An extension of area K83, this landing is shown on map 11.

> This forty-foot-long corridor connects two spiral stairways, one leading up and the other descending into the depths of Castle Ravenloft. Hanging from an iron rod bolted to the eastern wall is a dusty, ten-foot-square tapestry depicting knights on horseback charging across a battlefield under a bloodred sky. The lead knight rides a black horse and wears a fur-lined black cloak, dark gray armor, and a visored helm shaped like a wolf's head. His sword glows with the light of the sun.

The stairs at the north end of the west wall descends to a door leading to area K78. The stairs at the south end of the west wall lead up, ending at door that opens into area K37.

### TREASURE

The tapestry depicts Strahd's father, King Barov, leading his fearsome knights into glorious battle. The tapestry weighs 10 pounds and is worth 750 gp intact. If it becomes damaged while in the party's possession, it is worthless unless mended.

## K84. CATACOMBS

> Buried deep beneath the keep of Ravenloft lie ancient catacombs, with arched ceilings supported by wide, hollow columns that double as crypts. Cobwebs hang limp in the musty air. A thick fog clings to the floor, which is covered in putrid waste. The black ceiling is moving.

The catacombs fill an area roughly 110 feet east to west by 180 feet north to south, and the floor is covered in several inches of bat guano. The catacombs are made up of 10-foot-wide arched walkways running between 10-foot-square crypts, which serve as pillars that support the 20-foot-high ceiling. The area has five means of entry and exit:

- The door adjacent to crypt 1 (connecting with area K81)
- A barred archway to the north (connecting with area K85)
- A barred archway to the south (connecting with area K86 but warded by teleport traps)
- A barred archway to the east (connecting with area K87)
- The high tower stair (area K18) or the shaft (area K18a) to the west

Each crypt is sealed with a chiseled stone "door"—actually a tight-fitting stone slab measuring 3 feet wide, 5 feet tall, and 3 inches thick. Removing or resetting a stone slab requires an action and a successful DC 15 Strength check.

Each crypt houses the remains of the person or persons whose epitaph is inscribed on the front of the slab. The crypts are described in the following sections, their epitaphs noted under the crypt's number in italics.

Unless noted otherwise, each crypt contains a 3-foot-by-6-foot rectangular bier of marble, 3 feet high, with a skeleton draped in rags lying atop it.

The catacombs are home to tens of thousands of bats. The bats hang here during daytime hours and fly out in the evening through the high tower's central shaft (area K18a) to hunt at night. They will not attack intruders unless they are provoked or are specifically commanded to do so by Strahd. If one or more bats within a 10-foot square on the map are attacked or caught in the area of a harmful spell, 2d4 **swarms of bats** form in that area and attack. No more swarms can be formed in that square until the next dawn, when more bats arrive to replenish those that were killed.

### TELEPORT TRAPS

Invisible teleport traps are located between crypts 37 and 38, between crypt 37 and the wall south of it, and between crypt 38 and the wall south of it. The traps can't be perceived except with a *detect magic* spell, which reveals an aura of conjuration magic in the trapped areas. Although the traps can't be disarmed, a successful casting of *dispel magic* (DC 16) on a trap suppresses its magic for 1 minute, allowing characters to move safely through its area. A trap is also suppressed while wholly or partly in the area of an *antimagic field*.

These teleport traps form a protective ring around the entrance to Strahd's tomb (area K86). Any creature that enters one of these 10-foot-square spaces is instantly teleported away, switching places with one of the wights in crypt 14. The wight materializes in the creature's previous location and attacks any living creature it sees.

## CRYPT 1
*Herein lie the ones who walk the path of pain and torment*

The stone door connects not with a crypt, but with a hewn tunnel of stone (area K81).

## CRYPT 2
*Artista DeSlop — Court Ceiling Painter*

> The domed ceiling of this crypt is painted with an image of imps holding bouquets of colorful flowers. A skeleton draped in rags lies atop a marble slab in the center of the crypt. A wooden box is tucked under one bony hand.

The box is unlocked. It contains seven wood-handled paintbrushes and seven small gourds of dried-up paint.

## CRYPT 3
*Lady Isolde Yunk (Isolde the Incredible): Purveyor of antiques and imports*

> A skeleton draped in rags lies atop a marble slab in the center of the crypt. Piled all around it, covering the floor, are heaps of old baskets, braziers, bundled tapestries, candlesticks, chairs, chests, cooking utensils, cressets, curtain rods, decanters, dishes, jugs, lamps, scroll cases, tankards, and tinderboxes. None of the junk looks valuable. An old chandelier hangs from the domed ceiling.

Characters could spend hours searching the crypt. Though the antiques here might fetch a fair amount of coin, they are hardly worth the trouble to transport.

## CRYPT 4
*Prince Ariel du Plumette (Ariel the Heavy)*

If the characters open the door to this crypt, read:

> The apparition of a large, rotund man forms within the dark crypt, its eyes wild with insanity. Large, artificial wings unfold from its back.

Prince Ariel was a terrible man who longed to fly. He attached artificial wings to a harness and empowered

the device with magic, but the apparatus still couldn't bear his weight, and he plunged from the Pillarstone of Ravenloft to his death. His evil **ghost** attacks the characters on sight. If Ariel succeeds in possessing a character, his host climbs the high tower (area K18) until it reaches the peak (area K59), then hurls itself down the tower's central shaft (area K18a), screaming, "I can fly!" the whole way down.

## CRYPT 5
*Artank Swilovich: Friend and member of the Barovian Wine Distillers Guild*

> You are greeted by the faint smell of wine. A skeleton draped in rags lies atop a marble slab in the center of the crypt. Heaped around it, covering the entire floor, are thousands of empty wine bottles.

Each bottle's label shows that it is from the Wizard of Wines winery, and the label names the wine inside: Champagne du le Stomp, Red Dragon Crush, or Purple Grapemash No. 3.

### FORTUNES OF RAVENLOFT
If your card reading reveals that a treasure is here, it is buried under the wine bottles. A character who searches under the bottles finds the treasure automatically.

## CRYPT 6
*Saint Markovia: Dead for all time*

The 10-foot-square section of floor in front of this crypt is a pressure plate that releases four poison darts hidden in tiny holes in the north wall. (See "Sample Traps" in chapter 5, "Adventure Environments," of the *Dungeon Master's Guide* for the rules on how this trap functions.) The trap resets when the weight is lifted and can be triggered a total of four times before its supply of darts is depleted.

If the door to the crypt is opened, read:

> This crypt smells of roses. The remains atop its marble slab have disintegrated, except for one thighbone.

If the characters disturb Saint Markovia's remains, add:

> A ghostly form appears above the dust, so faint that you can barely discern more than part of a face. From this apparition comes the faintest of whispers: "The vampire must be destroyed. Use me as your weapon." With that, it fades away.

**Treasure.** A *detect magic* spell reveals that the thighbone radiates an aura of evocation magic. See appendix C for more information on *Saint Markovia's thighbone*.

## CRYPT 7

> The stone door of this crypt lies on the floor, its inscription obscured by fog. The crypt gapes open. A skull, some bones, and a few bits of rusted armor lie atop a marble slab with a leering stone gargoyle squatting at each end.

The epitaph on the door reads "Endorovich (Endorovich the Terrible): What the blood of a hundred wars did not do, the spurn of a woman accomplished."

Endorovich was a ruthless soldier and self-aggrandizing noble who loved a woman named Marya, but she loved another man. As Marya and her lover were dining, Endorovich put poison into the man's wineglass. The glasses were mixed up, and Marya drank the poison instead. The lover was hanged for murdering Marya and buried at the Ivlis River crossroads (chapter 2, area F). Endorovich never got over his guilt and, out of madness, killed many in his lifetime.

Endorovich's spirit is trapped inside one of the gargoyles. If anyone disturbs the bones on the slab, one of the **gargoyles** awakens and attacks. If the gargoyle is reduced to 0 hit points, Endorovich's spirit moves to the second gargoyle, which then awakens and attacks. Both gargoyles have maximum hit points (77). Once the second **gargoyle** is destroyed, Endorovich's spirit is laid to rest.

### FORTUNES OF RAVENLOFT

If your card reading reveals that a treasure is here, it is contained in a secret compartment under Endorovich's remains. Once his bones and dust are swept away, the compartment can be found and opened without an ability check.

## CRYPT 8

*Duchess Dorfniya Dilisnya*

> A skeleton draped in rags lies atop a marble slab in the center of the crypt. Hanging on the back wall is a handsome quilt that depicts a royal feast.

The quilt is magically preserved but not valuable.

## CRYPT 9

*Pidlwick — Fool of Dorfniya*

> A small skeleton wearing the remains of a fool's costume lies atop a stumpy marble slab in the center of the crypt.

If Pidlwick II (see area K59) is with the party, it refuses to enter the crypt. The slab in this crypt is 4 feet long (instead of the usual 6 feet long). The bones atop the slab belong to the fool servant of Duchess Dorfniya Dilisnya (see crypt 8).

**Treasure.** If the characters explore this crypt after summoning the ghost of Pidlwick in area K36, they find a small, flat wooden box on the marble slab next to Pidlwick's bones. The box contains a full *deck of illusions*.

## CRYPT 10

*Sir Leonid Krushkin (Sir Lee the Crusher): Bigger than life, he loved his jewelry*

> An oversized skeleton draped in jewelry and rags lies atop an elongated marble slab in the center of the crypt. Leaning against the slab is a bloodstained maul strung with cobwebs.

Sir Lee stood well over seven feet tall. His maul might give the characters pause, but it is harmless and nonmagical.

**Treasure.** Three jeweled necklaces (worth 750 gp each) are lying across Sir Lee's skeleton.

## CRYPT 11

*Tasha Petrovna — Healer of Kings, Light unto the West, Servant, Companion*

> A skeleton wearing tattered priestly vestments lies atop a marble slab in the center of the crypt. The domed ceiling overhead is painted with a glorious sun mural.

Creatures that would take damage from exposure to sunlight (such as vampires) have disadvantage on all ability checks, attack rolls, and saving throws while inside this crypt.

**Treasure.** Draped around the neck of the skeleton is a sun-shaped holy symbol (worth 25 gp). A good-aligned character who picks up the holy symbol hears a ghostly female voice. It whispers the following message:

> "There is a grave to the west, with roses that never die, in a place built by healers, in a village called Krezk. When all turns to darkness, touch this holy symbol to the grave to summon the light and find a treasure long lost."

The message refers to a gravestone in the Abbey of Saint Markovia (chapter 8, area S7).

## CRYPT 12

*King Troisky — The Three-Faced King*

> There are no bones atop the marble slab in this crypt, only a steel helm with a visor shaped like an angry face.

The helm has three evenly spaced visors crafted to look like human faces—one sad, one happy, and one angry. Only the angry visage is visible from the crypt's doorway. King Troisky wore this three-faced helm in battle, earning him the moniker of Three-Faced King. The helm is nonmagical and weighs 10 pounds.

The slab upon which the helm rests is weight-sensitive. If the helm is removed from the slab without 10 pounds of weight immediately being added, poisonous gas pours out of the slab's hollow interior and fills the crypt. A character who searches the slab for traps and succeeds on a DC 12 Wisdom (Perception) check spots tiny holes bored into the slab's marble base. It's from these holes that the gas spews forth.

A creature in the crypt when the gas is released must make a DC 14 Constitution saving throw, taking 22 (4d10) poison damage on a failed save, or half as much damage on a successful one.

## CRYPT 13

*King Katsky (Katsky the Bright): Ruler, inventor, and self-proclaimed time traveler*

> A skeleton draped in rags lies atop a marble slab in the center of the crypt. Lying amid the bones is a stoppered drinking horn, a fat pouch, and a weird-looking scepter made of metal and wood. Above the bones, hanging from the domed ceiling by wires, is a wooden flying contraption that looks like a set of folding dragon wings fitted with leather straps, metal buckles, and taut leather wing flaps.

The stoppered drinking horn is a water-resistant powder horn loaded with gunpowder, and the "weird-looking scepter" is a musket. The fat pouch contains 20 silver marbles (silvered bullets for the musket). For more information on firearms and explosives, see chapter 9, "Dungeon Master's Workshop," of the *Dungeon Master's Guide*.

**Glider.** Any Small or Medium humanoid can wear the dragon-wing glider. (It takes 1 minute to don or doff the glider.) It can't support more than 80 pounds, although the amount of weight it can carry is not evident. A character who inspects the glider in an attempt to discern its maximum weight allowance can do so accurately with a successful DC 15 Intelligence check.

If its wearer is light enough (accounting for gear), the apparatus can be used to glide, but only in wide-open spaces where there is room to maneuver. The wearer can become airborne by stepping or jumping off a high place, or by performing a high jump to take off from level ground. While aloft, the wearer gains a flying speed equal to its walking speed, with the following limitations: except in a significant updraft, the wearer can't use the glider to gain altitude, and the glider descends 1 foot for every 10 feet of horizontal distance covered. At the end of the flight, the wearer lands on its feet and the glider is intact. If the wearer tries to accelerate the rate of descent, the glider breaks, and the wearer falls.

The glider has AC 12, 1 hit point, and a 15-foot wingspan. Any damage causes it to break and become inoperable. A *mending* cantrip can repair the damage, provided all the broken pieces are present.

## CRYPT 14

*Stahbal Indi-Bhak: A truer friend no ruler ever had. Here lies his family in honor.*

If the characters open the door to this crypt, read:

> A ten-foot-square shaft plunges into darkness. The sound of slowly dripping water echoes up the shaft.

Characters who have darkvision or a sufficient light source can see that the shaft descends 40 feet to some kind of vault deep in the Pillarstone of Ravenloft. Stones protrude from the shaft at regular intervals, offering handholds and footholds. The stones are slippery, however, so a character who tries to scale the wall without the aid of magic or the use of a climber's kit must make a successful DC 10 Strength (Athletics) check.

**Vault.** When the characters reach the bottom of the shaft, read:

> At the bottom of the shaft is a dank vault with a ten-foot-high ceiling. The room is awkwardly shaped and smells of rotten meat. Fifteen stone coffins are scattered throughout the vault, all oriented with their heads pointed north. The floor is covered with human bones and rusty swords.

If a character teleports into a coffin from one of the teleport traps that protect Strahd's tomb (area K86), read the following to that character's player:

> A flash of light explodes around you, and then you are plunged into absolute darkness, suddenly lying in a confined space choked with dust.

This vault contains fifteen **wights** (one per coffin), minus any that have been teleported away (see "Teleport Traps" at the start of this section). Lifting a coffin's lid requires an action and a successful DC 15 Strength check.

Each wight remains inactive until it is teleported away or until its coffin is opened, whereupon it attacks.

The bones and rusty swords cover the floor to a depth of 6 inches, and are the remains of servants who swore to avenge Stahbal Indi-Bhak's family. Whenever a wight is killed in this vault, some of the bones knit together, forming 2d6 animated human **skeletons**. These skeletons attack intruders on sight but have no ranged attacks. There are enough bones and swords in the room for one hundred skeletons to form in this manner.

## CRYPT 15

*Khazan: His word was power*

> A skeleton draped in rags lies atop a marble slab in the center of the crypt. The skull has black opals set in its eye sockets and shards of amber where its teeth should be.

Khazan was a powerful archmage who unlocked the secrets of lichdom, then later tried to become a demilich and failed. Neither his skull nor his bones pose any threat, but the gems embedded in the skull are valuable.

**Treasure.** The skull's black opal eye-gems are worth 1,000 gp apiece. The skull also has eight amber teeth worth 100 gp each.

Any creature that stands inside the crypt and boldly speaks the name "Khazan" causes the Pillarstone of Ravenloft to tremble as a *staff of power* materializes above the marble slab and hovers in place. The first creature to grab hold of the staff must make a DC 17 Constitution saving throw, taking 44 (8d10) lightning damage on a failed save, or half as much damage on a successful one. Afterward, the *staff of power* can be held and used normally. If no one grabs the staff within 1 round of its appearance, it vanishes, never to return.

## CRYPT 16
*Elsa Fallona von Twitterberg (Beloved Actor): She had many followers*

A skeleton draped in rags lies atop a marble slab in the center of the crypt. Nine shallow alcoves are carved into the surrounding walls. The back wall of each alcove is painted with a full-body image of a handsome man. Some of the men wear fine clothes; others wear armor. At the feet of each painting rests a skull atop a pile of bones.

The bones in the niches belong to Elsa's nine consorts. There is nothing of value here.

## CRYPT 17
*Sir Sedrik Spinwitovich (Admiral Spinwitovich): Confused though he was, he built the greatest naval force ever assembled in a landlocked country*

An eleven-foot-long funeral barge dominates this crypt, wedged diagonally into the available space. Lying in the boat is a skeleton draped in rags, with hundreds of gold coins piled around it.

The coins are made of clay painted gold and are worthless. The funeral barge, which was assembled inside the crypt, is too big to fit through the door.

## CRYPT 18
The stone door of this crypt has been carefully laid to one side. Through the swirly mists of the perpetual fog, freshly engraved letters spell out the words "Ireena Kolyana: Wife."

The crypt is empty and has been swept clean. This is where Strahd intends to keep Ireena once he turns her into a vampire spawn.

## CRYPT 19
*Artimus (Builder of the Keep): Thou standest amidst the monument to his life*

A skeleton draped in rags lies atop a marble slab in the center of the crypt.

This crypt contains nothing of interest.

## CRYPT 20
*Sasha Ivliskova — Wife*

Webs as thick and pale as linen cover a shapely female form lying atop a marble slab in the center of this dusty, web-filled crypt. You hear a voice issue from the darkness.

"My love, have you come to set me free?"

The woman rises, the shroud of webs clinging to her in a ghastly fashion.

This **vampire spawn** is an old wife of Strahd's. Once she realizes that the characters aren't her husband, Sasha tears away her web shroud like an unloved wedding dress and attacks.

## CRYPT 21
*Patrina Velikovna — Bride*

The creature inside this crypt attacks as soon as the door is opened.

From the darkness comes a horrifying visage, a spectral elf maiden twisted by the horror of her undead existence. She wails, and the very sound claws at your soul.

The spectral elf is a **banshee** that attacks the characters on sight, using her wail immediately. Once awakened, the banshee is free to roam Castle Ravenloft, but she can't travel more than 5 miles from this crypt.

In life, Patrina Velikovna was a dusk elf who, having learned a great deal about the black arts, was nearly a match for Strahd's powers. She felt a great bond with him and asked to solemnize that bond in a dark marriage. Drawn to her knowledge and power, Strahd consented, but before he could drain all life from Patrina, her own people stoned her to death in an act of mercy to thwart Strahd's plans. Strahd demanded, and got, Patrina's body. She then became the banshee trapped here.

Reducing the banshee to 0 hit points causes it to discorporate. Patrina's spirit can't rest, however, until she is formally wed to Strahd; the banshee re-forms in her crypt 24 hours later. Casting a *hallow* spell on the crypt prevents the banshee from returning for as long as the spell lasts.

***Treasure.*** Read the following text when the characters investigate Patrina's crypt:

> In the center of the crypt, a skeleton draped in rags lies atop a marble slab, surrounded by thousands of coins.

Patrina's crypt contains 250 pp, 1,100 gp, 2,300 ep, 5,200 sp, and 8,000 cp. The coins are of a mixed origin. The platinum and electrum coins have Strahd's profiled visage stamped on them. Buried under the coins is Patrina's spellbook, which has carved wooden covers. It contains all the spells listed for the **archmage** in the *Monster Manual*.

 ***Development.*** If she is restored to life by her brother (see "Kasimir's Dark Gift" in the "Special Events" section in chapter 13), Patrina (NE female dusk elf) returns as an **archmage** with no spells prepared. If the characters have her spellbook, she kindly asks them to give it back to her so that she can prepare her long-forgotten spells and help destroy Strahd (a lie). If the characters oblige, she repays their kindness by learning as much about them as possible before pursuing her own goals.

## CRYPT 22
*Sir Erik Vonderbucks*

> A gilded man lies atop a marble slab in the center of this otherwise barren crypt.

Sir Erik Vonderbucks was a wealthy noble whose dying wish was to have his corpse dipped in molten gold.

 ***Treasure.*** The thin layer of gold, if peeled from Sir Erik's desiccated corpse, is worth 500 gp.

## CRYPT 23
The first time the characters happen upon this crypt, they see one of their names (determined randomly) etched into the door. Opening the crypt releases a horrid stench of decay and reveals a corpse lying on the marble slab within. The corpse looks like the character named on the door. Touching the corpse causes it to melt away, whereupon the inscription fades. On later visits to this crypt, the door is unmarked and the crypt is empty.

## CRYPT 24
*Ivan Ivliskovich, Champion of Winter Dog Racing: The race may go to the swift, but vengeance is for the loser's relatives*

> A skeleton draped in bits of fur lies atop a marble slab in the center of the crypt. The walls and ceiling are covered with plaster painted to make the crypt seem as if it stands in an evergreen forest, surrounded by snow. The plaster has peeled and fallen away in many places, shattering the illusion.

This crypt contains nothing of interest.

## CRYPT 25
*Stefan Gregorovich: First Counselor to King Barov von Zarovich*

> A skeleton draped in rags lies atop a marble slab in the center of the crypt. Most of the bones appear dusty and neglected, but the skull is well polished.

A *detect magic* spell cast here reveals that Stefan's skull radiates a faint aura of necromancy magic. As long as the skull remains in the crypt, it will answer up to five questions put to it, as though a *speak with dead* spell had been cast on it. This property recharges each day at dawn. In life, Stefan was neither observant nor well informed. If the skull is questioned about Strahd or Castle Ravenloft, all the information it provides is untrue.

## CRYPT 26
*Intree Sik-Valoo: He spurned wealth for the knowledge he could take to heaven*

> A skeleton draped in rags lies atop a marble slab in the center of the crypt. Most of the bones appear dusty and neglected, but the skull is well polished.

A *detect magic* spell cast here reveals that Intree's skull radiates a faint aura of necromancy magic. As long as the skull remains in the crypt, it will answer up to five questions put to it, as though a *speak with dead* spell had been cast on it. This property recharges each day at dawn. Unlike Stefan Gregorovich in crypt 25, Intree was well educated and astute. If the skull is questioned about Strahd or the castle, the information it provides is true.

## CRYPT 27

> This crypt is missing its door.

Three **giant wolf spiders** infest this otherwise empty crypt. The spiders make no noise and leap out to attack anyone who moves in front of the crypt's gaping doorway.

## CRYPT 28
*Bascal Ofenheiss — Chef Deluxe*

> A skeleton draped in white linen lies atop a marble slab in the center of the crypt, clutching a bell to its sunken chest. Fitted over its skull is a tall chef's hat.

If the bell is rung inside the crypt, magic fire sweeps through the crypt to scorch Chef Ofenheiss's bones. A creature in the crypt must make a DC 17 Dexterity saving throw, taking 22 (4d10) fire damage on a failed save, or half damage on a successful one. Any creature that fails its save catches fire, taking 5 (1d10) fire damage at the end of each of its turns until it or another creature uses an action to douse the flames.

**Treasure.** Tucked under the chef's hat is an electrum spork with a bejeweled handle (worth 250 gp).

## CRYPT 29
*Baron Eisglaze Drüf*

> Opening the door causes the air around you to turn as cold as the coldest hell you can imagine. Every surface inside the crypt is covered with thick, brownish mold.

A patch of brown mold (see "Dungeon Hazards" in chapter 5, "Adventure Environments," of the *Dungeon Master's Guide*) fills the crypt. Characters within 5 feet of the crypt's open doorway are affected.

If the brown mold is killed off, characters can dig through the moldy crust to find the bones of Baron Drüf lying atop a marble slab.

**Treasure.** Hidden under the brown mold next to the baron's bones is a *luck blade* with one wish remaining. If a creature uses the wish to try to escape from Barovia, the spell fails. If a creature uses the sword to wish for Strahd's destruction, the wish doesn't destroy Strahd but rather teleports him to within 5 feet of the sword.

## CRYPT 30
*Prefect Ciril Romulich (Beloved of King Barov and Queen Ravenovia): High Priest of the Most Holy Order*

> A marble slab in the center of the crypt displays a skeleton draped in red vestments, a golden holy symbol clutched in one bony hand. The domed ceiling fifteen feet above is painted to look like a canopy of trees with bright autumn leaves. A narrow stone ledge encircles the crypt ten feet above the floor. Perched on it are dozens of stone ravens, their eyes fixed on the marble slab.

The carved ravens are ominous yet harmless.

**Treasure.** The prefect's gold holy symbol is festooned with tiny gemstones and is worth 750 gp. If touched by an evil creature, the holy symbol is consumed in a blast of intense light that deals 11 (2d10) radiant damage to all creatures within 5 feet of it. Characters familiar with Barovian religion recognize the symbol as that of the Morninglord.

## CRYPT 31
*We knew him only by his wealth*

> This crypt is empty. Its walls are painted to depict mountains of gold coins.

The floor of the crypt is actually the cover of a 30-foot-deep spiked pit. The cover opens if 100 pounds of weight or more are placed on it. It splits down the middle, east to west, and its doors are spring-loaded. After a victim or victims fall into the pit, its doors snap shut. (See "Sample Traps" in chapter 5, "Adventure Environments," of the *Dungeon Master's Guide* for the rules on locking pits and spiked pits.) The spikes at the bottom of the pit are made of iron but aren't poisoned.

**Treasure.** A human skeleton (the remains of a dead adventurer) wrapped in bits of studded leather armor lies amid the spikes at the bottom of the pit. A shattered lantern and a rusty crowbar lie nearby. Tied to the corpse's leather belt is a 50-foot coil of hempen rope, a dagger in a worn scabbard, a pouch containing 25 pp, and a stoppered wooden tube containing a *spell scroll* of *magic circle*.

### FORTUNES OF RAVENLOFT
If your card reading reveals that a treasure is here, it is lying next to the skeleton at the bottom of the pit.

## CRYPT 32
The door to this crypt has no name or epitaph on it.

> This crypt is empty except for two alcoves in the back wall. Above the alcoves are carved the following words: PASS NOT THESE PORTALS YE FOOLISH MORTALS

A *detect magic* spell reveals that both alcoves radiate strong auras of conjuration magic.

Creatures that enter the eastern alcove of this crypt are teleported to the eastern alcove of Strahd's tomb (area K86). Stepping into the western alcove of this crypt has no effect, but any creature that teleports from the western alcove of area K86 appears here.

## CRYPT 33
*Sir Klutz Tripalotsky: He fell on his own sword*

> In the center of this crypt, atop a marble slab, human bones lie amid the empty shell of a suit of rusty plate armor. Plunged through the armor's breastplate is a longsword.

Neither Sir Klutz's armor nor his longsword are magical or valuable.

If the sword is pulled from the armor, Sir Klutz appears as a **phantom warrior** (see appendix D), thanks whoever pulled his weapon free, and agrees to fight alongside that character for the next seven days. Sir Klutz perished years before Strahd became a vampire, so the phantom warrior knows nothing of Strahd's downfall or the curse afflicting Barovia.

## CRYPT 34
*King Dostron the Hellborn*

> Resting in the center of this crypt is a seven-foot-long gilded sarcophagus, its lid painted with the likeness of a screaming king wearing a crown of horns. Looming behind the sarcophagus is a stuffed owlbear frozen in a roar, with claws outstretched.

King Dostron was an ancient ruler of this land, long before the arrival of Strahd. He claimed descent from a duke of the Nine Hells, and his deeds did justice to this ancestry. His sarcophagus is made of beaten lead and encased in gold (see "Treasure" below). Its lid can be pried open with a crowbar or similar tool, revealing nothing but dust within. The stuffed owlbear is a late addition to the crypt's decor—a gift given to Strahd that wound up here. It looks almost alive but is harmless.

An invisible **imp** is perched atop the owlbear. If someone tries to open the sarcophagus, the imp says in Common, "I wouldn't do that if I were you!" The imp is magically bound to King Dostron's remains and must watch over them for several more centuries before its contract are fulfilled. It isn't obligated to protect the contents of the crypt (so it will not attack), and it delights in telling lies and engaging in mischief. For instance, it warns the characters that the sarcophagus is trapped, and that opening the lid will free a pit fiend bound within.

**Treasure.** Characters who take the time to pry the gold from the sarcophagus can amass 500 gp worth of the precious metal, weighing 10 pounds.

## CRYPT 35
*Sir Jarnwald the Trickster: The joke was on him*

> A charnel stench fills this empty crypt.

The floor here is an illusion that hides a 20-foot-deep pit. The sides of the pit are polished smooth; a creature without a climbing speed can't move along them without the aid of magic or a climber's kit. At the bottom of the pit are six starving **ghouls**. A permanent *silence* spell suppresses sound in the pit. The silence can be dispelled, as can the illusory floor (DC 14 for both).

**Treasure.** Sir Jarnwald was "entombed" here, so far as he was pushed into the crypt and devoured by the ghouls. What remains of him lies scattered on the pit floor: a few scraps of clothing, a handful of teeth, and a signet ring that bears a stylized "J" (worth 25 gp).

## CRYPT 36
Claw marks obliterate the name on this crypt's door.

> A skeleton draped in rags lies atop a marble slab in the center of the crypt.

This crypt contains nothing of interest.

## CRYPT 37
*Gralmore Nimblenobs — Wizard Ordinaire*

> Lying on a marble slab in the center of this crypt is the corpse of a man with a long white beard. His skin clings tightly to his skull and bones, and he wears dusty red robes. Clutched to his chest is a wooden staff that has a brass knob on one end and a marble knob on the other.

The staff is a nonmagical quarterstaff.

Inspection of the marble slab reveals a shallow, concave recess at one end. If the marble-knobbed end of Gralmore's staff is placed in the recess, the slab levitates 5 feet upward, revealing a compartment underneath (see "Treasure" below). The slab slowly sinks back into place after 1 minute. If the brass-knobbed end of the staff is placed in the recess, the holder of the staff takes 22 (4d10) lightning damage.

**Treasure.** The compartment under the slab holds a small, black leather case containing three *spell scrolls* (*cone of cold, fireball,* and *lightning bolt*).

### FORTUNES OF RAVENLOFT
If your card reading reveals that a treasure is here, it is in the compartment with the other treasure.

## CRYPT 38
*General Kroval "Mad Dog" Grislek (Master of the Hunt): A leader of hounds and men*

When the characters open the door to this crypt, read:

> The stench of brimstone and burnt fur spills from this crypt. In its darkness are three pairs of glowing red eyes.

Three **hell hounds** lunge forth and attack, fighting to the death. In the round after they attack, General Grislek's **wraith** emerges from the crypt, uttering commands to the hounds in Infernal. Once these evil creatures are slain, the characters can inspect the crypt more closely.

> Bits of incinerated bone lie strewn atop a marble slab in the center of the crypt. Lying amid the bones are fragments of a shattered spear with a silvered head. The walls and domed ceiling of the crypt are covered with scorched murals that depict legions of infantry and cavalry clashing on battlefields.

A *mending* cantrip can repair the spear, which is broken into three pieces of roughly equal length. If repaired, it can be wielded as a silvered, nonmagical spear.

### FORTUNES OF RAVENLOFT
If your card reading reveals that a treasure is here, it is in a secret compartment under Grislek's remains. Once his charred bones are cleared away, the compartment can be found and opened without an ability check.

## CRYPT 39

*Beucephalus, the Wonder Horse: May the flowers grow ever brighter where he trods*

The door to this crypt is larger than all the others, 6 feet wide by 8 feet tall. Removing or resetting the slab requires a successful DC 20 Strength check. When the door is opened, read:

> Dry, hot air and smoke billow from the crypt as a black horse with a flaming mane and fiery hooves emerges. Smoke billows from its nostrils as it rears up to attack.

The **nightmare**, Beucephalus, is Strahd's steed. It has 104 hit points. If the characters slay it, Strahd hunts them down mercilessly. When the steed wants to leave the castle, it flies up the central shaft of the high tower (area K18a), exiting through the gash in the tower roof (area K59).

## CRYPT 40

*Tatsaul Eris — Last of the Line*

> A skeleton draped in rags lies atop a marble slab in the center of the crypt. Mounted on the north, east, and south walls are three unlit torches in iron brackets.

When a creature enters this tomb for the first time, the torches burst into flame and continue to burn until they are spent or extinguished.

Examination of the skull and bones reveals that they are plaster facsimiles.

## K85. SERGEI'S TOMB

A portcullis is closed in the archway into this tomb. Lifting it requires a successful DC 25 Strength check.

> White marble steps descend to a tomb that has a vaulted ceiling thirty feet overhead. A stillness—a calm amid the storm—is felt here. In the center of the tomb, a white marble slab supports an intricately inlaid coffin. Chiseled into the slab is a name: Sergei von Zarovich. To the north, behind the coffin, are three alcoves. A beautifully carved statue stands in each alcove—a stunning young man flanked by two angels—looking as polished and new as the day each was placed there. An iron lever protrudes from the south wall, west of the tomb's entrance.

Raising the lever lifts the portcullis at the top of the stairs. Pulling it down lowers the portcullis.

The coffin opens easily to the touch of a lawful good creature. Otherwise, opening it requires a successful DC 15 Strength check. Sergei's flesh has been magically preserved, and at first glance it looks like he is sleeping in his casket.

ESCHER AND THE THREE BRIDES

### TREASURE

Sergei's embalmed body is clothed in shining *+2 plate armor*.

### FORTUNES OF RAVENLOFT

If your card reading reveals that a treasure is here, it is inside the coffin next to Sergei's body.

If your card reading indicates an encounter with Strahd in this area, he is lying across Sergei's coffin, weeping.

## K86. STRAHD'S TOMB

A heavy portcullis stands closed in the archway leading to this tomb. Lifting it requires a successful DC 25 Strength check.

> Black marble steps descend to a dark tomb that has a vaulted ceiling thirty feet overhead. The essence of evil permeates the very air. The smell of freshly turned earth is here. Settled into the dirt on the floor is a shining black coffin of finely waxed wood. The coffin's fittings are of brilliant brass, and the lid is closed. South of the coffin are three gloomy alcoves. An iron lever protrudes from the north wall, east of the tomb's entrance.

Raising the lever lifts the portcullis at the top of the stairs. Pulling it down lowers the portcullis.

Lying under the earth near the east wall of the tomb are three **vampire spawn** brides dressed in soiled gowns and wearing dirt-encrusted jewelry (see

"Treasure" below). They rise to attack anyone who approaches Strahd's coffin.

A *detect magic* spell reveals that the western and eastern alcoves radiate strong auras of conjuration magic. The central alcove is nonmagical.

Creatures that enter the western alcove are instantly teleported to the western alcove of crypt 32 in area K84. Stepping into the eastern alcove has no effect, but any creature that teleports from the eastern alcove of crypt 32 appears here.

### TREASURE

Strahd lavished many fine gifts on his three brides.

Ludmilla Vilisevic wears a soiled white wedding gown, a gold tiara (worth 750 gp), and ten gold bracelets (worth 100 gp each).

Anastrasya Karelova wears a stained and tattered red wedding gown, a black and crimson silk head scarf sewn with precious jewels (worth 750 gp), and a platinum necklace with a black opal pendant (worth 1,500 gp).

Volenta Popofsky wears a faded gold wedding gown, a platinum mask shaped vaguely like a skull (750 gp), and ten platinum rings set with gemstones (worth 250 gp each).

### TELEPORT DESTINATION

Characters who teleport to this location from area K78 arrive at the bottom of the stairs, just inside the tomb.

### FORTUNES OF RAVENLOFT

If your card reading reveals that a treasure is here, it lies in the center alcove.

If your card reading indicates an encounter with Strahd in this area, he is in his coffin, ready to attack anyone who opens the lid.

## K87. GUARDIANS

The following text assumes that the characters are approaching from area K84. If they approach this area from area K88, references to descending stairs should be changed to ascending stairs.

> Wide steps descend to a landing flanked by two alcoves. Within each alcove, taking up the full thirty-foot height of the ceiling, is a bronze statue of a warrior holding a spear. A soft blue curtain of light flows between the two alcoves. Dimly visible on the other side of the curtain are more descending stairs.

The curtain has no effect on creatures that move east to west (from area K88 to area K84).

A creature of lawful good alignment that moves west to east through the curtain can do so without difficulty, but creatures of other alignments that do so are teleported back to the top of the stairs behind them. A Small creature can squeeze behind and around one of the bronze statues to circumvent the light curtain.

## K88. TOMB OF KING BAROV AND QUEEN RAVENOVIA

> This tomb rests in hushed silence. Tall, stained glass windows dominate the eastern walls, allowing dim light to fall on two coffins resting atop white marble slabs. The one against the north wall is marked King Barov von Zarovich, and the one against the south wall is marked Queen Ravenovia van Roeyen. The vaulted ceiling thirty feet overhead is inlaid with a beautiful gold mosaic.

The stained glass windows are so dirty on the outside as to be nearly opaque. The windows don't open, but they can be smashed easily. Anyone who looks upward through a window can see, 110 feet above, the castle's stone overlook (area K6). Anyone who falls out a window here plummets almost 900 feet to the base of the Pillarstone of Ravenloft.

Prying the gold from the ceiling of this tomb would be a long and tedious effort for little reward.

The north coffin holds a beautifully sculpted, life-sized wax effigy of Strahd's father, King Barov. The old king's bones lie in a compartment beneath his effigy.

The south coffin holds the skeleton of Strahd's mother, Queen Ravenovia. (The magic that was meant to preserve her earthly remains failed years ago.) A tattered white shroud covers her bones.

### FORTUNES OF RAVENLOFT

If your card reading reveals that a treasure is here, it lies atop Queen Ravenovia's coffin.

If your card reading indicates an encounter with Strahd in this area, he is in a frenzy of rage and despair.

KING BAROV AND
QUEEN RAVENOVIA

# CHAPTER 5: THE TOWN OF VALLAKI

OCATED CLOSE TO THE SHORES OF LAKE Zarovich, the town of Vallaki (pronounced vah-*lah*-key) seems like a safe haven against the evils of the Svalich Woods, if not Strahd himself. The town lies beyond the sight of Castle Ravenloft and doesn't, at first blush, seem as depressed (or oppressed) as the village of Barovia farther east. Characters who spend time in Vallaki, however, quickly realize that there is no happiness here, only false hope—which Strahd himself cultivates.

Vallaki was founded not long after Strahd's armies conquered the valley by an ancestor of the town's current burgomaster, Baron Vargas Vallakovich. The Vallakoviches have royal blood in their veins and have long believed themselves superior to the Zarovich line. Baron Vallakovich has deluded himself into believing that hope and happiness are the keys to Vallaki's salvation. If he can make everyone in Vallaki happy, the burgomaster thinks that the town will somehow escape Strahd's grasp and return to the forgotten world whence it came. He stages one festival after another to bolster the spirits of the townsfolk, but most Vallakians consider these festivals to be pointless, meaningless affairs more likely to incur Strahd's wrath than to provide any hope for the future.

In the last festival, Baron Vallakovich had townsfolk parade through the streets with the severed heads of wolves on pikes. His next event, which the burgomaster has dubbed the Festival of the Blazing Sun, is soon to get under way (see the "Special Events" section at the end of this chapter). Weatherworn garlands from previous festivals still hang from the eaves of Vallaki's buildings, and work has begun on a large wicker sun, to be set ablaze in the town square on the day of the festival. In the days leading up to the festival, Baron Vallakovich has begun arresting local malcontents and throwing them in the stocks so that his efforts aren't ruined by "those of little hope or faith."

---

THERE IS NO LIGHT IN THE *eyes of the men that feed off this land. They are as dead as the dead.*

—Strahd von Zarovich

---

## APPROACHING THE TOWN

When the characters first approach Vallaki, read:

> The Old Svalich Road meanders into a valley watched over by dark, brooding mountains to the north and south. The woods recede, revealing a sullen mountain burg surrounded by a wooden palisade. Thick fog presses up against this wall, as though looking for a way inside, hoping to catch the town aslumber.
>
> The dirt road ends at a set of sturdy iron gates with a pair of shadowy figures standing behind them. Planted in the ground and flanking the road outside the gates are a half-dozen pikes with wolves' heads impaled on them.

A 15-foot-high wall encloses the town, its vertical logs held together with thick ropes and mortar. The top of each log has been sharpened to a point. Wooden scaffolding hugs the inside of the palisade twelve feet off the ground, enabling guards to peer over the wall there.

## TOWN GATES

Three tall gates made of iron bars lead into town:

- The north gate is sometimes called the Zarovich Gate, or "the gate to the lake," because it leads to Lake Zarovich (chapter 2, area L).
- The west gate is referred to as the Sunset Gate, even though no living person in Vallaki has seen an undimmed sunset. A few abandoned cottages line the road outside this gate.
- The east gate is also known as the Morning Gate, or, as some locals like to call it, the Mourning Gate.

Heavy iron chains with iron padlocks keep the gates shut at night. During the day, the gates are closed but not typically locked.

Two town **guards** (LG male and female humans) stand just inside each gate. Instead of spears, they carry pikes (reach 10 ft., 1d10 + 1 piercing damage on a hit). These weapons are long enough to stab creatures through the bars of the gate. The guards greet all visitors with suspicion, particularly those who arrive at night. If the characters arrive at night, one or more of them must succeed on a DC 20 Charisma (Persuasion) check to convince the guards to unlock the gate and let them enter.

If trouble breaks out at one of the gates, the guards there cry out, "To arms!" Their shouts are echoed across Vallaki, putting the entire town on alert within minutes. Vallaki has twenty-four human **guards**, half of whom are on duty at any given time (six stand watch at the gates, six patrol the walls). The town can also muster a militia of fifty able-bodied human **commoners** armed with clubs, daggers, and torches.

## HOUSE OCCUPANTS

If the characters explore a residence other than the burgomaster's mansion (area N3), roll a d20 and consult the following table to determine the house's occupant.

| d20 | Occupant |
| --- | --- |
| 1–3 | None |
| 4–5 | 2d4 **swarms of rats** |
| 6–18 | Vallakian townsfolk |
| 19–20 | Vallakian cultists |

### RATS

A house infested with rats appears abandoned at first. The rats are servants of Strahd and attack if the characters explore the interior of the house.

### TOWNSFOLK

A house of Vallakian townsfolk contains 1d4 adults (male and female human **commoners**) and 1d8 − 1 children (male and female human noncombatants). Anyone who listens at the door hears chatter from within. Townsfolk won't willingly invite strangers into their homes, but they will speak with characters from behind closed doors or while standing in their vestibules.

### CULTISTS

A cult haven contains 2d4 Vallakian adults (LE male and female **cultists**) and one **cult fanatic** (LE male or female) who leads them in prayer or orchestrates ritual sacrifices. These cultists worship devils and consider Lady Fiona Wachter (see area N4) to be their spiritual leader.

## VALLAKI LORE

In addition to the information known to all Barovians (see "Barovian Lore" in chapter 2), Vallakians know the following bits of local lore:

- The Blue Water Inn (area N2) offers food, wine, and shelter to visitors. A stranger with pointed ears is staying there. He came to Barovia from a distant land, riding into town on a carnival wagon.
- The burgomaster, Baron Vargas Vallakovich, has decreed that the Festival of the Blazing Sun will be held in the town square (area N8) in three days. The previous festival, which he called the Wolf's Head Jamboree, was less than a week ago.
- Vallaki has endured at least one festival every week for the past several years. Some Vallakians believe that the festivals keep the devil Strahd at bay. Others think they provide no protection or benefit whatsoever. Most consider them dismal affairs.
- Those who speak ill of the festivals are declared by the burgomaster to be in league with the devil Strahd and arrested. Some are thrown in the stocks (area N8), while others are taken to the burgomaster's mansion so that the baron can purge them of their evil.
- The burgomaster's henchman, Izek Strazni, has a history of violence as well as a fiendish deformity: a monstrous arm with which he can conjure fire. Fear of Izek keeps the baron's enemies at bay.
- No one hates the burgomaster more than Lady Fiona Wachter, who is often quoted as saying, "I'd rather serve the devil than a madman." She owns an old house in town (area N4) but rarely leaves her estate. Her two adult sons, Nikolai and Karl, are local troublemakers. Lady Wachter also has a mad daughter whom she keeps locked away. The burgomaster doesn't confront Fiona or her offspring because he is afraid of Lady Wachter, whose family has old ties to Strahd.
- Purple flashes of light have been seen emanating from the attic of the burgomaster's mansion.
- Wolves and dire wolves prowl the woods and aren't afraid to attack travelers on the Old Svalich Road. Well-armed groups of hunters and trappers have managed to kill several of the wolves, but more keep coming.
- It's too dangerous to go fishing on Lake Zarovich (chapter 2, area L), but the threat of Strahd's wolves hasn't stopped Bluto Krogarov, the town drunk, from trying. He sets out each morning and returns every evening, but hasn't caught any fish in a while.
- There have been no recent sightings of the Mad Mage of Mount Baratok (chapter 2, area M). Folks used to see him skulking along the north shore of Lake Zarovich, shooting lightning bolts into the water to kill the fish. (If the characters seem interested in meeting this wizard, locals recommend that they use the fishing boats on the south shore to cross the lake, because it's shorter and a lot less dangerous than walking around the lake.)
- There's a Vistani camp in the woods southwest of town (area N9). The Vistani there aren't very friendly. Vistani aren't welcome in Vallaki.
- West of town is a haunted mansion (see chapter 7, "Argynvostholt"). Legend has it that a dragon died there long, long ago.
- South of town is a village that has been abandoned for decades. Its burgomaster committed some terrible offense and incurred the wrath of Strahd.

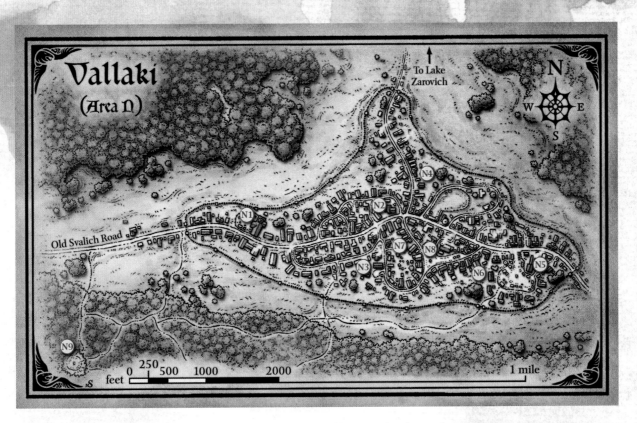

## Areas of Vallaki

The following areas correspond to labels on the map of Vallaki above.

### N1. St. Andral's Church

No map of the church is provided. If one becomes necessary, assume that this church has the same configuration as the one in the village of Barovia (chapter 3, area E5), but without the undercroft.

> This slouching, centuries-old stone church has a bulging steeple in the back and walls lined with cracked, stained glass windows depicting pious saints. A fence of wrought iron encloses a garden of gravestones next to the church. A thin mist creeps among the graves.

This church is dedicated to the Morninglord and named after St. Andral, whose bones once rested under the altar (see the "Bones of St. Andral" section).

Father Lucian Petrovich (LG male human **priest**) oversees the church and does his best to raise spirits. Assisting him is an orphan and altar boy named Yeska (LG male human noncombatant). A brawny lad with a perpetually furrowed brow named Milivoj (see below) tends the grounds and digs graves.

At night, the church is packed with 2d6 + 6 frightened Vallakian adults (male and female human **commoners**) and 2d6 equally terrified Vallakian children (male and female human noncombatants). Father Lucian offers his nightly congregation his prayers and the promise of St. Andral's protection. Among Father Lucian's nightly flock is a sad old woman named Willemina Rikalova.

Her son, the shoemaker Udo Lukovich, has been imprisoned for speaking out against the burgomaster (see area N3m). She prays that her son will be set free.

Milivoj (N male human **commoner**) is rarely seen without a shovel, which he wields like a club. Modify his statistics as follows:

- His Strength is 15 (+2).
- His melee weapon attack bonus is +4, and he deals 4 (1d4 + 2) bludgeoning damage when he hits with the blunt head of his shovel.

Milivoj rejects the burgomaster's proclamation that "All will be well!" and is frustrated that he can't protect his younger siblings. He wants to be free of Barovia's curse but sees no hope of escape.

#### Bones of St. Andral

Until recently, the church was protected from Strahd's depredations by the bones of St. Andral, which were sealed in a crypt beneath the church's main altar. But now the church is at risk because someone broke into the crypt a few nights ago and stole the bones. Until recently, Father Lucian was the only person in Vallaki who knew about the bones, but he recalls mentioning them to Yeska over a month ago to put the fearful boy at ease. After the bones were stolen, Father Lucian asked Yeska if he told anyone else about the bones. The boy nodded but wouldn't divulge a name.

The culprit is Milivoj, whom Father Lucian correctly suspects. But the priest has been reluctant to confront Milivoj because the lad is so temperamental. Father Lucian has not reported the theft for fear of the distress that the news might cause, and he doesn't want to ruin the burgomaster's festival. If the party includes a good-aligned cleric or paladin, Father Lucian mentions the

MILIVOJ

theft in the hope that the characters can provide assistance. St. Andral's crypt is a 10-foot-square, 5-foot high chamber beneath the chapel. To reach the crypt, Milivoj used his shovel to pry up the chapel floorboards. (The boards have since been replaced.) If one of the characters confronts Milivoj and succeeds on a DC 10 Charisma (Intimidation) check, he admits that Yeska told him about the bones. He also admits to passing along the information to Henrik van der Voort, the local coffin maker (area N6), and to stealing the bones for Henrik in return for money to help feed his younger sisters and brothers.

The theft of the bones has left the church vulnerable to attack by Strahd's minions (see "St. Andral's Feast" in the "Special Events" section at the end of this chapter). If the bones are returned to their resting place, St. Andral's church once again becomes hallowed ground, as though the building was protected by a *hallow* spell.

## N2. BLUE WATER INN

> Gray smoke issues from the chimney of this large, two-story wooden building with a stone foundation and sagging tile roof, upon which several ravens have perched. A painted wooden sign hanging above the main entrance depicts a blue waterfall.

The Blue Water Inn is Vallaki's main gathering place for locals, especially at night. The innkeeper, Urwin Martikov, considers the inn a sanctuary from the evils of this land. In the event of trouble, the windows and doors can all be barred shut from within.

A bed for the night costs 1 ep. Characters looking for something to eat are fed hot beet soup and fresh bread at no additional charge. A cooked wolf steak costs 1 ep.

The inn offers a pint of Purple Grapemash No. 3 wine for 3 cp, or a pint of the superior Red Dragon Crush wine for 1 sp. Urwin is hurt if the characters complain about the wines, for his family makes them.

The inn's wine supply is almost depleted, and the latest delivery from the Wizard of Wines winery is over-

due. If the characters claim to be adventurers, Urwin asks them if they would be so kind as to find out what's holding up the latest shipment, promising them free room and board if they return with the wine.

### KEEPERS OF THE FEATHER

Urwin Martikov (LG male human) is a **wereraven** (see appendix D) and a high-ranking member of the Keepers of the Feather, a secret society of wereravens that opposes Strahd. Urwin's wife and business partner, Danika Dorakova (LG female human), is also a **wereraven**, as are their two sons, Brom and Bray. The boys have only 7 hit points each and, at ages eleven and nine, are too young to be effective combatants.

At any given time, another 1d4 **wereravens** (members of the Keepers of the Feather) are present at the inn, either perched on the rooftop in raven form or huddled inside in human form. These wereravens are loyal friends of the Martikovs and help protect the inn.

If the characters earn the trust of the wereravens in Vallaki, the Keepers of the Feather will watch their backs. The next time the characters get themselves in serious trouble, you can have a group of 1d4 **wereravens** show up to rescue or otherwise help them.

### FORTUNES OF RAVENLOFT

If your card reading reveals that a treasure is hidden at the inn, the Keepers of the Feather don't reveal where the treasure is until they know the characters are capable of protecting it. As a way of testing their abilities, Urwin gives the characters the following quest:

> Urwin takes you aside and keeps his voice low. "My supply of wine is nearly gone, and the next shipment is overdue. I'll give you what you seek if you bring me my wine. The vineyard and winery is a few miles west of here. Just follow the Old Svalich Road and the signs."

Urwin fails to mention that his cantankerous father, Davian Martikov, owns the local winery and vineyard, the Wizard of Wines (chapter 12). There's bad blood between Urwin and his father (whom Urwin and Danika refer to as "the old crow"). Although Urwin could easily visit the winery himself, he considers dealing with his father to be a worthy test of the characters' competence, and he makes good on his promise if they complete the quest and return with his wine shipment.

Urwin sends a **wereraven** in raven form to observe the party's progress from a distance. If the characters get in trouble, the wereraven reports to Urwin at once.

### N2A. WELL

A 3-foot-high stone rim surrounds the mouth of this 40-foot-deep, moss-lined well. The inn draws fresh water from this well.

### N2B. OUTSIDE STAIRCASE

A wooden staircase hugs the outer wall of the inn and leads up to guest quarters on the upper floor (areas N2l and N2m). The sturdy wooden door at the top of the stairs can be barred from the inside.

# Blue Water Inn
## (Area N2)

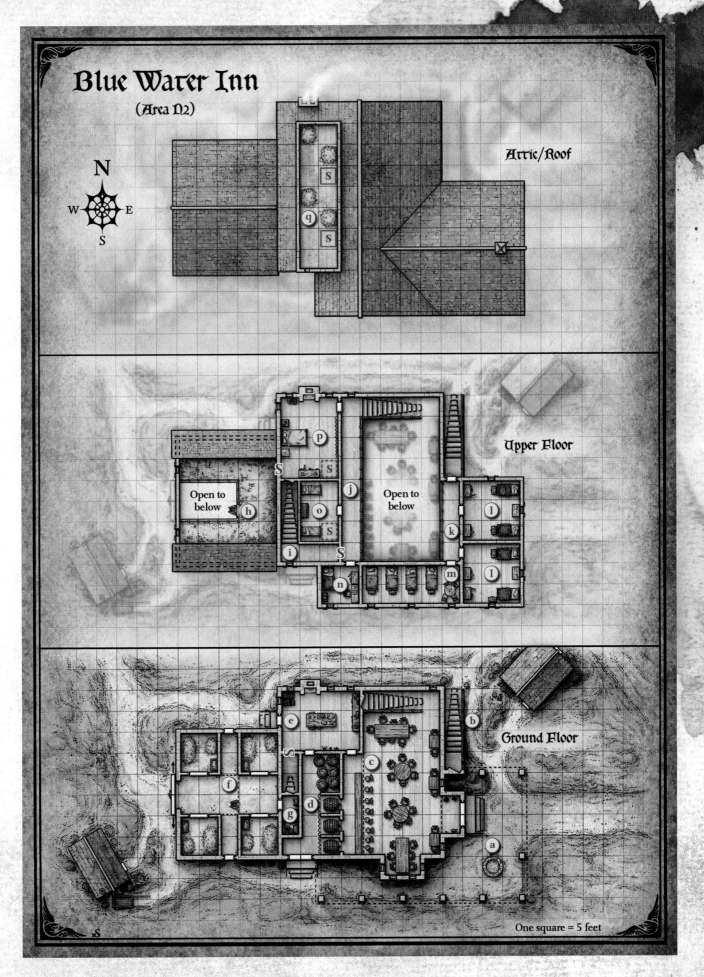

N W E S

Attic/Roof

q

s

s

Upper Floor

Open to below

h

i

p

S

s

o

s

S

j

Open to below

k

l

l

m

n

Ground Floor

e

S

c

b

d

g

f

a

One square = 5 feet

Damp cloaks hang from pegs in the entrance portico. The tavern is packed with tables and chairs, with narrow paths meandering between them. A bar stretches along one wall, under a balcony that can be reached by a wooden staircase that hugs the north wall. Another balcony overhangs an entrance to the east. All the windows are fitted with thick shutters and crossbars. Lanterns hanging above the bar and resting on the tables bathe the room in dull orange light and cast shadows upon the walls, most of which are adorned with wolf heads mounted on wooden plaques.

SZOLDAR
SZOLDAROVICH

YEVGENI KRUSHKIN

The double doors leading into the taproom can be barred shut from within.

Mounted on braces and tucked into alcoves behind the bar are three wine barrels, each one three-quarters empty. Two of the barrels contain Purple Grapemash No. 3 (a cheap wine), and the third contains Red Dragon Crush (a fine wine). A brass spigot is hammered into each barrel.

Danika Martikov usually tends bar while her husband busies himself in the kitchen (area N2e). Their boys, Brom and Bray, scamper about and easily get underfoot.

Between dawn and noon, there are no patrons here, and the Martikovs are upstairs in their bedrooms (areas N2o and N2p) or in the attic (area N2q).

From noon to dusk, the taproom holds 2d4 local patrons (male and female **commoners**). Between dusk and midnight, 2d8 Vallakians are here. In addition, one or more of the following people might be present during this time.

**Wolf Hunters.** Szoldar Szoldarovich and Yevgeni Krushkin (N male human **scouts**) are local hunters who frequent the Blue Water Inn. They kill wolves and sell the meat for a living, and their work is dangerous and bloody. Both men are grim and have haunted looks in their eyes.

These two are dour fellows, but they seldom pass up an opportunity to earn coin. If the characters are looking for guides or information about the land of Barovia, Szoldar and Yevgeni can be of service. They aren't afraid to venture beyond Vallaki's walls during the day, and they know the woods and valley well. They're willing to serve as guides for 5 gp per day, or to provide directions to important landmarks in exchange for free drinks. They think it's foolish to travel "this cursed realm" at night and won't do so unless their payment is exorbitant (100 gp or more).

On rare occasions when he has something to say, Szoldar speaks brusquely, while Yevgeni usually parrots his friend in not so many words. Szoldar has a notch in his bow for every wolf he's killed, while Yevgeni adds a new swatch to his wolfskin cloak every time he makes a kill. Both men have families but spend most of their time together, either drowning their sorrows or hunting in the woods. Most of the wolf heads that adorn the tavern walls are the result of their handiwork.

**Wachter Brothers.** Nikolai and Karl Wachter (N male human **nobles**) are brothers of noble birth. They are brash drunkards always looking for trouble, though they are smart enough not to pick fights with well-armed strangers. Their mother, Fiona Wachter (see area N4), is an influential figure in town, but her sons never talk about her. They'd rather listen to tales of the characters' harrowing adventures or hear about how the characters plan to free Vallaki from the burgomaster's madness.

**Rictavio.** The lone guest of the Blue Water Inn at present is a colorfully dressed half-elf bard who goes by the name **Rictavio**—a false identity adopted by the legendary vampire hunter Rudolph van Richten (see appendix D). He regales tavern patrons with stories so outrageous as to be hardly believable, yet he asserts they are true indeed. Rictavio claims to be a carnival ringmaster from a distant land. He's been staying at the inn for almost a month, taking advantage of Urwin Martikov's generosity and good nature. When he arrived, he was accompanied by a monkey named Piccolo. The monkey wasn't welcome at the inn, so Rictavio gave it to the local toymaker (see area N7).

Rictavio admits to having no musical talent but manages to entertain locals nonetheless with his stories of faraway places. Twice each day, at dawn and again at dusk, he leaves the inn with a couple of apples and a cooked wolf steak wrapped in a handkerchief. He claims the food is for his portly friend, "the destitute toymaker" (area N7) and his pet monkey. In fact, the apples are for his horse Drusilla (area N2f), and the steak is for his captured saber-toothed tiger (area N5).

During his stay at the inn, Rictavio is quietly gathering information on the Keepers of the Feather, trying to figure out the identities of all the wereravens in town. He's also trying to learn as much as he can about the Vistani, particularly the ones living in the camp just outside town (area N9). Once he concludes that they are in league with Strahd, Rictavio plans to unleash his trained saber-toothed tiger upon them, with or without the support of the wereravens.

Rictavio wears a *hat of disguise* and a *ring of mind shielding* to conceal his identity. He carries an iron key that unlocks the door to his carnival wagon (area N5).

## N2D. WINE STORAGE

> This hallway contains three curtained alcoves as well as a larger area stuffed with wine barrels.

The Martikovs store their wine here. Tucked behind red curtains are three alcoves, each one containing a half-emptied wine barrel lying on its side in a wooden brace. Twelve empty wine barrels are piled two high near the door to the kitchen (area N2e). All the barrels have the Wizard of Wines name burned into them.

Nine of the fifteen barrels, including two of the barrels in the curtained alcoves, have the following label burned into their sides, under the winery's name: Purple Grapemash No. 3. Six of the fifteen barrels, including one of the barrels in the curtained alcoves, have a different label: Red Dragon Crush.

The double doors that lead outside can be barred shut from within.

## N2E. KITCHEN

> This room looks like the kitchen of someone who loves to cook. It has piles of pots, walls lined with utensils and shelves of ingredients, and all manner of pleasant odors. Two lanterns hang above a sturdy pine worktable in the middle of the clutter. A pot of soup bubbles on the hearth.

Urwin Martikov, who prepares most of the meals, is found here throughout the day. He occasionally receives help from his two boys, but they are easily distracted. A cupboard against the east wall holds most of the inn's supply of cutlery and dishware, none of it valuable. A door in the west wall leads outside and is usually barred from the inside.

A secret door at the west end of the south wall can be pushed open to reveal a wooden staircase that leads up to area N2i.

## N2F. STABLE

The sliding wooden doors on the west wall of this room are held shut by an iron lock and chain. Urwin carries the key to the lock. The doors to the north and south can be barred shut from the inside but are usually unlocked.

> You hear the squawking of birds and the plaintive whinny of a horse as you peer inside this stable. The stalls are clean and well maintained. One of them contains a gray mare. A small door is set into the east wall, and a wooden ladder gives access to a loft overhead. Perched on the wooden railing that encloses the loft are dozens of ravens.

Any character who has a horse can keep it here for 1 sp per night. The gray mare is a **draft horse** named Drusilla, and she likes apples. The horse belongs to Rictavio (see area N2c).

The small door in the east wall can be pulled open to reveal area N2g. The loft is described in area N2h.

## N2G. STORAGE

This small room lies under a wooden staircase (area N2i). Hanging from wooden pegs are saddles and barding to equip two horses. In an unlocked wooden chest are a dozen horseshoes, a wooden mallet, and a mound of horseshoe nails.

## N2H. RAVENS' LOFT

> Dim light spilling in through a pair of dirt-encrusted windows reveals piles of hay with pitchforks sticking out of them. Ravens rule this roost—you can see hundreds of them.

Characters who search the loft thoroughly find three pitchforks and a locked wooden chest buried under a pile of hay (see "Treasure" below), next to a secret door. If the characters tamper with the chest, the ravens gather into four **swarms of ravens** and attack. If two swarms are killed, the others flee. Otherwise, they cease their attacks if the characters leave the chest alone. If the fighting continues for more than 3 rounds, Urwin Martikov and two other wereravens hear the ruckus and investigate (in human form).

A secret door in the back of the loft can be pushed open to reveal a bedchamber (area N2p) beyond. No ability check is required to spot the secret door, because light in the room beyond slips through the door's cracks.

**Treasure.** Inside the locked chest are 140 ep, 70 pp, two *elixirs of health*, three *potions of healing*, and a gray *bag of tricks*. The coins are embossed with the profiled likeness of Strahd von Zarovich.

## N2I. SECRET STAIRS AND HALL

> A wooden staircase to the north descends fifteen feet to a landing. A window dimly illuminates a short, wood-paneled hallway that runs west to east.

Guests aren't told about the inn's secret hallway. Rictavio knows of its existence because he has heard the

Martikov boys opening and closing the secret door closest to his room (area N2n).

At each end of this area is a secret door, each of which is easy to spot from inside the hallway (no ability check required). The northern secret door, at the bottom of the staircase, can be pulled open to reveal the kitchen (area N2e) beyond. The eastern secret door can be pulled open to reveal a balcony (area N2j) that overlooks the taproom.

## N2j. Great Balcony

A wooden balcony stretches the full length of the taproom, enclosed by a wooden railing carved with raven motifs. The taproom's many lanterns illuminate the rafters and cast ominous shadows on the peaked ceiling.

The balcony floor is 15 feet above the taproom floor.

A secret door at the south end of the western wall can be pushed open to reveal a wood-paneled hallway (area N2i) beyond.

## N2k. Guest Balcony

This twenty-foot-long balcony provides a clear view of the bar and has a wooden railing carved with raven motifs. The taproom's many lanterns illuminate the rafters and cast ominous shadows on the peaked ceiling.

The balcony floor is 15 feet above the taproom floor.

## N2l. Guest Rooms

These two rooms have identical furnishings.

Two cozy beds with matching footlockers rest in the far corners of this fifteen-foot-square room. Wolf furs are heaped atop each bed. Between the beds, a lamp sits on a table under a shuttered window. Two tall black wardrobes stand against the wall by the door.

The door to this room can be locked from the inside, and each guest gets a key. Urwin and Danika carry spare keys. The footlockers and wardrobes are empty and are for the use of guests.

## N2m. Guest Room

Four plain beds with straw mattresses line the north wall of this well-lit room. Each bed comes with a matching footlocker to store clothing and other belongings. A table and four chairs occupy the corner across from the door. An oil lamp resting on the table casts a bright yellow flame.

The door to this room can be locked from the inside, and each guest receives a key. Urwin and Danika carry spare keys. The footlockers are empty and are for the use of guests.

## N2n. Private Guest Room

Rictavio has a key to this room, which is locked at all times. Urwin and Danika carry spare keys. The door's lock can be picked, but discretion is called for because the door is in plain view of the taproom below.

This small guest room contains a bed heaped with wolf furs, a footlocker, a tall wardrobe, and a writing desk with matching chair. An oil lamp rests atop the desk near a journal bound in a red leather jacket.

Rictavio sleeps here between midnight and dawn. At dawn, he leaves to check on his horse (area N2f) and his wagon (area N5), returning to the inn around noon. Between noon and dusk, there's a 40 percent chance he is here; otherwise, he's in the taproom (area N2c). At dusk, he leaves the inn to tend to his horse and his wagon again, then returns to his room to retire for the night.

Rictavio is too clever to leave anything valuable or incriminating in his room. The footlocker and the wardrobe contain nothing but common clothes and travel wear.

***Rictavio's Journal.*** The journal on the desk is a bit of artifice that Rictavio created to perpetuate the illusion that he is an entertainer in search of new acts for his traveling carnival. His writing makes frequent mention of conversations with Drusilla (which the journal fails to mention is the name of Rictavio's horse) and recounts many long and tedious journeys by wagon. Rictavio has also written about various "oddities" he has seen in his travels, including the following:

- A "werehare" child (a boy who transforms into a rabbit on nights of the full moon)
- A half-orc woman named Gorabacha who could chew through iron chains
- A giant, man-eating plant that had the most remarkable singing voice
- A pair of conjoined goblins
- A small man with no legs named Filmore Stunk, who could drink whole casks of wine without getting drunk

## N2o. Boys' Bedroom

A large, painted toy box rests between two small, cozy beds. Murals of ravens in flight are painted on the walls above the wood paneling.

Brom and Bray Martikova don't spend much time in this room. The toy box contains a pile of neglected toys, many of them etched with the slogan "Is No Fun, Is No Blinsky!" The toys include the following:

- A miniature puppet theater with appropriately sized marionettes of a king, a queen, a prince, a princess, an

executioner, a tax collector, a dunce, a vampire, and a vampire hunter
- A garish toy Vistani wagon hitched to a wooden horse and filled with tiny wooden Vistani figures
- A pair of painted wooden clown masks, one displaying a mean scowl and the other a frightened expression
- A wooden top painted with images of scarecrows chasing children through the forest
- A stuffed (real) bat on puppet strings

A hidden trapdoor in the 8-foot-high ceiling opens into a secret attic (area N2q).

## N2p. Master Bedroom

> Matching end tables flank a large wood-framed bed with a red silk canopy. Across from the bed hangs a tapestry depicting a beautiful mountain valley. The other walls are dominated by a fireplace and a wardrobe.

Urwin and Danika retire to this room every night before heading to the attic (area N2q) to sleep. This room is for appearances only and contains no valuables.

A secret door at the west end of the south wall can be pulled open to reveal the loft beyond (area N2h).

A hidden trapdoor in the 8-foot-high ceiling opens into a secret attic (area N2q).

## N2q. Secret Attic

> This ten-foot-wide, thirty-five-foot-long attic has a ceiling that slants down toward the west, dropping from a height of eight feet to a height of five feet. Four straw nests

> cover the floor, and a locked iron strongbox sits against the north wall. A small square opening in the south wall leads outside. Two trapdoors with iron hinges are set into the floor.

The Martikovs sleep here at night in hybrid form. The opening in the south wall is just big enough for a raven or other Tiny creature to pass through. The wereravens can use this opening as an escape route.

The strongbox is described in "Treasure" below.

Two trapdoors, clearly visible on the floor, can be pulled open to reveal the bedchambers (areas N2o and N2p) that lie directly beneath them.

**Treasure.** Urwin carries the key to the locked iron strongbox. The lock can be picked with thieves' tools and a successful DC 20 Dexterity check. The box contains a sack of 150 ep (each coin bearing the profiled visage of Strahd von Zarovich), six pieces of jewelry (worth 250 gp each), and three *potions of healing*.

### Fortunes of Ravenloft

If your card reading reveals that a treasure is here, it is in the iron strongbox.

## N3. Burgomaster's Mansion

> This mansion has walls of plastered stone that display many scars where the plaster has fallen away from age and neglect. Drapes cover every window, including a large, arched opening above the mansion's double entrance doors.

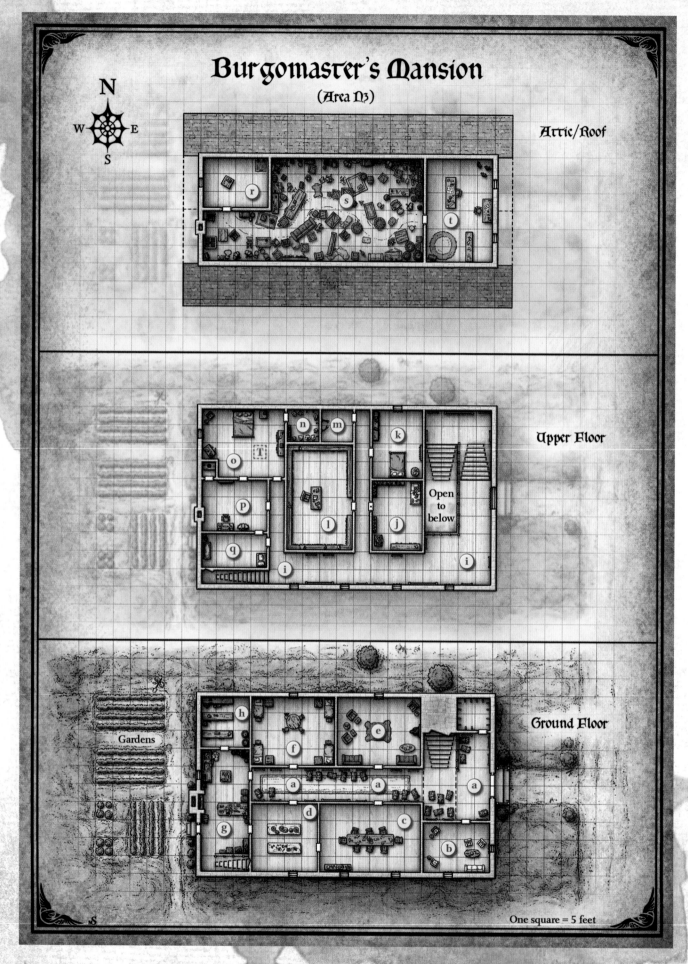

# Burgomaster's Mansion
## (Area N3)

Attic/Roof

Upper Floor

Open to below

Ground Floor

Gardens

One square = 5 feet

People come and go from the mansion at all hours during the day. Guards bring criminals cited for "malicious unhappiness." Men and women arrive carrying bundles of twigs, which are piled about the mansion's grand foyer (area N3a) until the construction of the wicker sun for the Festival of the Blazing Sun gets under way.

If the characters knock on the front doors, a maid (LG female human **commoner**) lets them in, escorts them to the den (area N3e), and leaves to fetch the baron.

### ROLEPLAYING THE VALLAKOVICH FAMILY

Use the following information to roleplay the burgomaster and his family.

**The Baron.** The burgomaster, Baron Vargas Vallakovich (NE male human **noble**), is a ruthless heel who prides himself on his good breeding and finely honed leadership skills. He stages repeated celebrations to foster happiness, and his "All will be well!" catchphrase has become a sad and tiresome punchline. Baron Vallakovich has convinced himself that if he can make everyone in Vallaki happy, the town will slip free of Strahd's dark grasp.

The baron has a brittle ego, and he lashes out at anyone who pokes fun at his festivals or treats him disrespectfully. He has two pet mastiffs that follow him everywhere, as well as a murderous and deformed henchman named **Izek Strazni** (see appendix D). In addition to his weapons, Izek carries an iron ring of keys that unlock the stocks in the town square (area N8).

If the characters get on his bad side, the baron accuses them of being "spies of the devil Strahd" and sends twelve **guards** to arrest them, seize their weapons, and run them out of town. If the guards fail in their duty, the baron sends Izek to rally a mob of thirty **commoners** to lynch the party. If the commoners also fail, the baron summons the twelve remaining guards to defend his mansion, giving characters the run of the town.

If the characters get on his good side, he insists that they join him in the next festival as special guests and asks that they tell everyone that all will, indeed, be well.

Two members of the baron's household staff have vanished in the past week: the butler and the baroness's lady-in-waiting. The baron has charged Izek with finding out what happened to them, but investigation isn't Izek's forte. Searches have been organized, to no avail.

**The Baroness.** At the risk of sacrificing her sanity, the baron's wife, Lydia Petrovna (LG female human **commoner**), has embraced her husband's philosophy of happiness. She laughs at the baron's every comment, to the extent that it has become a nervous reflex, and she tries to spread good cheer by throwing daily tea-and-sandwich parties in the parlor for her "dearest friends," many of them poor folk who tolerate the baroness only because they crave something warm to eat and drink. Lydia is a gods-fearing woman and the younger sister of the town priest, Father Lucian Petrovich. She is a descendant

of Tasha Petrovna, a priest entombed in Castle Ravenloft (chapter 4, area K84, crypt 11).

**The Baronet.** The baron's miserable son, Victor Vallakovich (NE male human **mage**), has confined himself to the attic (area N3t), where he is content to avoid the unwanted attention of his mother and the disapproving glares of his father. Years ago, Victor found an old spellbook in the mansion's library and used it to teach himself magic. He has been busy constructing a *teleportation circle* in the hope of escaping Barovia and leaving his parents to their doom.

## N3A. ENTRANCE HALL AND VESTIBULE

> Framed portraits adorn the walls of this grand foyer, which features a wide staircase with a sculpted railing. A long, carpeted hall attached to the foyer stretches almost the length of the mansion and has several doors leading away from it, including one at the far end. Bundles of twigs are heaped against the walls.

The twigs are being stored here until they can be fashioned into a wooden effigy of the sun (for the Festival of the Blazing Sun).

The stairs climb to the upstairs gallery (area N3i).

The portraits depict the baron, his family, and their ancestors. Close inspection reveals that some of the people portrayed look very much alike.

Tucked in the northeast corner of the foyer is a vestibule packed with fine cloaks, coats, and boots.

THE BARONESS
AND THE BARON

## N3b. Parlor

> This parlor contains a fine array of furnishings and draperies, with an overall feminine touch.

The baroness sometimes entertains guests here.

## N3c. Dining Room

Characters can hear the chatter of female voices as they approach this room. The first time they peer inside, read:

> A chandelier of wrought iron fitted with wax candles hangs above a polished wooden dining table. Around the table are seated eight women of various ages in comfortable, high-backed chairs. They wear faded clothes, drink tea, and devour cake while a ninth woman, well dressed and very pleased with herself, circles the table and talks excitedly about decorations for the impending festival.

The women seated at the table are eight Vallakian peasants (female **commoners**) invited to spend time with the baroness, Lydia Petrovna, who is bribing them with tea and cake. Lydia has assigned these women the task of stitching children's costumes and weaving together a wicker sun for the Festival of the Blazing Sun.

Lydia assumes that the characters are here at the invitation of her husband, the burgomaster. She calls for the maid to take them to the den (area N3e) and then to inform Baron Vallakovich (see area N2l) that his guests have arrived.

A serving table stands in one corner of the dining hall.

## N3d. Preparation Room

> White sheets cover two plain wooden tables in the center of this room. Neatly arranged atop one table is a complete set of polished silverware. The other table is covered with wicker baskets containing turnips and beets.

The beets and turnips are for the Festival of the Blazing Sun (see the "Special Events" section at the end of this chapter).

***Treasure.*** The silverware set is worth 150 gp.

## N3e. Den

Characters who ask to see the burgomaster are brought here.

> Padded chairs and couches line the walls of this cozy, carpeted den. The room reeks of pipe smoke, and mounted on the east wall is the head of an angry-looking brown bear.

The mounted bear's head is meant to unnerve visitors. It serves as a subtle warning not to antagonize the burgomaster, who spends most of his time in the library (area N3l). Although the burgomaster claims that his father killed the bear, the head was actually a gift given to his family by the late Szoldar Grygorovich, father of the wolf hunter Szoldar Szoldarovich (area N2).

## N3f. Servants' Quarters

> This room contains four simple beds and an equal number of plain wooden trunks.

The household staff consists of a maid (LG female human **commoner**) and a cook (LG male human **commoner**). The other two beds belonged to the butler and the baroness's lady-in-waiting, both of whom have gone missing (see area N3t). The trunks contain the staff's clothing and uniforms.

## N3g. Kitchen

> A cook wearing a white apron over a black smock busies himself in this warm, well-appointed kitchen. A staircase in one corner climbs to the upper floor.

The staircase leads to the upstairs gallery (area N3i). A door in the west wall leads to a garden outside. The door is usually locked, and both the cook and the burgomaster carry keys to unlock it.

## N3h. Pantry

> This pantry contains shelves of foodstuffs, although half of the shelves are bare. Two barrels of wine stand against the east wall.

The pantry has not been fully stocked for as long as anyone can remember. The two barrels contain a fine wine called Red Dragon Crush, created by the Wizard of Wines winery—facts burned into the side of each barrel.

## N3i. Upstairs Gallery

If the characters arrive here from the entrance hall (area N3a), read:

> The staircase climbs twenty feet to a beautifully appointed gallery that continues toward the west, running almost the length of the mansion. Framed landscape paintings line the walls, and red silk drapes cover a ten-foot-tall arched window of leaded glass.

If the characters arrive here from the kitchen (area N3g), read:

> The staircase climbs to a ten-foot-wide gallery that stretches almost the length of the mansion. Breathtaking paintings of landscapes line the walls. Two separate, narrow hallways lead away from the gallery to the north.

## N3J. IZEK'S BEDROOM

The door to this room is locked. Izek Strazni carries the only key.

The following description assumes the characters have met Ireena Kolyana (see chapter 3, area E4). If the characters haven't met her, don't read the last sentence.

> Dolls. This room is full of pretty little dolls with powder-white skin and auburn hair, some of them dressed beautifully, others plainly. Some of the dolls fill a long bookshelf, and others are arranged in neat rows on wall-mounted shelves. Still others are piled atop a bed and a heavy wooden chest. What's most odd is that all of the dolls, apart from their clothing, look the same. They all look like Ireena Kolyana.

The burgomaster's monstrous henchman, **Izek Strazni** (see appendix D), sleeps here at night. During the day, he is in town taking care of his master's business. Izek's chest is unlocked and contains a heap of wrinkled clothes, under which is a nonmagical shortsword.

A thorough search of the room reveals a few empty wine bottles under the bed. The label on each bears the winery's name, the Wizard of Wines, and wine's name, Purple Grapemash No. 3.

***Izek's Doll Collection.*** Each doll has a small tag stitched into its clothing that reads "Is No Fun, Is No Blinsky!" Izek had the local toymaker, Gadof Blinsky (area N7), craft the dolls in Ireena's likeness.

## N3K. VICTOR'S BEDROOM

> This handsomely appointed room contains a canopied bed, a low bookshelf, and a full-length mirror in a wooden frame on the wall across from the door. Set into the north wall is an arched window of leaded glass. Nothing here seems unusual.

Nothing about his bedroom betrays Victor's deviant nature or magical proclivities. The books include collections of Barovian fables and tomes about mythology, heraldry, and other innocuous subjects.

## N3L. LIBRARY

> Floor-to-ceiling shelves line every wall of this windowless room, and the number of books contained here is nothing short of astounding.

> A brass oil lamp sits atop a large desk in the center of the room. The chair behind the desk is comfortably padded and has the symbol of a roaring bear stitched into its back cushion.

If the burgomaster has not been drawn elsewhere, he is here. Add:

> Standing behind the chair, holding an open book, is a bear of a man. His breastplate, rapier, silk tunic, and greasy beard glisten in the lamplight. Resting on small rugs to his left and right are a pair of black mastiffs.

Baron Vargas Vallakovich never goes anywhere without his two **mastiffs**. A paranoid man, he wears his breastplate and rapier even while relaxing in his library. Two of his servants, the butler and his wife's lady-in-waiting, have vanished without a trace in the past week, so he has good cause to be worried.

The baron believes that everyone else is beneath him, and those who question his word or challenge his authority must be humbled. He won't pick a fight with well-armed strangers, however. If he can't make the characters yield to his authority, he swallows his pride until he can circle around with Izek Strazni and assemble his guards to run them out of town.

The baron's desk contains three drawers stuffed with blank sheets of parchment, jars of ink, and writing quills. It also holds thick books of tax records dating back to the times of the baron's father, grandfather, and great-grandfather.

The baron wears a signet ring and carries three keys: one that unlocks the outside door in area N3g, and two keys for the door and the manacles in area N3m.

***Treasure.*** The Vallakovich book collection contains old, leather-bound tomes on virtually every subject. Use the Random Books table (see chapter 4, area K37) to determine the subject matter of a particular book.

## N3M. LOCKED CLOSET

The door to this room is locked. The baron carries the key.

> Chained to the back wall of this otherwise empty closet is a badly beaten man wearing nothing but a loincloth. The iron shackles have cut into his wrists, causing blood to trickle down his hands.

The man is a Vallakian shoemaker named Udo Lukovich (LN male human **commoner**). He was arrested during the Wolf's Head Jamboree for carrying a sign that suggested that Vallakians should feed the baron to the wolves.

Baron Vallakovich has the key to Udo's manacles. The manacles break if they take 10 damage or more from a single weapon attack.

If the characters release Udo, his first desire is to return to his home. Later, he plans to tell Father Lucian (see area N1) of his ill treatment in the burgomaster's estate. If the baron discovers that Udo has escaped or been set free, he sends Izek to find the shoemaker and bring him back for further questioning. Under great duress, Udo provides the names or descriptions of those who liberated him, turning the burgomaster against the characters.

### N3n. Master Bedroom Closet

Cloaks, coats, gowns, and other fancy apparel hang from hooks in this closet. Arranged on low shelves are many fine shoes, slippers, and boots.

### N3o. Master Bedroom

Time has faded the grandeur of this master bedroom. The furnishings have lost some of their color and splendor. A short pull-rope hangs from a wooden trapdoor in the ceiling.

The baron and the baroness sleep in one bed at night. Nothing of value is kept here.

The trapdoor in the ceiling can be pulled down to reveal an attic room (area N3r). An unfolding wooden ladder allows easy access.

### N3p. Bridal Gown and Spirit Mirror

This room smells of powder and fine perfume. A vanity with a mirror stands against one wall next to a faceless wooden mannequin wearing a white bridal gown. Mounted on another wall is a full-length mirror with a gilded frame. A door in one corner leads to a garderobe.

The baroness used to while away long hours in this room, fondling her perfume collection and searching for solace in her own reflection. Since her lady-in-waiting went missing several days ago, the baroness has spent almost no time here.

**Bridal Gown.** The white gown stored here belongs to the baroness. It reminds the her of happier times.

**Magic Mirror.** A *detect magic* spell reveals that the gilded mirror on the wall radiates an aura of conjuration magic. None of the mansion's current occupants are aware of this fact, because the mirror's magic hasn't been used in generations. Casting an *identify* spell on the mirror reveals that an assassin's ghost is magically bound to it. The spell also reveals the forgotten rhyme needed to summon the ghost:

*Magic mirror on the wall,*
*Summon forth your shade;*
*Night's dark vengeance, heed my call*
*And wield your murderous blade.*

The entity in the mirror is the spirit of a nameless assassin who once belonged to a secret society called the Ba'al Verzi. If a creature speaks the rhyme while standing within 5 feet of the mirror and staring at its own reflection, the assassin's ghost appears nearby. The form that the spirit takes depends on the alignment of the one who summoned it:

**Non-evil Summoner.** If the summoner isn't evil, the spirit assumes solid form, appearing as a darkly handsome thirty-year-old man with bloodshot eyes. He has the statistics of an **assassin** but doesn't speak, and he disappears into the ether if reduced to 0 hit points. The assassin's summoner can command him to kill one living creature within Strahd's domain that the summoner mentions by name. The assassin automatically knows the distance and direction to the named target. The assassin attacks any other creature that tries to prevent him from completing his assignment. Once he completes his task, the assassin disappears. If commanded to attack a creature that is either dead or undead, or if he isn't given an appropriate name within 1 round of being summoned, the assassin disappears.

**Evil Summoner.** If the summoner is evil, the ghost manifests as a pair of floating, bloodshot eyes and strong, spectral hands. The hands try to wrap themselves around the summoner's neck. The spectral eyes and hands have the statistics of a **ghost**, but without the Etherealness and Possession actions. The ghost attacks its summoner until one or the other drops to 0 hit points, at which point it disappears.

Once the power of the mirror is used, the mirror becomes dormant until the next dawn. The mirror has AC 10, 5 hit points, and immunity to poison and psychic damage. Destroying it lays the assassin's spirit to rest, causing the manifestation to disappear if it is present.

The mirror corrupts those who use it to do evil. Summoning the assassin isn't evil, but using him to commit murder is. Each time a creature uses the mirror for this purpose, there is a cumulative 25 percent chance that the creature's alignment shifts to neutral evil.

If a character touches the mirror and speaks Strahd's name, there is a 50 percent chance that Strahd takes notice and appears on the mirror's surface. In this form, the vampire can't be harmed. He tries to charm one humanoid he can see within 30 feet of the mirror. Whether the target resists the effect or not, Strahd's smiling visage invites the characters to dine at Castle Ravenloft, then fades away. A creature charmed by Strahd feels compelled to accept the vampire's invitation.

### N3q. Bathroom

An iron tub with clawed feet stands against the back wall. Neatly folded towels rest atop a table near the door.

### N3r. Attic Room

Characters are most likely to enter this room via a trapdoor in the ceiling of the master bedroom (area N3o).

> This dusty, twenty-foot-square room has a high-pitched ceiling that reaches its peak twenty feet above. The wooden rafters are shrouded in cobwebs. Except for an old table with a lantern on it, the room is empty.

A door in the south wall can be pulled open to area N3s.

## N3s. Attic Storage

> This large attic is full of old, forgotten things draped in white sheets. Piled around them are barrels, crates, trunks, and old furnishings covered with cobwebs and dust. You see a clear footpath through the maze.

Characters can follow a single set of human footprints in the dust that lead to area N3t.

Searching through the junk in this attic uncovers a few old paintings and antiques, but nothing of value.

### Fortunes of Ravenloft

If your card reading reveals that a treasure is here, the item is hidden in a trunk. Each character has a cumulative 20 percent chance of finding the item for every hour the character spends searching the attic.

### N3t. Victor's Workroom

Victor spends most of his time here, leaving only when he needs food or spell components. When the characters first set eyes on the door to this room, read:

> Someone has carved a large skull into this door. Hanging from the doorknob is a wooden sign that reads "ALL IS NOT WELL!" You hear a young man's voice beyond.

Anyone who inspects the carving and succeeds on a DC 14 Intelligence (Investigation) check notices a small, nearly invisible glyph etched into the skull's forehead. This is a *glyph of warding* (5d8 lightning damage) that triggers if anyone other than Victor opens the door.

The voice belongs to Victor. He is reading aloud from his spellbook. Anyone who listens at the door and succeeds on a DC 14 Intelligence (Arcana) check can tell he's badly pronouncing some kind of teleportation spell.

If the characters open the door, read:

> Someone has taken old, mismatched furniture and created a study is this dusty, lamplit chamber. Tables are strewn with pieces of parchment, on which strange diagrams are drawn, and a freestanding bookshelf holds a collection of bones. A dusty rug covers the floor in front of a pine box, on which lounges a skeletal cat. Several more skeletal cats skulk about. Most unnerving of all is the sight of three small children standing with their backs to you in the northeast corner of the room.

If the characters trigger the *glyph of warding* or otherwise announce their arrival, Victor casts a *greater invisibility* spell on himself and hides in a corner. Otherwise, he's visible. If the characters can see Victor, read:

> In the center of the room, perched on a stool, is a thin young man with a premature streak of gray in his dark hair. He cradles an open leather-bound book in his arms.

Victor found a spellbook in his father's library and is using it to teach himself the art of spellcasting. Only recently has he been able to decipher some of its high-level spells. He's a weird, awkward, and off-putting fellow who is dangerous only if threatened.

For practice and for fun, Victor dug up some old cat bones behind the Wachter estate (see area N4) and animated them, creating six cat skeletons (use the **cat** stat block, but give them darkvision out to a range of 60 feet and immunity to poison damage, exhaustion, and the poisoned condition). The skeletons attack only when Victor commands them to.

The "children" standing in the corner are painted wooden dolls dressed in clothing that Victor wore as a child. He pretends they are his disobedient pupils.

The sheets of parchment are covered with elaborate diagrams of teleportation circles. Victor drew them in an effort to learn the *teleportation circle* spell, which he's still trying to master (see "Teleportation Circle" below).

The trunk contains several bolts of silk cloth, needles and thread, and a half-finished wizard's robe. Victor started to make the robe for himself but found the work tedious and stopped.

***Teleportation Circle.*** Victor's spellbook contains incomplete text for a *teleportation circle* spell, along with the sigil sequences of three permanent teleportation circles, the locations of which aren't described. There's not enough text to prepare the spell properly, but that hasn't stopped Victor from trying to learn to cast it.

Victor recently inscribed his own version of a teleportation circle on the floor. It's hidden under the rug so that his parents don't find it. In the past couple of weeks, Victor has managed to imbue the circle with magic, but he failed to account for several factors. His circle doesn't fade after use, nor does it function like the *teleportation circle* spell. If the circle is used in the casting of a *teleportation circle* spell, whether the actual spell or Victor's version of it, any creature standing on the circle when the spell is cast takes 3d10 force damage and isn't teleported anywhere. If this damage reduces the creature to 0 hit points, the creature is disintegrated. Any character who studies the circle and succeeds on a DC 15 Intelligence (Arcana) check realizes that Victor's circle is horribly flawed and potentially deadly when used.

Victor has tested his circle on two reluctant servants (compelled by his *suggestion* spell), in both cases linking his circle to one of the other circles whose sigils are in his spellbook. Each servant was torn apart before Victor's eyes before vanishing in a flash of purple light. Victor doesn't know how to fix the circle but plans to make more modifications to it before testing it again.

**Treasure.** Victor's spellbook contains all the spells Victor has prepared (see the **mage** stat block in the *Monster Manual*) as well as the following spells: *animate dead, blight, cloudkill, darkvision, glyph of warding, levitate, remove curse,* and *thunderwave.*

# N4. WACHTERHAUS

> This house seems disgusted with itself. A slouching roof hangs heavy over furrowed gables, and moss-covered walls sag and bulge under the weight of the vegetation. As you study the house's sullen countenance, you hear the edifice actually groan. Only then do you realize the extent to which the house hates what it has become.

The Wachter family, once an influential noble line in Barovia, owns and occupies a mansion in Vallaki. The house's reigning governess, Fiona Wachter, is a loyal servant of Strahd. She seeks to supplant Baron Vallakovich as the town burgomaster.

## ROLEPLAYING

Use the following information to roleplay Lady Wachter, her family, and her associates.

**Lady of the House.** Lady Fiona Wachter (LE female human **priest** with AC 10 and no armor) makes no secret of her family's long-standing loyalty to the von Zarovich line. She believes that Strahd von Zarovich is no tyrant but, at worst, a negligent landlord. She would happily serve Strahd as burgomaster of Vallaki, but she knows that Baron Vargas Vallakovich won't give up his birthright without a fight.

Fiona conspired to wed her young daughter, Stella, to the baron's son, Victor, as part of a plot to gain a foothold in the baron's mansion, but Stella found Victor to be demented, and he showed no interest in Stella whatsoever. In fact, he spoke such unkind words to Stella that she went mad, and Fiona had to lock her daughter away (see area N4n).

Lady Wachter's latest scheme to gain control of Vallaki is far more diabolical. She has started a cult based on devil worship and has written a manifesto that she reads to her "book club," which is made up of the most fanatical group members. Inspired by her words, these zealots have created smaller cults of their own. Once her cult has enough members, Fiona plans to take the town by force. To reward her most loyal followers, she has her pet imp stand invisibly in the center of a pentagram, then performs a false ritual that calls upon "princes of darkness" to lavish their appreciation upon the cultists. The imp then sprinkles onto the floor a few electrum coins, which Lady Wachter allows the cultists to keep.

Another secret of Fiona's is that she sleeps with the corpse of her dead husband, Nikolai, who died of sickness nearly three years ago and whom Fiona cherished. Lady Wachter casts *gentle repose* spells on the corpse to keep it from deteriorating.

If the characters come to Wachterhaus looking for help to overthrow the burgomaster, Lady Wachter is all ears and suggests they start by killing the baron's evil henchman, Izek Strazni. She's happy to take care of the rest. If they come looking for a way to defeat Strahd, Lady Wachter turns them away, stating in no uncertain terms that she is not, nor ever will be, Strahd's enemy.

Lady Wachter has a different list of prepared spells from that of the priest in the *Monster Manual*:

Cantrips (at will): *light, mending, thaumaturgy*
1st level (4 slots): *command, purify food and drink, sanctuary*
2nd level (3 slots): *augury, gentle repose, hold person*
3rd level (2 slots): *animate dead, create food and water*

**Fiona's Sons.** Fiona sees a lot of her husband in her sons, Nikolai and Karl (N male human **nobles**), who have grown into young men with a fondness for wine and trouble. They aren't home during the day, because they don't like attending to their mother or listening to her tiresome prattle. The characters might encounter them at the Blue Water Inn (area N2) or wandering about town. The brothers are home most nights, passed out in their beds after hours of heavy drinking.

Nikolai and Karl have none of their mother's ambition or mean temper. They are aware of her cult, but they don't know that she sleeps with their dead father. This would be unwelcome news and probably turn them against their mother. They want only to spend their mother's money and make the most of their miserable situation, trapped as they are within the walls of Vallaki under the control of Strahd and his puppet, the baron.

**Fiona's Spy.** Fiona employs a money-grubbing **spy** named Ernst Larnak (LE male human) to keep her informed about everything that happens in town. Ernst knows Lady Wachter's secrets, and he would blackmail her in a heartbeat if their relationship went sour.

## N4A. FRONT DOOR AND VESTIBULE

The front door is locked and reinforced with bronze bands. All of the servants carry a key, as do Lady Wachter and Ernst Larnak. The door can be forced open with a successful DC 20 Strength check.

If the characters knock on the front door, a servant opens a small window cut into the door at eye height and asks their business. Suspicious-looking strangers aren't invited inside, in case they're vampires.

> The front door opens into a narrow vestibule. Three stained-glass doors in wooden frames lead from it.

Two closets flank the front door. The western closet contains Lady Wachter's outdoor clothes; the eastern one contains coats and boots that belong to her children.

## N4B. STAIRCASE

> A wooden staircase leads up to a balcony. At the foot of the stairs is a landing with three stained-glass doors in wooden frames.

The staircase climbs 15 feet to the upstairs hall (area N2l).

# Wachterhaus

### (Area N4)

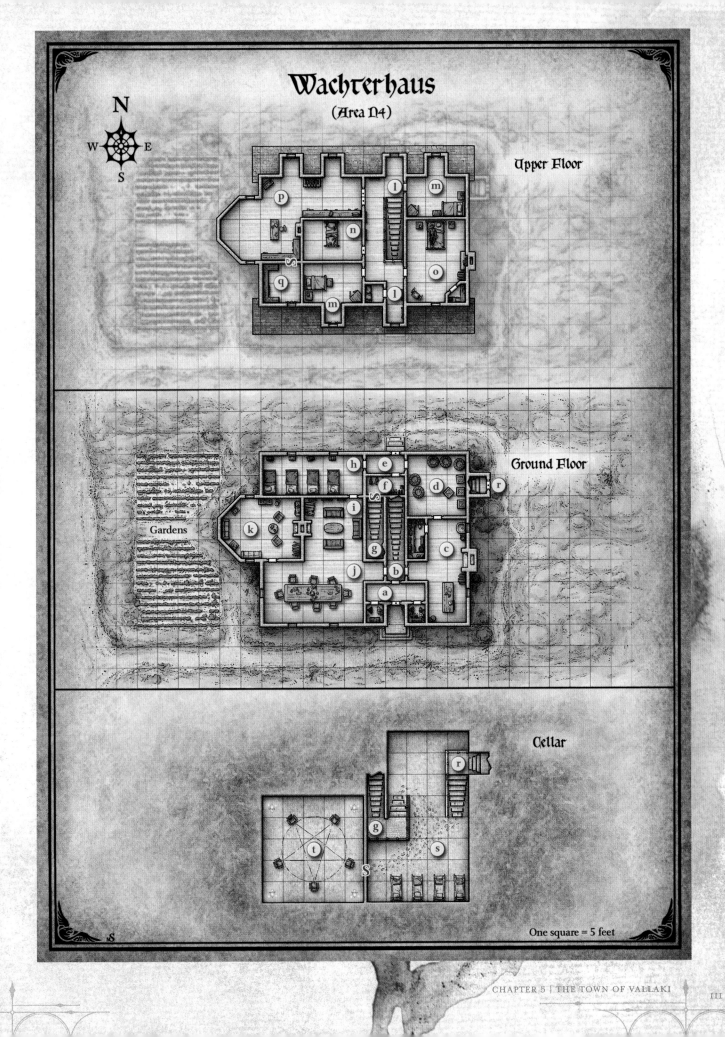

Upper Floor

Ground Floor

Gardens

Cellar

One square = 5 feet

FIONA WACHTER
AND MAJESTO

The stairs connect the servants' closet (area N4f) with the cellar (area N4s). Lady Wachter uses this staircase to reach her secret cult lair (area N4t).

## N4H. SERVANTS' QUARTERS

> The furnishing in this room are bereft of imagination: four simple beds with equally austere wooden chests.

Lady Wachter's four servants (N male and female **commoners**) sleep here at night. They include a cook named Dhavit, two maids named Madalena and Amalthia, and a valet named Haliq. The servants know Lady Wachter's secrets, but they would sooner die than betray her.

## N4I. PARLOR

Lady Wachter greets her guests here, under the watchful eyes of her dead husband.

> Here three elegant couches surround an oval table made of black glass. All are set in front of a blazing hearth, above which hangs the portrait of a smirking nobleman sporting a broken nose and a tangle of hair graying at the temples. Several smaller portraits hang on the north wall.

The portrait above the mantel depicts Lord Nikolai Wachter, Fiona's late husband (of whom his sons are the spitting image). The other portraits depict Lady Wachter, her sons, her daughter, and various deceased family members.

The parlor shares the fireplace with the den (area N4k). Ernst Larnak lurks in the den and eavesdrops on any conversation that Lady Wachter has with the characters, so that he can advise her after they depart.

## N4J. DINING ROOM

> An ornate dining table stretches the length of this room, a crystal chandelier hanging above it imperiously. The silverware is tarnished, the dishes chipped, yet all are still quite elegant. Eight chairs, their backs adorned with sculpted elk horns, surround the table. Arched windows made of a latticework of iron and glass look out onto the small, fog-swept estate.

If the characters aim to oppose the burgomaster, Lady Wachter offers them a warm meal in the dining room as a token of her support and allegiance.

## N4K. DEN

> Wood paneling, embroidered rugs, colorful furnishings, and a blazing fire make this chamber stifling. Mounted above the mantel is an elk's head. Across from the hearth, tall, slender windows look out over dead gardens.

## N4C. KITCHEN

The house cook (see area N4h) rushes about this spotless kitchen most of the day, preparing meals or cleaning up after himself. A washbasin stands in the northeast corner. A slender door in the west wall leads to a small pantry.

## N4D. STORAGE ROOM

This room holds crates of old clothing, as well as three barrels of drinking water, two empty wine barrels, and one full wine barrel. The wine barrels are emblazoned with the winery name, the Wizard of Wines, and the wine's name, Red Dragon Crush.

## N4E. BACK VESTIBULE

The back door is locked and similar to the front door (area N4a) in every respect. The vestibule has plain wooden doors leading to areas N4d, N4f, and N4h.

## N4F. SERVANTS' CLOSET

> Servants' coats and aprons hang from hooks in this room, and boots are neatly lined up against the wall.

Anyone who searches the closet and makes a successful DC 10 Wisdom (Perception) check finds a secret door in the south wall. The door can be pulled open to reveal a stone staircase (area N4g) that leads to the cellar.

## N4G. SECRET STAIRCASE

> Iron torch sconces cling to the wall of a stone staircase that cuts its way through the heart of the old house.

Ernst Larnak, Lady Wachter's spy, lounges here when he's not out spying on her behalf.

**Treasure.** The room contains several items of value, including a golden goblet (worth 250 gp) from which Ernst drinks wine, a crystal wine decanter (worth 250 gp), four electrum candelabras (worth 25 gp each), and a bronze urn with frolicking children painted on its sides (worth 100 gp).

## N4L. UPSTAIRS HALL

> A hallway with a window at each end wraps around the staircase railing. Framed portraits and mirrors festoon the walls, surrounding you with judging looks and dark reflections. You hear something scratching at one of the many doors.

The scratching noise comes from the door to area N4n, which is locked. If the characters call out, a plaintive female voice meows like a cat and says, "Can little kitty come out to play? Little kitty is sad and lonely and promises to be good this time, really she does." A closet at the south end of the hallway holds blankets and linens.

## N4M. BROTHERS' ROOMS

> This bedroom contains nothing out of the ordinary: a neatly made bed, a table with an oil lamp on it, a handsome wooden chest, a slender wardrobe, and a window box with drapes.

These two rooms belong to Lady Wachter's sons, Nikolai and Karl. There's a 25 percent chance that one of the maids (see area N4h) is here, tidying up.

## N4N. STELLA'S ROOM

The door to this room is locked from both sides, and only Lady Wachter has a key.

> This room is musty and dark. An iron-framed bed fitted with leather straps stands near a wall. The place has no other furnishings.
>
> Scurrying away from you on all fours is a young woman in a soiled nightgown. She leaps onto the bed and hisses like a cat. "Little kitty doesn't know you!" she shouts. "Little kitty doesn't like the smell of you!"

The young woman is Stella Wachter (CG female human **commoner**), Lady Wachter's insane daughter. A *greater restoration* spell rids her of the madness that makes her think she's a cat. If she is cured of her madness, she blames her mother for treating her horribly and using her as a pawn to seize control of the town. Stella knows none of her mother's secrets, apart from her mother's desire to overthrow the burgomaster. Stella has nothing kind to say about the burgomaster or his

son, Victor, whose very name makes her cringe. With her wits restored, Stella feels she has no one in Vallaki she can count on. She latches onto any character who is kind to her. If the party takes her to St. Andral's church (area N1), Father Lucian offers to look after her, and she agrees to stay with him.

## N4O. MASTER BEDROOM

The door to this room is locked. Lady Wachter and her servants carry keys. A ghastly sight awaits those who peer into the room:

> Across from the door, a fire sputters and struggles for life in the hearth, above which hangs a framed family portrait: a noble father and mother, their two young sons, and a baby daughter in the father's arms. The sons are smiling in a way that suggests mischief. The parents look like uncrowned royalty.
>
> Wood paneling covers the walls of the room. A closet and a framed mirror flank a curtained window to the south. To the north, a wide, canopied bed lies pinned between matching end tables with oil lamps. Stretched out on one side of the bed is a man dressed in black, his eyes each covered with a copper piece. He bears a striking resemblance to the father in the painting.

Lady Wachter's husband, Nikolai, lies in his bed, impeccably dressed, quite deceased, and under the effect of the *gentle repose* spell. Nothing of value is on him.

The closet contains shelves of fancy footwear and many fine garments, including a black ceremonial robe with a hood (similar to the ones worn by the cult fanatics in area N4t). On a high shelf rests a locked iron chest. Lady Wachter hides the key to the chest on a tiny hook in the fireplace, under the mantel. A character who takes a minute to search the fireplace finds the key with a successful DC 10 Wisdom (Perception) check. Use of the key disables a poison needle trap hidden in the lock (see "Sample Traps" in chapter 5, "Adventure Environments," of the *Dungeon Master's Guide*). A creature that triggers the trap and fails the saving throw against the needle's poison falls unconscious for 1 hour instead of being poisoned for 1 hour.

The iron chest is lined with thin sheets of lead and contains the bones of Leo Dilisnya, an enemy of the Wachter family. Leo was one of the soldiers who betrayed and murdered Strahd on the day of Sergei and Tatyana's wedding. He escaped from Castle Ravenloft, only to be hunted down and killed by the vampire Strahd. The Wachters keep his bones under lock and key so that Leo can't be raised from the dead.

### FORTUNES OF RAVENLOFT

If your card reading reveals that a treasure is here, it is in the iron chest that contains Leo Dilisnya's bones.

## N4P. LIBRARY

The double doors to this room are locked. Lady Wachter and her servants carry keys.

This room is crawling with cats. Bookshelves hug the walls, but most of the shelves are bare. Other furnishings include a desk, a chair, a table, and a wine cabinet. The room has an irregular shape, and none of its angles seem quite right, as though the shifting of the house has set the whole place on edge.

Eight **cats** have the run of the library. These family pets have vicious dispositions, attacking anyone who tries to pick them up. Characters who have a passive Wisdom (Perception) score of 10 or higher notice that one cat has a small key hanging from its collar. The key opens the locked chest in area N4q.

There is a 25 percent chance that one of the maids is here, dusting the bookshelves.

The cabinet holds a fine collection of wineglasses. The desk contains blank pieces of parchment, quill pens, jars of ink, wax candles, and a wax seal.

Most of the Wachter family's book collection was sold off years ago to cover debts, and the books that remain aren't particularly valuable. Use the Random Books table (see chapter 4, area K37) to determine the subject matter of a particular book.

A section of the bookshelf that stretches along the southernmost wall is actually a secret door on hidden hinges. The bookshelf can be pulled outward, revealing an open doorway that leads to area N4q.

## N4Q. STORAGE ROOM

Behind the hinged panel in the bookcase lies a dusty, ten-foot-square room with a curtained window and shelves lining three walls. On the bottom shelf rests an iron chest. The other shelves are bare.

The key to the chest can be found in the library (area N4p). Use of the key disables a poison needle trap hidden in the lock (see "Sample Traps" in chapter 5, "Adventure Environments," of the *Dungeon Master's Guide*).

**Treasure.** The iron chest contains several items:

- A silk bag containing 180 ep, each coin bearing Strahd's stern visage in profile
- A leather bag containing 110 gp
- A wooden pipe that has been passed down through many generations of Wachter patriarchs
- Five scrolls—notarized deeds for parcels of land given to the Wachter family by Count Strahd von Zarovich nearly four centuries ago
- A supple leather case containing an unbound manuscript titled *The Devil We Know*—a poetic manifesto written by Lady Fiona Wachter attesting that the worship of devils can bring happiness, success, freedom, wealth, and longevity
- A blasphemous treatise bound in black leather titled *The Grimoire of the Four Quarters*, written by the infamous diabolist Devostas, who was drawn and quartered for his fell practices yet did not die (this is a forgery; the actual grimoire would drive a reader mad)

- A very old letter to Lady Lovina Wachter (an ancestor) from one Lord Vasili von Holtz, thanking Lovina for her hospitality, loyalty, and friendship over the years

Characters who have the *Tome of Strahd* (see appendix C) realize that the handwriting in Lady Lovina's letter is identical to Strahd's handwriting, suggesting that Strahd and Lord Vasili are one and the same.

## N4R. CELLAR ENTRANCE

If the characters approach the cellar door from the outside, read:

A slanted, wooden cellar door with an iron pull ring and iron hinges stands against the foundation of the house.

The door is unlocked. On the other side of the door are stone steps leading to a stone landing with a wooden railing. A longer staircase extends south from the landing, leading down to the cellar.

## N4S. CELLAR

This large root cellar has a dirt floor. Two ascending flights of stone steps enclosed by wooden railings stand across from one another. Tracks in the earth lead from one staircase to the other, and other trails go from both staircases to the center of the bare west wall. Four neatly made cots are set in a row against the south wall.

Buried under the earthen floor are eight human **skeletons**—the animated remains of dead Vallakians that were stolen from the church cemetery (area N1) and animated by Lady Wachter. They rise up and attack intruders who cross the floor. The skeletons don't attack anyone who utters the phrase "Let the dead remain at rest" before setting foot on the floor. Only Lady Wachter, her sons, her servants, and her loyal cult fanatics know the pass phrase.

The cots are here for cultists to spend the night.

The footprints in the dirt give away the location of a secret door in the center of the western wall. Consequently, no ability check is required to locate it. The door is soundproof and pivots open on a central axis.

## N4T. CULT HEADQUARTERS

Flickering candles in iron holders fill this room with light and shadows. This room has a ten-foot-high ceiling and a large black pentagram inscribed on the stone floor. At each point of the pentagram rests a wooden chair. Seated in four of the five chairs are men and women in black robes with hoods: a young man who has the face of an angel; a balding hulk of a man; a squat, middle-aged woman; and a taller, younger woman with an unsettling glare. They rise to confront you.

The four people are town residents (LE male and female human **cult fanatics**) whom Lady Wachter has seduced with promises of power, wealth, and long life. They are members of her "book club," eagerly waiting for Lady Wachter to join them, read passages from her manifesto (see area N4q), and maybe conjure up a few coins. Resting on the fifth chair, quietly eavesdropping on the cultists, is the lady's invisible **imp**, Majesto.

The cultists are gathered here in secret and attack the characters to protect their identities. They are evil Vallakians of no great importance who are tired of living in fear and poverty. Use the "Barovian Names" sidebar in chapter 2 to generate names for them, if needed.

The imp doesn't get involved in the fighting unless Lady Wachter is drawn into the conflict, in which case it fights to protect its mistress.

The pentagram is a nonmagical decoration, though Lady Wachter would have her cultists believe otherwise.

## N5. Arasek Stockyard

> This large stockyard has several locked sheds along its periphery and lies adjacent to a roomy warehouse. A wooden sign above the front gate reads "Arasek Stockyard."
>
> Parked at the south end of the stockyard is a sturdy carnival wagon, its colorful paint peeling off. Faded lettering on its sides spells out the words "Rictavio's Carnival of Wonders." A heavy padlock secures the back door.

The stockyard is a general store and a facility where storage sheds can be rented. It is owned by a middle-aged married couple, Gunther and Yelena Arasek (LG male and female **commoners**). They sell items from the Adventuring Gear table in the *Player's Handbook* that have a price of 25 gp or less, but at five times the price.

### Rictavio's Carnival Wagon

The colorful half-elf bard Rictavio (see area N2 and appendix D) paid Gunther and Yelena a generous amount of gold to watch his carnival wagon, no questions asked. If the characters approach the wagon, read:

> The wagon suddenly lurches, as though something big has thrown itself against the inside wall. You hear the cracking of wood, the scraping of metal, and the snarl of something inhuman. Upon closer inspection, you see that the sides of the wagon are spattered with dry blood. You also see an inscription on the wagon's door frame that reads, "I bring you from Shadow into Light!"

Rictavio carries the key to the wagon door. The lock can be picked but is rigged with a poison needle trap (see "Sample Traps" in chapter 5, "Adventure Environments," of the *Dungeon Master's Guide*).

Inside the wagon is a **saber-toothed tiger** with 84 hit points. It is clad in specially fitted half plate (AC 17) and has been trained to hunt Strahd's Vistani servants. This tiger has a challenge rating of 3 (700 XP).

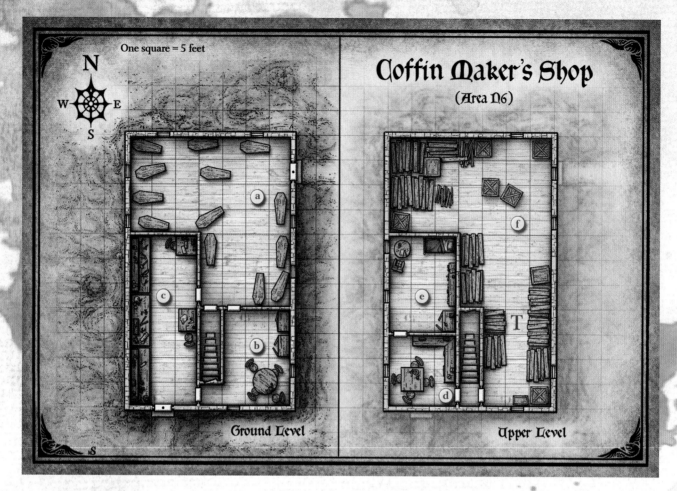

One square = 5 feet

N W E S

## Coffin Maker's Shop
### (Area N6)

Ground Level

Upper Level

The wagon also contains the torn-up remains of a doll. A character who makes a successful DC 10 Intelligence (Investigation) check discovers that the doll was once a colorfully dressed Vistani effigy. Stitched into its tattered pants is a slogan: "Is No Fun, Is No Blinsky!"

Rictavio isn't ready to unleash the tiger on the Vistani just yet. He feeds it by dropping wolf steaks down a 1-foot-square hatch in the wagon's roof. A character who climbs atop the wagon can spot the hatch without needing to make an ability check.

If the tiger is released, it begins stalking through the streets until its keen sense of smell locates either Rictavio (area N2) or Piccolo (area N7). The tiger doesn't attack anyone who isn't a Vistana except in self-defense. It attacks Vistani on sight. Rictavio can make the tiger break off its attack and lure it back into the wagon.

### TREASURE

The front seat of the wagon conceals a secret compartment that requires a successful DC 15 Wisdom (Perception) check to find and open. The compartment holds several items:

- An unlocked wooden coffer containing 50 ep bearing Strahd's profile and six gemstones (worth 100 gp each)
- A small prayer book (worth 50 gp) with a green leather cover and indecipherable notes in the margins
- A healer's kit
- Three wooden holy symbols inlaid with silver and in the shape of a sunburst (worth 50 gp each)

- A silvered shortsword
- A hand crossbow inlaid with mother-of-pearl (worth 250 gp)
- A bundle of twenty silvered crossbow bolts
- A worn leather case with gold buckles (worth 100 gp) containing three sharpened wooden stakes, a sack of garlic, a jar of salt, a box of holy wafers, six vials of holy water, a polished steel mirror, and a bone scroll tube with a silver stopper and chain (worth 25 gp). The tube contains a *spell scroll* of *protection from fiends* and a *spell scroll* of *protection from undead*.

### FORTUNES OF RAVENLOFT

If your card reading reveals that a treasure is here, it is hidden with the other items under the front seat of the wagon, in a lead-lined box.

## N6. COFFIN MAKER'S SHOP

> This uninviting shop is two stories tall and has a sign shaped like a coffin above the front door. All of the window shutters are closed up tight, and a deathly silence surrounds the establishment.

Henrik van der Voort (LE male human **commoner**) is a mediocre carpenter and a troubled, lonely man. He profits from the deaths of others, and no one desires his company, because of the ghastly nature of his handiwork. One night several months ago, Strahd visited Henrik in the guise of an imposing, well-dressed nobleman named Vasili von Holtz and promised the coffin maker "good business" in exchange for his help. Since then, Henrik's workshop has become the lair of a pack of vampire spawn—former adventurers who were turned by Strahd. These vampires are lying low for the time being.

The vampires plan to attack St. Andral's church (see "St. Andral's Feast" in the "Special Events" section at the end of this chapter). When Henrik learned about the sacred bones buried under the church, the vampire spawn ordered him to steal the bones, which Henrik paid Milivoj the gravedigger (see area N1) to do.

Every window of Henrik's shop is a latticework of iron fitted with squares of frosted glass and locked from the inside. The outside doors of the shop are barred shut from within. If the characters knock on one of them, Henrik shouts, "We're closed! Go away!" without opening the door. If the characters accuse Henrik of stealing the bones of St. Andral, he shouts again, "Go away! Leave me alone!"

If the characters break into the store, Henrik offers no resistance. He tells them where to find the bones (in the upstairs bedroom wardrobe, area N6e) and the vampire nest (in the upstairs wood storage room, area N6f).

If the characters report the theft of the bones to the burgomaster, Baron Vallakovich dispatches four **guards** to arrest Henrik and retrieve the bones. If the guards show up during daylight hours, Henrik surrenders himself and the bones without a fight, claiming that vampires forced him to steal the bones. If the guards come at night, Henrik surrenders himself and tells the guards where the bones are hidden, but he won't retrieve the bones himself for fear of being killed by the vampires.

### N6a. Coffin Storage

> Arranged haphazardly about the floor of this musty, L-shaped room are thirteen wooden coffins.

Henrik stores and displays the coffins he has made in this room. All of them are empty.

### N6b. Junk Room

> A table with four chairs is in one corner of this room, with a lantern hanging from a chain directly above. Two well-made cabinets stand against the east wall.

The cabinets are packed with worthless items that Henrik has collected over the years.

### N6c. Workshop

> This workshop contains everything a carpenter needs to make coffins and furniture. Three sturdy worktables stretch the length of the west wall.

Henrik builds coffins and keeps his carpenter's tools in this room.

### N6d. Kitchen

> This kitchen contains a square table surrounded by chairs and shelves of provisions.

Henrik prepares his meals here.

### N6e. Henrik's Bedroom

> This modest bedchamber holds a cot and several well-made pieces of furniture, including a table, a padded chair, a bookshelf, and a wardrobe.

Henrik sleeps here, at night and well into the morning. The bookshelf contains a handful of storybooks and carpenters' manuals that have been handed down from previous generations.

***Treasure.*** The wardrobe in the southeast corner has a secret compartment in its base, requiring a successful DC 15 Wisdom (Perception) check to find. Inside the compartment are two sacks—a large one containing the bones of St. Andral and a small one containing 30 sp and 12 ep. All of the coins bear the profiled visage of Strahd von Zarovich.

HENRIK
VAN DER VOORT

## N6f. Vampire Nest

> This large, drafty room is strung with cobwebs and takes up most of the upper floor. Stacks of wooden planks lie amid several crates marked "JUNK."

The two southernmost crates contain old junk that Henrik has accumulated over the years. The six crates in the northern part of the room are packed with earth and serve as resting places for the six **vampire spawn** that lair here. If the characters open one of the occupied crates, all of the vampire spawn burst forth and attack.

**Teleport Destination.** Characters who teleport to this location from area K78 in Castle Ravenloft arrive at the point marked T on the map.

## N7. Blinsky Toys

> This cramped shop has a dark entrance portico, above which hangs a wooden sign shaped like a rocking horse, with a "B" engraved on both sides. Flanking the entrance are two arched, lead-framed windows. Through the dirty glass, you see jumbled displays of toys and hanging placards bearing the slogan "Is No Fun, Is No Blinsky!"

Vallaki's toymaker, Gadof Blinsky (CG male human **commoner**), calls himself "a wizard of tiny wonders," but he has been consumed by despair lately because no one seems to like him or want his toys. His fascination for eerie playthings causes most other locals to avoid him. The burgomaster enables Blinsky to stay in business by giving him a couple of gold pieces a month to make festival decorations.

Blinsky is a heavyset man who wears a moth-eaten jester's cap during store hours, more out of habit than to humor visitors. In the past six months, the only paying customer who has set foot in the store is a visitor from a faraway land named Rictavio (see area N2), who came in two weeks ago and bought a stuffed Vistana doll. Realizing that the toymaker was lonely, Rictavio gave Blinsky his pet monkey, Piccolo (use the **baboon** stat block in the *Monster Manual*). Overjoyed, Blinsky has begun training the monkey to fetch toys from hard-to-reach shelves. The toymaker has also fitted Piccolo with a custom-tailored ballerina tutu.

When he meets new customers, Blinsky recites a well-rehearsed greeting: "Wyelcome, friends, to the House of Blinsky, where hyappiness and smiles can be bought at bargain prices. Perhaps you know a leetle child in need of joy? A leetle toy for a girl or boy?"

### Creepy Toys

Blinsky believes the burgomaster is right—that the only way to escape from Barovia is to make everyone in town "hyappy." Blinsky would like to do his part by making sure that all the children in Barovia have fun toys. On display are a few of his creations:

GADOF BLINSKY AND PICCOLO

- A headless doll that comes with a sack of attachable heads, including one with its eyes and mouth stitched shut (price 9 cp)
- A miniature gallows, complete with trapdoor and a weighted "hanged man" (price 9 cp)
- A set of wooden nesting dolls; the smaller each one gets, the older it gets, until the innermost doll is a mummified corpse (price 9 cp)
- A wood-and-string mobile of hanging bats with flapping wings (price 9 cp)
- A wind-up musical merry-go-round with figures of snarling wolves chasing children in place of prancing horses (price 9 sp)
- A ventriloquist's dummy that looks like Strahd von Zarovich (price 9 sp)
- A doll that looks remarkably like Ireena Kolyana (not for sale; see below)

**Ireena Kolyana Dolls.** Blinsky makes special dolls for the burgomaster's henchman, Izek Strazni (see area N3 and appendix D). Izek doesn't pay for the dolls but instead threatens to burn down Blinsky's shop unless the toymaker delivers a new doll every month. Every doll is modeled on a description given to Blinsky by Izek, and each doll has been closer to capturing Ireena's likeness than the last. Blinsky doesn't know that the doll is meant to be modeled after anyone in particular. If Ireena is with the party, however, Blinsky realizes that she is the inspiration for Izek's dolls.

**Von Weerg's Masterpiece.** Blinsky considers himself a student of a great inventor and toymaker named Fritz von Weerg. Blinsky has heard rumors that von Weerg's greatest invention—a clockwork man—lies somewhere in Castle Ravenloft. If the characters seem intent on going there, Blinsky asks if they would be so kind as to find the clockwork "myasterpiece" and "dyeliver" it to him, in exchange for which Blinsky offers to make them any toy they desire. Because "byusiness" has not been good, he says, he has no other reward to offer except, perhaps, his new monkey companion.

The shops and homes that enclose the town square are decorated with limp, tattered garlands and painted wooden boxes filled with tiny, dead flowers. At the north end of the square stands a row of stocks, locked in which are several men, women, and children wearing crude, plaster donkey heads.

In the center of the square, peasants in patchwork clothes eye you suspiciously as they use cups and vases to draw water from a crumbling stone fountain. Standing tall at the center of the fountain is a gray statue of an impressive man facing west. All around the square are posted proclamations:

> Come one, come all,
> to the greatest celebration of the year:
> THE WOLF'S HEAD JAMBOREE!
> Attendance and children required.
> Pikes will be provided.
> ALL WILL BE WELL!
> — The Baron —

The Wolf's Head Jamboree has already occurred, making the square's proclamations out of date. If the characters linger, they see the burgomaster's henchman, **Izek Strazni** (see appendix D), arrive with two town **guards**. Izek orders one guard to tear down all of the old proclamations while the other posts the following new one:

> COME ONE, COME ALL,
> to the greatest celebration of the year:
> THE FESTIVAL OF THE BLAZING SUN!
> Attendance and children required.
> Rain or shine.
> ALL WILL BE WELL!
> — The Baron —

Most Vallakians have no idea whom the statue in the square represents. The burgomaster claims it is Boris Vallakovich, his ancestor and the town's founder, but there's no noticeable family resemblance.

### DONKEY-HEADED CRIMINALS

The townsfolk in the stocks were arrested for "malicious unhappiness" (spreading negative opinions about the upcoming festival). An iron padlock secures each set of stocks, and Izek Strazni carries the keys on an iron ring.

Three men, two women, and two boys are trapped in the stocks—all of them tired, wet, and famished. The five adults have the statistics of human **commoners**, and the children are noncombatants. The plaster donkey heads they wear are meant to encourage ridicule.

Freeing one or more prisoners without the baron's consent is a crime. If the characters are witnessed doing

so, Izek rallies the town **guards** (twenty-four in all) and orders the characters to leave town at once or suffer the consequences. If the characters stand their ground, Izek orders the guards to beat them into submission, seize their weapons, and cast them out of Vallaki to be "food for the wolves."

If the characters are exiled from Vallaki without their weapons, the Keepers of the Feather (see area N2) snatch the party's belongings from under Izek's nose and see them safely returned to the characters.

If the guards fail to waylay the characters, Izek (if he's still around) flees to the burgomaster's mansion, giving the characters the run of the town. The townsfolk lock themselves in their homes, fearful that the characters aim to murder them.

## N9. VISTANI CAMP

Several footpaths and horse trails lead to this location in the woods southwest of Vallaki.

The woods part to reveal an expansive clearing: a small, grass-covered hill with low houses built into its sides. Fog obscures the details, but you can see that these buildings feature elegantly carved woodwork and have decorative lanterns hanging from their sculpted eaves. Atop the hill, above the fog, is a ring of barrel-topped wagons that surround a large tent with a column of smoke pouring out through a hole in the top. The tent is brightly lit from within. Even at this distance, you can smell the odors of wine and horses that emanate from this central area.

This natural clearing serves as a permanent campsite for the Vistani and their dusk elf allies.

### ROLEPLAYING THE VISTANI AND THE ELVES

Use the following information to roleplay the Vistani and the dusk elves that occupy the camp.

***Vistani.*** The Vistani in this camp all serve Strahd. The elders have died, leaving a pair of brothers named Luvash and Arrigal in charge. Both men are evil and willing to do whatever Strahd demands of them.

These Vistani have two problems. First, Luvash's seven-year-old daughter, Arabelle, recently disappeared from the camp. Consequently, half of the Vistani are out searching for her when the characters arrive. Second, the Vistani have exhausted their supply of wine and are eager to obtain more. Characters who help them with either problem earn the Vistani's respect.

***Dusk Elves.*** The dusk elf race is all but forgotten, and the few survivors live in secret places such as this. They have dark skin and hair, but otherwise they are similar to wood elves (as described in the *Player's Handbook*). One of Strahd's old brides, Patrina Velikovna, used to live here. Her brother, Kasimir Velikov, still does.

The dusk elves reside in small homes built into the hillside and are mostly self-sufficient. They are skilled trackers, and many of them are away from camp when the characters arrive, helping the Vistani search for

# Vistani Camp
## (Area N9)

One square = 10 feet

Arabelle. Strahd has tasked the Vistani with keeping an eye on the dusk elves, and the dusk elves know they aren't safe in Barovia without the Vistani's "protection." Strahd has also forbidden the Vistani from helping the dusk elves escape his domain.

There are no women or children among the dusk elves. Strahd had all the female dusk elves put to death around four centuries ago as a punishment for Patrina's murder. Thus, the remaining elves can't procreate. A broken people, they are aware of the vampire's absolute hold over the land of Barovia. They keep a low profile and have no desire to incur Strahd's wrath again.

## N9A. KASIMIR'S HOVEL

If the characters approach the house at the base of the hill on the eastern perimeter of the camp, read the following text:

> Standing quietly in front of this house, bathed in the warm light of its lanterns, are three sullen, gray-cloaked figures, their angular features and black, flowing hair half-hidden under their cowls.

The cloaked figures are three **guards** (N male dusk elves). If the characters seem friendly and are looking for someone to talk to, the guards direct them inside to Kasimir or point them toward the Vistani camp on the hilltop.

**Kasimir Velikov** (see appendix D) is the leader of the dusk elves. His hovel has a decorated vestibule and a comfortable room beyond with a fireplace. Wooden statuettes of elven deities stand in cubbyholes along one wall. A tapestry of a forest hangs on the opposite wall.

Kasimir confesses that he is burdened by dreams sent to him by his dead sister, Patrina Velikovna, whose spirit has languished in the catacombs below Castle Ravenloft for centuries. Kasimir believes that Patrina has repented for her many sins, and he yearns not only to free her but also to restore her to life.

If the characters seem intent on destroying Strahd, Kasimir tells them about the Amber Temple. Without divulging too much of the dreams sent to him by Patrina, Kasimir informs the characters that the secret to breaking Strahd's pact and freeing Barovia from its curse might be hidden there. Kasimir doesn't know whether this claim is true or not, but he states it as a way of persuading the characters to accompany him to the temple; his main objective, he says, is to find something there that he can use to bring Patrina back from the dead.

**Treasure.** Kasimir wears a *ring of warmth* and has a leather-bound spellbook containing all the spells he has prepared (see appendix D) plus the following spells: *arcane lock*, *comprehend languages*, *hold person*, *identify*, *locate object*, *nondetection*, *polymorph*, *protection from evil and good*, and *wall of stone*.

### FORTUNES OF RAVENLOFT

If your card reading reveals that a treasure is here, it is in Kasimir's possession. He relinquishes it if the characters promise to accompany him to the Amber Temple

and help him find a way to bring his sister Patrina back from the dead.

## N9B. DUSK ELF HOVELS

Six simple houses ring the base of the hill, three protruding from the north side and three from the south side.

> A grim, gray-cloaked figure stands in front of the door to this house.

The cloaked figure is a **guard** (N male dusk elf). If the characters appear friendly and are looking for someone to talk to, the guard directs them to Kasimir's hovel (area N9a). Under no circumstances does the guard willingly allow strangers to enter the house he protects.

Each hovel is configured similarly to Kasimir's hovel. All are currently unoccupied. (Except for the nine guards left behind to watch the homes, the dusk elves are out searching for Arabelle.)

## N9C. VISTANI TENT

> Piled outside the wagon are several empty casks of wine. From inside the tent comes the crack of a whip followed by the howls of a young man. Three sputtering campfires fill the tent with smoke, and through the haze you see six Vistani passed out in various places on the dead grass. A barely conscious and shirtless teenager hugs the central tent pole, his wrists bound with rope and his back streaked with blood. An older, larger man in studded leather armor lashes the young man with a horsewhip, causing him to scream again. Standing in the bigger man's shadow is a third man also clad in studded leather. "Easy, brother," he says to the whip-wielding brute. "I think Alexei has learned his lesson."

The two men in studded leather armor are the leaders of the Vistani camp—the brothers Luvash (CE male human **bandit captain**) and Arrigal (NE male human **assassin**). If you used the "Plea for Help" adventure hook, the characters have already met Arrigal. Luvash is the older of the two and the brother whom the other Vistani fear most. Each brother carries a key that unlocks one of the padlocks of the treasure wagon (area N9i).

Luvash is punishing a Vistana named Alexei (CN male human **bandit** with 3 hit points remaining) for failing to keep a watchful eye on his daughter. The characters' arrival distracts Luvash, and he forgets about Alexei long enough to play the role of host—until such time as the characters become tiresome or threatening. Alexei blames himself for not watching the little brat more closely and has accepted his punishment. If the characters try to rescue him, he screams at them to stop, not wanting to appear weak in front of Luvash and Arrigal.

In addition to Luvash, Arrigal, and Alexei, there are six intoxicated Vistani (CN male and female human

LUVASH

ARRIGAL

**bandits**) lying unconscious in the tent. A drunk Vistana awakens only if the Vistana takes 5 damage or more and has at least 1 hit point remaining afterward.

***Dealing with Luvash.*** Luvash is unhappy because his seven-year-old daughter, Arabelle, has vanished. She's been gone for a little more than a day. Because everyone in the camp was drunk and Arrigal was away, no one remembers seeing or hearing anything strange. Luvash is determined to find her, no matter what the cost, and most of his camp is out scouring the woods when the characters arrive. (Missing from the camp are twelve **bandits**. Each hour that passes, 1d4 of them return to camp with no news on Arabelle's whereabouts.)

If an alarm is sounded, nine Vistani **bandits** (NE male and female humans) emerge from three of the surrounding wagons (area N9g) and arrive at the tent with weapons drawn in 2 rounds.

Luvash won't meddle in the characters' affairs without Strahd's consent, and he is quite content to let the vampire deal with them. For a hefty price, he offers to sell the characters potions that allow safe passage through the deadly fog that surrounds the valley; he keeps them in the treasure wagon (area N9i). The potions don't work, of course.

If the characters rescue Arabelle from Lake Zarovich (chapter 2, area L) and see her safely returned to camp, Luvash is overjoyed and offers to repay the favor. He doesn't sell them the fake potions. ("Um, they aren't as potent as they could be.") Instead, he lets them choose a treasure from the Vistani treasure wagon (area N9i).

If the characters ask something of the Vistani but have not earned Luvash's goodwill, he agrees to do business with them if they accomplish one of two tasks: either find his missing daughter or procure six barrels of wine and bring them to the camp. Luvash suggests they can

get the wine in Vallaki, or go straight to the source—the Wizard of Wines winery. He isn't picky when it comes to the quality of the wine.

***Dealing with Arrigal.*** Arrigal is a much more dangerous creature than his brute of a brother. If the characters have something in their possession that is either useful or harmful to Strahd and Arrigal becomes aware of it, he tries to deprive the characters of this item, stalking them if necessary and going as far as to kill one or more of them if he thinks he can escape with the item in his possession. If he succeeds, he takes one of the riding horses (area N9d) and delivers the item to Strahd at Castle Ravenloft.

## N9D. HORSES

> The hilltop is covered with steaming piles of horse dung. More than two dozen horses are tethered to stone blocks inside the circle of wagons but outside the tent. Most of the animals are draft horses, but a few of them are riding horses equipped with saddles.

Twenty-four **draft horses** and six **riding horses** are tethered here.

## N9E. LUVASH'S WAGON

> This barrel-topped wagon is nicer that the others. Drapes of golden silk hang in the windows, and the wheels have gold, sun-shaped hubcaps. An iron chimney pipe protrudes from the roof.

Luvash's wagon is a mess inside. Empty wineskins, dirty clothes, and mangy furs are strewn about. A small hammock strung across the width of the wagon under the driver's seat serves as Arabelle's bed. A burlap doll with button eyes lies in the hammock; Arabelle has no other possessions.

A small iron stove in the middle of the wagon keeps the interior warm.

***Treasure.*** The wagon's "golden sun" hubcaps are worth 125 gp apiece (500 gp total).

## N9F. WAGON OF SLEEPING VISTANI
There are four of these wagons at the camp.

> You hear heavy snores from within this barrel-topped wagon.

Each of these wagons contains 1d4 sleeping Vistani (CN male and female human **bandits**). These Vistani wake up if their wagon is shaken or if they take damage and have at least 1 hit point remaining.

## N9G. WAGON OF GAMBLING VISTANI
There are three of these wagons at the camp.

> Loud voices and laughter spill from this barrel-topped wagon.

Each of these wagons contains three Vistani (CN male and female human **bandits**). The Vistani are playing a dice game for favors, since they have no money. They respond to sounds of alarm by drawing their weapons and heading to the tent (area N9c).

### N9H. VISTANI FAMILY WAGON

There are three of these wagons at the camp.

> This barrel-topped wagon is filled with the raucous screams and laughter of children.

Each of these wagons contains one Vistani adult (male or female human **commoner**) and 1d4 + 1 Vistani children (male and female human noncombatants). The adult is watching the children playing games, teaching the children about their heritage, or telling a scary story to frighten the children.

### N9I. VISTANI TREASURE WAGON

> Two iron padlocks secure the door of this barrel-topped wagon.

The Vistani keep all their treasure in this wagon. The door to the wagon has two locks, each of which requires a different key. Luvash carries one key, Arrigal the other. Each lock is rigged with a poison needle trap (see "Sample Traps" in chapter 5, "Adventure Environments," of the *Dungeon Master's Guide*).

**Treasure.** The wagon contains the following items:

- A wooden chest containing 1,200 ep (each coin stamped with the profiled visage of Strahd)
- An iron chest containing 650 gp
- An onyx jewelry box with gold filigree (worth 250 gp) containing six pieces of cheap jewelry (worth 50 gp each) and a *potion of poison* in an unlabeled crystal vial (worth 100 gp)
- A wooden throne with gold inlay and decorative stones (worth 750 gp)
- A rolled-up 10-foot-square rug with an exquisite unicorn motif (worth 750 gp)
- A small wooden box containing twelve fake potions in stoppered gourds (the Vistani sell these nonmagical elixirs to naive strangers, claiming that they protect against the deadly fog surrounding Barovia)

#### FORTUNES OF RAVENLOFT

If your card reading reveals that a treasure is here, it is lying amid the other items in the wagon.

## SPECIAL EVENTS

Any of the following events can occur while the characters are staying in Vallaki.

## FESTIVAL OF THE BLAZING SUN

The Festival of the Blazing Sun takes place three days after the characters first arrive in Vallaki. You can delay the festival if the characters get waylaid or drawn elsewhere, or you can advance the timeline if the characters seem to be in a hurry.

> Under threatening skies, a parade of unhappy children dressed as flowers trudges through the muddy streets, leading the way for a group of sorry-looking men and women carrying a ten-foot-diameter wicker ball. The burgomaster and his smiling wife, who holds a sad bouquet of wilting flowers, follow the procession on horseback. As weary spectators watch from their stoops, the ball is borne to the town square. There, it is hoisted and hung from a fifteen-foot-high wooden scaffold, and townsfolk take turns splashing it with oil. Before the wicker sun can be set ablaze, the sky tears open in a sudden downpour. "All will be well!" cries the burgomaster as he brandishes a sputtering torch and marches defiantly through the rain toward the wicker ball, only to have his torch go out as he thrusts it into the sphere.
>
> A singular laugh erupts from the crowd, drawing the burgomaster's fiery gaze as well as gasps from the townsfolk.

The laugh comes from Lars Kjurls (LG male human **guard**), a member of the town militia. The other guards are aghast at Lars's ill-timed outburst. The burgomaster immediately has Lars arrested for "spite." Unless the characters intervene, Lars is bound at the ankles and wrists, then dragged behind the burgomaster's horse for the "amusement" of all. The burgomaster rides the horse himself.

### DEVELOPMENT

If the characters challenge the burgomaster in any way, he orders them banished from Vallaki. If they protest, he orders the guards to arrest them, deprive them of their weapons, and force them out of Vallaki at sword point.

If the characters lose their weapons, the Keepers of the Feather (see area N2) eventually steal back the weapons and return them to the characters.

If the guards fail in their duty, the burgomaster retreats to his mansion and the townsfolk flee to their homes, giving the characters free rein in town.

## TYGER, TYGER

Karl and Nikolai Wachter (see areas N2 and N4) are young, foolish men from a proud noble family. The drunken brothers sneak into Arasek's Stockyard (area N5) while everyone else is attending the festival in the town square. On a dare, one of them rocks the wagon. The saber-toothed tiger locked inside becomes enraged and smashes through the wagon door. The characters and everyone else in town hear the screams of the young men as the tiger escapes. The tiger flees the stockyard without harming the Wachters and begins to prowl the streets, looking for an escape. Reports of a tiger running loose in the streets ruin the festival and send townsfolk scurrying for their homes.

The saber-toothed tiger doesn't harm anyone until it takes damage, whereupon it attacks the perceived source of the damage. If he is still alive, Izek Strazni gathers six town guards and hunts down the beast with the intention of killing it. Meanwhile, Rictavio does his best to lure the beast back to his wagon while assuring townsfolk that it won't harm them.

### DEVELOPMENT

If he's still in power, the burgomaster conducts an investigation to find out where the tiger came from. Guards and local witnesses are questioned. The Wachter boys feign innocence, insisting that they were at the festival, but Gunther and Yelena Arasek (area N5) admit to hearing "evil growls" and scratching sounds coming from inside the carnival wagon parked in their stockyard. When pressed, the Araseks admit to seeing the wagon's "weird owner" routinely drop food into the wagon through a hatch in the roof. They also confess that the half-elf paid them for their silence.

After the burgomaster learns that the tiger belongs to Rictavio, he commands his guards to arrest the mysterious bard. If Rictavio thinks the characters can help him, he asks them to distract the burgomaster and the guards while he gathers his horse, wagon, and tiger (in that order). If the characters ask Rictavio where he plans to go, he tells them about an old tower to the west where he can lie low (see chapter 11, "Van Richten's Tower").

## LADY WACHTER'S WISH

Ernst Larnak (see area N4) begins shadowing the characters. Characters who have a passive Wisdom (Perception) score of 14 or higher notice him doing so. If they confront him, he claims that he keeps a watchful eye on all strangers, though he doesn't mention the name of his employer. If the characters threaten him, he backs off and reports to Lady Wachter after he believes he's not being watched or pursued.

Lady Wachter is looking for powerful allies to help her oust the burgomaster. If Ernst tells her that he thinks the characters fit the bill, Lady Wachter has Ernst or her sons invite the characters to a private dinner at Wachterhaus. During the dinner, Lady Wachter determines whether the characters have the ability and the resolve to crush the baron.

If the characters refuse her invitation, or if they profess to be enemies of Strahd, Lady Wachter marks them as her enemies and sets out to destroy them without incriminating herself.

### DEVELOPMENT

Once she determines that the characters are her enemies, Lady Wachter hands Ernst a bag of 100 gp (taken from area N4q) and instructs him to deliver it to the Vistani camp outside town (area N9), along with a letter from her that asks the Vistani to dispose of the characters once they have left town. The Vistani burn the letter after reading it, as per Lady Wachter's request.

If the characters have rescued Arabelle (see chapter 2, area L), the Vistani return Lady Wachter's gold to Ernst and do nothing.

Otherwise, a Vistana bandit watches the road east of Vallaki and reports back to camp if the characters are sighted leaving. The Vistani, worried that the characters might be more than a match for them, send one emissary on horseback to race ahead of the characters and inform Strahd. If Arrigal is alive, he makes the ride himself. Otherwise, the rider is a young Vistana bandit named Alexei (see area N9c).

## ST. ANDRAL'S FEAST

The characters can prevent this special event from occurring by returning the bones of St. Andral to the church (area N1) or by destroying the vampire spawn hiding in the coffin maker's shop (area N6). If the characters stay in Vallaki for three days or more and don't retrieve the bones or destroy the vampire spawn, Strahd visits the coffin maker's shop the following evening and orchestrates an attack on the church.

The vampire spawn begin the attack that night. They cling to the outer walls and roof of St. Andral's church while four **swarms of bats** enter the church through the belfry and terrify the congregation. As the townsfolk flee the church, the vampire spawn leap down and attack them.

During the chaos, Strahd enters the church in bat form, then reverts to vampire form and attacks Father Lucian. Unless the characters intervene, Strahd kills the priest before returning to Castle Ravenloft.

If Father Lucian dies, locals bury his body in the church cemetery, whereupon it rises the following night as a **vampire spawn** under Strahd's control. If Rictavio (area N2) learns of the priest's death, he suggests that the characters burn the priest's body to ensure that it doesn't rise from the dead.

### DEVELOPMENT

The attack on St. Andral's church terrorizes and demoralizes the town. After a few days, fear turns to misdirected rage as townsfolk blame the burgomaster. Baron Vallakovich's "All will be well!" mantra can't protect him from their wrath. Barring intervention by the characters, the burgomaster's mansion is set ablaze, and the baron, his wife, and his son are dragged to the town square, thrown in the stocks, and stoned to death. If he is alive, Izek Strazni flees the town to avoid a similar fate. Where he hides is up to you, but likely locations include Old Bonegrinder (chapter 6), Argynvostholt (chapter 7), or the ruins of Berez (chapter 10).

If the characters thwart the attack on the church and protect Father Lucian, Strahd pays a visit to Wachterhaus (area N4) and there composes a letter, which he asks Lady Wachter to deliver to the characters. The letter is written in Strahd's hand and extends an invitation to the characters to come to Castle Ravenloft. Lady Wachter orders her spy, Ernst Larnak, or one of her sons to take the letter to the characters. If the characters open and read it, show the players "Strahd's Invitation" in appendix F. If the characters head toward the castle, they have no threatening random encounters on the way.

# CHAPTER 6: OLD BONEGRINDER

NCE A GRAIN MILL THAT SERVED VALLAKI, this slouching windmill is now home to three night hags: Morgantha and her wretched daughters, Bella Sunbane and Offalia Wormwiggle. The hags are trapped in Barovia, but they like it here. Using their Change Shape action to look like Barovian women—a frumpy mother and her two homely daughters—the hags snatch children, devour them, and use the windmill's grindstone to crush their little bones into powder. This powder is a key ingredient in the hags' dream pastries, which they offer to Barovian adults who are desperate to escape Strahd's domain.

Made with the bones of the innocent, the hags' dream pastries allow Barovians to enter a trance, wherein they can escape to heavenly places full of joy. When adults can no longer afford the hag's dream pastries, the hags offer to trade their pastries for the Barovians' children, thus preying on the adults' selfishness while acquiring the ingredients they need to make more pastries. This is how the hags sow corruption in Strahd's domain and why they don't take the children by force. The hags are interested only in children who have souls. They prick each child with a needle; if the child cries, that's a sign that the infant has a soul.

## MORGANTHA'S COVEN

The hags possess the shared spellcasting abilities of a coven (see the "Hag Covens" sidebar in the hags entry in the *Monster Manual*). If one or more hags die, the coven is broken. Morgantha tolerates her daughters only because they help her complete the coven. If one of them dies, Morgantha sets out to abduct and consume a human child so that she can give birth to a new daughter (as described in the *Monster Manual*).

Morgantha gave her coven's *hag eye* to Cyrus Belview, Strahd's disfigured manservant (see chapter 4, area K62), so that she could spy on Castle Ravenloft and keep an eye on the vampire. The hags are fearful of Strahd and respect his dominion over this land. For more information on the *hag eye*, see the hags entry in the *Monster Manual*.

DREAMS ARE FOR THE LIVING.
—Strahd von Zarovich

## DREAM PASTRIES

These pastries look and taste like small mincemeat pies. A creature that eats one in its entirety must succeed on a DC 16 Constitution saving throw or fall into a trance that lasts for 1d4 + 4 hours, during which time the creature is incapacitated and has a speed of 0 feet. The trance ends if the affected creature takes any damage or if someone else uses an action to shake the creature out of its stupor.

While in the trance, the creature dreams of being in some joyous place, far removed from the evils of the world. The places and characters in the dream are vivid and believable, and when the dream ends, the affected creature experiences a longing to return to the place.

## APPROACHING THE WINDMILL

The windmill's stone walls are easily climbed. Wooden floors separate the various levels. There are no lights within, since the hags have darkvision.

> The Old Svalich Road transitions here from being a winding path through the Balinok Mountains to a lazy trail that hugs the mountainside as it descends into a fog-filled valley. In the heart of the valley you see a walled town near the shores of a great mountain lake, its waters dark and still. A branch in the road leads west to a promontory, atop which is perched a dilapidated stone windmill, its warped wooden vanes stripped bare.

Closer investigation of the windmill yields a few more details:

> The onion-domed edifice leans forward and to one side, as though trying to turn away from the stormy gray sky. You see gray brick walls and dirt-covered windows on the upper floors. A decrepit wooden platform encircles the windmill above a flimsy doorway leading to the building's interior. Perched on a wooden beam above the door is a raven. It hops about and squawks at you, seemingly agitated.

A character who succeeds on a DC 12 Wisdom (Insight) check senses that the **raven** is trying to warn the party. After delivering its message, the raven flies off toward Vallaki, the town in the valley below (see chapter 5).

Beyond the windmill is the forest. Once atop the windmill's hill, the characters can see a ring of four squat megaliths at the forest's edge. Ravens can be seen circling in the air above the stones, which are described at the end of the chapter.

## Areas of the Windmill

The following areas correspond to labels on the map of Old Bonegrinder on page 127.

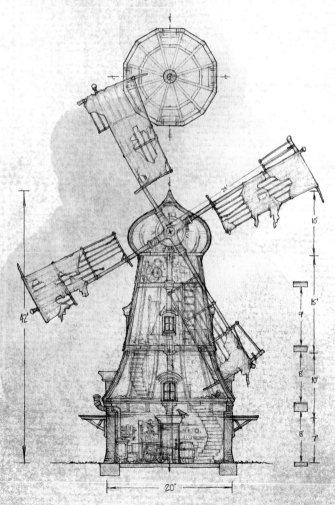

## O1. Ground Floor

> The ground floor has been converted into a makeshift kitchen, but the room is filthy. Baskets and old dishware are piled everywhere. Adding to the clutter is a peddler's cart, a chicken coop, a heavy wooden trunk, and a pretty wooden cabinet with flowers painted on its doors. In addition to the clucking of the chickens, you hear toads croaking.
>
> The sweet smell of pastries blends horridly with a stench that burns your nostrils. The awful odor comes out of an open, upright barrel in the center of the room.
>
> Warmth issues from a brick oven against one wall, and a crumbling staircase ascends the wall across from it. Shrieks and cackles from somewhere higher up cause the old mill to shudder.

The ceiling here is 8 feet high. If the characters explore the room, read:

> Small human bones litter the flagstone floor.

Baking in the oven are a dozen dream pastries. Morgantha checks on them every 10 minutes. The staircase curls up to area O2.

The barrel holds glistening, greenish-black demon ichor. Morgantha can use the barrel as a font for a *scrying* spell. She can also knock on the barrel three times as an action to summon a **dretch**. The demon crawls out of the barrel at the end of Morgantha's turn and obeys the night hag's commands for 1 hour, after which it dissolves into a pool of ichor. Morgantha can summon up to nine dretches in this manner before the ichor is gone.

Morgantha's cabinet contains wooden bowls full of herbs and baking ingredients, including flour, sugar, and several gourds of powdered bone. Hanging on the inside of the cabinet doors are a dozen locks of hair. Amid various concoctions are three small, labeled containers that hold elixirs. The first elixir, labeled "Youth," is a golden syrup that magically makes the imbiber appear younger and more attractive for 24 hours. The second elixir, labeled "Laughter," is a nonmagical red tea that infects the imbiber with cackle fever (see "Diseases" in chapter 8, "Running the Game," of the *Dungeon Master's Guide*). The third elixir, a greenish milky liquid labeled "Mother's Milk," is actually a dose of pale tincture (see "Poisons" in chapter 8 of the *Dungeon Master's Guide*).

The chicken coop contains three chickens, a rooster, and a few laid eggs.

The wooden trunk has tiny holes bored into its lid and contains a hundred croaking **toads**. Several toads escape if the lid is lifted, but they are harmless.

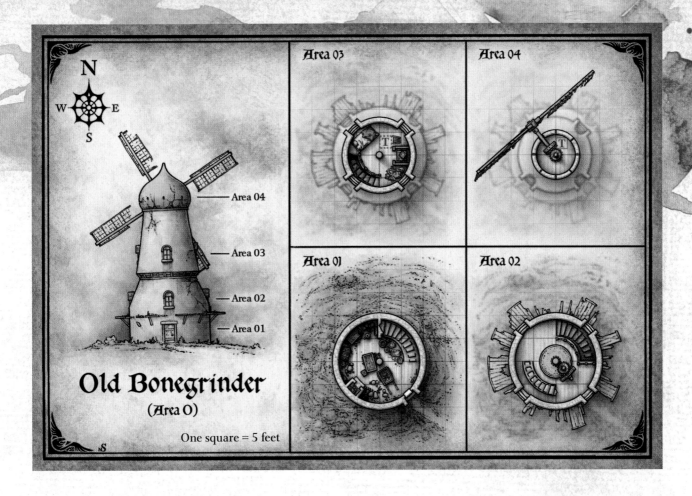

**Old Bonegrinder**
(Area O)

N
W E
S

One square = 5 feet

Area 03

Area 04

Area 01

Area 02

Area 04

Area 03

Area 02

Area 01

## O2. Bone Mill

Unless she has been lured elsewhere, Morgantha is encountered here. This is where she grinds children's bones to make the powder for her dream pastries.

> A haggard, heavyset old woman with a face as wrinkled as a boiled apple sweeps the floor, pushing around a few old bones and stirring up a cloud of white dust with her broom. She wears a bloodstained, flour-caked apron. A long, sharp bodkin impales her bundled-up mound of gray hair.
>
> The dirt-caked windows allow very little light to enter this eight-foot-high chamber, most of which is taken up by a large millstone connected to a wooden gear shaft that rises through the ceiling in the center of the room. A stone staircase continues up, toward the sound of loud cackling.

The old woman is Morgantha, a **night hag**. She doesn't mind visitors, as long as they've come to do business. She tries to sell her latest batch of dream pastries, charging 1 gp for each one. She's proud of her confections and claims that she uses only the finest ingredients. If the characters seem uninterested in her wares, she bellows, "Begone!" If they attack or refuse to leave, she calls out to her daughters and turns to fight.

The hags operate the millstone manually, since the arms of the windmill no longer function.

## O3. Bedroom

The **night hags** Bella Sunbane and Offalia Wormwiggle are here, unless they have been drawn elsewhere.

> Dancing around a thick wooden gear shaft in the center of this cramped, circular room are two ugly young women wearing silk shawls and gowns of stitched flesh. Long needles stick out of their tangled mops of black hair. The women cackle with glee.
>
> In a rotting wooden closet are three crates, stacked one atop another, with small doors set into them. Next to the closet is a heap of discarded clothing. A ladder climbs to a wooden trapdoor in the nine-foot-high ceiling. A moldy bed with a tattered canopy stands nearby.

Morgantha's daughters are repulsive even in their human guises. When they are not singing, dancing, or telling terrible jokes to one another, they are pricking captured children with needles to make them cry. Any attempt to free the children incurs the hags' wrath.

The discarded clothing belongs to children whom the night hags have already devoured. The trapdoor in the ceiling can be pushed open to reveal area O4.

Each crate is 3 feet square. The top one is empty, but the middle and lower ones each contain a captive child.

The outward-facing side of each crate is fitted with a small door that has an iron latch and iron hinges. It can be unlatched and opened easily from the outside.

The two captured children (LG male and female noncombatants) were taken from the village of Barovia after being given to the hags by their parents in exchange for dream pastries. The boy, Freek, is seven years old. The girl, Myrtle, is barely five. Their crates are full of crumbs, as the hags are fattening them up. If freed, neither child wants to go home, because of what their parents did. They both speak kindly of Ismark and Ireena in Barovia, hoping to be taken to them.

### Treasure

The hags don't use the bed for sleeping, but they store their treasure in it. Six pieces of cheap jewelry (worth 25 gp each) are stuffed in the moldy straw mattress.

## O4. Domed Attic

> You've reached the windmill's peak—a domed chamber filled with old machinery. There's not much room to move around. Light slips into this attic through small holes in the walls.

Characters searching this space find a few old, abandoned bird's nests.

### Fortunes of Ravenloft

If your card reading reveals that a treasure is here, it's easy to find, either tucked in a bird's nest or buried under some dirt in a corner.

## The Megaliths

The four ancient stones near the windmill were erected centuries ago by the valley's original human inhabitants. Each moss-covered stone bears a crude carving of a city, each of which is associated with a different season. The city of winter is shown covered with snow, the city of spring is arrayed in flowers, the city of summer has a sunburst overhead, and the city of autumn is covered with leaves. If the characters ask any of the priests or scholarly NPCs in Barovia about the stones, the characters are told that ancient legends tell of the Four Cities, said to be the cities of paradise where the Morninglord, Mother Night, and the other ancient gods first dwelled.

Several ravens circle overhead, and one pecks at something on top of the stone that depicts the city of autumn. Upon inspection, the characters see the raven is pecking at a dream pastry, and on the ground in the center of the stone circle is a small pile of children's teeth. The hags placed these here to desecrate the stones and as an offering to the entity they worship, the wicked archfey Ceithlenn of the Crooked Teeth.

# CHAPTER 7: ARGYNVOSTHOLT

WHEN STRAHD DROVE HIS ENEMIES INTO the valley long ago, determined to annihilate them, the last thing he expected to encounter was a silver dragon.

The dragon, who called himself Argynvost, had come to the valley years earlier in the guise of a nobleman named Lord Argynvost. The dragon didn't lair in the valley solely because of its idyllic beauty. He knew of a place called the Amber Temple—a repository of evil power guarded by the forces of good. Argynvost wanted to make sure that whatever was trapped inside the Amber Temple wouldn't be allowed to escape, so he built his fortified mansion, Argynvostholt, close by.

Like many silver dragons, Argynvost was extraordinarily wealthy, and he was comfortable living among humans while disguised as one of them. He used his resources to attract other champions of good, and valorous knights flocked to the valley to join Lord Argynvost's prestigious Order of the Silver Dragon. Only those who were initiated into the order were told of Lord Argynvost's true nature.

During the war between Strahd and his foes, the Order of the Silver Dragon drove away malefactors searching for the Amber Temple. It also sheltered Strahd's enemies and proved more than a match for Strahd's battle-weary soldiers. But the early victories of the order didn't win the war. Even with Argynvost on their side, the knights were ultimately overwhelmed when Strahd's reinforcements swept into the valley. Those forces slew the last of the knights and battled the dragon inside Argynvostholt. After the dragon was slain, Strahd had its corpse hacked to pieces, stripped to the bone, and transported to Castle Ravenloft as a trophy.

Since the dragon's death, Argynvostholt has become a haunted ruin, a former bastion of nobility and light turned into a place of desolation and unrest.

## THE ORDER OF THE SILVER DRAGON

The death of Argynvost enraged the spirit of Vladimir Horngaard, the greatest of the dragon's knights. Horngaard returned as a revenant and swore to avenge the destruction of the order. His zeal was so great that it also brought back the spirits of several other knights, who rose as revenants under Vladimir's command.

The vengeful revenants killed many of Strahd's soldiers, and whenever the undead knights were cut down, their spirits found new corpses to inhabit. Though the knights were grossly outnumbered, they waged war for months and slew hundreds of foes.

When Strahd died and became a vampire, Vladimir's knights should have gone to their everlasting rest, but their spirits couldn't leave Strahd's domain. They marched to Castle Ravenloft and were confronted by the Vistani seer Madam Eva, who told them Strahd had died, only to become a prisoner in his own land, tormented by the death of his beloved Tatyana and the murder of his brother Sergei.

After receiving that news, Vladimir ceased his advance and led his knights back to Argynvostholt. He realized that Strahd had already died and been damned to a hell of his own creation. With nowhere else to go and nothing else to do, Vladimir set his knights to killing Strahd's agents and anyone else who might help to ease Strahd's torment. Consumed by hatred, the knights have lost their honor and nobility. Their redemption hinges on whether Vladimir can set aside that hatred. The undead knight can be found brooding in the ruins of Argynvostholt.

I WAS LOOKING AT DEAD MEN. BEFORE *another hour passed, I'd send them wailing on their way to rotting hell. All of them.*

—Strahd von Zarovich
in *I, Strahd: The Memoirs of a Vampire*

129

The spirit of the dragon Argynvost isn't at rest, either. It can sense that the knights have been corrupted, and it reaches out to the characters, hoping they will help the knights find peace. If the characters retrieve the dragon's skull from Castle Ravenloft and place it in the mausoleum of Argynvostholt, the dragon's spirit ascends to the highest tower of the mansion and transforms into a beacon of light that flashes across Barovia. The light of the beacon reminds Vladimir Horngaard of what he has lost, enabling him and his fellow knights to let go of their hatred and find both redemption and rest.

# APPROACHING THE MANSION

A winding branch of the Old Svalich Road meanders up the forested slope of a mountain spur to the old mansion, which is perched on high ground overlooking the Svalich Woods and the Luna River valley.

When the characters first come within sight of Argynvostholt, read:

> High above the river valley juts a quiet promontory upon which looms a sepulchral mansion, its turrets capped with fairytale cones, its towers lined with sculpted battlements. A third of the structure has collapsed, as has part of the roof, but the rest appears intact. A dark, octagonal tower rises above the surrounding architecture.
>
> Out of the fog comes a distant peal of thunder, quickly accompanied by the howling of wolves in the woods below, but the house stands silent, seeming like the fossilized remains of some long-dead thing smote upon the mountainside.

# AREAS OF ARGYNVOSTHOLT

The following areas correspond to labels on the maps of Argynvostholt on page 131 and 137.

## Q1. DRAGON STATUE

> Perched atop a ten-foot-wide, ten-foot-high cube of granite is a moss-covered statue of a dragon, its wings tucked close to its body. The statue looks east, toward the mansion.

The fog makes it hard to see the dragon's features from a distance, but close inspection reveals that it's a silver dragon of noble bearing, its spiny frill cracked and broken in many places. The statue is 10 feet tall but looks much more imposing perched on the granite block.

If scrutinized with a *detect magic* spell, the statue radiates an aura of evocation magic. The dragon statue used to breathe a cone of cold as part of a magic trap, but the trap no longer works (see area Q2).

## Q2. MAIN ENTRANCE

> Flagstone steps flanked by stone railings climb to a landing in front of a pair of tall, wooden doors with rusted iron bands and knockers shaped like small dragons. Carved into the lintel above the entrance is the word ARGYNVOSTHOLT.

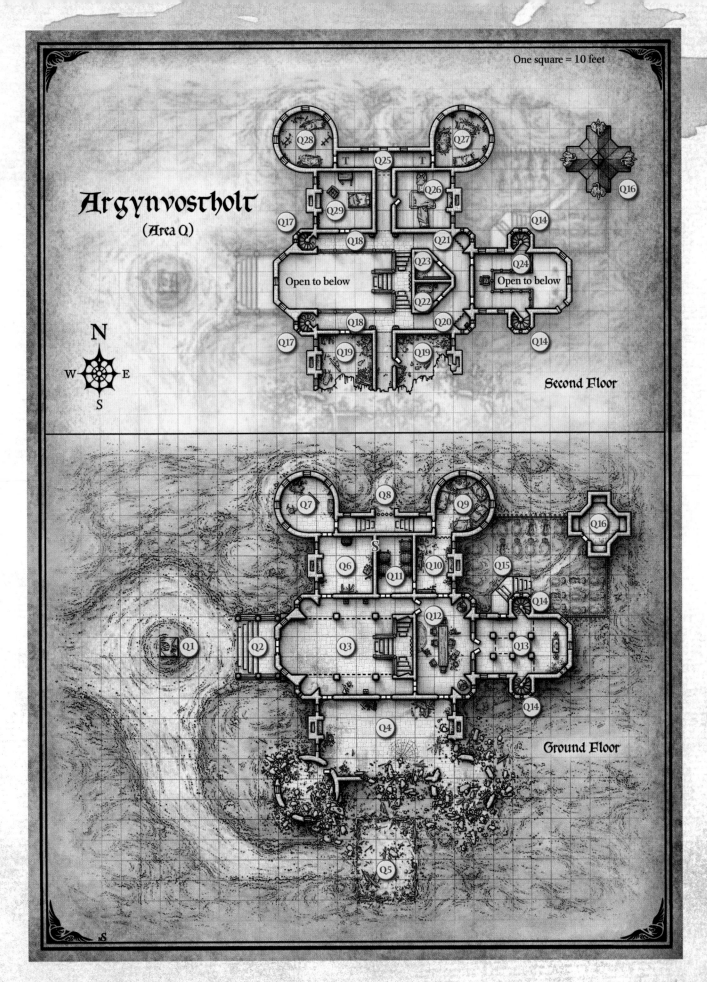

# Argynvostholt
## (Area Q)

One square = 10 feet

Second Floor

Ground Floor

N
W · E
S

If a creature climbs the steps or sets foot on the landing, the dragon statue (area Q1) opens its mouth and exhales a 60-foot cone of harmless cold air, then closes its mouth and doesn't activate again until the next dawn. At one time, the statue would breathe a cone of ice and hail, but its magic has deteriorated over the years.

The doors are unlocked and can be pushed open to reveal a dark foyer (area Q3).

## Q3. DRAGON'S FOYER

> This room feels like a king's tomb. A grand staircase leads up to stone balconies held aloft by stone pillars and arches. A tall, faded tapestry depicting a nobleman in silver armor hangs from an iron rod above the staircase landing.
>
> Six sets of double doors lead from this foyer. Along the walls, displayed on marble pedestals, are three alabaster busts of handsome men. A fourth bust and its pedestal have been knocked over, and their shattered remains lie strewn across the mosaic floor. Two chandeliers of wrought iron hang from the ceiling like monstrous black spiders.

The tapestry is torn in places and worthless. It is a portrait of Lord Argynvost. The alabaster busts depict several of the dragon's other human guises. The stairs lead up to the second-floor balconies (area Q18).

### SHADOW OF ARGYNVOST
The first time the characters pass through this foyer, read:

> A great shadow with wings moves across the walls and disappears. You hear the soft bestial hiss in the darkness.

The draconic shadow is ominous yet harmless.

## Q4. SPIDERS' BALLROOM

> Rubble is strewn throughout much of this vast chamber, caused by the partial collapse of the rooms above it. On the pink marble floor, fallen chandeliers lie amid broken chairs and other furnishings. Thick webs stretch from wall to wall, and moving among them are too many giant spiders to count!

Nine **giant spiders** nest here. They attack anyone who gets too close.

## Q5. RUINED STABLE

> Here lie the blackened beams of a wooden stable, burned to its stone foundation. Looming above the wreckage is the partially collapsed south end of the mansion, all three of its floors exposed to the elements.

There is nothing of value in the stable.

## Q6. DRAGON'S DEN

> This wood-paneled den has been ransacked, its furnishings tossed about. A cold, dark hearth dominates the west wall between two narrow windows. Standing upright against the north wall is a sarcophagus made of black wood with a queen's effigy carved into its lid.

Argynvost had the empty sarcophagus converted into a wine cabinet. Now, only shattered wineglasses and decanters are to be found on the shelves. The den's other furnishings include rotted divans, broken chairs, overturned ottomans, and smashed oil lamps.

A secret door at the north end of the east wall can be pushed open to reveal a storage room (area Q11).

### LIVING FIRE
If the beacon of Argynvostholt (area Q53) has not been lit, read the following text when the characters approach the fireplace for the first time:

> A fire erupts in the dead hearth and assumes a draconic form. It hisses, crackles, and unfurls its smoky wings.

Have the player characters roll initiative. The fire acts on initiative count 10 and has AC 15, 1 hit point, and immunity to fire, poison, and psychic damage. If it is reduced to 0 hit points, it explodes and fills the room with fire, setting fire to the dry furnishings. Each creature in the room must make a DC 12 Dexterity saving throw, taking 22 (4d10) fire damage on a failed save, or half as much damage on a successful one.

The fire doesn't attack. On its first turn, if it has not been reduced to 0 hit points, it speaks:

> The fiery dragon hisses as it addresses you. "My knights have fallen into darkness. Save them if you can. Show them the light they have lost!" With that, the fire burns out.

The dragon refers to the Order of the Silver Dragon and the beacon (area Q53).

## Q7. Parlor

> Tattered velvet drapes cover the tall, slender windows that encircle this parlor. The furnishings are covered with dust and cobwebs, and lie in disarray. A damaged brass chandelier hangs from the ceiling, which is covered with a faded mural that depicts metallic dragons and colorful birds flying beneath white clouds.

Time and neglect have damaged the furnishings, leaving nothing of value.

## Q8. Iron Gate

An iron gate, chained shut, closes off a 10-foot-tall archway on the north wall of the mansion. The key to the chain's padlock was lost long ago, but the lock can be picked by someone who uses thieves' tools and makes a successful DC 20 Dexterity check. The old lock can be smashed by a character who uses a bludgeoning or slashing weapon on it and makes a successful DC 15 Strength check.

Ten-foot-high flights of stone steps to the west and east of the archway lead up to landings and doors that provide access to areas Q7 and Q9.

## Q9. Servants' Quarters

> Tattered brown drapes cover the windows of this circular room, and a heavy curtain hangs across an archway to the south. Strewn about the floor is the wreckage of half a dozen beds and other pieces of furniture.

Lord Argynvost's household staff once slept here. The room contains nothing of value. Beyond the curtain lies the kitchen (area Q10).

## Q10. Kitchen

> This kitchen has been plundered, its tables overturned. The floor is littered with rusted utensils and smashed crockery. Narrow windows flanking a hearth look out over a cemetery. An open iron pot hangs from a hook inside the blackened fireplace. It rattles on its hook and bobs up and down, as though something is inside it.

The iron pot contains an ordinary **bat**. When the characters get close, it flies out and flaps about the room.

## Q11. Wine Storage

> Five barrels lie in wooden braces along the walls of this dark, moldy storage room.

Hiding behind the barrels is a wounded elf named Savid (N male dusk elf **scout**). He has 4 hit points remaining and is grateful for any healing the characters can provide.

Savid lives with the other dusk elves of Barovia in the Vistani camp outside Vallaki (chapter 5, area N9). He was searching the woods for a missing Vistani girl named Arabelle when a wandering mob of needle blights accosted him. He was forced to take refuge in the mansion.

Savid, who is more than four hundred years old, volunteers the following useful information:

- Argynvost was a silver dragon that liked to assume human forms. Argynvostholt was the dragon's home.
- In human guise, the noble dragon led a group of knights called the Order of the Silver Dragon. They gave shelter to refugees who had come to the valley to escape Strahd's army. Strahd's soldiers slew the dragon, destroyed the order, and sacked the mansion.
- Vistani and dusk elves avoid the mansion, believing that the dragon's ghost haunts it.

The wine in the barrels turned to vinegar and evaporated long ago. Emblazoned on the barrels' sides are the name of the winery, the Wizard of Wines, and the name of the wine, Champagne du le Stomp.

A secret door at the north end of the west wall can be pulled open to reveal a den (area Q6).

## Q12. Dining Hall

> A twenty-foot-long table with sculpted dragons for legs stands in the center of this hall. The chairs that surround the table have backs carved to resemble folded dragon wings, and several of the chairs have been overturned or smashed to pieces. Suspended above the table is a crystal chandelier that glows with a soft white light. Standing in windowed alcoves are two life-sized statues depicting knights with dragon-winged helms and shields.
>
> Rainwater trickles through cracks in the ceiling, flowing down the west wall and adding to a large puddle on the floor.
>
> Five sets of wooden doors lead to this hall. The doors in the northeast corner hang open. A pair of leaded glass doors, their panes cracked and broken, stand open between panels of stained glass set into the east wall. These panels depict silver dragons in flight. Beyond the glass doors lies a dark, misty room that appears to be a chapel.

A *continual light* spell was cast on the crystal chandelier long ago and has never been dispelled. The knight statues are lifelike but inanimate.

## Q13. Chapel of Morning

> Cracked wooden pillars support a wooden, U-shaped balcony that overhangs this stone-walled chapel. Narrow archways lead to spiral staircases that curl up to the balcony, and a door set into the north wall has a wooden beam barring it. At the east end of the chapel rests a stone altar flanked by iron candelabras. The altar is carved with a rising sun bas-relief. Tall, arching windows set with panels of stained glass decorate the walls behind the altar. One of the windows has been shattered, covering the chapel floor with shards of colored glass and allowing thick fog to enter and fill the room.

If the beacon has not been lit (see areas Q16 and Q53), add:

> Through the fog, you see three armored figures kneeling before the altar.

The figures are three **revenants** clad in tattered chain mail that affords the same protection as leather armor. Each revenant wields a longsword. If the beacon is lit, the revenants are cleansed of their hatred and laid to rest, and the characters find three armored corpses with longswords lying on the floor in front of the altar.

The revenants, if still active, are blinded by their hate and attack the characters on sight, seeking to drive them out of Argynvostholt. As an action, a revenant attacks twice with its longsword, wielding the weapon with both hands and dealing 15 (2d10 + 4) slashing damage on a hit.

Characters who study the room's iconography and orientation (the fact that it draws light from the east) can determine, with a successful DC 10 Intelligence (Religion) check, that the chapel is dedicated to a god of the dawn. Anyone familiar with Barovian religion can conclude that the god in question is the Morninglord.

The balcony (area Q24) is 20 feet high and can be reached by climbing either spiral staircase (area Q14).

Characters who stand near the altar and look up can see the hollow interior of the beacon tower. The tower's lower landing (area Q50) is 60 feet above the chapel floor, and the upper landing (area Q51) is another 20 feet above that.

The bar across the north door is easily lifted from this side. Once the bar is removed, the door can be pulled open to reveal a stone staircase leading down to a cemetery (area Q15).

## Q14. Chapel Staircases

> Narrow windows allow dim light to enter this five-foot-wide spiral staircase.

The staircase leads from the chapel (area Q13) to the chapel's balcony (area Q24) and climbs another 20 feet to a small, empty room with a window that looks down on the chapel.

## Q15. Cemetery

> Tucked behind the mansion is a fog-shrouded cemetery enclosed by a seven-foot-tall fence of wrought iron. In the northeast corner stands a mausoleum.

If the beacon has not been lit (see areas Q16 and Q53), read the following text when the characters cross the cemetery for the first time:

> You suddenly feel like someone or something is watching you. Looking up, you spot a well-dressed man with a thick mane of thistledown hair observing you from a high tower window. He draws the curtain and disappears from view.

The strange man watches the characters through the southeast window of area Q42. He is merely an apparition intended to lure the characters to that room.

The mausoleum is described in area Q16.

The thick fog obscures the fact that five of the graves have been dug up. Closer inspection and a successful DC 10 Wisdom (Perception) check reveals that the corpses buried there crawled out of the earth. Of the missing corpses there is no sign, but the surrounding fence is intact, which suggests that no one got into the cemetery from outside. (These corpses were animated by the spirits of revenants and clawed their way out.)

A stone staircase curls up the outside of a turret to a flagstone landing in front of a sturdy wooden door. The door is barred from the inside and opens into the chapel (area Q13).

## Q16. Dragon's Mausoleum

> Tarnished, silver-plated gargoyles shaped like dragon wyrmlings cling to the stone-tiled roof of this mausoleum. An eight-foot-tall, four-foot-wide white marble door set into the southwest wall is engraved with a name: Argynvost.

The dragon-shaped gargoyles are harmless statuary. The stone door can be pulled open with a successful DC 15 Strength check.

> The interior of the mausoleum is dark and dusty. You see four empty alcoves with raised floors. Etched into the far wall is a verse written in Draconic.

Characters who can read the Draconic script can decipher the writing on the wall:

> Here lie the bones and treasures of
> Argynvost, lord of Argynvostholt and
> founder of the Order of the Silver Dragon.

### DEVELOPMENT

If the skull of Argynvost is brought from Castle Ravenloft (see chapter 4, area K67) and sealed inside the mausoleum, the dragon's spirit transforms into a brilliant light at the top of the tower (see area Q53).

## Q17. WEST STAIRCASES

> Narrow windows illuminate this dusty, five-foot-wide spiral staircase.

These staircases connect the second-floor balconies (area Q18) to areas Q30 and Q36 on the third floor.

## Q18. BALCONIES

> Two stone balconies flank the main foyer. Balusters carved to resemble knights in shining armor support their elegantly carved stone railings. Weapons and shields festoon the walls along each of these walkways, while alabaster busts of handsome men flank hallways that lead north and south away from the foyer. At the west end of each balcony is an archway that leads to a spiral staircase going up.

The balcony is 20 feet above the floor of the foyer (area Q3). The weapons and shields hanging on the walls are nonmagical. The busts, displayed atop wooden pedestals, depict various human guises of the dragon Argynvost. Their eyes seem to watch the characters as they walk by, but the effect is an optical illusion.

## Q19. RUINED BEDCHAMBERS

There are two of these rooms.

> The south end of this room has collapsed, exposing the chamber to the elements. A few furnishings lie broken under fallen debris from the level above.

The wooden floor creaks underfoot. Although it is safe to walk on, doing so attracts the giant spiders from area Q4. The spiders crawl up into the room and attack. The floor here is 20 feet above the floor of the ballroom.

## Q20. SOUTH ALCOVE

> A red velvet curtain hangs in front of an alcove in the southeast corner of this hall. It ripples ever so slightly.

One of the narrow windows in the back of the alcove has a broken glass pane through which a slight breeze passes, causing the curtain to move. When the characters look behind the curtain, read:

> A black cloth covers something atop a white marble pedestal.

Beneath the black cloth is the severed head of a randomly determined character—an illusion created by Strahd's consciousness. In actuality, it's an exquisite alabaster bust of a handsome, middle-aged human with a neatly trimmed mustache and beard (Lord Argynvost). The illusion is too strong to be disbelieved, but it can be dispelled if the bust is broken or covered up again.

## Q21. NORTH ALCOVE

> A red velvet curtain hangs in front of an alcove in the northeast corner of this hall.

The alcove is empty except for the narrow windows in the back walls. Whenever the characters part the curtain and leave, the curtain is closed when they return. Only by removing the curtain from its rod can they prevent the curtain from closing on its own.

## Q22. BATHROOM

> The room contains an iron tub and has wood paneling on the walls that rises to a height of three feet. Above the paneling, the walls are painted with a continuous, faded mural of a mountainscape.

The mural accurately depicts the Balinok Mountains.

## Q23. STORAGE ROOM

> Rainwater seeps through cracks in the ceiling and flows into a pool on the sagging wooden floor. The pool fills about half the room. Bare stone shelves line the walls.

This room has been thoroughly looted. The wooden floor is soft and spongy, and it can't support more than 100 pounds of weight. If more weight is applied, the floor collapses, and any creature in the room falls 20 feet, taking damage as normal and landing in area Q12.

## Q24. Chapel Balcony

This wooden balcony overhangs the mansion's chapel. An exquisitely carved wooden throne rests at the west end between two doors, and narrow archways lead to spiral staircases going up and down. Hanging from the high ceiling is an iron chandelier with candle holders shaped like tiny silver dragons.

The doors behind the throne lead to areas Q20 and Q21. A wooden railing surrounds the balcony, which is 20 feet above the floor of the chapel (area Q13).

## Q25. Trapped Hallway

This T-shaped hallway has branches to the west, east, and south. Three arched windows in the north wall look out over the foggy grounds.

The ceiling in the hall is 20 feet high. The wooden doors to areas Q27 and Q28 are locked, requiring a successful DC 20 Strength check to break down. The 10-foot squares in front of the doors (marked T on the map) are trapped. When a character enters one of these squares, a floor-to-ceiling wall of stone (created by the spell of the same name) magically appears across the opening on the south wall. At the same time, the **phantom warriors** in areas Q27 and Q28 rush through the doors (which can be freely opened from their side) and attack.

The wall of stone vanishes after 10 minutes, at which time the trap resets. Characters who cast a *detect magic* spell in the hall can perceive hazy auras of evocation magic in front of the doors.

## Q26. Northeast Guest Room

The door to this room hangs open.

Two beds with torn canopies stand against opposite walls with a tattered rug lying on the floor between them. Set into the far wall is a fireplace black with soot. A soft hiss issues from the hearth.

When one or more characters approach within 10 feet of the fireplace, add:

A small, hissing dragon made of ash and smoke erupts from the fireplace, filling the room with soot as it beats its wings.

The smoky dragonet has the statistics of a **smoke mephit** but fights only in self-defense. If left alone, it flies out of the room at a speed of 30 feet, up the spiral staircase (area Q17), through the curtain at area Q30, over the rubble in area Q33, and into area Q36. Once there, it lands on the back of Vladimir's throne and disappears.

## Q27. Knights' Quarters

This room is littered with the wreckage of ancient bunk beds. Five dirt-caked windows allow precious little light to enter, and between them are four empty armor stands. Empty torch sconces line the walls.

Four **phantom warriors** (see appendix D) haunt this room. They manifest only when the characters enter the room or trigger the magic trap in area Q25. They fight until destroyed.

## Q28. Knights' Quarters

Tattered and faded drapes cover the windows of this circular room, and empty torch sconces line the walls. Broken bunk beds and armor stands are strewn on the floor.

Three **phantom warriors** (see appendix D) haunt this room. They manifest only when the characters enter the room or trigger the magic trap in area Q25. They fight until destroyed.

### Treasure
Buried under the wreckage is a small wooden coffer containing four *potions of invulnerability*. A search of the room yields this lost cache.

## Q29. Northwest Guest Room

The contents of this room are draped in cobwebs. Between curtained windows stands a black marble hearth with a sculpted mantelpiece, above which hangs a framed portrait of a handsome, well-dressed man with a wry smile and a thick mane of thistledown hair. Opposite the fireplace is a large bed with a rotting mattress and wooden posts carved to resemble dragons. Across from the double doors stands a tall wardrobe, its doors hanging open, revealing a dark and empty cavity. The only other piece of furniture is an overstuffed leather chair that faces the hearth.

The portrait depicts the silver dragon Argynvost in its guise as the human noble Lord Argynvost.

## Q30. Curtained Staircase

A tattered black curtain conceals an archway leading to a spiral staircase that descends to area Q17.

At the top of the stairs is a secret door that can be pulled open to reveal area Q36 beyond.

# Argynvostholt
## (Area Q)

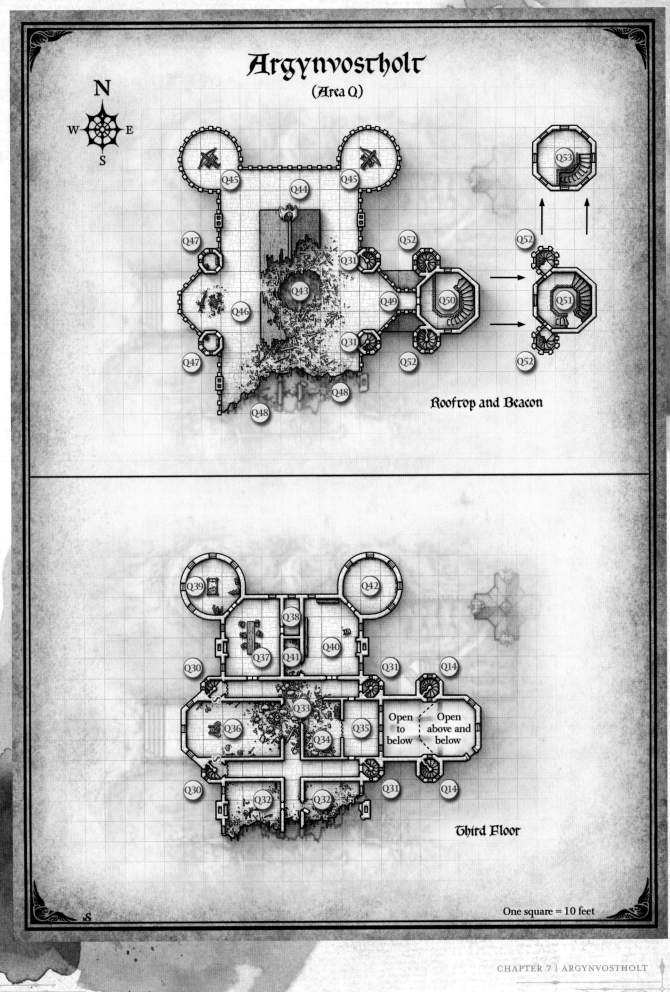

N
W · E
S

Q45
Q44
Q45
Q47
Q31
Q52
Q52
Q53
Q43
Q46
Q49
Q50
Q51
Q52
Q47
Q31
Q48
Q52
Q48

Rooftop and Beacon

Q39
Q42
Q38
Q30
Q40
Q37
Q41
Q31
Q14
Q33
Open
to
below
Open
above and
below
Q36
Q35
Q34
Q30
Q32
Q32
Q31
Q14

Third Floor

One square = 10 feet

## Q31. East Staircases

A round-topped wooden door opens to reveal a spiral staircase with narrow windows set into its walls. The stair connects the third floor and the mansion's roof.

## Q32. Ruined Bedchambers

These two rooms stand across from each other, separated by a ruined corridor that abruptly ends to the south of their doors.

> Most of this chamber has collapsed. The wooden floor is strewn with rubble and falls away into a foggy abyss to the south. The roof overhead is jagged and broken.

The floor here is 40 feet above of the floor of the ballroom (area Q4). The roof is 20 feet overhead.

## Q33. Collapsed Ceiling

> The roof over this part of the mansion has collapsed, creating a twenty-foot-diameter gaping hole with broken rafters bisecting it. Dark storm clouds roll across the sky overhead. The floor is piled with rocks, broken tiles, shattered beams, and other debris. Beneath the rubble lie a sagging floor and puddles of rainwater.

The ceiling here is 20 feet high, and the rubble is difficult terrain.

Vladimir Horngaard (see area Q36) can hear visitors climbing over the rubble and can't be surprised by them.

## Q34. Ruined Bathroom

> This room has a tiled floor and an iron bathtub filled with debris from the collapsed roof. A torn curtain hangs in an open doorway in the center of the east wall.

## Q35. Upstairs Gallery

> This room has dark wood paneling on the walls that rises to a height of three feet. Above the paneling, the walls are painted with murals of religious figures performing holy rites. In the center of the west wall is a tattered curtain hanging in an open doorway. Three tall, slender stained-glass windows set into the opposite wall depict figures in white robes with orange sunrises behind their heads.

From north to south, the three stained-glass windows portray Saint Andral, the Morninglord, and Saint Markovia.

## Q36. Dragon's Audience Hall

> The west wall of this fifty-foot-long, thirty-foot-wide audience hall has crumbled, leaving a gaping hole and a pile of rubble. Weapons and shields that once hung from the walls have fallen to the floor and succumbed to rust. A large, wooden throne carved to resemble a dragon with unfolding wings faces three tall windows to the west. Slumped in the throne is a gaunt, armored figure with one gauntlet wrapped around the hilt of a greatsword.

Vladimir Horngaard (see appendix D), commander of the fallen Order of the Silver Dragon, is slumped in the throne. If the beacon of Argynvostholt (see area Q53) has been lit, the corpse is lifeless, and characters can plunder it freely (see "Treasure" below).

If the beacon has not been lit, the body is serving as a host for the revenant. If the characters approach it, it says, "Go away." If they don't leave immediately, read:

> The creature's grip on the greatsword tightens. "If you have come to destroy me, know this: I perished defending this land from evil over four centuries ago, and because of my failure, I am forever doomed. If you destroy this body, my spirit will find a new corpse to inhabit, and I will hunt you down. You cannot free me from my damnation, nor would I wish it.
>
> "If you have come to free this land from the creature that feasts on the blood of the innocent, know this: There is no monster I hate more than Strahd von Zarovich. He slew Argynvost, broke the life of the knight I loved, and destroyed the valiant order to which I devoted my life, but Strahd has already died once. He can't be allowed to die again. Instead, he must suffer eternally in a hell of his own creation, from which he can never escape. Whatever can be done to bring him misery and unrest, I will do, but I will destroy anyone who tries to end his torment."

Vladimir fights in self-defense. He also rises from his throne and attacks if the characters fail to heed his warning and press him for help destroying Strahd. The first time Vladimir takes damage, six **phantom warriors** (see appendix D) materialize and join the fray, coming to his defense.

Hatred so clouds Vladimir's mind that he can't remember that Sir Godfrey (area Q37) was his beloved in life. If Sir Godfrey helps the characters and faces Vladimir, anguished recognition shines in Vladimir's eyes, yet only lighting the beacon can free him.

### Treasure

Vladimir Horngaard wields a *+2 greatsword*.

Vladimir wears a platinum holy symbol of the Morninglord (worth 250 gp) around his neck, underneath his half plate armor.

If your card reading reveals that a treasure is here, it's in Vladimir's possession, and he doesn't part with it willingly unless the beacon of Argynvostholt has been lit (see area Q53).

## Q37. KNIGHTS OF THE ORDER

The leaders of the Order of the Silver Dragon used to convene here.

> Through the dust and cobwebs, you see faded war banners adorning the walls of a spacious chamber, in the center of which stands a heavy wooden table. An iron chandelier hangs above the table, which is surrounded by six high-backed chairs with wood-carved dragons perched atop them. Slumped in five of the chairs are skeletal humans in tattered chainmail.

If the beacon in area Q53 has been lit, the spirits of these revenants are laid to rest, leaving behind their inanimate corpses. If the beacon has not been lit, add the following:

> The corpses tilt their heads in your direction. One of them growls, "Why do you the living disturb the dead?"

The skeletal figures are five **revenants**. All five are lawful evil. They are awaiting orders from Vladimir (area Q36) and fight only in self-defense. The revenants wear broken chainmail that affords as much protection as leather armor, and they wield longswords. As an action, a revenant attacks twice with its longsword, wielding the weapon with both hands and dealing 15 (2d10 + 4) slashing damage on a hit.

One of the revenants, Sir Godfrey Gwilym, is a spellcaster with a challenge rating of 6 (2,300 XP) and the following additional feature:

***Spellcasting.*** Sir Godfrey is a 16th-level spellcaster. His spellcasting ability is Wisdom (spell save DC 15). Sir Godfrey has the following paladin spells prepared:

1st level (4 slots): *command, detect magic, divine favor, thunderous smite*
2nd level (3 slots): *aid, branding smite, magic weapon*
3rd level (3 slots): *blinding smite, dispel magic, remove curse*
4th level (2 slots): *aura of purity, staggering smite*

Characters who inspect the fireplace notice a shield-shaped patch on the wall above the mantelpiece. A magic shield once hung there, but it was taken when Strahd's soldiers plundered the mansion. It now rests in Castle Ravenloft's treasury (chapter 4, area K41).

### DEVELOPMENT

Sir Godfrey can sense that the spirit of Argynvost isn't at rest and isn't happy that the order has been reduced to such a state. If the characters petition the revenants for aid, Sir Godfrey (speaking in a scratchy voice) relates all the information presented at the start of the chapter concerning Argynvost and the rise and fall of the Order of the Silver Dragon. Neither he nor the other revenants can help the characters in any meaningful way, however, because of the oaths they have sworn to Vladimir Horngaard.

### FORTUNES OF RAVENLOFT

If your card reading reveals that Sir Godfrey is Strahd's enemy and the characters persuasively ask him for help, he offers to join the fight against the vampire. Fate has unlocked his memory of the love that he and Vladimir once shared, and the power of that memory drives Godfrey to help fight Strahd and restore the order's honor.

If the beacon in area Q53 has not been lit, Godfrey's decision incurs the wrath of the other revenants, triggering an armed conflict.

If the beacon in area Q53 has been lit, Sir Godfrey remains a revenant even after all the other revenants (including Vladimir) are laid to rest, except that his alignment changes to lawful good. Although Sir Godfrey is unaware of the tarokka card reading, he somehow senses that he must perform one final task before his spirit can rest with Vladimir's, and thus he agrees to help the characters face Strahd in Castle Ravenloft.

## Q38. CLOSET

> This dusty closet has a slender window set into the north wall. The room is otherwise empty.

SIR GODFREY GWILYM

## Q39. Vladimir's Bedroom

> Light enters this circular room through five cracked windows. The light falls on a large, dust-covered bed in the center of the room, its posts topped with wood-carved dragons. Two large animals flank the double doors. One is a brown bear standing on its hind legs, its claws outstretched. The other is a dire wolf, its face frozen in an evil snarl. Near the wolf lies an empty wooden chest.

This room once served as a bedchamber for Sir Vladimir Horngaard and Sir Godfrey Gwilym. The bear and the dire wolf are stuffed and harmless. Looters ransacked the chest long ago, leaving nothing of value.

## Q40. Argynvost's Study

> This room is a haven for dust and cobwebs. Three narrow windows allow slivers of light to illuminate bare oak shelves along the walls and a torn, padded chair lying on its side near a cavernous hearth. A picture above the mantel has been slashed, its lower half hanging down below the frame like a torn piece of flesh. An iron door set in the south corner of the west wall hangs open on one hinge.

Strahd's soldiers forced open the iron door that once sealed Argynvost's vault (area Q41). They also took every book in this study but one. (Many of the books taken from here can be found in Strahd's study in Castle Ravenloft.)

The sole remaining volume lies on the floor behind the overturned chair. Titled *The Oath Celestial*, the book has been partially burned, and its cover was slashed by a sword. Leafing through the crumbling book reveals that it is a devotional text for knights from a place called the Holy Empire of Valentia. Most of the knights who joined Argynvost against Strahd came from that empire—now lost beyond the mists.

### Journal Page

As the characters cross the room, read:

> You hear the soft flapping sound of wings, but can't discern its origin. A single piece of parchment blows off the top of a bookshelf, spirals lazily in the air, and lands gently at your feet.

The sheet of parchment is the last page of Argynvost's journal, the rest of which was destroyed. If the characters look at the torn page, show the players the "Journal of Argynvost" in appendix F.

### Slashed Picture

If the characters study the whole picture above the mantelpiece, read:

> The picture shows the mansion in better days, under clear winter skies with snow-capped mountains in the background. The top of the chapel tower glows like a silver beacon.

The picture radiates an aura of transmutation magic under the scrutiny of a *detect magic* spell, but the aura is weak. If the characters repair the picture using a *mending* cantrip, read:

> The beacon in the picture flashes with a brilliant silver light, and the spectral form of a huge silver dragon fills the room. "My skull lies in the fortress of my enemy," it says, "displayed in a place of ill omen. Return my skull to its rightful crypt, and my spirit will shine here forever, bringing hope to this dark land." With that, the dragon's apparition fades away.

The spectral dragon isn't the spirit of Argynvost, but a spell-like effect. Once the dragon has spoken, the picture no longer glows and becomes nonmagical.

## Q41. Dragon's Vault

The iron door leading to this room hangs open on a single rusty hinge. It has obviously been forced open and no longer closes properly.

> The walls of this room are lined with lead. Emptied chests and shattered vases lie strewn upon the floor, their contents plundered.

This vault once held a dragon's trove but was stripped of all valuables long ago.

## Q42. Argynvost's Bedroom

> Rich drapes, faded by time and neglect, hide the windows of this otherwise empty room.

Argynvost preferred to sleep in his dragon form. Thus, there is no furniture here.

## Q43. Hole in Roof

This 20-foot-diameter hole in the mansion's roof is directly above area Q33, the floor of which is 20 feet below. The rubble on the roof surrounding the hole is difficult terrain. The roof is sloped and covered with cracked stone tiles. Climbing the tiled roof requires a successful DC 10 Strength (Athletics) check. A failure by 5 or more causes the climber to slide down to the parapet, landing prone but taking no damage.

## Q44. Dragon Gargoyle

Perched on the rooftop overlooking the parapet is a silver-plated gargoyle shaped like a dragon wyrmling.

The silver dragon wyrmling statue is 10 feet above the parapet and has a *magic mouth* spell cast on it. When a character passes in front of it, the spell is activated, and the wyrmling whispers the following short verse in the Common tongue:

*When the dragon dreams its dream*
*Within its rightful tomb,*
*The light of Argynvost will beam*
*And rid this land of gloom.*

## Q45. Ancient Ballista

An ancient ballista, rotted by time and weather, stands behind the battlements on this tower rooftop.

The ballista falls apart if disturbed.

## Q46. Destroyed Ballista

Strewn atop the roof toward the front of the mansion is the wreckage of a ballista. Flanking the wreckage are two stone turrets with conical rooftops and narrow doors.

The turrets are described in area Q47.

## Q47. Roof Turrets

Cobwebs hang from the rafters of this turret, which is empty except for a wooden bench and an iron stove. Arrow slits look down upon the foggy grounds in front of the mansion.

The knights who once guarded the rooftop used these turrets for warmth and shelter on rainy days and cold nights.

## Q48. Roof's Edge

Beyond a ragged edge of stone is a sixty-foot plunge to the rubble-strewn ground below. A few rafters stick out from beneath the stone.

The edge of the roof is sturdy enough to walk on, and not in danger of further collapse. It's 20 feet down to area Q32, 40 feet down to area Q19, and 60 feet down to area Q4.

## Q49. Beacon Tower Door

The parapet narrows to a width of ten feet, ending before a sturdy wooden door set into the wall of the eastern tower.

This door is barred from the inside. The phantom warriors in the tower's turrets (area Q52) make ranged attacks against characters who try to force their way into the tower. These spectral defenders have three-quarters cover behind the arrow slits.

## Q50. Beacon, Lower Landing

A rickety wooden landing and a staircase cling to the walls of this tower. The stairs lead up to another landing twenty feet above, and the floor of the chapel lies sixty feet below.

The landing and the stairs creak and shudder underfoot, but they are safe.

## Q51. Beacon, Upper Landing

Creaky stairs climb to a wooden landing with three windows that look out over the roof of the mansion. Flanking the windows are two narrow wooden doors.

The landing creaks and groans underfoot, much like in area Q50, but here things aren't so safe. The 10-foot-long section marked T on the map is particularly weak, collapsing under 50 or more pounds of weight. A creature on this section of the landing when it collapses must succeed on a DC 15 Dexterity saving throw or fall 20 feet to the landing below (area Q50). The collapse of this section creates a 10-foot gap in the landing.

The doors lead to the rooftops of the turrets (area Q52).

## Q52. Beacon Turrets

A stone battlement encloses the roof of this turret. A spiral staircase descends to the level below.

These turret rooftops are 80 feet above ground level. The spiral stairs descend 20 feet to archers' posts—small rooms lined with arrow slits. Standing guard in each of these rooms is a **phantom warrior** (see appendix D) with a spectral longbow that shoots arrows of force energy. The two phantom warriors gain the following action options:

*Multiattack.* The phantom warrior makes two attacks with its spectral longsword or spectral longbow.

*Spectral Longbow. Ranged Weapon Attack:* +2 to hit, range 150/600 ft., one target. *Hit:* 4 (1d8) force damage.

## Q53. Beacon of Argynvostholt

> Wooden stairs climb to the tower's peak, which has a stone floor and a thirty-foot-high pitched roof. Ravens roost on crisscrossing rafters, coming and going through small holes in the roof. Ten-foot-high, five-foot-wide arched windows are evenly spaced around the walls. Each window consists of a lead latticework fitted with small panes of transparent glass.

The **ravens** that roost here are harmless, but they watch the characters with great interest. If the characters look out the windows, you can use the following text to describe what they see in the distance.

> To the north and east lies a mist-shrouded valley with dark woods, a small town, and a lonely windmill on a precipice. To the south, a river flows through a foggy marsh. To the west, between rocky hills, you glimpse an abbey perched on a snowy mountainside beyond a long stretch of fog-smothered pines.

The small town is Vallaki (chapter 5). The windmill is Old Bonegrinder (chapter 6). The abbey is the Abbey of Saint Markovia in Krezk (chapter 8).

### Lighting the Beacon

When the skull of Argynvost is placed in the dragon's mausoleum (area Q16), the dragon's spirit transforms into a brilliant light that fills this room and flashes across the valley like the beacon of a lighthouse. Even if the tower is cast down, the light of Argynvost remains where it is, flashing in the sky. Although the mountains prevent the beacon's light from reaching Castle Ravenloft directly, Strahd can see the light's glow in the sky to the west.

The beacon can be seen in Vallaki (chapter 5), Krezk (chapter 8), and Berez (chapter 10), as well as from Old Bonegrinder (chapter 6), Van Richten's Tower (chapter 11), and the werewolf den (chapter 15).

The beacon's light can be "felt" even by creatures that are blind. The light allows good-aligned creatures to experience glimmers of hope and joy, while evil creatures find the light disconcerting.

***Beacon of Protection.*** While the beacon shines, characters and other creatures that oppose Strahd gain a +1 bonus to AC and saving throws for as long as they remain in Barovia.

***Revenants at Rest.*** Vladimir Horngaard and the other revenants that haunt Barovia see the light as a reminder of all that was once good and noble about the knightly order to which they once belonged. They let go of their hatred and their corporeal bodies, leaving corpses behind as their spirits find rest at long last. Henceforth, any random encounter with a revenant should be treated as no encounter.

### Fortunes of Ravenloft

If your card reading reveals that a treasure is here, it's resting on the west windowsill.

## Special Events

You can use one or both of the following events as the characters explore Argynvostholt.

### Special Delivery

This encounter occurs while the characters are inside Argynvostholt. Those who have a passive Wisdom (Perception) score of 11 or higher hear the clopping of horse hooves and the crunch of wagon wheels on gravel.

A cart pulled by a **draft horse** and driven by a mad Vistana named Kolya (CN male human **bandit**) stops in front of the mansion. After relieving himself on the statue of Argynvost (area Q1), Kolya untethers the horse and rides back to the Vistani camp outside Vallaki (chapter 5, area N9), leaving the cart and its cargo: a plain wooden coffin.

The coffin was made in Vallaki by the local coffin maker, Henrik van der Voort (see chapter 5, area N6). It has the name of one of the characters (determined randomly) neatly chiseled into its lid. Opening the coffin releases a **swarm of bats** from within. The swarm attacks the character whose name is engraved on the coffin. If that character isn't in sight, the swarm flies away.

### Arrigal's Hunt

**Ezmerelda d'Avenir** (see appendix D) arrives at Argynvostholt on the back of a **riding horse** stolen from the Vistani camp outside Vallaki (chapter 5, area N9). She has heard that the reportedly haunted mansion might harbor enemies of Strahd and contain secrets to the vampire's destruction.

Once she arrives, Ezmerelda releases the horse (which flees back to its camp) and quietly makes her way through the mansion until she reaches the characters.

Hot on Ezmerelda's trail are the Vistani leader Arrigal (NE male human **assassin**) and two Vistani bodyguards (CE female **bandits**). Arrigal rides a black **riding horse**, while the bandits ride two **dire wolves**. These dire wolves are servants of Strahd and can't be charmed or frightened.

Arrigal is determined to capture Ezmerelda and haul her back to the Vistani camp to face punishment for horse theft. He does nothing to antagonize the characters, however, and returns to the Vistani camp if he can't convince them to give up Ezmerelda. For more information on Arrigal, see chapter 5, area N9c.

# CHAPTER 8: THE VILLAGE OF KREZK

THE FORTIFIED VILLAGE OF KREZK LIES near the edge of Strahd's domain, and the wall of mist that marks the border is clearly visible above the treeline. Yet even here there is no escaping the vampire. In fact, the villagers are so terrified of Strahd and his wolves that they never venture away from the village. Within their walls, they grow trees that provide ample wood to keep them warm on cold nights, and they draw water from a blessed pool. They have chickens, hares, and small pigs, as well as gardens of beets and turnips. The only thing they depend on from the outside world is wine. The burgomaster, Dmitri Krezkov, comes from a noble family and regularly has wine delivered from the nearby winery, the Wizard of Wines (chapter 12), to keep the locals' bellies warm and their spirits up.

Looming high above Krezk is the Abbey of Saint Markovia, once a convent and hospital, now a madhouse overrun with wickedness. After Saint Markovia and her followers failed to overthrow Strahd, the abbey became a fortress closed off from the rest of the world. Strahd ruthlessly preyed on the fears of the clerics and nuns holed up inside, but ultimately it was their isolation and greed that doomed them. The clergy began fighting over food and wine. By the time their supplies ran out, they had either been killed by each other's hands or driven hopelessly insane by Strahd's acts of terror against them. For years afterward, the villagers of Krezk avoided the place, fearing that the abbey was cursed, haunted, or both.

Then, over a century ago, a pilgrim from a distant land came to Krezk and insisted that he be allowed to reopen the abbey. The nameless man was strikingly handsome and extremely persuasive, and the villagers couldn't help but do as he commanded. Eternally young, he presides over the abbey to this day, and locals refer to him simply as the Abbot. Many villagers suspect that the Abbot is Strahd in disguise, for they've heard stories about Strahd appearing in other guises. The truth, however, is even more disturbing.

---

THE GLEAM IN HER EYES WAS LIKE *warm sunlight on a still pond. That light is gone forever. When I try to imagine those eyes, all I see is a mad abyss.*

—Strahd von Zarovich

---

## AREAS OF KREZK

The following areas correspond to labels on the map of Krezk on page 144.

### S1. ROAD JUNCTION

> The road branches north and climbs a rocky escarpment, ending at a gatehouse built into a twenty-foot-high wall of stone reinforced with buttresses every fifty feet or so. The wall encloses a settlement on the side of a snow-dusted mountain spur. Beyond the wall you see the tops of snow-covered pines and thin, white wisps of smoke. The somber toll of a bell comes from a stone abbey that clings to the mountainside high above the settlement. The steady chime is inviting—a welcome change from the deathly silence and oppressive fog to which you have grown accustomed. It's hard to tell at this distance, but there seems to be a switchback road clinging to the cliffs that lead up from the walled settlement to the abbey.

The Old Svalich Road continues west from this location for a little more than a mile before it plunges into the foggy curtain that surrounds Barovia (see chapter 2, "Mists of Ravenloft"). Characters who follow the road north arrive at the gatehouse (area S2).

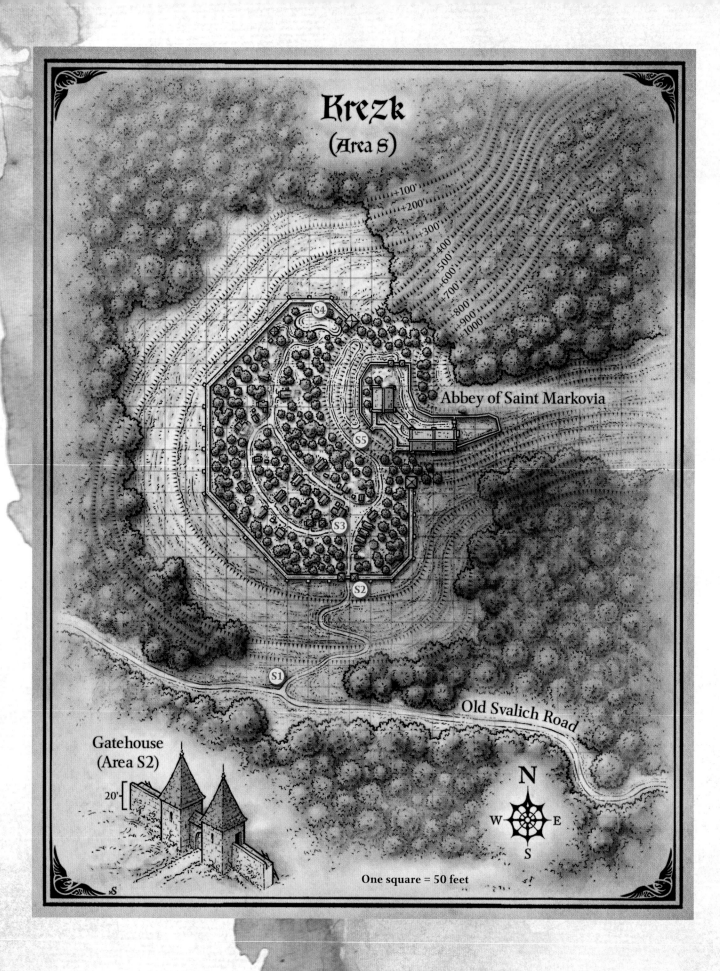

# Krezk
## (Area S)

+100'
+200'
+300'
+400'
+500'
+600'
+700'
+800'
+900'
+1000'

S4

**Abbey of Saint Markovia**

S5

S3

S2

S1

*Old Svalich Road*

## Gatehouse
## (Area S2)

20'

N
W    E
S

One square = 50 feet

## S2. Gatehouse

The map of Krezk includes a diagram of the gatehouse.

> The air grows colder as you approach the walled set-
> tlement. Two square towers with peaked roofs flank a
> stone archway into which is set a pair of twelve-foot-tall,
> ironbound wooden doors. Carved into the arch above the
> doors is a name: Krezk.
>
> The walls that extend from the gatehouse are twenty
> feet high. Atop the parapet you see four figures wearing
> fur hats and clutching spears. They watch you nervously.

Cut into the upper floor of each tower is an arrow slit 6 inches wide, 4 feet tall, and 1 foot deep. An open doorway leads from the archer's post in each tower to the adjacent parapet. Behind the walls, wooden ladders lead from the parapets to the ground 20 feet below.

Two archers (male and female human **scouts**) are stationed inside the gatehouse, one in each tower. Four **guards** (male and female humans) man the adjacent walls. If the characters are seen flying or climbing over the walls, the guards assume that the village is under attack and cry out in alarm. Five rounds after the alarm sounds, every able-bodied adult in the village arrives at the gatehouse, ready for battle. Krezk's militia consists of four more guards plus forty **commoners** (male and female humans) armed with handaxes.

The double doors are made of thick wood planks bound with iron bands and sealed shut with a heavy wooden bar held in iron brackets. The bar can be lifted with a successful DC 15 Strength check. The doors require a siege engine to break them open.

There aren't enough people in Krezk to adequately defend its outer wall. Every 300-foot stretch of wall is watched over by a lone **guard** (male or female human). The guards are trained to crouch behind the wall and sound the alarm at any sign of danger.

### Burgomaster Dmitri Krezkov

If the characters ask to be let inside or otherwise draw the attention of the guards on the wall, one of the guards fetches the burgomaster, Dmitri Krezkov (LG male human **noble**). His ancestors built Krezk at the foot of the abbey after Strahd's armies conquered the valley.

Dmitri is a lord and expects to be treated like one. He places the safety of his village above the welfare of strangers. He has seen adventurers before and assumes that the characters are Strahd's allies or enemies; either way, their presence spells trouble for Krezk. Dmitri isn't prepared to shelter Strahd's enemies any more than he is willing to humor Strahd's allies. The only way the characters can earn his favor is to help Krezk in some way, whereupon Dmitri is required by his oath of office and his honor as a Barovian noble to show them hospitality. If the characters ask what they can do, Dmitri asks them to secure a wagonload of wine from the Wizard of Wines winery to the south. His people have been without wine for days, and the next delivery is long overdue.

If the characters force their way into town using magic or strength of arms, Dmitri tells his guards to stand down, hoping to avoid bloodshed, and does everything he can to expedite the characters' departure.

A character who succeeds on a DC 12 Wisdom (Insight) check can discern that Dmitri is trying to hide the fact that he is distraught. He is grieving over the natural death of his youngest son, Ilya—the last of his children (see area S3).

## S3. Village of Krezk

When the characters get past the outer wall, read:

> The mist-shrouded village beyond the wall is nothing
> more than a scattering of humble wooden cottages along
> dirt roads that stretch between stands of snow-dusted
> pine trees—so many trees, in fact, as to constitute a for-
> est. To the northeast, gray cliffs rise sharply, and the road
> winding up to the abbey is easy to see from this vantage.

The village operates as a commune, with no exports or moneymaking businesses. Villagers grow trees and vegetables, cut wood to heat their homes, raise chickens and pigs, and share their food. A few villagers have cows and mules, but there are no horses in Krezk. The village has no inns or taverns. Characters who are willing to chop wood, milk cows, or perform other chores can spend the night in the burgomaster's cottage or some other residence.

### Cottages

Krezk's residences are single-story pine cottages with stone chimneys and thatch roofs. Pigs and chickens are kept in indoor pens and coops so that they don't freeze.

***Burgomaster's Cottage.*** The building closest to the outer gate is the burgomaster's cottage—the largest building in town but still a modest dwelling. Dmitri Krezkov and his fearless wife Anna (LG female human **noble**) have no living children. The last of their four children, Ilya, died of an illness seven days ago at the age of fourteen. Given their age, the Krezkovs are unlikely to have more children—a source of great consternation to everyone in the village, since that means the end of the Krezkov bloodline.

The burgomaster's cottage has a wine cellar (currently empty) and lots of space for pigpens and chicken coops. Behind the cottage is a graveyard where deceased members of the Krezkov family are interred. Dmitri and Anna's four children, all of whom died of illness, are buried here. Several of the family caskets are empty, their contents stolen in the night by the Abbot's mongrelfolk gravediggers (see area S6). Ilya's plot is fresh and undisturbed, since he was interred only four days ago.

***Commoner Cottages.*** A typical cottage is only 200 square feet yet contains 1d4 adults (male and female human **commoners**), 1d4 − 1 children (male and female human noncombatants), plus the family's pigs, hares, and chickens.

Every cottage has its own graveyard where family members are interred. All the caskets planted in the

past decade are now empty, thanks to the Abbot's sneaky mongrelfolk gravediggers (see area S6).

### Krezk Lore

In addition to the information known to all Barovians (see "Barovian Lore" in chapter 2), the villagers of Krezk (called Krezkites) know the following bits of local lore:

- Residents never leave the village for fear of being attacked by wolves, dire wolves, and werewolves.
- About once a month, a wagonload of wine arrives from the Wizard of Wines (chapter 12), the winery and vineyard to the south. The business is owned and operated by the Martikov family.
- Burgomaster Krezkov recently lost his fourteen-year-old son, Ilya, to illness. Ilya was the last of the four Krezkov children.
- A pool at the north end of the village provides fresh water throughout the year. Next to the pool, the village's ancestors built a shrine to the Morninglord in a gazebo. It's known as the Shrine of the White Sun.
- The Abbey of Saint Markovia is named after a priest of the Morninglord who took a stand against the devil Strahd. After a fierce uprising, Markovia and her most loyal followers stormed Castle Ravenloft, only to be destroyed.
- The abbey was once a hospital and a convent, but it fell on hard times after the land was swallowed up by the mists. Some of the clergy fell prey to Strahd, while others went mad and either starved themselves to death or turned to cannibalism.
- The head of the abbey, called simply the Abbot, arrived over a century ago and hasn't aged a day since. He occasionally visits the Shrine of the White Sun but doesn't talk much, and he demands tribute in the form of wine. No one knows his true name or where he came from, and many believe he's Strahd's servant or the vampire himself in disguise.

- No one from the village visits the abbey anymore. The abbey's bell rings at odd times, day and night, and the place is filled with baleful screams and horrible, inhuman laughter that can be heard throughout the village.

## S4. Pool and Shrine

> Even under gray skies, this pool at the north end of the village shimmers and sparkles. Near its shore sits an old gazebo on the verge of collapse. A wooden statue of a mournful, bare-chested man, its paint chipped and faded, stands in the gazebo with arms outstretched, as though waiting to be embraced.

The pool is fed by an underground spring and was blessed long ago by Saint Markovia. Its waters defy corruption, and anyone who drinks from it for the first time gains the benefit of a *lesser restoration* spell. (The water once had even greater magic but has weakened over the years.) The water otherwise tastes sweet and fresh.

The gazebo is so frail that it wouldn't take more than a strong wind to knock it over. It remains standing because it's protected from the elements by the surrounding trees, walls, and cliffs. The statue is a depiction of the Morninglord, positioned so that he is reaching toward the east (the dawn). Locals refer to the statue and gazebo as the Shrine of the White Sun, though they have no idea why their ancestors named it so.

### Fortunes of Ravenloft

If your card reading reveals that a treasure is here, the item is hidden under the gazebo. The gazebo must be torn down to reach it, and doing that doesn't sit well with the locals. If the characters damage the gazebo and don't repair it, any Charisma checks they make to shift the attitudes of the villagers have disadvantage.

## S5. Winding Road

> The switchback road that hugs the cliff is ten feet wide and covered with loose gravel and chunks of broken rock. The ascent is slow and somewhat treacherous, and the air grows colder as one nears the top.

The road climbs 400 feet, doubling back on itself twice before reaching area S6.

# Areas of the Abbey

The following areas correspond to labels on the maps of the Abbey of Saint Markovia on pages 149 and 153.

The mongrelfolk that infest the abbey are all descendants of one family—the Belviews—and all suffer from some form of madness. Whenever the characters interact with a mongrelfolk who isn't detailed here, roll on the Indefinite Madness table (see "Madness Effects" in chapter 8 of the *Dungeon Master's Guide*) or choose from the available options on the table to determine how that particular mongrelfolk's madness is expressed.

Most of the mongrelfolk in the abbey are locked up because they can't be trusted to wander about unsupervised. The only mongrelfolk who are free to move about are the Abbot's gravediggers, Otto and Zygfrek, and his faithful, two-headed manservant, Clovin.

Clovin Belview rings the abbey's bell (area S17) when the Abbot decides it's time for dinner. The toll of the bell causes all the other mongrelfolk in the abbey to hoot and holler with excitement as they wait to be fed.

The windows of the north wing are made of leaded glass that is translucent—good for letting in light but not good for seeing through. The windows of the east wing are broken outward and have damaged shutters.

## S6. North Gate

> The road from the village climbs above the mist to the wide ledge on which the abbey is perched. A light dusting of snow covers the trees and the rocky earth.
>
> The gravel road passes between two small, stone outbuildings, to either side of which stretches a five-foot-high, three-foot-thick wall of jumbled stones held together with mortar. Blocking the road are iron gates attached to the outbuildings by rusty hinges. They appear to be unlocked. Viewed through the gates, the stone abbey stands quiet. Its two wings are joined by a fifteen-foot-high curtain wall. A belfry protrudes from the rooftop of the closer north wing, which also sports a chimney billowing gray smoke.

The iron gates are unlocked but squeal loudly when someone opens them.

Two gate guards are on duty, but they aren't awake when the characters arrive (see below). Characters who succeed on a DC 12 Dexterity (Stealth) check can climb over the low outer wall without waking them. If one or more characters fail the check, or if the characters open the gates, the guards rouse themselves and stumble forth to confront the trespassers.

The gate guards are Otto and Zygfrek Belview, two lawful evil **mongrelfolk** (see appendix D). They sleep under piles of musty animal furs. Both are loyal servants of the Abbot, yet not so good at guarding. If the characters seem friendly, the mongrelfolk escort them to the courtyard (area S12) and ask the characters to wait there while they fetch the Abbot (area S13). If the characters seem hostile, the mongrelfolk let them enter but don't accompany them willingly.

Hanging on the inside wall of each guard post is a net woven from twigs and pine needles, as well as a shovel. Otto and Zygfrek cover themselves with the nets when they skulk through the village at night in search of fresh graves to dig up.

### Roleplaying the Mongrelfolk

Use the information below to roleplay the mongrelfolk guards, Otto and Zygfrek.

*Otto Belview.* Otto is 4 feet, 9 inches tall and squats instead of standing upright. He looks like a beardless dwarf with patches of donkey flesh covering his face and body. He has one human ear and one wolf's ear, and a protruding wolf's snout and fangs. His arms and hands are human, but his legs and feet are leonine, and he has a donkey's tail. He can barely speak Common, and his laugh sounds like a donkey's bray. He wears a plain wool cloak.

OTTO BELVIEW

ZYGFREK BELVIEW

Otto has the Standing Leap feature (see the mongrel-folk stat block in appendix D). His madness is embodied in the following statement: "I am the smartest, wisest, strongest, fastest, and most beautiful person I know."

***Zygfrek Belview.*** Zygfrek stands 4 feet, 7 inches tall. The left side of her face and body is covered with lizard scales, the right with tufts of gray wolf fur. Between these tufts is pale human skin. One of her eyes is that of a feline, and her fingers and hands resemble cat's paws with opposable thumbs. She has a gruff voice and wears a gray cloak with black fur trim.

Zygfrek has the Darkvision feature (see the mongrel-folk stat block in appendix D). Her madness is embodied in the following statement: "I don't like the way people judge me all the time."

## S7. GRAVEYARD

> Stunted pine trees grow out of the rocky earth in the graveyard near the foundation of the abbey's north wing. The windows of the structure are cracked panes of leaded glass. Ancient gravestones burst from a thin crust of snow in the yard. Beyond the low wall that surrounds the graveyard, the ground falls away. The village lies four hundred feet below, and the view is breathtaking.

Carved into each gravestone is the name of a long-dead priest or nun. Some of the names include Brother Martek, Brother Valen, Sister Constance, and Sister Lenora.

### SUN'S GRAVE

The gravestone marked X is carved with roses and bears a 3-inch-diameter sun-shaped indentation on its east side. Engraved beneath the indentation is the name PETROVNA. If Tasha Petrovna's holy symbol (see chapter 4, area K84, crypt 11) is placed in the indentation, both the holy symbol and the indentation vanish. Then read:

> A ray of golden sunlight breaks through the clouds to the west and shines upon the grave. The fog and the gloom shrink from its brilliance as the sunlight causes the gravestone to crack and crumble, revealing a ring within.

The sunray lasts for 1 minute. If the characters smash the gravestone without placing Tasha Petrovna's holy symbol in it first, they find nothing within its remains.

The ring is a *ring of regeneration*.

## S8. GARDEN GATEHOUSE

> A gatehouse stands at the entrance to the abbey gardens.

The gatehouse is empty.

## S9. GARDENS

> Nestled between rising and plunging cliffs are four rectangular garden plots enclosed by a five-foot-high wall of mortared stones. White rabbits nibble on turnips uprooted by the cold. Two lifeless scarecrows with stuffed gullets and sackcloth heads hang from wooden crosses pounded into the cold, hard earth.

If the characters haven't cleared out the east wing, add:

> The abbey's east wing looms over the garden, its shattered windows dark and disturbing. A door leads into this forlorn edifice, which apparently isn't as abandoned as one might have hoped. From within come the laughter and the wailing of things that should not be.

The rabbits and the scarecrows are harmless. The gardens contain a meager assortment of root vegetables and squash. The door leading to area S15 isn't locked.

### FORTUNES OF RAVENLOFT

If your card reading reveals that a treasure is here, the item is hidden in the straw-filled gullet of the southernmost scarecrow. If the treasure is removed from the scarecrow, seven **wights** erupt from the gardens and attack. They wear tattered livery of Strahd's house.

## S10. ABBEY ENTRANCE

> A fifteen-foot-high curtain wall joins the abbey's two wings. Behind its battlements, two guards stand at attention, their features obscured by fog. Below them, set into the wall, is a pair of ten-foot-tall, wooden doors reinforced with bands of steel. To the right of these doors, mounted on the wall, is a tarnished copper plaque.

The plaque bears the abbey's name, under which appear these words: "May her light cure all illness."

The "guards" on the wall are propped-up scarecrows that wear corroded chain shirts and clutch rusted spears (see area S18). A character who succeeds on a DC 10 Wisdom (Perception) check discerns the charade.

The double doors are heavy but unlocked. They can be pushed open to reveal a foggy courtyard (area S12).

## S11. INNER GATEHOUSES

These two empty buildings help support the curtain wall (area S18) that encloses the courtyard (area S12). The wooden doors that lead to them are unlocked.

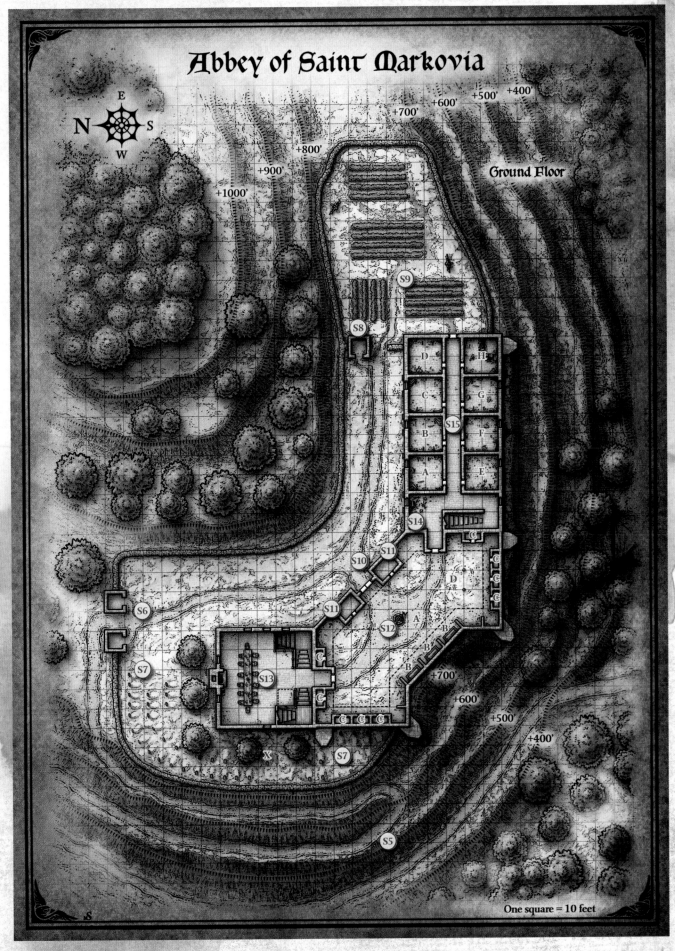

# Abbey of Saint Markovia

Ground Floor

+400'
+500'
+600'
+700'
+800'
+900'
+1000'

S9

S8

D
C
B
A

H
G
F
E

S15

S14

S11
S10

S11

S12

S6

S7

S13

S7

X

S5

+700'
+600'
+500'
+400'

One square = 10 feet

## S12. Courtyard

> The thick fog that fills this courtyard swirls, as if eager to escape. The courtyard is surrounded by a fifteen-foot-high curtain wall on which stand several guards with their backs to you—or so it seemed at first. It's clear now that these guards are merely scarecrows.
>
> Wooden doors to the north and east lead to the abbey's two wings. In the center of the courtyard is a stone well fitted with an iron winch, to which a rope and bucket are attached. Along the perimeter, tucked under the overhanging wall, are several stone sheds with padlocked wooden doors, as well as three shallow alcoves that contain wooden troughs. Two wooden posts pounded into the rocky earth have iron rings bolted to them, and chained to one of them is a short humanoid with bat wings and spider mandibles.
>
> The quiet is shattered by horrible screams coming from the sheds.

If the characters are escorted here by Otto and Zygfrek Belview (area S6), they are asked to wait in the courtyard while the mongrelfolk fetch the Abbot from area S13.

### S12a. Well

The well is 80 feet deep. Hiding 20 feet down is a chaotic evil **mongrelfolk** (see appendix D) named Mishka Belview. He clings to the wall of the shaft and scuttles up to attack anyone who shines a light down on him.

**Mishka Belview.** Mishka stands 5 feet tall and has a wiry, spindly build. He has three red spider eyes on the right side of his face, while the left side appears human. He has a frog's foot in place of his left hand and a taloned crow's foot where his right foot should be.

He has the Spider Climb feature (see the mongrelfolk stat block in appendix D). In his madness, he's discovered he enjoys killing people.

### S12b. Old Troughs

These three horse troughs are badly rotted and fall apart if handled or jostled.

### S12c. Chicken Sheds

Each of these sheds is fitted with an iron padlock. Clovin Belview (area S17) carries the keys to these locks.

If the characters open a shed, read:

> This shed holds the shattered remains of several chicken coops. Shackled to the back wall is a wretched humanoid with bestial deformities.

There are nine of these sheds, each one containing a howling or mewling **mongrelfolk** (see appendix D).

### S12d. Tethering Posts

Iron rings bolted to these wooden posts were once used to secure horses. Chained to one post is a chaotic neutral **mongrelfolk** (see appendix D) named Marzena Belview, the older sister of Mishka Belview (see area S12a).

If the characters approach Marzena, read:

> The creature chained to the post flaps its leathery wings and takes to the air, but doesn't get far before its chains go taut. She flutters about madly, screaming nonsense.

Marzena Belview is skittish and afraid of everyone and everything except for Clovin Belview (area S17), whom she allows to come close enough to feed her.

**Marzena Belview.** Marzena stands 4 feet, 5 inches tall and has a hunched posture. Long, stringy black hair hides much of her face, but clearly visible are the spider mandibles and teeth that replace her human mouth. She has the arms and wings of a bat, as well as a cloven hoof in place of her right foot. She doesn't allow anyone to get close enough to undo her shackles, but if her bonds are magically unlocked or if her chains are somehow broken, she flies away and never returns.

Marzena has the Flight feature (see the mongrelfolk stat block in appendix D). Her madness is embodied in the following statement: "I am convinced that powerful enemies are hunting me, and their agents are everywhere I go. I am sure they're watching me all the time."

## S13. Main Hall

> Gentle-sounding music trickles down from above, played on a single stringed instrument by some unseen master.
>
> The ground floor is one large, fifty-foot-square room with arched, leaded glass windows. A cauldron sits on an iron rack above a fire in a hearth, while above the fireplace mantel hangs a golden disk engraved with the symbol of the sun. In one corner, a wooden staircase climbs to the upper level, while in another corner a stone staircase descends into darkness.
>
> Several chairs surround a wooden table that stretches nearly the length of the room. Wooden dishware and gold candelabras are neatly arranged on the table, standing behind which is a young woman with alabaster skin dressed in a torn and soiled red gown. Her auburn hair is neatly bundled so as not to touch her soft shoulders. She seems lost in her own thoughts.

The Abbot is normally here. If he is here, add:

> A handsome young man in a brown monk's robe gently takes the woman by her hand. A painted wooden holy symbol that depicts the sun hangs from a chain around his neck. He moves with the grace of a saint.

The Abbot is a **deva** in disguise (see appendix D, as well as "Something Old" in the "Special Events" section at the end of this chapter). He wears a holy symbol of the Morninglord around his neck. The woman in the tattered red gown is Vasilka, a **flesh golem** that has been exquisitely put together to serve as Strahd's bride. Characters within 5 feet of Vasilka can see the seams in her powdered skin where disparate body parts stolen from Krezkite graves have been carefully stitched together.

The Abbot is teaching Vasilka the finer points of etiquette. He also intends to teach her how to dance. Vasilka obeys his every command. She can't speak but lets loose an unholy scream if harmed. If driven berserk, she fights until the Abbot reasserts control or until she is destroyed. She has the supernatural strength of a typical flesh golem despite her smaller size.

The Abbot has no desire to harm the characters. He knows that Strahd has brought them to Barovia for a reason and doesn't want to thwart Strahd's plans for them. His calm, pleasant demeanor changes if they become hostile or if they threaten Vasilka. He sheds his disguise and assumes his true angelic form, hoping that sight is enough to make them back down.

The Abbot would like to find a proper bridal gown for Vasilka. If the characters seem friendly, he asks them for help in locating one. In exchange, he offers his magic, agreeing to cast *raise dead* up to three times on their behalf, or give them each the benefit of his healing touch. If they decline to help or behave rudely, he orders them to leave the abbey at once, attacking them if they refuse and doing his utmost to keep Vasilka safe.

The music comes from upstairs (area S17). The stone staircase leads down to the wine cellar (area S16). The wooden stairs climb to the loft and belfry (area S17).

The stew pot in the fireplace contains several gallons of hot turnip and rabbit soup, intended for the mongrelfolk imprisoned in areas S12c and S15.

### ROLEPLAYING THE ABBOT

The Abbot believes he is righteous. He regrets transforming the Belviews into horrid mongrelfolk, and he considers their imprisonment to be necessary, to contain their madness. With regard to Strahd's bride, he believes that she is the key to freeing the land from its curse. The insane Abbot can't be convinced otherwise.

The Abbot shares his beliefs openly, claiming that his decisions are based on the Morninglord's guidance. He will give visitors a tour of the abbey if they seem friendly, but he turns hostile if they threaten him or his charges.

### TREASURE

The golden sun disk hanging above the fireplace is worth 750 gp. Taking the disk off the wall reveals a niche that contains a *potion of superior healing* in a crystal and electrum flask (worth 250 gp). Four gold candelabras (worth 250 gp each) rest atop the table.

### FORTUNES OF RAVENLOFT

If your card reading reveals that a treasure is here, it is hidden in the niche along with the potion.

## S14. FOYER

> This room used to be an office, as evidenced by the remains of a desk and a chair, both of which have been smashed to pieces. A hallway to the south leads to a staircase going up. A dark passage to the east is full of unnatural whispers, mad laughter, and bestial odors.

The stairs lead up to area S20.

If the characters enter this area making noise or carrying light sources, the golem in area S15 is drawn to them (unless they have already defeated it).

## S15. MADHOUSE

> This lightless corridor has multiple doors behind which lie creatures that shatter the quiet with their mad cackles and whispered curses. The stench is overpowering.

Before he set out to create a bride for Strahd, the Abbot tried his hand at creating a more rudimentary golem. This creature paces the hall, tirelessly guarding the abbey's madhouse and making sure no mongrelfolk escape. When the characters first see the golem, read:

> Even in the gloom, you can make out a monstrous shape lumbering down the hall. When the darkness can no longer hide its true nature, your eyes are treated to a terrifying, 7-foot-tall assemblage of human body parts.

This **flesh golem** attacks anyone who isn't in the company of the Abbot or Clovin Belview.

None of the doors leading from the hall are locked. If the characters open any and look inside, they see that the rooms on each side of the hall are dimly lit by natural light that filters through dirty, shuttered windows. The door at the east end of the hall leads outside and can be pulled open to reveal the gardens (area S9).

The sixty **mongrelfolk** confined here are fed at irregular intervals by Clovin Belview. Dinner is foretold by the ringing of the abbey bell (area S17). These mongrelfolk aren't restrained, but they refuse to leave their rooms for fear of being killed by the golem or cast out of the abbey and forced to fend for themselves. In addition to a dagger, each mongrelfolk has its own wooden soup bowl.

### S15A. FEARFUL MONGRELFOLK

> This room was once a shared bedchamber, but its furnishings have been destroyed. Three shrieking mongrels cower in the shadowy northwest corner. One of them cradles something shiny.

Three **mongrelfolk** are confined here. One of them cradles a polished brass candlestick as if it was a doll. Any attempt to take it causes the mongrelfolk to attack.

## S15b. Quarreling Mongrelfolk

> Four mongrel creatures brawl amid the wreckage of this bedchamber while a fifth watches and cackles behind a life-sized, painted wooden statue of a saintly woman in robes.

Five **mongrelfolk** are confined here. The four that are fighting aren't trying to kill each other, but they are trying to assert dominance. They stop fighting if a character separates them.

The statue is a little over 5 feet tall and carved from a single piece of wood. It depicts Saint Markovia. Close inspection reveals that it is covered with bite marks.

## S15c. Incanting Mongrelfolk

> Seven mongrels are seated in the middle of this room, forming a ring. They appear to be chanting a spell.

These seven **mongrelfolk** are trying to cast a spell that will cause the abbey's bell to ring, so that dinner will be served. They are speaking nonmagical gibberish.

## S15d. Hungry Mongrelfolk

> Nine mongrel creatures stand in the middle of this room, starting at the doorway in silence with hungry looks in their eyes.

These nine **mongrelfolk** haven't been fed in days because Clovin doesn't like them. They try to kill and devour any character who sets foot in the room.

## S15e. Mongrelfolk Horde

> This room is packed wall to wall with mongrels wallowing in their own filth. The floor is strewn with gnawed bones.

Sixteen screaming **mongrelfolk** are confined here. The bones are all that remain of mongrelfolk who perished and were eaten. The survivors beg for food.

## S15f. Singing and Dancing Mongrelfolk

> Eight mongrels caper about the wreckage of this bedchamber while singing a rhyme. One of them holds up a glittering gold statuette as it leads this mad parade.

The eight **mongrelfolk** sing the following rhyme:

*The devil dwells in his dark house,*
*Upon the misty pillar.*
*First he'll taste her sweet, sweet blood,*
*And then he'll have to kill her.*

They weep if their treasure is taken from them.

***Treasure.*** The golden statuette depicts Saint Markovia and is worth 250 gp. It grants any good-aligned creature that carries it a +1 bonus to saving throws.

## S15g. Mongrelfolk Babies

> Filthy mongrels cradle screaming young in the debris-strewn corners of this room while several more hoot, holler, roll on the floor, and whack each other with sticks.

This room contains ten **mongrelfolk**, three of which are tendng to noncombatant mongrelfolk babies.

## S15h. Mongrelfolk Fort

> This room contains a fort made out of piled bits of shattered furniture and torn draperies. From within the fort, you hear a mischievous cackle.

Two **mongrelfolk** live in the "fort" but refuse to come out unless baited with food. While hidden under the wreckage, they have three-quarters cover.

## S16. Wine Cellar

> The stone steps descend twenty feet to a cellar that contains ten barrels of wine and an L-shaped wooden rack packed with wine bottles.

The barrels in the center of the room are empty. The wine names are emblazoned on the barrels, as is the winery's name: the Wizard of Wines. The barrels against the east wall contain Purple Grapemash No. 3, a cheap wine. The four barrels against the south wall contain Red Dragon Crush, a fine wine.

The wine racks contain thirty-three bottles of Purple Grapemash No. 3 and twenty-four bottles of Red Dragon Crush.

### Treasure

Among the wine bottles on the rack is one with no stopper and a label that reads "Champagne du le Stomp." It contains a rolled-up *spell scroll* of *heroes' feast*.

## S17. Loft and Belfry

Anyone on the curtain wall (area S18) who listens at this room's door hear the soft tones of a stringed instrument.

The wooden stairs climb twenty feet to a loft with a pitched roof and a door in the center of the south wall. Unlit lanterns hang from the rafters, and a rope dangles from a bronze bell lodged in the belfry thirty feet overhead. The room is filled with the sound of beautiful music—a melody so enchanting that it adds a bit of much-needed warmth to the otherwise freezing room.

A black shroud covers a humanoid shape lying on a wooden table. The music does nothing to stir it.

A cot heaped with furs rests in the northeast corner, surrounded by empty wine bottles. An oil lamp burns atop a table nearby, silhouetting a squat creature that has two heads. It sits on the edge of the cot with a viol between its legs. With a crustacean, clawlike appendage, it grasps the neck of the instrument while running a bow gently across its strings with its human hand.

This loft is where the Abbot creates his flesh golems. Needles, thread, saws, and other tools lie on a small table in the northwest corner.

If anyone rings the bell, a cacophony erupts from the courtyard and the east wing as the mongrelfolk cry out, "Food!" The cries last until the creatures are fed.

Clovin Belview, the Abbot's manservant, a two-headed neutral evil **mongrelfolk** (see appendix D), resides here. He plays the viol beautifully when he is drunk, and the music help puts his half-formed head to sleep. Hidden under the furs of his cot are three bottles of Purple Grapemash No. 3. Several empty wine bottles are strewn about the floor around the cot.

## ROLEPLAYING CLOVIN

Clovin stands 4 feet, 7 inches tall and has a barrel-like shape. His right head is fully formed and combines the features of a patchy-haired man with those of a goat, complete with stubby horns. His left head is about half normal size and has a soft, cherubic face partly covered with crocodilian hide. Clovin has a crab's pincer in place of his left hand and a bear's paw where his right foot should be. He wears an ill-fitting monk's robe with a belt made of hempen rope.

Clovin is the Abbot's faithful martinet, but he is despised by the other mongrelfolk, who accuse him of hoarding food and slowly starving them to death. He would let them starve, but the Abbot has forbidden it.

Clovin has the Two-Headed feature (see the mongrelfolk stat block in appendix D). His madness is embodied in the following statement: "Being drunk keeps me sane." He is drunk most of the time, but not to the extent that it impedes his combat ability, and his musical performance improves when he is inebriated.

The larger head does all the talking. The smaller head has a forked snake's tongue and can't do anything except hiss and make other horrible sounds.

## TELEPORT DESTINATION

Characters who teleport to this location from area K78 in Castle Ravenloft arrive at the point marked T on the map.

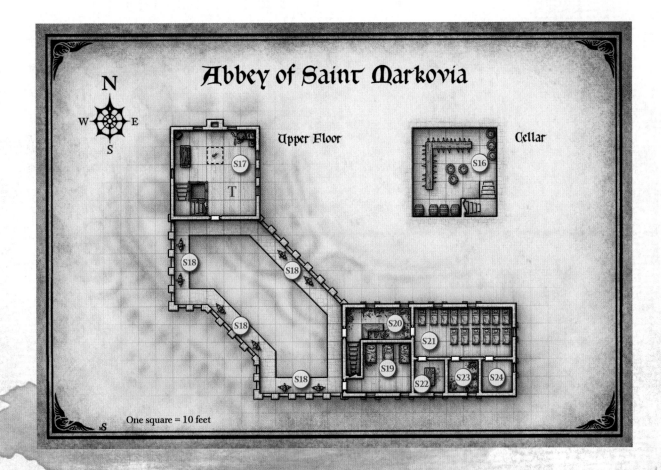

Abbey of Saint Markovia

Upper Floor

Cellar

One square = 10 feet

CLOVIN BELVIEW

### Thing on the Table

If the characters lift the black shroud covering the larger table, read:

> Beneath the shroud lies a creature made of stitched-together body parts. You recognize some of these parts as your own!

The creature on the table appears to be made from the body parts of the characters, which, of course, cannot be. Strahd's will is playing a trick on them. If a character touches the horrid creature, its true appearance is revealed:

> Your eyes play tricks, for what truly lies atop the table are chopped-up body parts, all of them taken from cold, gray, lifeless women, all of them waiting to be stitched together into something horrid.

The body parts were plundered from graves in Krezk. They are leftovers—pieces the Abbot didn't use in the creation of Strahd's bride (see area S13).

### S18. Curtain Wall

> Scarecrows line the abbey walls, looking outward. They wear tattered chain shirts and carry spears with rusty heads. The courtyard below is blanketed with fog.

The scarecrows are lashed to wooden stands. Though fearsome from a distance, they have no life to them.

It's a 15-foot drop from the top of the wall to the courtyard. Any creature that falls over the southwest wall tumbles 400 feet down the cliffside.

### S19. Barracks

> Bunk beds that have disintegrated with age lie in heaps along the walls of this moldy, thirty-foot-square room.

Long ago, the abbey employed guards to defend its walls, and they were quartered here.

#### EZMERELDA D'AVENIR

If the characters have not already encountered her elsewhere, the vampire hunter **Ezmerelda d'Avenir** (see appendix D) is here, plotting her next move.

Ezmerelda crept into Krezk unseen under cover of darkness and made her way to the abbey, in the hope of gaining knowledge about Strahd and his domain from the residents there. Having met the Abbot and Strahd's "bride" (area S13), Ezmerelda realizes the Abbot is insane. The Abbot told her that he is expecting Strahd to visit his bride-to-be. Ezmerelda has decided to wait for the vampire to come, so that she can destroy him away from Castle Ravenloft, far from his resting place. She is planning to create a magic circle in this room as an added precaution.

As the Abbot's guest, Ezmerelda is free to come and go as she pleases. If the characters seem committed to fighting Strahd, she abandons her plan and offers to join forces with them.

### S20. Upstairs Office

> A wooden counter shaped like an L stands at the front of this spacious office. All the other furniture has rotted away, leaving heaps of moldy wood and faded cloth.

The wood of the counter is old, soft, and easily broken. Nothing of value remains here. If the characters haven't already cleared out the madhouse (area S15), they can hear the whoops, laughter, and screams of the mongrelfolk below. The clamor continues as they explore areas S21–S24 to the east.

### S21. Haunted Hospital

> This spacious chamber contains bed frames of wrought iron arranged in two neat rows. Cobwebs and bits of rotten mattress cling to each frame.
>
> Three doors are spaced along the south wall, each with a plaque mounted on it. From west to east, the plaques read OPERATING ROOM, NURSERY, and MORGUE.

Six **shadows** haunt this room. They are the remnants of dark souls that perished here long ago. The creatures wait until one or more characters are at least 10 feet inside the room before moving out from within the normal shadows to attack. The shadows can't leave this room.

## S22. OPERATING ROOM

> A bloodstained table stands in the middle of this otherwise empty room.

The first time a character touches the table, read:

> A scream fills the room—a scream that echoes through time. It is followed by other, fainter screams of those who died under the knife. The screams fade until they are nothing more than haunting memories.

There is nothing of value here.

## S23. NURSERY

> This room contains the wreckage of old wooden cribs.

If the characters search the room, one of them (determined randomly) sees a figure reflected in the window glass: a nun in white robes, standing in the doorway. A look back toward the door reveals nothing there, and the reflection can't be seen again.

### FORTUNES OF RAVENLOFT
If your card reading reveals that a treasure is here, it is under the wreckage of one of the cribs.

## S24. MORGUE

> A raven perches on the windowsill of this otherwise empty room.

If the characters approach the **raven**, it flies to the shoulder of the nearest scarecrow in the garden (area S9).

A character who kills the raven is cursed. While cursed, the character has disadvantage on all attack rolls and ability checks. A *greater restoration* spell, a *remove curse* spell, or a similar effect ends the curse.

# SPECIAL EVENTS

You can use one or more of the following special events while the characters explore Krezk and the abbey.

## SOMETHING OLD

This event can occur if the characters don't or can't raise the burgomaster's son, Ilya, from the dead.

If alive, the Abbot learns that Ilya died recently and, in his human guise, visits the burgomaster's cottage. If one or more characters are staying there, they hear a knock at the door. Without bothering to introduce himself, the Abbot tells the burgomaster and his wife that he wants to raise their son from the dead. He claims that the "gods of light" want the Krezkov bloodline restored.

The characters can try to interfere in the raising of Ilya Krezkov. Otherwise, the burgomaster digs up his son's corpse. Without needing the requisite material components, the Abbot casts a *raise dead*, returning Ilya to life with 1 hit point. Anna Krezkova praises the Abbot and Saint Markovia for this generous act before tending to her son. The burgomaster, his grief dispelled, fears that he has misjudged the Abbot and has no way to repay him for this supreme act of kindness.

### DEVELOPMENT
Ilya Krezkov returns to life with a random form of indefinite madness (see "Madness Effects" in chapter 8, "Running the Game," of the *Dungeon Master's Guide*). The Abbot uses the raising of Ilya as leverage to get the burgomaster to undertake an unusual quest (see "Something Borrowed" below).

## SOMETHING NEW

The characters learn that a Krezkite woman named Dimira Yolensky (LG female human noncombatant) is about to give birth. A local midwife named Kretyana Dolvof (LG female human **commoner**) is summoned to the mother's cottage to deliver the newborn. In the absence of a priest, the burgomaster's wife, Anna Krezkova, is called upon to supervise the blessed event and offer prayers for the health of the mother and the child.

Dimira gives birth to a healthy baby boy, but the baby doesn't cry. While the mother coddles the infant, characters who succeed on a DC 10 Wisdom (Insight) check can see that Kretyana is deeply troubled. If the characters question the midwife, she tells them in confidence, "That child has no soul. Very sad."

Kretyana was raised to believe that newborns are soulless if they don't cry, and she has come to believe, rightly, that most Barovians lack souls.

## SOMETHING BORROWED

The Abbot needs a bridal gown. He doesn't trust the mongrelfolk to find one, so he pays a visit to Burgomaster Krezkov and instructs him to obtain a gown within a month, either as compensation for raising his dead son (see "Something Old" above) or on pain of death.

No one in Krezk can fashion such a gown, leaving the burgomaster with no choice but to look elsewhere. His wife, Anna, says she should personally lead a well-armed group of Krezkites to the east to Vallaki.

Anna Krezkova (LG female human **noble**) bids her husband farewell and leaves with two **guards**, four **commoners**, and a **mule** laden with provisions. If the characters are present, the burgomaster urges them to provide escort. If they agree, check for random encounters as they make their way along the Old Svalich Road, as normal. If the guards at Vallaki's gates can be convinced to let them in, Anna and the characters can begin searching for a bridal gown or a dressmaker. Local dressmakers are willing to fashion a gown for 50 gp, but Anna can't afford it, and the dress won't be finished in time. The dressmakers are quick to point out that Baroness Lydia Petrovna, the wife of Vallaki's burgomaster, owns a beautiful white bridal gown (see chapter 5, area N3p). The baroness, eager to please, is willing to give up her dress for a good cause, although her husband won't allow it and could care less about Krezk's problems.

If the characters don't accompany Anna on her quest, her expedition falls prey to the perils of the wilderness and never returns. Krezkov sends more villagers to find them, and these villagers are also lost. Unwilling to risk any more lives, Krezkov visits the abbey for the first time in his life and makes a desperate plea to the Abbot, who ignores the plea. Characters can escort the burgomaster to the abbey or eavesdrop on the burgomaster's conversation with the Abbot. If they do, they hear the Abbot promise "divine retribution" as punishment.

The evening after the burgomaster's visit, the Abbot releases all the mongrelfolk in the abbey's madhouse (area S15) and sets them on the village. They steal pigs, chickens, and anything else that's edible. None of the villagers are harmed, but their food supplies are depleted, and 2d6 mongrelfolk are killed. The surviving mongrelfolk return to the abbey with their plunder. The burgomaster is so distraught that he hangs himself from the rafters of his cottage a few days later.

The characters can stop all this from happening by delivering the dress to the Abbot. They can also stop the mayhem by halting the mongrelfolk as they descend from the abbey or by killing the Abbot beforehand.

### DEVELOPMENT

If Lydia Petrovna's bridal gown is delivered to the Abbot, he honors whatever deal he made with the characters. If the characters resort to magical trickery (for example, creating an illusory dress), the Abbot becomes hostile toward them once the deception is revealed.

## SOMETHING BLUE

This encounter occurs if the characters bring Ireena Kolyana to Krezk, as the priest Donavich suggested (see chapter 3, area E5f).

BARON KREZKOV

BARONESS KREZKOVA

Ireena hears a gentle voice calling to her. It leads her to the edge of the blessed pool (area S4). If the characters follow her, read:

> As Ireena reaches the pool's edge, an image appears in its sparkling blue waters: a handsome youth of kind and noble visage. The sadness in his eyes turns to sudden joy.
> "Tatyana!" he says. "It has been so long! Come, my love. Let us be together at last."
> Ireena gasps and puts a hand on her heart. "My beloved Sergei! In life, you were a prince and a man of faith. We were to be married long ago. Has this blessed pool called your spirit to me?" She reaches toward the water's surface as a hand of water rises up to take hers.

If the characters intervene, pulling Ireena away from the water's grasp, the hand sinks back into the pool, Sergei's image fades, and she cries as she screams his name.

If the characters allow her to take the hand, read:

> Ireena is pulled into the pool and embraces Sergei beneath the rippling water. You have never seen a happier couple as they both begin to fade from view.

The spirit of Sergei takes Ireena to a place where Strahd can't harm her. She is safe with him.

Whether or not Sergei takes Ireena, Strahd senses that the two have found each other. He reacts as follows:

> A peal of thunder shakes the land, and the dark clouds coalesce into a terrible visage. A deep, dark voice from beyond the mountains cries out, "She is mine!" A terrible crack resounds as blue lightning splits the sky and strikes the pool.

Each creature within 15 feet of the pool must make a successful DC 17 Dexterity check or be knocked prone. The blast knocks down the old gazebo as well. A creature in the water when the lightning strikes must make a DC 17 Constitution saving throw, taking 44 (8d10) lightning damage on a failed save, or half as much damage on a successful one.

Strahd's wrath destroys the blessing on the pool, rendering its waters nonmagical and preventing the spirit of Sergei from manifesting in them again.

### DEVELOPMENT

If Sergei and Ireena are brought together, Ireena is no longer within Strahd's grasp. Strahd blames the characters for his loss and seeks to destroy them from this moment on. Not long afterward, he has one of his servants deliver a letter to the characters, inviting them to Castle Ravenloft. If the characters open and read the letter, show the players "Strahd's Invitation" in appendix F. If the characters head toward the castle, they have no threatening random encounters on the way.

# CHAPTER 9: TSOLENKA PASS

TSOLENKA PASS IS A GRAVEL ROAD THAT hugs Mount Ghakis, climbing to great heights. The road starts at the Raven River crossroads (chapter 2, area R) and travels seven miles to a gatehouse (areas T1–T3) and a guard tower (areas T4–T6), as well as a stone bridge (areas T7–T9) that spans the Luna River. Wind and snow make the journey treacherous. Without some way to keep warm, characters who aren't dressed for cold weather suffer the effects of extreme cold at night (see "Weather" in chapter 5, "Adventure Environments," of the *Dungeon Master's Guide*).

## AREAS OF THE PASS

The following areas correspond to labels on the map of the Tsolenka Pass on page 158. These structures are made of tightly fitted stone and can't be scaled without the aid of magic or a climber's kit.

### T1. GATEHOUSE PORTCULLIS

When the characters approach from the west, read:

> The shelf of rock on which the mountain road clings grows narrow. To your left, the icy cliffs rise sharply toward dark, rolling clouds. To your right, the ground falls away into a sea of fog. Ahead, through the wind and snow, you see a high wall of black stone lined with spikes and topped by statues of demonic vultures with horned heads. Set in the center of the wall is a closed iron portcullis, behind which burns a curtain of green flame.
>
> On the other side of the dark wall, gripping the mountain's edge, is a guard tower of white stone topped by golden statues of mighty warriors.

The gatehouse is 30 feet high. The adjoining walls are 20 feet high and lined with stone spikes. If the characters circumvent the gate by flying or climbing over it, the statues on the gatehouse (area T2) animate and attack.

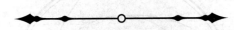

THE ROAD CURVED AND CLIMBED, MAKING *a lengthy switchback into this edge of Mount Ghakis. The air grew colder, not warmer, and patches of snow became more frequent until they were unbroken.*

—Strahd von Zarovich
in *I, Strahd: The Memoirs of a Vampire*

If the characters approach within 10 feet of the portcullis, it shrieks with the sound of metal on metal as it rises on its own. It stays open for 1 minute, then closes.

### T2. DEMON STATUES

These statues are actually two petrified **vrocks**. If they are attacked, or if the characters bypass the gatehouse, the vrocks revert to flesh and attack, pursuing prey that flees and fighting until slain.

### T3. CURTAIN OF GREEN FLAME

A curtain of green flame fills the eastern archway of the gatehouse. Any creature that enters the curtain for the first time on a turn or starts its turn in the green flame takes 33 (6d10) fire damage.

A successful casting of *dispel magic* (DC 16) suppresses the curtain for 1 minute. The curtain is also suppressed within an *antimagic field*.

### T4. GUARD TOWER, GROUND FLOOR

The tower door is made of ironbound wood and barred from within. A character can force open the door with a successful DC 22 Strength (Athletics) check.

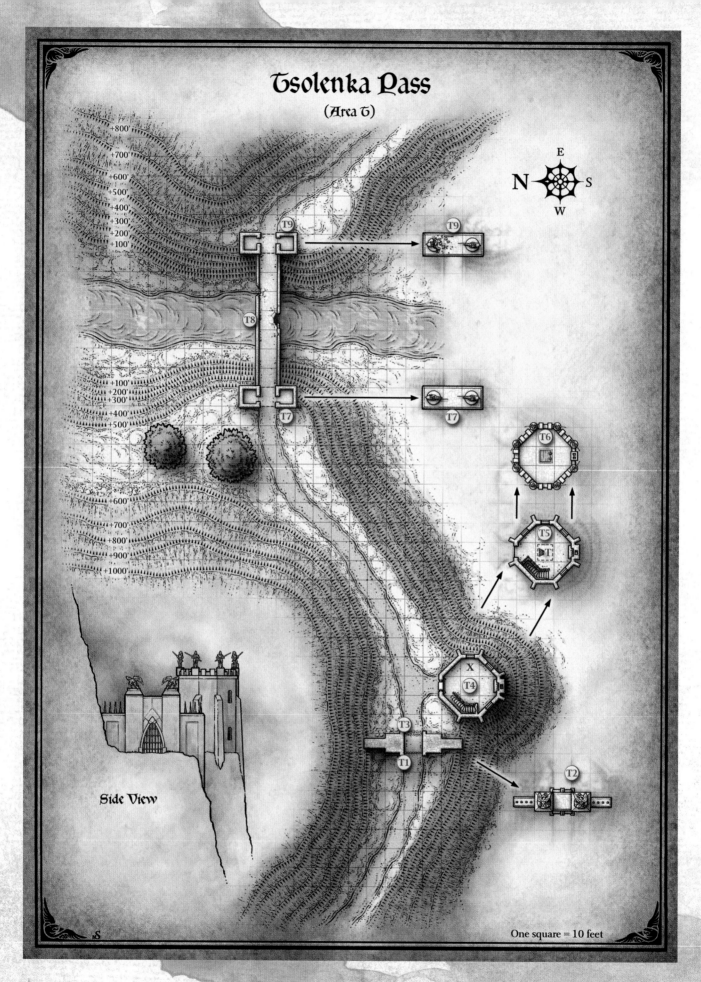

# Tsolenka Pass
## (Area T)

**Side View**

One square = 10 feet

A cold hearth stands across from the door, the wind howling down its chimney. A stone staircase is on the south wall. Three windows look out over a foggy sea.

The stairs climb 20 feet to area T5.

### TELEPORT DESTINATION

Characters who teleport to this location from area K78 in Castle Ravenloft arrive at the point marked X on the map.

## T5. GUARD TOWER, UPPER FLOOR

The upper level of the tower is an icebox with windows set in almost every wall. A rusted iron ladder bolted to the floor and ceiling leads up to a wooden trapdoor. Mounted above the stone hearth is a dire wolf's head. The wind coming down the chimney howls in its stead.

The trapdoor in the ceiling pushes open with a squeal, revealing the rooftop (area T6) and the stormy gray sky.

## T6. GUARD TOWER ROOFTOP

Ten-foot-tall, gold-plated statues stand atop the battlements, facing outward. Each one depicts a female human knight holding a lance. The cold wind stirs the snow, under which you see human skeletons clad in rusty mail.

The roof is 40 feet high and 540 feet above the misty valley below. A wooden trapdoor in the floor squeals as it is pulled open, revealing area T5 below.

The skeletons are the remains of four guards who held this post long ago. Characters who search the remains find tattered bits of cloth, broken longbows and arrows, rusted blades in ruined sheaths, and rusty chain mail.

### FORTUNES OF RAVENLOFT

If your card reading reveals that a treasure is here, read:

The swirling snow assumes the forms of thin, young women. The wind howls, "Begone! The treasure is ours!"

The forms are six snow maidens. Use the **specter** statistics, with the following modifications:

- The snow maidens have immunity to cold damage.
- The snow maidens' Life Drain attack deals cold damage instead of necrotic damage.

The snow maidens don't speak, nor are they interested in hearing what the characters have to say. If the characters don't leave at once, the snow maidens attack. When the last snow maiden is defeated, the treasure that the characters seek magically appears in the swirling snow on the rooftop.

## T7. WESTERN ARCH

When the characters approach the bridge, read:

The snowy pass comes to a gorge spanned by a stone bridge. At each end of the bridge is a thirty-foot-tall, thirty-foot-wide stone arch. Atop each one are two statues of armored knights on horseback with lances, charging toward one another. The wind bites and howls like wolves as it passes through the gorge.

The western arch contains empty guard posts, one on each side of the bridge. These 10-foot-wide chambers provide some protection against the howling wind.

## T8. STONE BRIDGE

The low walls that enclose the stone bridge have fallen away in a couple of places, but the bridge appears intact. A black-cloaked rider on a charcoal-colored horse guards the middle of the bridge.

The cloaked rider is a manifestation of Strahd von Zarovich—a grim warning to proceed no further. If the characters interact with the manifestation in any way, the rider and horse disperse like ash in the wind.

Five hundred feet below the bridge is the Luna River, barely visible through the fog. Though slippery in a few places, the 10-foot-wide, 90-foot-long bridge is safe to cross.

## T9. EASTERN ARCH

One of the statues atop this arch has crumbled, leaving only the hindquarters of the horse intact. The mountain pass continues beyond.

This arch contains 10-foot-square guard posts, one on each side of the bridge. Both rooms are empty.

Beyond this arch, Tsolenka Pass hugs the mountainside for three miles before branching north and south. The northern branch leads to the Amber Temple (chapter 13). The southern branch continues to wrap around Mount Ghakis until it ends at the deadly fog that surrounds Barovia (see chapter 2, "Mists of Ravenloft").

# SPECIAL EVENTS

You can use one or both of the following events as the characters make their way along Tsolenka Pass.

## ROC OF MOUNT GHAKIS

As the characters cross the stone bridge (area T8) from east to west—possibly on their way back from the Amber Temple (chapter 13)—they are spotted by a **roc** that has survived in the mountains for thousands of years. The

roc has a great nest on the top of Mount Ghakis to the southeast and feeds on fish in the nearby lake.

When the Roc of Mount Ghakis appears, read:

> Diving toward the bridge is a creature of unearthly size—a bird so monstrous that its wings blot out the sky.

The roc attacks a random creature on the bridge, snatching up a horse or a mule, if one is available. Otherwise, it attacks a party member. It can't reach characters who hide in the guard posts at either end of the bridge. If it has nothing to attack on its turn, the roc lets loose a horrible shriek and flies back to its nest.

## BLOODHORN'S CHARGE

As the characters make their way along Tsolenka Pass, they encounter a beast that the druids and berserkers of Barovia call Sangzor ("Bloodhorn"):

> The road ahead is cut out of the mountainside, rising steeply to one side and falling away on the other. Mist and snow greatly reduce visibility, and the howling wind cuts through you like a knife.

If no character has a passive Wisdom (Perception) score of 16 or higher, the party is surprised. Otherwise, read:

> A nine-foot-tall goat stands atop a crag above you, its gray fur blending perfectly with the rock of the mountainside. It lowers its head, and malice glimmers in its eyes.

Sangzor is a **giant goat** known for its supernatural resilience and evil disposition. Mountain folk have been hunting it for years. Modify its statistics as follows:

- It has an Intelligence of 6 (−2 modifier) and is chaotic evil.
- It has 33 hit points.
- It has resistance to bludgeoning, piercing, and slashing damage from nonmagical attacks.
- Its challenge rating is 1 (200 XP).

The giant goat charges down the mountainside (using its Charge feature) and rams a character. If the attack hits and the target fails its saving throw, it is sent tumbling down the mountainside, falling 100 feet onto a ledge.

The goat flees if it takes 10 damage or more. The mist and snowfall prevent seeing anything more than 60 feet away. Once the goat is out of sight, it disappears through a cleft.

### DEVELOPMENT

A character who wears Sangzor's pelt can command the respect of the berserkers who inhabit Strahd's domain. They will not attack the character or that character's companions unless provoked.

# CHAPTER 10: THE RUINS OF BEREZ

ONG BEFORE IREENA KOLYANA, THERE
was a peasant from Berez named Marina.
The vampire Strahd first met Marina
in this small village on the shore of the
Luna River. Marina bore a striking resemblance to Strahd's beloved Tatyana,
both in appearance and manner, and she
became Strahd's obsession. He seduced her in the dead
of night and feasted on her blood, but before she could
be turned into a vampire, the burgomaster of Berez, Lazlo Ulrich, with the aid of a local priest named Brother
Grigor, killed Marina to save her soul from damnation.
Enraged, Strahd slew the priest and the burgomaster,
then used his power over the land to swell the river,
flooding the village and forcing the residents to flee.
Later the marsh crept in, preventing the villagers from
returning. Berez has remained mostly abandoned since.

The ruins of Berez are now home to **Baba Lysaga** (see
appendix D), an almost mythic figure tied to Strahd's ancient past. A hermit, she spends most of her time craft-
ing and animating scarecrows to hunt down and kill the
ravens and the wereravens that infest Strahd's domain.
When she isn't working evil magic, Baba Lysaga sacrifices beasts to Mother Night and collects their blood,
then bathes in the blood on nights of the new moon in a
ritual to stave off the effects of extreme old age.

Baba Lysaga recently stole a magic gemstone from
the Wizards of Wines vineyard (chapter 12), in the hope
that the wereravens who protect the vineyard will try
to reclaim it. She keeps it in her hut as bait to lure her
enemies to their deaths. The gem has given her hut a
semblance of life.

## APPROACHING THE RUINS

The following boxed text assumes that the characters
approach Berez from the north, along the trail leading
from the Old Svalich Road. If they approach from a different direction, don't read the first sentence.

> The trail hugs the river for several miles. The dirt and
> grass soon turn to marsh as the trail dissolves into
> spongy earth pockmarked with stands of tall reeds and
> pools of stagnant water. A thick shroud of fog covers
> all. Scattered throughout the marsh are old peasant
> cottages, their walls covered with black mildew, their
> roofs mostly caved in. These decrepit dwellings seem to
> hunker down in the mire, as though they have long since
> given up on escaping the thick mud. Everywhere you
> look, black clouds of flies dart about, hungry for blood.
>
> The fog is much thinner on the far side of the river,
> where a light flashes amid a dark ring of standing stones.

The river ranges in depth but is never more than 10
feet deep. Muriel Vinshaw, a wereraven in human form,
lurks amid the circle of standing stones (area U6) and
is using a lantern to signal the heroes. In the village
proper, fog prevents a creature from seeing any other
creature or object more than 120 feet away.

I HAD NOTHING LEFT TO GIVE
*but my own life's blood, but it*
*was hers to take. She would at*
*last be my bride.*

—Strahd von Zarovich
in I, Strahd: The Memoirs
of a Vampire

A few sections of dirt road have survived, and these places are not difficult terrain. The marsh, however, is difficult terrain. Whenever the characters take a short or long rest in the marsh, even if they barricade themselves in a ruined building, they are accosted by 1d4 swarms of hungry flies (use the **swarm of insects** [wasps] stat block in the *Monster Manual*). The swarms don't trouble characters in areas U3 or U5.

## Marsh Scarecrows

Seven **scarecrows** stand guard in the marsh. They appear to be ordinary, nonmagical scarecrows stuffed with raven feathers until one or more of them are attacked, until Baba Lysaga commands them to attack, or until someone activates the howling skulls that surround Baba Lysaga's goat pen (see area U2).

# Areas of Berez

The following areas correspond to labels on the map of Berez on page 164.

## U1. Abandoned Cottages

As you approach this cluster of ruined cottages separated by low stone walls, you see a short stretch of dirt road that has remained intact.

The cottages contain rotted furnishings and nothing of value. The walls that separate the cottages are 3 feet tall and easily scaled or circumvented.

## U2. Ulrich Mansion

Toward the south end of the village lie the remains of a mansion built on higher ground. It has been reduced to piles of stone and rotting timber. Empty, arched windows stare at you. South of the ruin, an untamed garden runs rampant, surrounded by broken walls that are no longer able to contain it. East of the ruin, someone has erected a crude wooden fence, forming a circular yard in which several goats are penned. Surmounting the fence posts are human skulls.

The ruined mansion is littered with the rotted remains of furniture and decor. The last burgomaster of Berez, Lazlo Ulrich, haunts the ruin as a **ghost**. If the characters search the mansion, the ghost appears before them:

A ghost takes shape in the fog, assuming the form of a giant of a man, his features mutilated and his entrails hanging out like frayed ropes. Despite its intimidating presence, the apparition has a cringing light in its eyes. "Why do you invade my home? Begone, I beseech you!"

Strahd refuses to let Burgomaster Ulrich's spirit find rest because of what he did to poor Marina. The ghost recounts Marina's sad tale if prompted. Only by convincing Ulrich that Marina has been reborn in the form of Ireena Kolyana can the characters put the tortured spirit to rest. The ghost must see Ireena in the flesh, and it can't travel beyond the confines of the crumbled mansion.

Ulrich's ghost is neutral good. It attacks if threatened or if the characters begin searching the ruined mansion for treasure. If the ghost is reduced to 0 hit points, it reforms after 24 hours. The characters receive experience points for the ghost only if they lay Ulrich's spirit to rest, not if they defeat the ghost in combat.

### Fortunes of Ravenloft
If your card reading reveals that a treasure is hidden in Berez, Ulrich's ghost points the characters to the treasure's true location, saying these words as it fades away:

"Travel west. Two hundred paces from the mansion lies a monument to my folly and the treasure you seek."

Characters who follow Ulrich's directions end up at area U5.

### Cellar
Buried under rubble inside the mansion is a stone staircase that leads down to an intact cellar. A single character can clear the rubble in 4 hours, and multiple characters working together can reduce the time proportionately. The cellar is a 30-foot-square room with mortared stone walls, a 10-foot-high ceiling supported by wooden beams, and a floor submerged under 3 inches of stagnant water. The cellar contains two dozen empty, rotted casks from the Wizard of Wines winery. Each cask is labeled Champagne du le Stomp.

### Garden
The garden behind the ruined mansion has run wild. Hidden behind tall weeds and thorny vines are nude sculptures of handsome men and beautiful women, as well as carved stone benches.

Four **giant poisonous snakes** attack characters who venture more than 10 feet inside the garden.

### Goat Pen
Baba Lysaga captures goats and uses their blood in her rituals of longevity. Nine **goats** are trapped behind this fence. Fifty human skulls are mounted on the tops of the fence posts, spaced 10 feet apart.

There is no gate in the fence, and Baba Lysaga uses her flying skull (see area U3) to enter and leave the pen. If the characters try to set the goats free by dismantling or damaging part of the fence, the skulls atop the fence posts begin howling and continue to howl for 1 minute. The racket attracts Baba Lysaga, who arrives in her flying skull on initiative count 20 in 2 rounds. The howling skulls also attract the seven **scarecrows** in the marsh (see "Marsh Scarecrows" above). Roll initiative once for all the scarecrows.

## U3. Baba Lysaga's Hut

Someone has built a ramshackle wooden hut on the stump of what was once an enormous tree. The rotting roots of the stump thrust up from the mire like the legs of a gigantic spider.

An open doorway is visible on one side of the hut, beneath which floats the upside-down, hollowed-out skull of a giant. Flanking the hut's doorway are two iron cages that dangle like hideous ornaments from the eaves. Scores of ravens are trapped in each one. They squawk and flutter their wings excitedly as you approach.

**Baba Lysaga** (see appendix D) is inside her hut unless she has been drawn forth by activity elsewhere. The squawks of the birds are music to her ears, but the noise makes it impossible for her to hear anyone approaching. Only the howling of the skulls in area U2 or sounds of combat nearby are loud enough to be heard over the squawking.

Inside each cage is a **swarm of ravens** that fiercely attacks Baba Lysaga and her scarecrows if released. Each cage is held shut by one of Baba Lysaga's *arcane lock* spells, and opening it requires a *knock* spell or a successful DC 20 Strength check. A character can also pick the lock with thieves' tools and a successful DC 20 Dexterity check.

### Giant Skull

The upside-down skull that floats next to the hut is a hill giant's skull that Baba Lysaga has hollowed out and transformed into a vehicle. It hovers in place until Baba Lysaga commands it to fly, which she can do only while inside it. It has a flying speed of 40 feet. No one else can control the skull. A creature inside the skull has three-quarters cover against attacks made from outside the skull. The skull is big enough to hold one Medium creature. It has AC 15, 50 hit points, and immunity to poison and psychic damage.

### Hut Interior

The hut is fifteen feet on a side and packed with old furniture, including a wooden cot, a wicker cabinet, a slender wardrobe, a wooden table, a stool, a barrel-topped wooden chest reinforced with brass bands, and an iron tub stained with blood. In the middle of the room is a ghastly wooden crib with a small, angelic child sitting in it. All the furnishings except for the crib are bolted to the floor. Beneath the crib, green light seeps up through cracks between the rotting floorboards.

The child and the crib are illusions created by Baba Lysaga using a *programmed illusion* spell. Baba Lysaga refers to the child as "Strahd" and created the illusion

**Baba Lysaga's Creeping Hut**
One square = 5 feet

out of madness, because she considers herself a protective mother.

Beneath the hut's rotting floorboards is a 3-foot-deep cavity containing the magic, green-glowing gem that Baba Lysaga took from the Wizard of the Wines winery. This gem animates the hut (see "The Creeping Hut" in the "Special Events" section below). The floorboards can be ripped up or smashed with a successful DC 14 Strength check. Characters can also break through the floor by dealing 10 damage to it. The hut doesn't give up the gemstone easily, however (see "Baba Lysaga's Creeping Hut" in appendix D). If the gem is destroyed or removed from the cavity, the hut becomes incapacitated.

Baba Lysaga keeps soiled robes in the wardrobe and assorted spell components in the wicker cabinet. The tub is where she ritually bathes in blood to prevent aging (see "Gifts of Mother Night" in the "Baba Lysaga" section in appendix D). If the characters approach the hut at an appropriate time without being noticed, they can see Baba Lysaga bathing.

### Treasure

The wooden chest in the hut is protected by a *glyph of warding* that requires a successful DC 17 Intelligence (Investigation) check to find. The glyph deals 5d8 thunder damage when triggered. Opening the lid releases four **crawling claws** that fight until destroyed. Also contained in the chest are various items that Baba Lysaga has taken from dead adventurers over the years:

- 1,300 gp
- Five 500 gp gemstones
- A vial containing *oil of sharpness*
- Two *spell scrolls* (*mass cure wounds* and *revivify*)
- A pouch containing ten *+1 sling bullets*
- A set of *pipes of haunting*
- A *stone of good luck*

### Fortunes of Ravenloft

If your card reading reveals that a treasure is here, it's in the chest with the other items.

# Berez
## (Area U)

**Scarecrows**

N
W · E
S

One square = 100 feet

---

## U4. Churchyard

> Through the fog you see the empty shell an old stone church, north of which is a cemetery of leaning gravestones enclosed by a disintegrating iron fence. Half of the cemetery has sunk into the mire.

Rotted coffins and moldy bones are buried in the graveyard. Characters who explore the gutted church find the rotten remains of a pulpit and an old iron bell half immersed in the marsh, lying amid the remains of a collapsed steeple.

## U5. Marina's Monument

Strahd had this monument erected after Marina's death. The monument is hidden in the marsh, and the characters aren't likely to find it on their own unless they scour the area thoroughly. If they lay Burgomaster Ulrich's spirit to rest (see area U2), it points them to this location before fading away. Without Ulrich's guidance, the characters must enter the square in which the monument is located and search that area. A character who searches the area for 10 minutes can make a DC 15 Wisdom (Perception) check, finding the monument on a success. If the monument isn't found, the check can be repeated after another 10 minutes of searching.

The following boxed text assumes that the characters have met Ireena Kolyana. If they have not, don't read the sentence that mentions her.

Hidden by the fog and elevated a few feet above the surrounding marsh is a raised plot of land, barely ten feet on a side, enclosed by a disintegrating iron fence. In the center of the plot is a life-sized stone monument carved in the likeness of a kneeling peasant girl clutching a rose. Although her features are gray and weatherworn, she bears a striking resemblance to Ireena Kolyana. Carved into the monument's base is an epitaph.

The epitaph reads as follows: Marina, Taken by the Mists.

## FORTUNES OF RAVENLOFT

If your card reading reveals that a treasure is here, it is hidden in a cavity underneath the monument, which can be tipped over or moved aside by someone who makes a successful DC 15 Strength check.

If the characters disturb the monument, read:

The croaking frogs and chirping crickets fall silent, and the stench of decay grows strong. You hear the trudge of heavy footsteps through mud and water as bloated gray shapes shamble out of the fog.

Seven distended human corpses have risen from the mire west of the monument. These walking corpses are 60 feet away when first seen. Use the **commoner** statistics for the corpses, but reduce their walking speed to 20 feet and give them immunity to the charmed and frightened conditions. When a corpse is reduced to 0 hit points, it splits open, disgorging a **swarm of poisonous snakes**. The snakes are hungry and fight until slain.

Characters can take the treasure and flee, easily outpacing the snake-swollen corpses.

## U6. STANDING STONES

A dozen moss-covered menhirs form a near-perfect circle in the spongy earth. These weathered stones range in height from 15 to 18 feet. A couple of them lean inward as if to share some great secret with their inscrutable neighbors. A wary-looking peasant woman lurks behind the tallest stone, a rusty lantern clutched in one gnarled hand and a dagger clutched in the other.

The woman is Muriel Vinshaw, a **wereraven** (see appendix D) and friend of the Martikov family (see chapters 5 and 12). A resident of Vallaki, Muriel spies on Baba Lysaga for her fellow wereravens. However, she avoids the village proper, preferring to lurk on the outskirts. If the characters allow her to speak, Muriel warns them about the dangers of Berez and arms them with the following information:

- Berez was abandoned long ago after the river rose and flooded the village.
- An ancient and powerful hag named Baba Lysaga lives in a hut in the middle of the village. When not in her hut, Baba Lysaga flies around in a giant skull.
- The scarecrows of Berez are murderous creatures under the hag's control. They surround Baba Lysaga's hut and serve as an early warning system.
- Baba Lysaga periodically sends her scarecrows to attack the Wizard of Wines, a winery and vineyard west of Berez. She's made enemies of the Martikov family, which owns and operates the winery and vineyard.
- The hag has trapped several mountain goats in a pen near the ruins of an old mansion. (Muriel assumes that Baba Lysaga feeds on these animals.)

Muriel avoids combat and flees if attacked. She conceals her lycanthropic nature for as long as possible, and she doesn't willingly identify other wereravens with whom she's acquainted. She can't be persuaded to accompany the characters if they decide to confront Baba Lysaga. However, Muriel knows Barovia well enough to point out other nearby locations that might interest the adventurers, including the ruined mansion of Argynvostholt (see chapter 7) and the ancient burial ground known as Yester Hill (see chapter 14). Muriel grew up hearing stories about the druids of Yester Hill, specifically how they turned away from their ancient beliefs to worship the devil Strahd. Muriel knows that the druids visit the circle of standing stones from time to time, and she does her best to avoid them.

## CIRCLE OF STANDING STONES

This ring of menhirs is one of the oldest structures in the Balinok Mountains—older than the Amber Temple, and much older than Castle Ravenloft and the various Barovian settlements scattered throughout the valley. The menhirs were raised by the same ancient folk who carved the megaliths near Old Bonegrinder (see chapter 6). Characters who have seen those megaliths can, with a successful DC 10 Intelligence check, discern rudimentary similarities between those stones and the menhirs arranged here.

The circle is 100 feet across, and the menhirs are spaced apart at regular intervals. The stones located to the north, west, south, and east are taller than the other eight stones, which have weatherworn glyphs carved into them that represent different animals. Characters who inspect the smaller menhirs can discern the following animal shapes carved into them: bear, elk, hawk, goat, owl, panther, raven, and wolf.

The standing stones are nonmagical. However, druid characters who enter the circle can sense that powerful gods once blessed this site, and that it still holds some measure of power. They can also sense one of its properties, namely that creatures within the circle can't be targeted by any divination magic or perceived through magical scrying sensors.

The circle has another property that druid characters can't sense but might discover when they use the Wild Shape feature within the circle's confines. Any druid that uses the Wild Shape feature within the circle gains the maximum number of hit points available to the new form. For example, a druid character using the Wild Shape feature to assume the form of a giant eagle would have 44 (4d10 + 4) hit points while in that form.

At your discretion, the circle might have other strange properties that have been forgotten over time. Although she knows something of the circle's history, Muriel is unaware of its properties.

# SPECIAL EVENTS

You can use one or both of the following special events while the characters are exploring the ruins of Berez.

## CREEPING HUT

Baba Lysaga has given a semblance of life to her hut using a magic gemstone stolen from the Wizard of Wines vineyard. If the characters overstay their welcome, she commands the hut to animate and attack them. If this happens, read:

> The giant roots beneath the hut come to life and pull themselves up out of the mire. The hut and the roots lurch and groan, becoming a lumbering mass that cracks as it walks, crushing all in its path.

**Baba Lysaga's creeping hut** (see appendix D) is a ponderous construct that heeds Baba Lysaga's instructions and no one else's. It fights until destroyed or until the gemstone that animates it is removed or destroyed. Baba Lysaga does everything she can to keep the characters from obtaining the gemstone, without which the hut is incapacitated.

## LOST BATTLEFIELD

This event occurs as the characters travel north of Berez after leaving the ruins.

> You hear sounds of battle, but the fog has grown so thick that you can barely see more than sixty feet in any direction. Suddenly, the fog takes on the forms of soldiers on horseback charging across the field. They collide with armored pike-bearers wearing devil-horned helms. As each soldier falls in battle, it turns to fading mist. Hundreds more soldiers collide in a storm of screams and clashing metal.

Characters can move through this ghostly battlefield unscathed, and they can't harm the foggy forms around them. The soldiers aren't solid enough for the characters to discern emblems or insignia, but it's clear that both armies are human.

If the characters have not yet explored Argynvostholt (chapter 7), add:

> You hear a thunderous roar, and seconds later a huge dragon made of silver mist glides overhead, dispersing enemy soldiers with each flap of its mighty wings. Its long, reptilian tail slices through the air above you as the dragon carves a swath through the fog, affording you a fleeting glimpse of a dark mansion overlooking the valley.

The dragon, like the soldiers, is a harmless phantom. The mansion that the characters see is Argynvostholt.

# CHAPTER 11: VAN RICHTEN'S TOWER

ONE OF THE MEN EMPLOYED BY STRAHD TO raise Castle Ravenloft was an archwizard named Khazan. After his work on the castle was complete, Khazan retired to the Barovian valley and built a tower for himself on a small island on Lake Bara-tok. With the help of some engineers and laborers, he also built an earth-and-gravel causeway connecting the island with the nearby shore.

In his waning years, Khazan visited the Amber Temple (chapter 13) and discovered the secret to becoming a lich. He returned to his tower and was able to complete the transformation. Some years later, after Strahd became a vampire, Khazan paid a visit to Castle Ravenloft with the notion of challenging Strahd for rulership of Barovia. Instead, much to Khazan's surprise, Strahd persuaded him to serve as an advisor in matters of magic. When not advising Strahd, the lich spent most of his time in the Amber Temple, trying to master the secret of demilichdom in the hope of finding a way to magically project his spirit beyond the confines of Strahd's realm. His efforts failed, and Khazan destroyed himself. His remains lie entombed in the catacombs of Ravenloft.

Khazan's tower stood empty for ages, it seemed, and would have collapsed under the weight of neglect were it not for the magic wards placed on it long ago. Recently, the tower was taken over by the legendary vampire hunter Rudolph van Richten, who used it as a base from which to explore Barovia. He has since relocated to the nearby town of Vallaki, where he hides in plain sight.

Following in the vampire hunter's footsteps is his protégé, Ezmerelda d'Avenir, who has taken to living in the tower while she searches for her mentor. She isn't present when the characters arrive, however.

*VAN RICHTEN HAS RETURNED, the old fool. He tries to hide from me, but I shall find him. He and I have much to discuss.*

—Strahd von Zarovich

## APPROACHING THE TOWER

The Svalich Woods have swallowed up the road that once led to the tower. Now only a wide dirt trail remains.

> You come to a cold mountain lake enclosed by misty woods and rocky bluffs. Thick fog creeps across the dark, still waters. The trail ends at a grass-covered causeway that stretches a hundred yards across the lake to a flat, marshy island with a stone tower on it. The tower is old and decrepit, with collapsing scaffolds clinging to one side where a large gash has split the wall. Timeworn griffon statues, their wings and flanks covered with moss, perch atop buttresses that support the walls.
>
> Parked near the base of the tower, within sight of the entrance, is a barrel-topped wagon spattered with mud.

The tower stands 80 feet tall. It has four levels (each 20 feet high) and a mostly intact slate tile roof. The second, third, and fourth floors have arrow slits that are 6 inches wide, 3 feet tall, and 1 foot thick. The tower's uppermost level overhangs the levels below it and has window boxes in addition to arrow slits.

The mossy griffons atop the buttresses are nothing more than decorative statues.

## KHAZAN'S SPELL DRAIN

Khazan warded his tower so that he alone could cast spells near or within it. The effect is identical to an *antimagic field* centered on the tower and extending 5 feet from it in all directions. The effect doesn't apply to magic traps and constructs created by Khazan, including the trap on the tower door in area V2, the golems in areas V4, and the animated suit of armor in area V7.

# Areas of the Tower

The following areas correspond to labels on the map of Van Richten's Tower on page 170.

## V1. Ezmerelda's Magic Wagon

Ezmerelda's wagon is parked in front of the tower. If the characters investigate the wagon, read:

> Under layers of mud, this wagon sports a fresh coat of purple paint, and its wheels have fancy gold trim. A brass lantern hangs from each corner, and red drapes cover a tombstone-shaped window on each side. A steel padlock secures the back door, hanging from which is a cheap wooden sign that reads, "Keep out!"

The wagon radiates an aura of conjuration magic if it is scrutinized with a *detect magic* spell. A character who casts an *identify* spell on the wagon learns the command words needed to operate it.

Anyone who sits in the driver's seat and speaks its command word ("Drovash") summons a pair of quasi-real draft horses, which are magically tethered to the wagon and can't be separated from it. The horses and wagon have a speed of 30 feet, and the horses heed the driver's simple commands. The driver can dismiss the horses with a second command word ("Arvesh"). The horses can be dispelled (DC 15) but not harmed.

The wagon has a hidden trapdoor in its underbelly that can be detected by a character who scuttles under the wagon and succeeds on a DC 13 Wisdom (Perception) check. The trapdoor opens into the wagon and is the only safe way inside.

## Booby Trap

The inside handle of the door has a wire looped around it, and the wire is connected to a flask of alchemist's fire hanging from the wagon's ceiling. When the door is opened, the flask falls and explodes, igniting one hundred more flasks of alchemist's fire that dangle from wires like ornaments along the wagon's interior walls. A creature within 30 feet of the wagon when it explodes must succeed on a DC 12 Constitution saving throw, taking 55 (10d10) fire damage on a failed save, or half as much damage on a successful one. Creatures inside the wagon or within 5 feet of it have disadvantage on the saving throw. The wagon is reduced to flinders by the explosion, and the contents of the wagon (see "Treasure" below) are destroyed as well.

A character inside the wagon spots the trap automatically (no ability check required) and can disable it with a successful DC 10 Dexterity check. A failed attempt to disable the trap triggers it.

## Treasure

The interior of the wagon contains the following items:

- A wooden trunk covered with claw marks that holds a battleaxe, a flail, a morningstar, a light crossbow, and 10 silvered crossbow bolts
- A narrow wardrobe containing three sets of fine clothes, two sets of traveler's clothes, several pairs of shoes, a harlequin mask, and three wigs
- A climber's kit, a disguise kit, a healer's kit, and a poisoner's kit
- A lyre with golden strings (worth 50 gp)
- A sculpted wooden cage holding a chicken and a silver ewer (worth 100 gp) with five chicken eggs in it
- A tiny wooden box containing a deck of tarokka cards (see appendix E) wrapped in silk

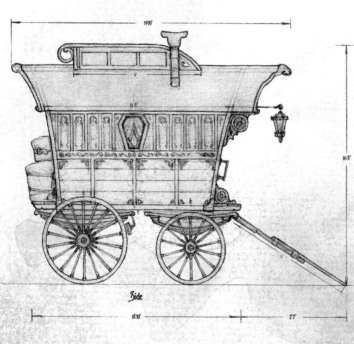

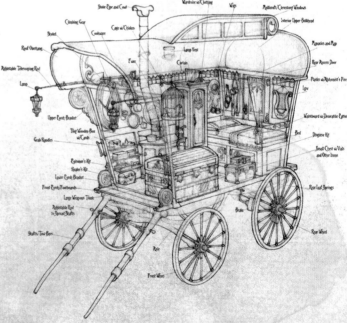

- A set of copper pots and pans (worth 50 gp)
- Three sets of manacles
- A shovel
- A wooden chest containing a gold holy symbol of the Morninglord (worth 100 gp), three vials of holy water, three vials of perfume, two vials of antitoxin, a 50-foot coil of hempen rope, a tinderbox, a steel mirror, a sharpened wooden stake, and a spyglass
- Two *spell scrolls* (*major image* and *remove curse*)
- A map of Barovia (showing all the locations marked on this adventure's map of Barovia)
- A charred page from van Richten's journal (show the players "Journal of Rudolph van Richten" in appendix F).

## V2. TOWER DOOR

> The tower door is made of iron, with no visible handles or hinges. In the middle of the door is a large, embossed symbol—a connected series of lines with eight stick figures set around it. Carved into the lintel above the door is a word: KHAZAN.

Show the players the door symbol to the right. The door is magically locked and trapped, and the symbol on the door is the key to disabling the trap. Magic that would normally unlock the door is neutralized by the tower's spell drain effect (see "Khazan's Spell Drain" earlier in the chapter).

A creature that touches the door without first disabling the trap causes lightning to envelop the tower. Any creature outside the tower and within 10 feet of it must succeed on a DC 15 Dexterity saving throw, with disadvantage if it is wearing armor made of metal, taking 22 (4d10) lightning damage on a failed save, or half damage on a successful one. As long as the effect persists, any creature that enters the lightning for the first time on a turn or starts its turn there takes 22 (4d10) lightning damage. The lightning lasts for 10 minutes.

The third time this trap is triggered, the magic fails and causes the tower to collapse. Each creature inside the tower when it collapses takes 132 (24d10) bludgeoning damage, while those within 20 feet of the tower must succeed on a DC 15 Dexterity saving throw or take 44 (8d10) bludgeoning damage from falling debris. The collapse not only destroys the tower but also most of its contents, including the animated armor in area V7. The wooden chest in area V7 (as well as the severed head inside it) remains intact but requires 1d8 + 2 hours of digging through rubble to find. The clay golems in area V4 are undamaged but buried under piles of debris. Every hour the characters spend searching through the rubble, they have a 10 percent chance of accidentally unearthing a berserk clay golem.

### OPENING THE DOOR

Each stick figure embossed on the door has differently positioned arms—either bent up or down at the elbow, or sticking straight out to the side. When a creature standing within 5 feet of the door uses an action to imitate the arm positions of all eight stick figures in the proper sequence, the trap is disabled and the door swings open on rusty hinges for 10 minutes. The lines of the symbol on the door reveal the proper sequence. The dance can be performed in one of two ways; a creature must trace the path of the lines, starting at either endpoint. All eight sets of arm positions must be performed, with no repeats, for the sequence to be complete.

If the arm positions are done out of order, a **young blue dragon** magically appears within 30 feet of the door and attacks all creatures it can see. The characters can keep trying to open the door while the dragon is attacking them. The dragon disappears if it is reduced to 0 hit points or if the characters open the door.

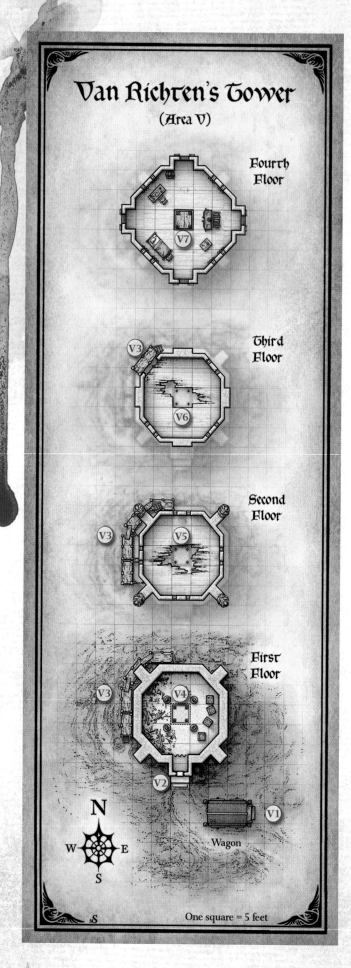

**Van Richten's Tower**

(Area V)

Fourth Floor

V7

Third Floor

V3

V6

Second Floor

V3

V5

First Floor

V3

V4

V2

V1

Wagon

N
W E
S

One square = 5 feet

## Vestibule

Beyond the door is a 5-foot-square vestibule with a tattered curtain that conceals area V4 beyond. The iron door leading outside can be safely opened from this side. It magically closes after 1 minute unless held open.

## V3. Rickety Scaffolding

Rotting wooden beams support the scaffolding, which groans and creaks with the slightest breeze. A series of ladders and platforms lead to a hole in the northwest wall on the third floor.

The scaffolding can't support more than 200 pounds of weight. If it collapses, anyone standing on it falls 20 feet to the ground, taking 1d6 bludgeoning damage per 10 feet fallen plus an additional 2d6 piercing damage from the debris. A creature underneath the scaffolding must succeed on a DC 13 Dexterity saving throw or take 14 (4d6) bludgeoning damage from falling debris.

## V4. Tower, First Floor

The flagstone floor is strewn with debris, and a few old crates stand near the east wall. A torn curtain to the south partially obscures the tower vestibule.

A five-foot-square indentation in the center of the floor contains four pulleys attached to taut iron chains that stretch up through a similarly sized hole in the rotted wooden ceiling. Standing next to the chains are four tall clay statues.

The four statues are **clay golems** that defend themselves if attacked. Otherwise, their sole purpose is to operate the elevator, which they do by pulling on the chains. The chains attach to a 5-foot-square wooden platform that normally rests on the fourth floor.

If it appears that a creature wants to use the elevator, the golems lower the platform, then raise it to whichever level the creature specifies. They also heed commands issued from above. They obey only commands having to do with raising and lowering the elevator.

The elevator isn't a smooth ride. The platform rises or lowers 5 feet per round, and its movements are jerky. If even one clay golem is destroyed, the remaining golems can no longer operate the elevator and remain motionless until attacked.

The crates in this room are all empty.

## V5. Tower, Second Floor

Dust and cobwebs fill this otherwise empty room, the wooden floor of which is badly rotted and partially collapsed.

In the middle of the room is a 5-foot-square hole in the floor and ceiling, with a rusty chain near each corner. The chains are part of the tower's elevator mechanism (see area V4). The 5-foot-square sections of floor that surround the central shaft are weak. Each 5-foot section can support 150 pounds; any more weight causes the section to collapse, and any creatures standing on that section fall 20 feet to the ground floor.

## V6. Tower, Third Floor

> Time and the elements have all but destroyed this chamber, leaving a gash in the northwest wall and slimy black mildew on the walls. The wooden floor is completely rotted and has begun to fall away in places.

In the middle of the room is a 5-foot-square hole in the floor and ceiling, with a rusty chain near each corner. The chains are part of the tower's elevator mechanism (see area V4). The 5-foot-square sections of floor that surround the central shaft are weak. Each 5-foot section can support 50 pounds; any more weight causes the section to collapse, and any creatures standing on that section fall 40 feet to the ground floor, smashing through the second floor on the way down.

## V7. Tower, Fourth Floor

> Unlike the levels below, this room shows signs of recent habitation, and although the place reeks of mold and mildew, it has plenty of creature comforts, including a cozy bed, a desk with matching chair, bright tapestries, and a large iron stove with plenty of wood to feed it. Light enters through arrow slits as well as through dirt-caked windows with broken shutters. Other features of the room include a standing suit of armor and a wooden chest. Old wooden rafters bend under the weight of the tower roof, which has somehow remained intact. Mounted to the rafters are pulleys around which hang iron chains that support the tower's elevator platform.

Van Richten spent several months in this room, reviewing a lifetime's worth of research on Strahd von Zarovich—notes that, once he committed them to memory, he burned in the stove. He also burned his journals. Ezmerelda searched the room, hoping to find a clue to her mentor's plan or whereabouts. Among the things she found here was a rolled-up map of Barovia and a burned page from van Richten's journal, which she took and hid in her wagon (area V1).

The standing armor is a suit of **animated armor**. It is incapacitated until someone speaks the command word ("Khazan") within 10 feet of it, whereupon the armor follows the commands of the one who activated it. If 24 hours pass without its receiving a new instruction from its controller, the animated armor becomes incapaci-

tated until someone reactivates it. If it is reduced to 0 hit points, the armor falls to pieces and is destroyed.

A lavender aroma emanates from the wooden chest, which is unlocked and safe to open. It contains the severed head of a human Vistana named Yan. Its flesh has a waxy complexion and has been embalmed with magic oils. If a *speak with dead* spell is cast on his head (which would need to be taken somewhere away from the tower's *spell drain effect*), Yan reveals that he was banished from his clan for stealing. A half-elf bard named Rictavio offered Yan a ride in his carnival wagon. The two traveled together for several days, but their time together was tense. When it was clear that Rictavio was looking for a road to Barovia, Yan tried to steal the wagon as well as Rictavio's pet monkey, but Rictavio got the better of him and drove a sword through his gullet.

The magic oils preserving Yan's head allow it to remember conversations it has while under the effect of *speak with dead*. Rictavio has cast *speak with dead* on the head twice to ask questions about the Vistani of Barovia. Yan believes that the half-elf plans to cause great harm to the Vistani and begs the characters to warn his people. He doesn't know where his body is.

### Fortunes of Ravenloft

If your card reading reveals that a treasure is here, it's in a narrow compartment hidden in the wall behind the suit of armor. If the armor is activated and commanded to retrieve the treasure, it pulls the stones out of the wall, revealing the treasure beyond.

If the characters have collapsed the tower (see area V2), they find the treasure after 1d8 + 2 hours of searching through the rubble. For each hour they spend searching, they have a 10 percent chance of accidentally unearthing a **clay golem** (see area V4) that withstood the collapse. The golem, which took no damage from the collapsing tower, is berserk and attacks until destroyed.

# SPECIAL EVENTS

You can use one or both of the following special events while the characters are exploring Van Richten's Tower.

## PACK ATTACK

If the characters blew up Ezmerelda's wagon, activated the lightning sheath around the tower, or caused the tower to collapse, the sound of their handiwork echoes through the valley as far west as Krezk and as far east as Vallaki. The disturbance attracts the attention of a pack of werewolves, which arrives after 1 hour.

The werewolves haunt the Svalich Woods west of Van Richten's Tower. They come running in wolf form, hoping to trap prey on the island by cutting off access to the causeway.

Leading the hunt is Kiril Stoyanovich, a **werewolf** with 90 hit points. Accompanying him are six normal **werewolves** and nine **wolves**. While in wolf form, the werewolves are indistinguishable from ordinary wolves. They either remain in wolf form or assume hybrid form.

If the characters were drawn into Barovia by the "Werewolves in the Mist" adventure hook, this encounter represents a climactic confrontation between the characters and the werewolf pack that has been terrorizing settlements in the Forgotten Realms. The werewolves know that the tower has magical defenses, so they are cautious. Kiril tries to lure the characters outside for a final showdown, but pulls his pack into the woods if the characters start lobbing spells or making ranged attacks from the tower.

### DEVELOPMENT

A captured werewolf can be forced to divulge the whereabouts of the children kidnapped by the pack. They are being held in a cave to the west (see chapter 15, "Werewolf Den").

## EZMERELDA'S RETREAT

**Ezmerelda d'Avenir** (see appendix D) returns to Van Richten's Tower after confronting Strahd in Castle Ravenloft and barely escaping with her life. She arrives on the back of a **riding horse** stolen from the Vistani camp outside Vallaki (chapter 5, area N9).

Ezmerelda hopes that the arsenal of weapons in her wagon will be enough to protect her from the vampire's wrath. If the characters blew up the wagon, she is understandably annoyed and retreats to the tower. (She

knows the trick to bypassing the trap on the tower door.) If the tower has also been destroyed, she doesn't stick around unless the characters are clearly her best hope of survival.

Ezmerelda's altercation with Strahd has left her with only 30 hit points. She graciously accepts any healing the characters have to offer.

### DEVELOPMENT

From this moment on, Strahd gains a new goal: kill Ezmerelda d'Avenir. Knowing that his Vistani spies might be conflicted at the thought of slaying one of their own, Strahd relies on the druids and the werewolves of the Svalich Woods, as well as human spies and vampire spawn hidden in Barovia's settlements, to help him find and kill Ezmerelda. If Strahd learns that she and the characters are working together, he invites the characters to Ravenloft, expecting that Ezmerelda will accompany them. The characters receive their invitation in the form of a letter delivered by one of Strahd's spies. If the characters open and read the letter, show the players the "Strahd's Invitation" handout in appendix F. If the characters head toward the castle, they have no threatening random encounters on the way.

Interior of Top Floor

Plan View

Side

Front

# CHAPTER 12: THE WIZARD OF WINES

INE IS THE LIFEBLOOD OF THE BAROVIAN people. It is one of the only indulgences left to them. Without it, many Barovians would lose their last shred of hope and succumb to utter despair.

Although the Vistani often bring wine from distant lands, they share it infrequently. Thus, most of Barovia's wine comes from one source: the Wizard of Wines winery and vineyard.

The Wizard of Wines was founded by a mage whose name is buried in the annals of history. The wizard fashioned three magic gems, each one as big as a pinecone, and planted them in the rich valley soil. These "seeds" gave rise to healthy grapevines, which produced sweet, plump grapes. Even after Strahd's curse settled over Barovia, the gems kept the vines and their grapes from succumbing to the darkness.

Strahd bequeathed the winery and vineyard to the noble Krezkov family as a reward for the family's loyalty. Later, an arranged marriage between the Krezkovs and the Martikov family led to the land being taken over by a Martikov descendant. The winery and vineyard have been tended by the Martikovs ever since. At some point, the Martikov family became infected with widespread lycanthropy. The current patriarch, Davian Martikov, is a wereraven, as are his children and grandchildren.

The wereravens provide the wine to Barovian taverns for free, knowing the good it brings to the Barovian people.

The winery is known for three wines: the unremarkable Purple Grapemash No. 3, the slightly more tantalizing Red Dragon Crush, and the rich Champagne du le Stomp. Ten years ago, one of the vineyard's magic gems was dug up and stolen, and as a result, the winery stopped producing its best vintage, the champagne. No one knows what happened to the gem. Davian Martikov blames his middle son, Urwin (see chapter 5, area N2), for the loss because Urwin was on watch the night the gem was taken. Davian is convinced that Urwin shirked his duty to spend time with his betrothed, and the two men have been at odds ever since. To this day, Urwin steadfastly denies his father's accusation.

Adding to Davian's misery, the wereravens have been fending off frequent attacks by Baba Lysaga's scarecrow constructs. Three weeks ago, during one such attack, another gem was found, dug up, and taken. Davian believes that it is in the possession of Baba Lysaga (see chapter 10, area U3).

Davian's belief is correct. The gem was a lucky find for Baba Lysaga, who had previously suspected that magic was the root of the vineyard's health but knew nothing of its source. Even after this great discovery, Baba Lysaga continues to send her scarecrows against the winery, antagonizing the wereravens like a bad neighbor.

Five days ago, evil druids stole the third and final gem and bore it to Yester Hill (chapter 14). The wereravens launched a counterattack on Yester Hill, hoping to get it back, but to no avail. The druids and their blights proved more than a match for the lycanthropes.

Two days ago, the druids returned with a horde of blights and drove Davian's family from the winery. They've also poisoned the fermentation vats, leaving the winery with only a few bottles and barrels of drinkable wine.

Even if the characters succeed in helping the Martikovs reclaim the winery, wine production in the valley will eventually stop as the vineyard dies off. Only by recovering the magic gems and replanting them in the soil can the characters ensure that the Barovians aren't without wine to comfort them on dark, wretched nights.

WHY, IT IS NOTHING TO BECOME AN *animal, for that is the true nature of every man. We are not meant to wear crowns and drink from goblets.*
—Strahd von Zarovich

## APPROACHING THE VINEYARD

A branch of the Old Svalich Road leads to the vineyard. If the characters approach along this path, read:

> After a half mile, the road becomes a muddy trail that meanders through the woods, descending gradually until the trees part, revealing a mist-shrouded meadow. The trail splits. One branch heads west into the valley, and the other leads south into dark woods. A wooden signpost at the intersection points west and reads, "Vineyard."

If the characters head west on the trail toward the vineyard, read:

> A light drizzle begins to fall. Unpainted fences blindly follow the trail, which skirts north of a sprawling vineyard before bending south toward a stately building. The fog takes on ghostly forms as it swirls between the neatly tended rows of grapevines. Here and there, you see rope-handled half-barrels used for hauling grapes. North of the trail is a large stand of trees. A man wearing a dark cloak and cowl stands at the edge of the trees, beckoning you.

The beckoning figure is one of nine **wereravens** (LG male and female humans) hiding in the grove north of the vineyard. If the characters ignore the cloaked figure and continue on to the winery, the wereravens keep their distance and wait to see what happens.

### THE MARTIKOV FAMILY

If the characters head toward the cloaked figure, the other wereravens emerge from the stand of trees and greet them in human form. They wear dark leather rain cloaks and cowls.

One of them is the current owner of the winery and vineyard, Davian Martikov, who is an old and suspicious man. Until he trusts the characters, he says nothing about the stolen gems but tells them that evil druids and blights have attacked the winery and forced his family to take refuge in the woods.

If the characters rid the winery of its invaders, Davian is grateful. Only then does he tell them that the vineyard's three magic "seeds" have been stolen. He describes them as gems the size and shape of pinecones, each one containing a glowing green light as bright as a torch. For the good of all Barovia, he urges the characters to travel to Berez (area U) and Yester Hill (area Y) to retrieve two of them. He has no idea what happened to the third gem.

Davian's group includes the following people:

- Davian
- Adrian, his eldest son

- Elvir, his youngest son
- Stefania, his adult daughter
- Dag Tomescu, Stefania's husband

All five are members of the Keepers of the Feather (see chapter 5, area N2). Also present are Stefania and Dag's four children: a teenage son named Claudiu, two young boys named Martin and Viggo, and a baby girl named Yolanda. The three youngest children are noncombatants; the boys are wereravens with 7 hit points each, and Yolanda is effectively a human with 1 hit point (she can't assume other forms yet).

If the characters come to the vineyard looking to obtain wine, Adrian can confirm that there are three barrels in the loading dock (area W2), plus another three barrels and several wine bottles in the cellar (area W14). There is more wine still fermenting (area W9).

## APPROACHING THE WINERY

If the characters continue toward the winery, read:

> Situated in the midst of the vineyard, the winery is an old, two-story stone building with multiple entrances, thick ivy covering every wall, and iron fencing along its roofline. The trail ends at an open loading dock on the ground floor.
>
> A wooden stable of more recent construction is attached to the east side of the winery, next to the loading dock. West of the winery is a crumbling well and a wooden outhouse.

When the characters reach the winery, read:

> You hear the rustle of dead vines all around you. Inhuman shapes emerge from the vineyard, their limbs cracking as they trudge forth through the mist and rain.

Thirty **needle blights** (in six groups of five) emerge from the surrounding vineyard and make their way toward the characters and the winery. The blights are 120 feet away when they first become visible, and they have a walking speed of 30 feet. Characters can either barricade themselves inside the winery, thus keeping the needle blights at bay, or stand and fight. If they stay outside and fight, druids and blights from inside the winery join the battle on the rounds shown below.

| Round | Creatures |
|---|---|
| 3 | 1 **druid** and 24 **twig blights** (from area W9) |
| 4 | 1 **druid** and 5 **needle blights** (from area W14) |
| 5 | 1 **druid** and 2 **vine blights** (from area W20) |

The druid lurking in area W16 carries a *Gulthias staff* (see appendix C). If the staff is destroyed, all blights within 300 feet of it instantly wither and die.

# Wizard of Wines Winery
## (Area W)

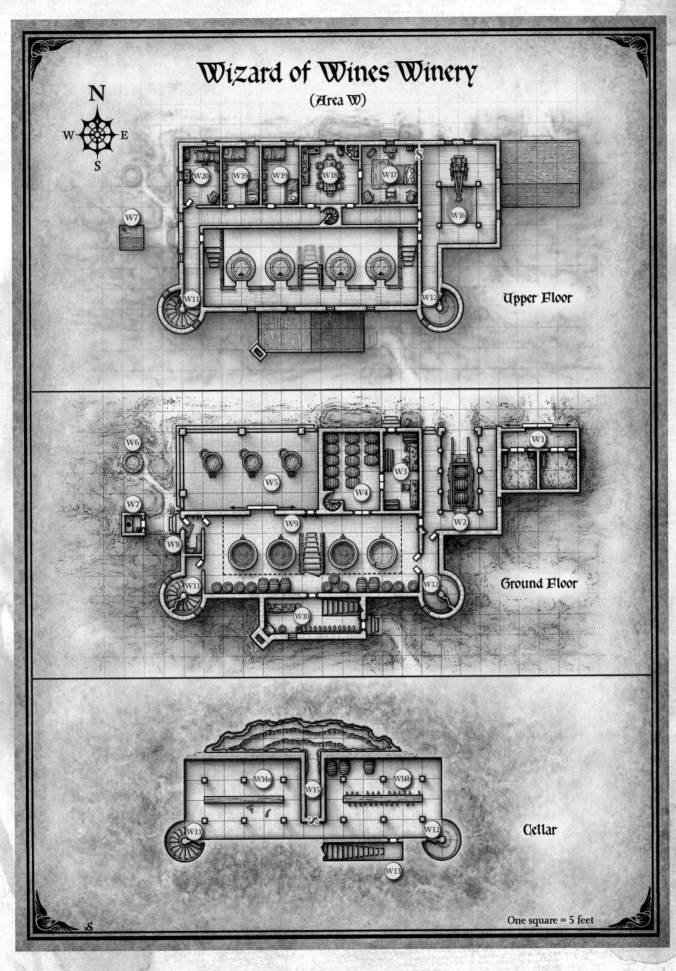

N
W • E
S

W7

W20  W19  W19  W18  W17

W16

S

W11  W12

**Upper Floor**

W6

W7

W8

W5  W9  W4  W3

W1

W2

W11  W12

W10

**Ground Floor**

W14a  W15  W14b

W11  W12

W13

**Cellar**

One square = 5 feet

# Areas of the Winery

The following areas correspond to labels on the map of the winery on page 175.

## W1. Stables

The Martikovs keep two **draft horses** here and use them to pull their wine wagon.

## W2. Loading Dock

Parked in the loading dock is a wagon with three barrels set in braces on the bed. A raised wooden walkway runs along the west, south, and east walls. Through a hole in the ceiling you see the wooden arm of a loading crane with ropes and hooks dangling from it.

Wine barrels in the cellar (area W14) are rolled up a ramp (area W12) to the crane on the upper floor (area W16), then lowered into the wagon from above. Empty barrels are rolled off the back of the wagon and stored in area W9. The three barrels on the wagon hold Purple Grapemash No. 3.

The south door has been forced open and hangs ajar. It can't be closed properly until repaired, though it can be barricaded.

## W3. Barrel Maker's Workshop

Strips of iron and wood lie in neat piles on the floor of this workshop, the walls of which are lined with tools. Two worktables stand against the east wall.

Wine barrels are made here. The north door is barred from the inside.

## W4. Barrel Storage

Rows of new barrels fill this room. A narrow stone staircase spirals upward in the southwest corner.

The room contains thirteen empty barrels.

## W5. Veranda

Resting on a flagstone veranda are three five-foot-diameter wooden tubs, their insides stained with grape juice. Each tub has a short ladder bolted to its side and a catch basin tucked underneath.

At the back of the veranda is a large set of sliding wooden doors as well as a normal-sized wooden door. Stone pillars and arches support the upper floor above.

This veranda is where grapes from the vineyard are crushed into juice. The sliding wooden doors are chained shut from the inside, and the smaller door is barred shut from the inside. Breaking through either requires a successful DC 20 Strength check.

## W6. Well

A ring of tight-fitting, moss-covered stones encloses this 40-foot-deep well.

## W7. Outhouse

Sweet-smelling herbs hang from the eaves of this ram-shackle wooden outhouse, which has a small crescent moon carved into its door.

The outhouse contains no surprises.

## W8. Storage

Bare hooks line the walls of this storage room. Shelves to the south hold several pairs of stained wooden sandals with oversized soles. Both doors to this room hang open. The one to the west is fitted with iron brackets and leads outside into the rain. Lying on the floor next to it is a five-foot-long wooden beam.

Before fleeing the winery, the wereravens took the leather rain cloaks stored here, but they left behind the wooden sandals that they wear when crushing grapes on the veranda (area W5).

The wooden beam on the floor can be used to bar the outer door.

## W9. Fermentation Vats

The rich smell of fermenting wine fills this large, two-story chamber, which is dominated by four enormous wooden casks, each one eight feet wide and twelve feet tall. A wooden staircase in the center of the room climbs to a ten-foot-high wooden balcony that clings to the south wall, which has four windows set into it at balcony level. Stacked against the wall underneath the balcony are old, empty barrels with "The Wizard of Wines" burned into their sides. The balcony climbs another five feet as it continues along the west and east walls, ending at doors leading to the winery's upper level. Underneath these side balconies are several doors, some of which hang open. Beneath the sloping roof stretch thick rafters, upon which scores of ravens have quietly gathered. They watch you with great interest.

Four **swarms of ravens** perch on the rafters but don't attack the characters under any circumstances.

Unless they have been drawn outside, twenty-four **twig blights** and one **druid** (NE female human) are also present. If they are here, read:

> The balcony creaks, drawing your eye to a wild-looking figure hunched over the westernmost cask, pouring a flask of thick syrup into it. She wears a gown made of animal skins and a headdress with goat horns, and her hair is long and unkempt. Suddenly, you see something skittering across the floor. It looks like a tiny creature made of twigs. It moves from its hiding place under the stairs and disappears behind the easternmost cask.

The four containers are fermentation vats, where grape juice is mixed with other ingredients and turned into wine. The easternmost cask has split in the back, creating a 6-inch-wide, 6-foot-high opening through which the twig blights can pass. All twenty-four twig blights are hidden in the cask, ready to emerge and attack when commanded to do so. While inside the cask, they have total cover against attacks that originate outside the cask.

The druid is poisoning the fermentation vats. The three westernmost vats contain poisoned wine, enough to fill a total of twenty barrels. Drinking the poisoned wine has the same effect as drinking a *potion of poison*. Pouring antitoxin into a vat neutralizes the poison, but it also spoils the taste of the wine. Casting a *purify food and drink* spell on a vat neutralizes the poison without spoiling the wine.

In addition to her animal skin gown and horned headdress, the druid wears necklaces of human teeth. If the characters attack the druid, she calls forth her twig blights. When that happens, the swarms of ravens descend from the rafters and begin attacking the blights. Each swarm tears apart one twig blight on each of its turns.

The sliding wooden doors along the north wall (leading to area W5) are chained shut from the inside. The key to the padlock can be found in the office (area W20).

The single door leading to area W5 is barred shut from the inside, as is the single door leading to area W2.

## W10. GLASSBLOWER'S WORKSHOP

> A dirty window in the south wall allows dim light to enter this room. Wine bottles are manufactured here, as evidenced by the tools lying about, the wooden rack full of freshly blown glass bottles along the south wall, the hearth built into the southwest corner, and the barrel of sand standing next to it. A staircase descends underground, and between it and the rack of bottles stands a barred door.

The stairs lead down to area W13. The bottles stored in the rack don't have labels. The east door is barred from the inside.

### FORTUNES OF RAVENLOFT

If your card reading reveals that a treasure is here, it's buried in the barrel of sand. Emptying the barrel or digging through the sand reveals the treasure without the need for a check.

## W11. SPIRAL STAIRCASE

> This turret contains a stone spiral staircase. Windows in the outer wall allow light to enter.

The stairs connect all three levels of the winery.

## W12. RAMP

> This turret has a sloping, wooden floor that spirals from the cellar to the upper levels. Scratch marks suggest that barrels are rolled up and down the ramp on a routine basis.

The spiraling ramp connects all three levels of the winery. The evil druids who have taken over the winery use this ramp to move between levels.

TWIG BLIGHT

## W13. Back Staircase

> Thick moss covers the walls of this underground staircase. At the foot of the steps is a landing with an arched wooden door set into the north wall.

This staircase connects areas W10 and W14.

## W14. Wine Cellar

In the winery's heyday, the wine cellar was packed with barrels awaiting shipment, but those days are long gone.

> Wooden pillars and beams support the ten-foot-high ceiling of this ice-cold cellar, which is split in two by a five-foot-thick brick wall. A thin mist covers the floor. Each half of the cellar features an eight-foot tall wooden partition that doubles as a wine rack. The western rack stands empty, but the eastern one is half filled with wine bottles.

Unless they have been drawn outside, five **needle blights** and one **druid** (NE male human) lurk in the eastern portion of the cellar. If they are here when the characters enter that part of the cellar, read:

> Something moves behind the eastern wine rack. Through the holes, you glimpse a half dozen humanoid figures, one with a full rack of antlers. You hear a gravelly voice mutter the words of a spell.

On his first turn, from behind the wine rack, the druid casts a *thunderwave* spell, which shatters 1d20 + 10 of the wine bottles as it resounds throughout the cellar. The druid then orders the needle blights to attack.

The cellar gets markedly colder the closer one gets to the north wall. Against that wall in the eastern portion of the cellar rest three frosty barrels containing Purple Grapemash No. 3, a fact that is emblazoned on each barrel's side. A single bottle of Purple Grapemash No. 3 lies on the flagstone floor in the western half of the cellar.

The wine rack in the eastern half of the cellar holds forty bottles, the labels of which show that the wine is the winery's Red Dragon Crush.

A secret door between the two halves of the wine cellar can be pushed open to reveal a freezing cold passageway (area W15).

## W15. Brown Mold

If the characters open the secret door, read:

> It takes some effort to push open the secret door, and you are greeted by a blast of cold air. A dark tunnel stretches for fifteen feet, ending at an archway beyond which lies a shallow cave.

Characters who have a light source can see brown mold covering the walls, floor, and ceiling around the archway and the cave beyond. Growing throughout this area, keeping the wine cellar cool, are ten patches of brown mold (see "Dungeon Hazards" in chapter 5, "Adventure Environments," of the *Dungeon Master's Guide*). The characters are safe from the mold as long as they keep their distance.

## W16. Loading Winch

> This room has a wooden floor with a ten-foot-square hole cut into the middle of it. Looming over the hole is a wooden winch. Perched atop it is a man with wild hair, rotted teeth, and skin painted red with blood. He waves a gnarled staff made from a black branch and babbles at you.

The man is a **druid** (NE male human) who fights only if cornered. Otherwise, he tries to flee by dropping onto the wagon in the loading dock (area W2). He then looks for a place in the winery to hide. A character who understands Druidic can translate the his words: "Nature bows to my every whim, for I have the vampire's staff!"

A secret door in the north corner of the west wall can be pulled open to reveal a bedroom (area W17).

### Treasure

The druid wields a *Gulthias staff* (see appendix C), which can be used to destroy the blights in the winery.

## W17. Master Bedroom

This bedroom normally belongs to Davian Martikov but is currently being used by his daughter, Stefania, and son-in-law, Dag, while they raise their baby daughter.

> This room contains a four-poster bed, its headboard carved in the likeness of a giant raven. A soft black rug covers the floor between the bed and the door. In the corners of the south wall stand two slender wardrobes with a tapestry of a church hanging on the wall between them. Beneath the tapestry sits a handsomely carved rocking cradle. To the north, under a window, is a plain desk and chair. Other furnishings include a wooden chest and a freestanding mirror in a wooden frame.

One of the wardrobes contains Stefania's clothes, and the other contains Dag's. The desk holds manifests recording wine shipments for the past century. A cursory examination of recent records reveals that almost all shipments are made to the following locations:

- "BV" (the Blood o' the Vine tavern in the village of Barovia)
- "BW" (the Blue Water Inn in the town of Vallaki)
- "K" (Krezk)
- "VISTANI"

Characters who check the oldest records also find entries for "S" (Strahd).

The wooden chest is locked, and the key is hidden in a compartment in one of the bedposts. A character who searches the bed notices that a knob on one of the bedposts is loose and can be removed, revealing the compartment inside. The contents of the chest are described in the "Treasure" section below.

A secret door in the north corner of the east wall can be pushed open to gain access to the loading winch (area W16).

### Treasure

Inside the chest are 50 gp, 270 ep (each electrum coin stamped with the profiled visage of Strahd von Zarovich), and 350 sp. A secret compartment in the lid can be found with a successful DC 15 Wisdom (Perception) check. It holds a gold locket (worth 25 gp) containing a painted portrait of a beautiful woman (Davian's deceased wife, Angelika), as well as a pouch containing five 50 gp gemstones.

## W18. Kitchen and Dining Room

> This room contains a rectangular table surrounded by eight chairs, an L-shaped cupboard, and a floor-to-ceiling closet pantry. Next to the pantry is a small iron stove.

Davian Martikov

The cupboard holds dishware and eating utensils. The pantry holds cooking ingredients and the winery's stores.

## W19. Sleeping Quarters

> Two pairs of bunk beds occupy this room. Against the west wall rest four identical footlockers.

Davian, Adrian, and Elvir sleep in the westernmost room. Claudiu and his two younger brothers sleep in the easternmost room, where a few toys are scattered about. One of the toys seems to resemble a child's wooden rocking horse, except that the horse is black with wild eyes and has painted orange flames where its mane, tail, and hooves should be. Carved into the wooden nightmare is the name "Beucephalus" and, in smaller lettering, the slogan "Is No Fun, Is No Blinsky!"

The footlockers contain clothing and personal belongings, but nothing of value.

## W20. Printing Press

The door to this room hangs open.

> In this chamber are a desk, a chair, a tall wooden cabinet, and a strange contraption that takes up most of the northern end of the room.

Two **vine blights** and one **druid** (NE female human) are in the room unless they have been drawn elsewhere, If they are here, read:

> Three creatures are here. One appears human but is so caked with dirt and mud that it's hard to know for sure. Her hair is full of twigs, and her face is hidden behind a veil of moss. She is rooting through the contents of the cabinet and haphazardly tossing them onto the floor. Behind her stand two creatures made entirely of dead vines.

The druid and the vine blights fight to the death.

Inside the cabinet is a key hanging on a loop of twine. The key unlocks the padlock on the sliding doors between the veranda (area W5) and the fermentation vats (area W9).

The contraption standing near the north wall is a printing press, which Davian Martikov uses to make wine bottle labels. The ink is made from wine and stored in bottles in the cabinet, along with pieces of parchment and jars of glue.

## Special Events

You can use one or both of the following special events after the characters have rid the winery of its current menace.

## Wine Delivery

After restoring the Martikovs to their rightful positions, the characters might ask them to deliver wine to the Blue Water Inn (chapter 5, area N2), the Vistani in the camp outside Vallaki (chapter 5, area N9), or the burgomaster of Krezk (chapter 8, area S2). A grateful Davian sets his sons to the task immediately. Adrian Martikov brings the three remaining wine barrels up from the cellar and sets them on the wagon while Elvir Martikov secures the horses. Adrian and Elvir make the delivery themselves, but they welcome the party's escort. If the characters don't volunteer for guard duty, Davian Martikov suggests they go along with the wine wagon to ensure its safety.

If the characters escort the wagon, check for a random encounter once for each mile traveled. The wagon is also watched over by two **swarms of ravens** that swoop down to attack anything that threatens the wagon or the characters.

### Development

The characters can trade the six barrels of wine for a much-needed treasure in the possession of the Keepers of the Feather or the Vistani (see chapter 5, areas N2q and N9i), or they can use it to buy their way into the walled village of Krezk (chapter 8).

## Wintersplinter Attacks

If the characters leave the winery and return at a later time before dealing with Wintersplinter (see the "Druids' Ritual" section in chapter 14), the enormous **tree blight** (see appendix D) is sent from Yester Hill to ravage the vineyard and destroy the winery.

The characters arrive to find the grapevines trampled and the winery in ruins. Wintersplinter's tracks are clearly visible on the trail to the south. Characters who follow the tracks catch up with Wintersplinter as the blight slowly makes its way back to Yester Hill.

The Martikovs narrowly escape the carnage and flee to the Blue Water Inn in Vallaki (chapter 5, area N2). Davian Martikov is crushed by the loss of the winery, and morale in Vallaki sinks to an all-time low as word of the winery's destruction spreads through town.

### Development

Three days after Wintersplinter's attack, Baba Lysaga (see chapter 10, area U3) dispatches the seven **scarecrows** from Berez and orders them to take up positions in the vineyard, to discourage the wereravens from returning. These scarecrows attack anyone who crosses the vineyard or approaches the ruined winery.

# CHAPTER 13: THE AMBER TEMPLE

A SECRET SOCIETY OF GOOD-ALIGNED wizards built the Amber Temple in the Balinok Mountains more than two thousand years ago. They needed a vault in which to contain the evil vestiges (remnants of dead, malevolent entities) they had captured and the hoard of forbidden knowledge they had amassed. They dedicated the temple to a god of secrets, whom they trusted to keep it hidden from the rest of the world until the end of time. Unfortunately for the wizards, even the will of a god couldn't prevent other evil creatures from learning the temple's location. The wizards were forced to guard the temple themselves, to keep its secrets from falling into villainous hands. The evil forces that were imprisoned within the temple eventually corrupted the wizards, turning them against one another.

The wizards were dead and gone by the time an evil archmage named Exethanter arrived at the temple. He breached the temple's wards, spoke to a vestige trapped in amber, and discovered the secret to becoming a lich. After his transformation, the lich Exethanter took over the temple and turned the skulls of it previous defenders into flameskulls under his command. Exethanter then took it upon himself to watch over the temple, not to hoard its evil secrets but to share them openly. Meanwhile, the evils within the temple fed on each other, growing in power.

When Strahd came to the temple seeking immortality, Exethanter sensed that he was a man of destiny. The evil powers in the temple felt something much stronger: a darkness that eclipsed their own. Strahd communed with these evil vestiges and forged a pact with them. When Strahd later murdered his brother Sergei, that pact was sealed with blood. Strahd transformed into a vampire, and the Dark Powers turned his land into a prison.

Strahd has returned to the temple several times to learn new magic and to find a means of escaping his fate, but the Dark Powers have no intention of giving him up. These recent years have been difficult for Exethanter, whose body and mind have been falling apart. The lich has grown weak and forgetful. He no longer remembers his name or his spells. He knows only that the Dark Powers that created Strahd's domain were born in the temple, and that these entities feed on the evil that Strahd represents. Strahd is the darkness that sustains them.

Characters who visit the temple can sense the presence of great evil. The dark vestiges imprisoned within the temple will try to corrupt them, offering them secrets and gifts in exchange for a taste of the evil that lurks within their true hearts.

## EXTREME COLD

The Amber Temple is a cold, dark place carved out of the snowy slope of Mount Ghakis. The temperature throughout the complex is –10 degrees Fahrenheit (–23 degrees Celsius). Characters who don't have heat sources, cold weather gear, or magic to protect them are subject to the effects of extreme cold, as described in the "Weather" section in chapter 5, "Adventure Environments," of the *Dungeon Master's Guide*. If Kasimir Velikov (see chapter 5, area N9a) is with the party, his *ring of warmth* protects him from the effects of the extreme cold.

I WOULD NOT BE CALLED 'DEATH'
*so soon. I made a pact with death,
a pact of blood.*

—*Tome of Strahd*

# Amber Temple
## (Area X)

Upper Level

One square = 10 feet

# AREAS OF THE TEMPLE

The following areas correspond to labels on the maps of the Amber Temple on pages 182 and 190.

All the doors in the temple are fashioned from blocks of translucent amber with iron hinges and fittings. Unless otherwise noted, arrow slits in the temple are 5 inches wide, 4 feet tall, and 1 foot thick.

## X1. TEMPLE FACADE

A snow-swept gravel road climbs the mountainside as it travels north from Tsolenka Pass toward the temple. When the characters reach the end of this road, read:

> The road fades away under a covering of snow, but it takes you far enough to see the facade of some kind of temple carved into the sheer mountainside ahead. The front of the structure is fifty feet high and has six alcoves containing twenty-foot-tall statues. Each statue is carved from a single block of amber and depicts a faceless, hooded figure, its hands pressed together in a gesture of prayer. Between the two innermost statues is a twenty-foot-tall archway with a staircase leading down.

The amber statues are impervious to damage. Looking at one for long fills a viewer with unease.

## X1A. NARROW FISSURE

> A natural fissure has opened in the mountainside west of the temple's facade, creating a gap two feet wide, ten feet tall, and fifteen feet deep. You see light coming from a room beyond, and you hear human voices there as well.

The fissure leads to area X15. If the characters make a lot of noise outside, one of the creatures in that area investigates the disturbance.

## X2. ENTRANCE

If the characters pass through the archway between the statues, read:

> Icy steps descend ten feet to a time-ravaged hallway with arrow slits in the walls. Beyond the hall lies a vast, sepulchral darkness.

The hall connects areas X1 and X4. There are no guards in the rooms behind the arrow slits (areas X2a and X2b).

## X2A. GUARD ROOM

This empty room lies behind a secret door. The ceiling is 10 feet high. Two arrow slits are carved into the east wall.

## X2B. GUARD ROOM

This room lies behind a secret door.

> Two arrow slits are carved into the west wall of this 10-foot-high, twenty-foot-square room. Slumped in the northeast corner is a skeleton wearing a blue wizard's robe and clutching a wand to its chest.

The skeleton is all that remains of a wizard who froze to death. It poses no threat.

TREASURE
The skeleton clutches a *wand of secrets*.

## X3. EMPTY BARRACKS

> Shattered bits of wood cover the floor of this frigid, twenty-foot-square room.

The ceiling in each of these rooms is 10 feet high. The wood is all that remains of guards' bunks.

A secret door set in one wall of each room can be pulled open to reveal area X2a or X2b beyond.

## X4. OVERLOOK

> A twenty-foot-wide balcony of black marble with a shattered railing overlooks a vast temple. Black marble staircases at each end of the balcony descend thirty feet to the temple floor. The vaulted ceiling is thirty feet above the balcony. The walls and ceiling are covered in an amber glaze, lending the gloom a golden sheen. A set of amber doors stands closed at the west end of the balcony. A similar pair stands open to the east.

Anyone with a passive Wisdom (Perception) score of 12 or higher notice arrow slits in the walls overlooking the temple (see areas X8 and X17 for more information on these arrow slits). If the characters' light source or vision extends 90 feet or more, they can see a large, faceless statue at the far end of the temple (area X5a).

The open doorway to the east leads to area X6. The double doors to the west open into area X15. Characters who listen at the western doors hear gruff humanoid voices beyond, but can't discern what's being said.

## X5. TEMPLE OF LOST SECRETS

> Four black marble columns support the vaulted ceiling of the temple, at the north end of which stands a forty-foot-tall statue of a cowled figure in flowing robes. The statue's stony hands are outstretched as if in the midst of casting a spell. Its face is a void of utter blackness.

> The ominous statue stands between two black marble balconies, one of which has partially collapsed and fallen on the temple's black marble floor, in front of an open doorway. The walls of the temple are sheathed in amber, and the doors leading from it are made of amber as well. Arched hallways coated with amber lead away from the temple to the west and east. Flanking these exits are alcoves that hold white marble statues of robed human wizards with pointed hats and golden staffs. One of them has toppled over and lies shattered on the floor.

An **arcanaloth** named Neferon guards this temple from within the hollow head of the great statue (area X5a) and attacks characters on sight with its longer-ranged spells. Thanks to its truesight, the arcanaloth can see the invisible and can see through magical darkness. Characters can't see Neferon unless they can penetrate the magical darkness that envelops the statue's face and head.

Once the arcanaloth begins casting spells, the three **flameskulls** in area X17 take up positions behind the arrow slits that overlook the temple and cast *magic missile* and *fireball* spells at characters they can see.

The temple ceiling is 60 feet high. Wide, black marble staircases ascend 30 feet to the southern balcony (area X4). The balconies that flank the statue (areas X11 and X23) are 30 feet high as well.

Arrow slits cut into the walls of the upper galleries (areas X8 and X17) and archer posts (areas X13 and X25) look down on the temple. The amber glaze that covers the temple walls makes these arrow slits difficult to spot. Characters who have a passive Wisdom (Perception) score of 12 or higher notice them. Creatures behind the arrow slits gain three-quarters cover.

The marble wizard statues stand 8 feet tall. Their 9-foot-tall golden staffs are made of wrought iron coated in peeling gold paint. The northeast statue fell over when an earth tremor collapsed the wall of its alcove.

## X5A. GOD OF SECRETS

This 40-foot-tall statue, carved out of granite, depicts a faceless god of secrets. At the base of the statue, in the back, is a secret door that can be found with a successful DC 20 Wisdom (Perception) check. It can be pulled open to reveal a spiral staircase that climbs to a stone trapdoor set into the floor of the statue's hollow head.

### STATUE'S HEAD

Neferon the **arcanaloth** lairs inside the statue's hollow head, within a field of magical darkness that fills the interior of the head and hides the statue's humanlike face. The darkness can be dispelled (DC 17).

A pair of 2-foot-wide eyeholes provides an unobstructed view of the temple floor south of the statue, as well as the southern balcony (area X4). Looking through the eyes, one can't see the northern balconies (areas X11 and X23), the areas beneath them, or anywhere behind or directly above the statue. The eyeholes grant the arcanaloth three-quarters cover against attacks that originate outside the head.

Neferon wears gold spectacles and a magic robe (see "Treasure" below). It uses its *alter self* spell and Deception skill to pass itself off as an old human wizard with a long white beard named Heinrich Stolt. "Heinrich" feigns confusion. If the characters ask him why he attacked, he claims that he was guarding the temple. If the arcanaloth loses more than half of its hit points, it teleports to the temple floor, turns invisible, and flees by the safest route, attacking the characters again when it's safe to do so. The arcanaloth will not, under any circumstances, leave the Amber Temple.

### TREASURE

The arcanaloth carries a spellbook containing the wizard spells it has prepared (see its stat block in the *Monster Manual*). It wears small gold spectacles with pink crystal lenses (worth 250 gp) and a *robe of useful items* with the following eight patches remaining:

- Bag of 100 gp
- Iron door
- Wooden ladder
- Riding horse
- Pit
- Rowboat
- *Spell scroll* (*moonbeam*)
- Mastiffs

See the robe's description in the *Dungeon Master's Guide* for more information on each patch.

### FORTUNES OF RAVENLOFT

If your card reading reveals that a treasure is here, it's lying on the floor inside the statue's head.

## X5B. SECRET DOOR

Set into the middle of the temple's north wall is a secret door. A character who searches the wall for secret doors and succeeds on a DC 20 Wisdom (Perception) check detects seams in the amber glaze that covers the wall, hinting at the presence of the door. It is warded by an *arcane lock* spell that prevents it from being opened, but knocking on the door three times causes it to swing open for 1 minute, revealing a dusty stone staircase. The stairs climb 30 feet to another secret door that swings open automatically when a creature moves within 5 feet of it. The stairs lead to area X30.

## X5C. LOCKED DOORS

These amber doors are sealed with an *arcane lock* spell. The password to suppress it is "Etherna." A character can push open the doors with a successful DC 25 Strength check. The doors (AC 15, 60 hit points) can also be smashed. If they are reduced to 0 hit points, necrotic energy fills the 30-foot cube directly north of them. A creature in that area takes 22 (4d10) necrotic damage, turning to dust if reduced to 0 hit points. Beyond the doors lie the temple catacombs (area X31).

## X5D. AMBER REFLECTIONS

> This arched hall rises to a height of twenty feet. You can see your reflections in the amber glaze. But the images don't mirror your movements. Instead, they wave their arms and scream silent warnings to you.

The characters' bizarre reflections are illusions meant to discourage them from exploring the temple. The illusions can be dispelled (DC 15).

The east hall leads to area X32, the west hall to area X36.

## X6. Southeast Annex

> This room is featureless except for a rough-edged, 10-foot-diameter circular hole in the floor to the east and empty torch sconces along the walls. Double doors of amber stand open to the north and west. A single closed door lies just south of the western set of double doors.

The ceiling here is 20 feet high. Beyond the open doors to the north, the characters can see a long, wide hallway with amber-covered walls (area X8).

The hole in the floor forms a roughly hewn shaft that descends 20 feet, then breaks through the ceiling of area X33a. From the bottom of the shaft, it's another 10-foot drop to the floor of area X33a. The shaft has abundant handholds and can be climbed without an ability check, but characters must still drop the last 10 feet to reach the floor below. If the characters make a lot of noise, the three **flameskulls** in area X33a float up the shaft and attack them. The flameskulls also attack anyone they can hear attempting to descend the shaft.

A secret door in the south wall opens into area X7.

## X7. Secret Scroll Repository

> Carved into the south wall of this dusty space are cylindrical holes fit for scrolls or maps.

The wizards kept magic scrolls here in case the temple came under attack. The scrolls have crumbled to dust.

## X8. Upper East Hall

> Glazed amber covers the walls of this twenty-foot-wide, seventy-foot-long arched corridor. The amber doors at both ends of the hall stand open. A closed door is in the middle of the east wall, and three arrow slits are cut into the wall across from it. Cracks in the black marble floor run the length of the hall.

The cracks in the floor were made by the golem in area X10. The arrow slits are 5 inches wide, 2½ feet tall, and 1 foot thick. They look down on the temple (area X5).

## X9. Lecture Hall

> This chamber is brightly lit by red copper lanthorns that hang from the ceiling. The walls are sheathed in amber

that has been shaped into bas-reliefs of wizards with spellbooks. Stairs to the north and south descend twenty feet to an obsidian lectern, behind which a slab of black slate hangs from chains. Between the stairs are descending rows of red marble benches.

The hanging lanthorns have *continual light* spells cast on them. The black slate slab once served as a chalkboard and has a few chalk marks on it.

Hiding behind the lectern is Vilnius (NE male human **mage**) and his invisible **quasit** familiar. Characters who have a passive Wisdom (Perception) score of 17 or higher notice him. A character who actively searches the room for hidden occupants spots Vilnius with a successful DC 12 Wisdom (Perception) check.

Vilnius wears scorched robes, his unkempt hair is half burned away, and his face and arms are covered with blisters from magic fire. He is the apprentice of Jakarion, the dead wizard in area X17. After the flameskulls there incinerated his master, the wounded Vilnius retreated here. He eats vermin to survive. The amber golem has been patrolling the hallway outside (area X8), and Vilnius won't leave this room until he knows the golem has been destroyed.

Vilnius is a greedy, treacherous coward. He curses his dead master for leading them to this wretched land. If the characters try to befriend him, he is suspicious of their intentions. He would like to retrieve his dead master's staff and spellbook, but otherwise he has no interest in exploring more of the Amber Temple. He knows the following information about the place:

- The temple is a haven for forbidden knowledge.
- Flameskulls—constructs made from the remains of dead wizards—guard the temple.
- Barbaric mountain folk use the temple for shelter.

VILNIUS AND QUASIT

## Treasure

Vilnius carries his spellbook, which contains all the spells he has prepared. He also has a gold amulet shaped like an upside-down V hidden under his robes. Of exquisite design, the amulet is worth 1,000 gp. It is the control amulet for the shield guardian in area X35.

Although he can tell that the amulet is magical, he doesn't know its purpose. The amulet thrums when it comes within 10 feet of the shield guardian. If Vilnius realizes what the amulet does, he won't part with it.

## X10. Northeast Annex

> The walls and ceiling in the eastern portion of this bare stone room have collapsed. To the west and south are open amber doors. In the center of the room is a ten-foot-tall statue of a jackal-headed warrior made of cracked amber. It turns to face you and clenches its fists.

The ceiling here is 20 feet high, and the walls are lined with empty torch sconces. The statue is a damaged amber golem (use the stat block for the **stone golem** in the *Monster Manual*). It has 145 hit points and attacks any creature it sees, stopping only when it can't see any.

An earthquake collapsed the eastern part of the room long ago.

## X11. Northeast Balcony

> This black marble balcony, thirty feet above the floor, overhangs the northeast corner of the temple. The two amber doors leading from this balcony stand open.

Characters can see an arrow slit west of the northern set of doors (see area X13).

## X12. East Shrine

> This bare stone room consists of a foyer to the west and a shrine to the east. Four candlesticks lie on the dusty floor of the foyer. In the shrine, fragments of a shattered obsidian statue are scattered in a raised alcove at the eastern end of the chamber. Two pairs of empty alcoves line the north and south walls of the shrine.

The amber golem in area X10 knocked over the candlesticks and pulverized the obsidian statue, which depicted the same nameless god that stands in area X5. Amber doors in the west wall open into area X13.

A secret door is set into the back of one of the alcoves on the north wall. It can be pulled open to area X14.

## X13. East Archer Post

> This narrow room has an arrow slit in the center of the south wall.

The ceiling here is 10 feet high. The arrow slit looks down toward the temple floor (area X5), beneath the raised left arm of the great statue (area X5a).

## X14. North Staircase

When the characters open the secret door at the top of the stairs, read:

> A dusty corridor heads north, then bends to the east, descending a dark staircase. The air is thin, but heavy with the stench of death.

Three 10-foot-long staircases with landings between them descend a total of 30 feet to area X14a. The stench grows stronger down the stairs.

## X14a. Collapsed Lower Hall

> The stairs descend to a collapsed hall with a high ceiling and amber-glazed walls glazed. Rubble covers most of the floor, and a path through the rubble leads to an open doorway. A deathly stench seems to come from there.

This ruined area once connected to area X32, but an earth tremor caused the ceiling and walls to collapse. The ceiling here is 25 feet high.

Unless the characters douse their light sources and move quietly, the creatures in area X33c hear them approaching and prepare to attack.

## X15. Southwest Annex

This room contains a **gladiator** (CE female human), five **berserkers** (CE male and female humans), and one **dire wolf**. The gladiator and the berserkers are bloodthirsty mountain folk, the dire wolf a servant of Strahd. The dire wolf can't be charmed or frightened.

When they aren't expecting trouble, the gladiator and the berserkers sit on the floor, sharpening their weapons, while the dire wolf sleeps in the middle of the room. The gladiator and the berserkers fight to the death. The dire wolf flees the temple (heading east, through areas X4 and X2) if reduced to fewer than half its hit points.

> Torches in sconces light this bare stone room. Six bedrolls made of stitched animal furs cover the floor. Cold air enters through a fissure in the southwest wall.

Other than the berserkers' armor and weapons, there is nothing of value here. The berserkers are aware of the flameskulls ("fiery spirits") to the north and keep the doors to area X17 closed.

A fissure has formed in the southwest wall. The gap is 2 feet wide, 10 feet tall, and 15 feet deep. It leads outside (area X1a).

A secret door in the south wall opens into area X16. Neither the mountain folk nor the dire wolf knows of it.

### Development

The gladiator, Helwa, uses this room as a shelter while hunting in the mountains. She and her berserkers know nothing about the temple's history or purpose.

## X16. West Scroll Repository

Apart from its location, this room is identical to area X7.

## X17. Upper West Hall

> The walls of this twenty-foot-wide, seventy-foot-long arched corridor are sheathed in amber. The southern half of the hall is scorched by fire, and a charred corpse lies on the floor here, under a burned fur cloak. Several amber doors lead from this hall, and three arrow slits are cut into the east wall. Floating in the middle of the hall are three skulls wreathed in green flame.

Three **flameskulls** guard this hall, attacking creatures that enter. The flameskulls will not leave the hall.

The charred corpse is all that remains of a wizard named Jakarion, who came to the Amber Temple seeking power. The flameskulls incinerated the wizard.

The arrow slits look down on the temple (area X5).

### Treasure

Although the dead wizard's spellbook didn't survive, his staff did. It is a *staff of frost*. Imprinted on it is a fragment of the wizard's personality. The first character who touches the staff gains the following flaw: "I crave power above all else, and will do anything to obtain more of it." This flaw trumps any conflicting personality trait.

## X18. Hallway

> This twenty-foot-long, ten-foot-high hallway of bare stone has an amber door at each end.

Area X17 lies beyond the door to the east, area X21 beyond the door to the west.

## X19. Potion Storage

> Stone blocks resembling tables stand in the center of this room covered in dust. Carved into the stone walls are niches filled with hundreds of dusty bottles. Cobwebs hang from wooden ladders that lean against the walls.

The ceiling here is 15 feet high. The bottles contain the dried-up remains of potions that lost their efficacy long ago. The ladders were once used to reach the higher niches, but they can no longer support any weight.

A secret door is set in the north wall. It can be pulled open to reveal a staircase landing (area X21).

## X20. Architect's Room

> Dominating this room is a twelve-foot-tall model of a dark castle with high walls and tall spires. Behind it, tucked in a corner, are some ruined furnishings and a wooden chest.

In the months leading up to the construction of Castle Ravenloft, this room was occupied by the castle's architect, a wizard named Artimus. He built a scale model of the castle out of magically sculpted rock. Anyone who has seen the castle recognizes this replica for what it is.

The ceiling here is 15 feet high. A secret door in the south wall can be pulled open to a staircase landing (area X21).

### Treasure

The wooden chest contains an old map case in which Artimus kept floor plans of Castle Ravenloft, but the maps were lost long ago. The chest has a false bottom that can be found with a successful DC 10 Wisdom (Perception) check. Inside the hidden compartment is a *tome of understanding*.

### Fortunes of Ravenloft

If your card reading reveals that a treasure is here, it's hidden in the miniature castle. The characters must smash their way into the castle to reach it.

## X21. West Staircase

Three 10-foot-long staircases separated by 10-foot-square landings connect areas X18 and X36. Thick dust covering the stairs has not been disturbed in ages.

The uppermost landing has secret doors set into its north and south walls. The south door opens into area X19, and the north door opens into area X20.

## X22. Northwest Annex

When one of the doors to this room is opened, read:

> Torches in sconces illuminate a dining table in the center of the room. Covering the table is a magnificent feast that fills the hall with the rich smells of cooked meat, sweet vegetables, piping hot gravy, and wine.

The ceiling here is 20 feet high. Amber doors lead south to a hallway (area X18) and east to a shattered balcony (area X23).

The table is real, but the torches, the feast, and the chairs are illusions created by a *programmed illusion* spell that triggers when a door to the room is opened. The illusion can be dispelled (DC 17).

Hidden in plain sight amid the feast on the table is a green copper ewer embossed with images of dancing bears, elks, and wolves. The ewer, like the table, isn't illusory. A *detect magic* spell reveals an aura of transmutation magic around the ewer. If a character picks up the ewer, the illusions fade away (including the torches and their light), and seven **specters** materialize and attack whoever has the ewer.

### TREASURE

Any poisonous liquid poured into the ewer is instantly transformed into an equal amount of sweet wine. Furthermore, a creature that grasps the ewer's handle can command the ewer to fill with 1 gallon of wine, and it can't produce more wine until the next dawn.

Many unscrupulous Barovians and Vistani would kill to obtain this ewer. Others would gladly pay for it or accept it as a gift.

## X23. NORTHWEST BALCONY

> This black marble balcony overhangs the northwest corner of the temple, the floor of which lies thirty feet below. Nearly half of the balcony has fallen away, and obvious cracks have formed near its ragged edge.

This balcony is unsafe. Weight in excess of 250 pounds causes it to collapse. Any creature on the balcony when it collapses falls 30 feet to the temple floor below.

Characters can see an arrow slit east of the northern set of doors (see area X25).

## X24. WEST SHRINE

> This bare stone room consists of a foyer to the east and a shrine to the west. Candlesticks draped in cobwebs stand in the four corners of the foyer. In the shrine, a faceless obsidian statue stands in a raised alcove at the western end of the chamber. Slumped before the statue are two desiccated corpses in tattered garments. Two pairs of alcoves line the north and south walls of the shrine.

The obsidian statue is 4 feet tall, weighs 250 pounds, and depicts the same nameless god that stands watch in the main temple (area X5). Any living creature that enters this room must succeed on a DC 16 Wisdom saving throw or be drawn to the statue as though affected by the sympathy effect of an *antipathy/sympathy* spell. The corpses lying in front of the statue are the remains of two human wizards who came here separately, failed their saving throws, and starved to death while under the spell's effect. The lich in area X27 destroyed the wizards' spellbooks and other possessions. Covering the statue or removing it from this shrine suppresses its magic and ends its sympathy effect on anyone.

A pair of amber doors in the east wall open into area X25. A secret door is set in the back of one of the northern alcoves. Pulling it open releases hundreds of skulls (see area X26).

## X25. WEST ARCHER POST

> This narrow room has an arrow slit in the center of the south wall.

The ceiling here is 10 feet high. The arrow slit looks down toward the temple floor (area X5), beneath the raised right arm of the great statue (area X5a).

## X26. SECRET ALCOVE

Two secret doors lead to this room. When either door is pulled open, read:

> Hundreds of skulls fall out of a cavity behind the door.

This room has a 30-foot-high ceiling and is packed floor to ceiling with human skulls. It takes 5 minutes for a single character to clear a path into the room. Multiple characters can work together to clear a path more quickly. Once the skulls are cleared away, characters can search the room.

> Attached to the thirty-foot-high ceiling of this dark sepulcher is an upside-down iron chest with a barrel-shaped lid.

The iron chest on the ceiling is held in place with *sovereign glue*, and its lid is sealed with an *arcane lock* spell. The chest is impervious to weapon damage. Prying it open requires a successful DC 25 Strength check, assuming the characters can reach it. The inside of the chest is lined with lead.

If the chest's lid is opened, the floor of this room disappears (as if affected by a *disintegrate* spell), creating a 10-foot-square hole above area X39. Creatures standing on the floor when it disappears fall 30 feet, landing in the northwest corner of area X39.

The iron chest is empty.

## X27. LICH'S LAIR

> This fifteen-foot-high room contains the trappings of royalty: ornate furniture, exquisite rugs and tapestries, and decorative statuary. Everywhere you look are lit candelabras atop small tables. The beauty of the decor is undone by thick dust and cobwebs. Standing in the center of the room is a decrepit skeleton clad in tattered robes.
>
> Red pinpoints of light burn in the skeleton's eye sockets. "Do I know you?" it asks.

The **lich** has fewer hit points than normal (99 hit points), doesn't remember its name (Exethanter), and has forgotten all of its prepared spells. It does know its cantrips. In its current condition, the lich has a challenge rating of 10 (5,900 XP). A *greater restoration* spell restores the lich's memory and all of its spells. Another casting of the spell restores its normal hit point maximum (135).

If the characters restore its memory, the lich gives them the passwords to all the locked doors in the Amber Temple (with the exception of the door into area X28, where its phylactery is hidden). It also provides all the information pertaining to Strahd and the temple presented at the start of this chapter. If the characters think to ask, it provides them with the command words for any of the books in the library (area K30).

If the characters restore its body, it offers to escort them while they explore the temple. The other creatures that inhabit the temple don't threaten the characters as long as the lich is with them.

The lich defends itself if attacked and turns to dust if it is reduced to 0 hit points.

The lich assumes that the characters have come seeking knowledge and power. If it is inclined to help them, it tells them how the amber sarcophagi work (as explained in the "Amber Sarcophagi" sidebar). The lich has no alliance with or animosity toward Strahd, and no interest in challenging Strahd for control of Barovia.

The furnishings here are in poor condition and fall apart easily.

There are three secret doors in this room. The secret door to area X28 has an *arcane lock* spell cast on it. The password to suppress the spell is "Exethanter."

### Treasure

The lich's ancient, bronze-covered spellbook sits on a rotted divan, in plain view. Inscribed on its spine is a title: *The Incants of Exethanter.* The spellbook contains all the spells on the lich's list of prepared spells (see the **lich** stat block in the *Monster Manual*). The lich attacks anyone who tries to take its spellbook.

## X28. HIDDEN PHYLACTERY

The secret door to this room has an *arcane lock* spell cast on it (see area X27 for details).

Behind the secret door is a small, dusty room. Rising from the floor in the eastern half of the room is a scaly arm and claw clutching a small box made of bone.

The scaly arm is merely a carved pedestal. The bone box is Exethanter's phylactery. If it takes 20 or more radiant damage from a single source, the phylactery is destroyed.

## X29. SECRET ROOM

Dust and cobwebs fill this otherwise empty room.

The ceiling here is 10 feet high.

## X30. PRESERVED LIBRARY

This stone library has twenty-foot-high walls and a thirty-foot-high vaulted ceiling. Covering the ceiling is a fresco that depicts angels being set ablaze in a hell. A black marble railing encloses a gold marble staircase that spirals gently down a thirty-foot-wide, thirty-foot-deep shaft to the north. Against the gray walls stand six ten-foot-tall, black marble bookcases. On their shelves are hundreds of well-preserved tomes. Embroidered rugs, chairs, and lit candelabras fill the southern half of the room.

The spiral staircase descends 30 feet to area X42. Peering over the railing reveals crates in that area.

There are no ladders here to reach the high bookshelves. (The wizards who built this place used *mage hand* spells.) All the books appear to have blank covers and empty pages. Holding a book while speaking its secret command word causes the book's text to magically appear. Only the lich in area X27 knows the command word for each book, and only if its memory is restored. A *true seeing* spell also allows one to see the magically obfuscated text. The tomes mostly contain vile, forbidden lore. Many spellbooks are hidden here, collectively holding every wizard spell in the *Player's Handbook*.

A book that is taken from the library disintegrates as the magic that preserves it is dispelled. The room's furnishings, which are also magically preserved, deteriorate and become brittle if taken from the room.

The secret door in the center of the west wall can be pulled open to reveal an empty room (area X29). The one in the center of the south wall can be pulled open to reveal a staircase that descends 30 feet to another secret door leading to area X5.

## X31. CENTRAL CATACOMBS

These catacombs contain the moldy remains of the wizards who once defended the Amber Temple. Later generations of wizards who were corrupted by the evil of the temple smashed the amber sheaths covering the dead wizards' bodies and stole everything of value, leaving the formerly preserved corpses to rot.

You smell the horrid perfume of the ancient dead. Stone niches along the walls of these catacombs hold human-shaped amber husks, bones, and tattered shrouds.

If the characters enter these catacombs, add:

Tall, iron candlesticks stand in alcoves. Their candles ignite as you enter, casting flickering light upon the walls and causing the shattered amber to glitter.

The magic candles ignite when a living creature enters the catacombs and melt away if taken from the area.

# Amber Temple
## (Area X)

Lower Level

One square = 10 feet

## X31A. WEST CATACOMBS

> More skeletal remains fill niches in the walls of this smaller annex, the amber husks that once preserved them smashed beyond repair.

## X31B. EAST CATACOMBS

> The niches set into the wall of this annex lie empty, except for a thick coat of dust.

No wizards were entombed here. This annex is empty.

## X32. LOWER EAST HALL

> The walls and ceiling of this great hall are coated in amber that glistens like fresh honey. Dust covers the black marble floor. To the north, the hall has collapsed, leaving a wall of rubble.
>
> Many amber doors lead from this hall. Standing in front of the south door are three ugly women in tattered black gowns with brooms and black, pointed hats.

An earth tremor collapsed the northern part of the hall. Three **Barovian witches** (see appendix D) are trying to open the amber door to area X33a by trying different passwords, unaware that they could gain entry through the shaft in area X6. Frustrated by their lack of progress, they vent their rage by attacking the characters. The witches let loose their three **brooms of animated attack** (see appendix D) while they cast spells.

### DEVELOPMENT
If two of the witches are killed or incapacitated, the surviving witch attempts to escape by flying away on her broom. Only the witches can use the brooms of animated attack in this fashion.

## X33. AMBER VAULTS

Several of these amber-glazed rooms are located along the periphery of the complex. Each room contains two or more amber sarcophagi (see the "Amber Sarcophagi" sidebar).

### X33A. VAULT OF SHALX
The amber door to this room is sealed with an *arcane lock* spell. The password to suppress the spell is "Shalx." A character can push open the doors with a successful DC 25 Strength check. The door (AC 15, 30 hit points) can also be smashed. If the door is reduced to 0 hit points, necrotic energy fills the 30-foot cube directly in front of it. A creature in the area takes 22 (4d10) necrotic damage, turning to dust and bones if reduced to 0 hit points.

### AMBER SARCOPHAGI

An amber sarcophagus looks like a rough block of solid amber 8 feet tall, 5 feet wide, and 5 feet thick. Trapped inside the block is a sliver or wisp of utter darkness no more than a few inches long. The darkness is the vestige of a dead and hateful god—a shard of pure evil with shreds of sentience and awareness. The vestige can't be harmed or controlled, and it is immune to all conditions.

An amber sarcophagus has AC 16, 80 hit points, and immunity to poison and psychic damage. Destroying one causes the vestige trapped within it to disappear, leaving no trace. You choose whether it is banished or destroyed.

A creature that touches the amber sarcophagus forms a telepathic link with the vestige inside. The vestige offers the creature a dark gift. The creature must willingly accept the gift to gain its benefits. A dark gift is described to the creature in general terms; its precise game effect isn't revealed until the creature accepts the gift. For example, a creature that touches Fekre's sarcophagus in area X33a is offered the power to spread disease. That the gift grants the ability to cast the *contagion* spell is not articulated.

A dark gift functions like a charm (see "Supernatural Gifts" in chapter 7, "Treasure," of the *Dungeon Master's Guide*). A creature doesn't receive a dark gift if it is being manipulated or coerced, or if it declines the gift. Once it receives a dark gift, a creature can never receive that same dark gift again.

The instant a dark gift is bestowed, the creature receiving it undergoes a transformation, gaining a sinister physical trait or flaw, or one of each. Unless the text states otherwise, a trait or a flaw that accompanies this gift can't be removed by anything short of a *wish* spell or divine intervention.

Each time a non-evil creature accepts a dark gift, it must make a DC 12 Charisma saving throw. If the saving throw fails, the creature's alignment changes to evil. A character who turns evil becomes an NPC under the Dungeon Master's control, although the DM can allow the player to continue playing the evil character.

Adjust the following text if the creatures in this room have already been encountered and destroyed.

> This room has walls of glazed amber, a floor of red marble, and a rough-hewn shaft in the center of its ten-foot-high ceiling. Three amber sarcophagi stand in alcoves, and above each sarcophagus floats a human skull wreathed in green flame.

Three **flameskulls** guard this room. They attack intruders on sight.

The shaft in the ceiling is 10 feet wide and 20 feet long, with abundant handholds. No ability check is required to climb it. The shaft leads up to area X6.

Characters who touch the amber sarcophagi are offered dark gifts by the evil vestiges contained within them (see the "Amber Sarcophagi" sidebar).

***West Sarcophagus.*** The vestige within this sarcophagus offers the dark gift of Fekre, Queen of Poxes. Fekre's gift is the power of spreading disease. This dark gift allows its beneficiary to cast the *contagion* spell as an action. After it has been used three times, the dark gift vanishes.

The beneficiary of this dark gift reeks of filth.

**South Sarcophagus.** The vestige within this sarcophagus offers the dark gift of Zrin-Hala, the Howling Storm. Zrin-Hala's gift is the power to create lightning. This dark gift allows its beneficiary to cast the *lightning bolt* spell as an action. After it has been used three times, the dark gift vanishes.

As soon as this dark gift is received, one side of the beneficiary's face sags and loses all feeling.

**East Sarcophagus.** The vestige within this sarcophagus offers the dark gift of Sykane, the Soul Hungerer. Sykane's gift is the power to raise the recently deceased. This dark gift allows its beneficiary to cast the *raise dead* spell as an action. After it has been used three times, the dark gift vanishes.

As soon as this dark gift is received, the beneficiary's eyes glow a sickly yellow until the dark gift vanishes. The beneficiary also gains the following flaw: "If I help someone, I expect payment in return."

### X33b. Vault of Maverus

The amber door to this room is sealed with an *arcane lock* spell. The password to suppress the spell is "Maverus." The door is otherwise identical to the door of area X33a.

> This room has amber-glazed walls, a blue marble floor, and three amber sarcophagi standing in alcoves.

The ceiling here is 10 feet high. Characters who touch the amber sarcophagi are offered dark gifts by the evil vestiges contained within them (see the "Amber Sarcophagi" sidebar).

**North Sarcophagus.** The vestige within this sarcophagus offers the dark gift of Savnok the Inscrutable. Savnok's gift is the power to shield the mind. This dark gift takes the form of a *mind blank* spell cast on the beneficiary. The spell has an extended duration of 1 year, after which the dark gift vanishes.

The beneficiary's eyes melt away upon receiving this dark gift, leaving empty sockets that can still see.

**East Sarcophagus.** The vestige within this sarcophagus offers the dark gift of Tarakamedes, the Grave Wyrm. Tarakamedes's gift is the power of flight. The beneficiary of this dark gift grows skeletal wings and gains a flying speed of 50 feet.

The beneficiary of this dark gift must eat bones or grave dirt to survive. At dawn, if the creature has not eaten at least 1 pound of bones or grave dirt in the past 24 hours, it dies.

**South Sarcophagus.** The vestige within this sarcophagus offers the dark gift of Shami-Amourae, the Lady of Delights. Shami-Amourae's gift is the power of persuasion. This dark gift allows its beneficiary to cast the *suggestion* spell as an action, and saving throws against the spell have disadvantage. After it has been used three times, the dark gift vanishes.

The beneficiary of this dark gift gains an extra finger on each hand, as well as the following flaw: "I can't get enough pleasure. I desire others to create beauty for me at all times."

### X33c. Ghastly Vault

The amber door to this room hangs open, and the chamber reeks of death.

> This room has amber-glazed walls and a floor of dark green marble. Three amber sarcophagi stand in alcoves. Two feral humanoids with ghastly gray skin stare at you hungrily with three eyes—two normal eyes and a third lidless eye blinded by cataracts. Five more cling to the walls and ceiling.

The ceiling here is 10 feet high. The seven hungry **ghasts** that lair here fight to the death. The ghasts have the following additional feature:

**Spider Climb.** The ghast can climb difficult surfaces, including upside down on ceilings, without needing to make an ability check.

Characters who touch the amber sarcophagi are offered dark gifts by the evil vestiges contained within them (see the "Amber Sarcophagi" sidebar).

**North Sarcophagus.** The vestige within this sarcophagus offers the dark gift of Drizlash, the Nine-Eyed Spider. Drizlash's gift is the power to walk on walls and ceilings. This dark gift allows its beneficiary to climb difficult surfaces, including upside down on ceilings, without needing to make an ability check.

The beneficiary of this dark gift grows an extra eye somewhere on its body. The eye is blind and ever open.

**East Sarcophagus.** The vestige within this sarcophagus offers the dark gift of Dahlver-Nar, He of the Many Teeth. Dahlver-Nar's gift is the power to live many lives. Upon receiving this dark gift, the beneficiary instantly reincarnates when it dies, as though it was the target of a *reincarnate* spell. The new body appears within 10 feet of the old one. After it has been used three times, the dark gift vanishes.

The beneficiary of this dark gift loses all of its teeth until it reincarnates for the third and final time.

**South Sarcophagus.** The vestige within this sarcophagus offers the dark gift of Zantras, the Kingmaker. Zantras's gift is power that comes from great presence and force of personality. This dark gift increases the beneficiary's Charisma by 4, up to a maximum of 22.

The beneficiary of this dark gift gains the following flaw: "I won't take no for an answer."

### X33d. Breached Vault

The amber door to this room hangs open.

> This room has amber-glazed walls and a floor of purplish-black marble. Two amber sarcophagi stand in alcoves to the west and east. A third sarcophagus that once stood in the north alcove lies shattered on the floor. Clustered in the middle of the room are four loathsome, hunched creatures. Each one has a single large, baleful eye.

The creatures huddled in this room are four **nothics**—former wizards reduced to this evil state by their mad quest for forbidden lore. The nothics use their Weird Insight feature to pry secrets from the characters. Although this power is wickedly invasive, the nothics don't consider their prying to be offensive, and so they are taken aback if the characters retaliate. The nothics fight only if one of them is accosted, or if the characters try to destroy the amber sarcophagi.

Characters who touch the amber sarcophagi are offered dark gifts by the evil vestiges contained within them (see the "Amber Sarcophagi" sidebar).

***West Sarcophagus.*** The vestige within this sarcophagus offers the dark gift of Delban, the Star of Ice and Hate. Delban's gift is the power to unleash deadly cold. This dark gift allows its beneficiary to cast the *cone of cold* spell as an action. After it has been used seven times, the dark gift vanishes. Until it vanishes, the beneficiary also gains the benefits of a *ring of warmth*.

The beneficiary of this dark gift gains the following flaw: "Fire terrifies me."

***North Sarcophagus.*** This sarcophagus has been shattered in a way that suggests the vestige inside it somehow broke free.

***West Sarcophagus.*** The vestige within this sarcophagus offers the dark gift of Khirad, the Star of Secrets. Khirad's gift is the power of divination. This gift allows its beneficiary to cast the *scrying* spell as an action. After it has been used three times, the dark gift vanishes.

The beneficiary's voice becomes a low whisper, and its smile becomes cruel and evil.

### X33e. Vault of Harkotha

The amber door to this room is sealed with an *arcane lock* spell. The password to suppress the spell is "Harkotha." The door is otherwise identical to the door of area X33a.

> This room has amber-glazed walls, a black marble floor with red veins, and three amber sarcophagi standing in alcoves.

In the center of the room, a **death slaad** has cast *invisibility* on itself and stands ready with its greatsword in hand. The slaad attacks anyone who enters the room, fighting until slain. It can't leave the Amber Temple.

Characters who touch the amber sarcophagi are offered dark gifts by the evil vestiges contained within them (see the "Amber Sarcophagi" sidebar).

***North Sarcophagus.*** The vestige within this sarcophagus offers the dark gift of Yrrga, the Eye of Shadows. Yrrga's gift is the power of true seeing. This dark gift grants its beneficiary the benefits of truesight out to a range of 60 feet. These benefits last for 30 days, after which the dark gift vanishes.

The eyes of the beneficiary become starry voids until the dark gift vanishes. The beneficiary of this dark gift also gains the following flaw: "I believe that all life is pointless and look forward to death when it finally comes."

***West Sarcophagus.*** The vestige within this sarcophagus offers the dark gift of Great Taar Haak, the Five-Headed Destroyer. Taar Haak's gift is great strength. This dark gift grants its beneficiary the benefit of a *belt of fire giant strength*. This benefit lasts for 10 days, after which the dark gift vanishes.

The beneficiary of this dark gift the following flaw: "I like to bully others and make them feel weak and inferior."

***South Sarcophagus.*** The vestige within this sarcophagus offers the dark gift of Yog the Invincible. Yog's gift is one of physical resilience. This dark gift increases the beneficiary's hit point maximum by 30. This benefit lasts for 10 days, after which the dark gift vanishes.

Oily black fur covers the beneficiary's face and body.

### X33f. Vault of Thangob

The amber door to this room is sealed with an *arcane lock* spell. The password to suppress the spell is "Thangob." The door is otherwise identical to the door of area X33a.

> This room has amber-glazed walls, a floor of grayish marble with black veins, and three amber sarcophagi standing in alcoves.

Characters who touch the amber sarcophagi are offered dark gifts by the evil vestiges contained within them (see the "Amber Sarcophagi" sidebar).

***West Sarcophagus.*** The vestige within this sarcophagus offers the dark gift of Norganas, the Finger of Oblivion. Norganas's gift is the power to turn life into undeath. This dark gift allows its beneficiary to cast the *finger of death* spell as an action. After it has been used three times, the dark gift vanishes. When it vanishes, the beneficiary must succeed on a DC 15 Constitution saving throw or drop to 0 hit points.

This dark gift turns the beneficiary's blood pitch black and viscid, like tar.

***South Sarcophagus.*** The vestige within this sarcophagus offers the dark gift of Vaund the Evasive. Vaund's gift is the power of evasion. This dark gift grants its beneficiary the benefits of an *amulet of proof against detection and location* and a *ring of evasion*. These benefits last for 10 days, after which the dark gift vanishes.

The beneficiary of this dark gift becomes twitchy and nervous, and also gains the following flaw: "I can't give a straight answer to any question put to me."

***East Sarcophagus.*** The vestige within this sarcophagus offers the dark gift of Seriach, the Hell Hound Whisperer. Seriach's gift is the power to summon and control hell hounds. As an action, the beneficiary of this dark gift can summon and control two **hell hounds**. Both hounds appear at the same time. The beneficiary can summon hounds only once, and the dark gift vanishes when they die.

The beneficiary gains the ability to speak and understand Infernal, if he or she doesn't already know the language. (The hell hounds understand no other language.) Sulfurous smoke issues from the beneficiary's pores whenever he or she speaks Infernal.

## X34. Wizard's Bedchamber

A white marble bed stands in the center of this bare stone room, its mattress long since rotted away. Golden hawks perch atop the bed's corner posts. The room's remaining furnishings have been reduced to dust-covered heaps. Cobwebs cover arcane sigils carved into the walls.

The ceiling here is 10 feet high. The sigils that cover the walls were once wards designed to protect the room's contents from theft, but they have been bled of their magic and can no longer harm anyone.

### Treasure
The four golden hawks are worth 250 gp each.

## X35. Sleeping Guardian

The furnishings of this bare stone room have succumbed to decrepitude. Standing in the center of the room, its head scraping the ten-foot-high ceiling, is a vaguely man-shaped construct made of dark wood and riveted iron. Its helmed head stares blindly in your direction. Cobwebs stretch from this terrible artifice to the wrecked furniture that surrounds it.

This room was once a wizard's bedchamber. The construct is an incapacitated **shield guardian**. Its control amulet can be found in area X9.

## X36. Lower West Hall

Glistening amber coats the walls and ceiling of this enormous hall like sculpted honey, and dust covers the black marble floor. The vaulted ceiling is twenty-five feet high. Set into the walls at a height of five feet are amber ledges lined with life-sized alabaster statues of cats, frogs, hawks, owls, rats, ravens, snakes, toads, and weasels. Many of the statues have fallen off their perches and lie shattered on the floor.

An amber door in the north wall stands open. Four other amber doors to the west and south stand closed.

The animal statues represent different kinds of familiars, and they are harmless.

## X37. Wizard's Bedchamber

Furnishings made of ancient, colorless wood have collapsed under their own weight and now lie covered with cobwebs and dust.

## X38. Haunted Room

This room, once a bedchamber, is littered with broken furnishings. Scattered about the room are the remains of a bed, a wardrobe, two trunks, three tall candlesticks, a desk, a bookshelf, and several chairs. Torn-up books, old quill pens, and tattered clothes are also strewn about.

The ceiling here is 10 feet high. A poltergeist (see the **specter** entry in the *Monster Manual*) haunts this room and telekinetically hurls broken furnishings at intruders so as not to give away its location.

### Treasure
A search of the room yields a wooden scroll tube containing an intact *spell scroll* of *wall of fire*.

## X39. Plundered Treasury

The amber doors that once sealed this great stone room have been smashed, their pieces lying amid crushed bones, armor, and weapons.

The ceiling here is 30 feet high and flat. A 10-foot-square hole in the northwest corner of the ceiling magically forms if the iron chest in area X26 is opened.

An amber golem once stood guard here, but it escaped after thieves broke into the treasury and looted it. The golem has since made its way upstairs (see area X10).

Not all of the thieves escaped, and the pulverized remains of those who died here lie strewn upon the floor. Their restless spirits survive here as four poltergeists (see the **specter** entry in the *Monster Manual*). The poltergeists can't leave the room and fight until destroyed.

## X40. Sealed Treasury

The amber doors to the south are sealed with an *arcane lock* spell. The password to suppress the spell is "Dhaviton." A character can push open the doors with a successful DC 25 Strength check. The doors (AC 15, 60 hit points) can also be smashed. If the doors are reduced to 0 hit points, a *greater invisibility* spell is cast on the amber golem in this room. The spell lasts for 1 minute.

Piles of treasure are heaped against the west and east walls of this stone room.

If the golem is visible, add:

A ten-foot-tall statue carved from amber in the likeness of a hawk-headed humanoid stands in a wide alcove to the north. Behind it, a crack has formed in the wall.

The ceiling here is 30 feet high and flat. The statue in the northern alcove is an amber golem (use the stat block for the **stone golem** in the *Monster Manual*). It attacks any creature that disturbs the treasure. The golem can leave the room but can't leave the Amber Temple.

See area X41 for a description of the cracks in the south wall.

### TREASURE

Six piles of treasure are numbered on the map.

#### Pile 1

- 17,500 cp (loose)
- Thirty 50 gp gemstones
- Three rusted suits of plate armor (worthless)
- Nine rusted shields (worthless)
- A child-sized sarcophagus made of black wood inlaid with gold (worth 250 gp)

#### Pile 2

- 12,000 sp (loose)
- Five rusted suits of ring mail and six rusted breastplates (worthless)
- A silvered rapier with a pink glass hilt
- Four rusted greatswords (worthless)
- A gilded chariot (worth 750 gp)

#### Pile 3

- 6,600 ep (loose), each coin stamped with the profiled visage of Strahd
- Seventy-five empty bottles
- A trunk filled with six fine dresses and gowns (worth 25 gp each)
- Ten pieces of jewelry (worth 250 gp each) and 500 gp in a rotted wooden chest
- Eight painted ceramic statues of saints (worth 250 gp each and weighing 50 pounds each)

AMBER GOLEM

#### Pile 4

- A pile of iron ingots (worth 250 gp total and weighing 2,500 pounds)
- Thirty holy symbols (worth 5 gp each) of gods from various worlds
- A set of twelve copper chalices with silver filigree (worth 25 gp each)
- A gilded skull with red garnets in its eye sockets (worth 250 gp)
- Eight warhammers and six war picks

#### Pile 5

- 9,000 sp (loose)
- Six nonmagical crystal balls (worth 20 gp each)
- A bronze crown with tiny gem-eyed dragons for spires (worth 750 gp)
- A life-sized wooden pony (worth 25 gp)
- Six marble vases (worth 100 gp each and weighing 100 pounds apiece)

#### Pile 6

- 7,000 wooden coins painted gold (worthless)
- 15,000 cp in fifteen iron pots
- An obsidian scepter with gold filigree (worth 2,500 gp)
- Eleven rusted helms (worthless)
- Fifteen thin, leather-bound tomes, all of them signed copies of a storybook called *Snow Dwarf and the Seven Wights*, by Nitch Rackmay.

### FORTUNES OF RAVENLOFT

If your card reading reveals that a treasure is here, it's buried in a random pile of treasure (roll a d6).

## X41. FISSURE

An earth tremor split the rock between areas X40 and X42, creating two natural openings that are virtually side by side. The openings are 3 feet wide, 8 feet high, and 10 feet deep.

## X42. AMBER VAULT

> A golden marble staircase with a black marble railing hugs the north wall as it spirals gently up a thirty-foot-wide shaft. Lying in the middle of the room are six rotting wooden crates.
>
> The amber-covered walls are sculpted to look like tentacles that entwine around marble bas-reliefs of kings, queens, pharaohs, and sultans attended by myriad slaves.
>
> The west, south, and east walls contain alcoves, and standing in each alcove is a tall, rough block of amber. Two wide cracks have opened up in the south wall, spilling rubble and shattered pieces of amber onto the floor in the southeast corner of the room.

The spiral staircase climbs 30 feet to area X30. See area X41 for a description of the cracks in the south wall.

Inside the wooden crates, buried in earth, are six **vampire spawn** created by Strahd from a dead party of adventurers. As soon as they hear intruders in the room, the vampire spawn burst out of their crates and attack, fighting until destroyed.

### TELEPORT DESTINATION

Characters who teleport to this location from area K78 in Castle Ravenloft arrive at the point marked T on the map.

### AMBER SARCOPHAGI

Characters who touch the amber sarcophagi are offered dark gifts by the evil vestiges contained within them (see the "Amber Sarcophagi" sidebar earlier in this chapter). Kasimir will know when he touches the east sarcophagus in this area that he has found the dark gift he seeks.

***West Sarcophagus.*** The vestige within this sarcophagus offers "the dark gift of the Vampyr" to any humanoid creature of evil alignment that touches it. The Vampyr's gift is the immortality of undeath. If the dark gift is accepted, its effect doesn't occur until the following conditions are met, in the order given below. The creature becomes aware of the conditions only after accepting the dark gift.

- The beneficiary slays another humanoid that loves or reveres him or her, then drinks the dead humanoid's blood within 1 hour of slaying it.
- The beneficiary dies a violent death at the hands of one or more creatures that hate it.

When the conditions are met, the beneficiary instantly becomes a **vampire** under the Dungeon Master's control (use the stat block in the *Monster Manual*).

After receiving the dark gift, the beneficiary gains the following flaw: "I am surrounded by hidden enemies that seek to destroy me. I can't trust anyone."

***South Sarcophagus.*** The vestige within this sarcophagus offers "the dark gift of Tenebrous" to any humanoid creature of evil alignment that can cast 9th-level wizard spells. Tenebrous's gift is the secret of lichdom. This dark gift grants its beneficiary the knowledge needed to perform the following tasks:

- Craft a phylactery and imbue it with the power to contain the beneficiary's soul
- Concoct a potion of transformation that turns the beneficiary into a lich

Construction of the phylactery takes 10 days. Concocting the potion takes 3 days. The two items can't be crafted concurrently. When the beneficiary drinks the potion, he or she instantly transforms into a **lich** under the Dungeon Master's control (use the stat block in the *Monster Manual*, altering the lich's prepared spells as desired).

The beneficiary of this dark gift gains the following flaw: "All I care about is acquiring new magic and arcane knowledge."

***East Sarcophagus.*** The vestige within this sarcophagus offers the dark gift of Zhudun, the Corpse Star. Zhudun's gift is the power to raise the ancient dead. As an action, the beneficiary of this dark gift can touch the remains of a dead creature and restore it to life. The effect

is identical to that of the *resurrection* spell, except that it works regardless of how long the creature has been dead. After it has been used once, the dark gift vanishes.

The beneficiary of this dark gift takes on a corpselike appearance and is easily mistaken for an undead.

# SPECIAL EVENTS

Two dusk elves are drawn to the Amber Temple for different reasons. You can use one or both of the following special events while the characters explore the temple.

## RAHADIN'S PRAYER

Strahd's loyal chamberlain, **Rahadin** (see appendix D), believes that his master forged a pact with the nameless god of secrets to whom the Amber Temple is dedicated. The dusk elf comes to the temple on occasion to petition the dark god into releasing his master from his torment.

Rahadin rides a *phantom steed* along Tsolenka Pass to the Amber Temple and kneels before the great statue in area X5. (The arcanaloth that guards the temple knows Rahadin and doesn't harm him. The arcanaloth and the flameskulls don't attack other visitors until Rahadin is killed or leaves.) Rahadin then pulls out a live toad, swallows it whole as a sacrifice, and offers a gesture of supplication to the secret god.

### DEVELOPMENT

Rahadin knows that Strahd will deal with the characters when he sees fit. If the characters confront the dusk elf, he defends himself but won't cause them any permanent harm. Strahd's chamberlain would sooner die than allow himself to be captured. Rahadin doesn't divulge his reason for visiting the temple, or even who is he or what role he serves. Left to his own devices, he rides back to Castle Ravenloft.

## KASIMIR'S DARK GIFT

If **Kasimir Velikov** (see appendix D and chapter 5, area N9a) finds his way to area X42 and accepts the dark gift of Zhudun, he then asks the characters to accompany him to the catacombs of Castle Ravenloft so that he can restore the life of his centuries-dead sister, Patrina Velikovna (see chapter 4, area K84, crypt 21).

### DEVELOPMENT

If Kasimir succeeds in his quest, the newly resurrected Patrina (NE female dusk elf **archmage**) feigns repentance until she regains her strength and her spells, whereupon she travels to Castle Ravenloft and attempts to return to Strahd, seeking to become his vampire bride at last. The mutilation of her brother at the hands of Rahadin, Strahd's chamberlain, doesn't sit well with her. She hopes to avenge her brother and distract the characters by setting them on a path to killing Rahadin, who has long opposed her marriage to Strahd.

Strahd has lost interest in Patrina as a consort. Given the chance, he turns her into a vampire spawn and puts her back in her crypt—a fate she would do everything in her power to prevent. Her attraction to Strahd is outmatched by a desire to increase her own power. She is no one's plaything.

# CHAPTER 14: YESTER HILL

T HE DRUIDS WHO WORSHIP STRAHD AS lord of the land and master of the weather convene here, atop Yester Hill, on the very edge of Strahd's domain. This hill is also where the evil blights that walk the Svalich Woods are born, and where Strahd comes on occasion to glimpse his ancestral home.

## AREAS OF THE HILL

The following locations correspond to labels on the map of Yester Hill on page 199.

### Y1. TRAIL

> The trail through the thick woods leads to a hill covered with dead grass and cairns of black rock. Dark, ominous clouds gather high above, and a single bolt of lightning strikes the hilltop. West of the hill, the land, the woods, and the sky vanish behind a towering wall of fog.

The trail splits as it climbs the hillside, forming two concentric rings (area Y2). The trail also leads to the hilltop (areas Y3 and Y4). The wall of fog (area Y5) marks the edge of Strahd's domain.

### Y2. BERSERKER CAIRNS

> Dirt trails run along two concentric rings of cairns that encircle the hillside. Each cairn is a ten-foot-high mound of slimy black rocks.

BY DAY OR NIGHT, STRETCHING UP *to the limits of vision, the edges of my realm are marked by a great wall of mist. I was there at its birth.*
—Strahd von Zarovich
in *I, Strahd: The Memoirs of a Vampire*

These burial mounds predate the arrival of Strahd and the druids. They have remained undisturbed for centuries. Buried under the rocks are the moldy bones of an ancient tribe of berserkers that once lived in the mountains. (See "Blood Spear of Kavan" in the "Special Events" section below.)

### Y3. DRUIDS' CIRCLE

> Atop the hill is a wide ring of black boulders and smaller rocks that collectively form a makeshift wall enclosing a field of dead grass. Lightning strikes the edge of the ring from time to time, illuminating a ghastly, fifty-foot-tall statue made of tightly woven twigs and packed with black earth. The statue resembles a towering, cloaked man with fangs.

The ring of boulders that surrounds the field is 250 feet in diameter and ranges from 5 to 10 feet high. Any creature that climbs over the black boulders has a 10 percent chance of being struck by lightning, taking 44 (8d10) lightning damage. Characters can avoid the damage by sticking to the two trails that pass through the ring.

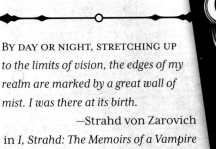

## Wooden Statue

The giant statue bears an eerie resemblance to Strahd von Zarovich. Close inspection reveals roots sprouting from the ground around its base. These roots are part of the Gulthias tree in area Y4. They wrap around the statue, providing added support and durability. The roots not only prevent the statue from being toppled but also allow the effigy to serve as a component in a ritual to create a tree blight (see "Druids' Ritual" in the "Special Events" section below). Planted in the "heart" of this wooden effigy is a magic gem stolen from the Wizard of Wines vineyard (chapter 12).

The statue has AC 10, 50 hit points, and immunity to poison and psychic damage. If the statue takes fire damage after being splashed with oil, it catches fire, taking 2d6 fire damage each round. If the statue is reduced to 0 hit points, it collapses, and the magic gem tumbles onto the field, glowing with a bright green light.

## Hidden Graves

Hidden throughout the field inside the boulders are six **druids** (CE male and female humans) and six **berserkers** (CE male and female humans), all descendants of the ancient mountain tribe whose members are buried on this hill and all covered head to toe in bluish-gray mud. They have long, tangled hair and wild-looking eyes. To honor their dark "god," they sleep in earthen graves hidden under covers made of sod and dead grass. Characters entering the circle who have a passive Wisdom (Perception) score of 16 or higher notice the dozen covered graves scattered throughout the field. The druids and the berserkers rise from their graves and attack if anyone approaches or damages the statue, or if they are discovered and attacked.

The druids are waiting to begin a ritual to summon forth an enormous tree blight. Only one druid is needed to complete the ritual, but the druids won't begin without Strahd's blessing. Thus, they are waiting for him to appear. The ritual can't be completed if the statue is destroyed or the magic gem is removed.

If the characters discern or divine the gem's location with the aid of magic, they can try to dig the gem out of the statue's chest. Climbing up the statue is a simple matter, requiring no ability check, and a character within reach of the chest cavity can use an action to dig into it. Have that character's player roll a d20: on a result of 13 or higher, the character unearths the gem and can take it as part of his or her action.

## Development

If the druids and the berserkers are killed, their numbers are replenished as others return from forays into the Svalich Woods. At the end of each day, at dusk, 1d4 − 1 druids and 1d4 − 1 berserkers arrive until there are six of each.

# Y4. Gulthias Tree

> At the south end of the hilltop is a sickly copse, a grove of dead trees and shrubs with a huge, misshapen tree at its core. Blood oozes like sap from its twisted trunk. Skulking around the tree are six gangly humanoid creatures covered with needles. Embedded in the tree is a shiny battleaxe, beneath which lies a humanoid skeleton.

The tree is a Gulthias tree (see the blights entry in the *Monster Manual*), the roots of which extend deep beneath the hill. Lurking among the dead trees and shrubs are three **vine blights**, six **needle blights**, and twelve **twig blights**. The needle blights are plainly visible, but the False Appearance feature of the vine blights and the twig blights allows them to hide in plain sight. The blights attack anyone who harms the Gulthias tree, which has no actions or effective attacks of its own.

The Gulthias tree has AC 15, 250 hit points, and immunity to bludgeoning, piercing, and psychic damage. If it is reduced to 0 hit points, it seems to be destroyed but isn't truly dead; it regains 1 hit point every month until it is fully healed. With a successful DC 15 Intelligence (Nature) check, a character can determine that the entire stump must be uprooted for the tree to truly die. The Gulthias tree withers and dies in 3d10 days if a *hallow* spell is cast in its area.

The Gulthias tree creates blights from ordinary plants and is the only tree of its kind in Barovia. If the Gulthias tree is killed, no new blights can be created within Strahd's domain. Award the party 1,500 XP for destroying the Gulthias tree.

The skeleton lying at the base of the Gulthias tree is all that remains of a human adventurer who was killed by blights while trying to cut down the tree.

## Treasure

The dead adventurer's tattered leather armor isn't salvageable, but the axe embedded in the tree is a magic battleaxe. Its handle is carved with leaves and vines, and the weapon weighs half as much as a normal battleaxe. When the axe hits a plant, whether an ordinary plant or a plant creature, the target takes an extra 1d8 slashing damage. When a creature of non-good alignment wields the axe, it sprouts thorns whenever its wielder makes an attack with it. These thorns prick the wielder for 1 piercing damage after the attack is made, and this damage is considered magical.

## Fortunes of Ravenloft

If your card reading reveals that a treasure is here, it's buried amid the roots of the Gulthias tree, beneath the skeleton of the dead adventurer. Characters who dig in the ground under the skeleton automatically find it.

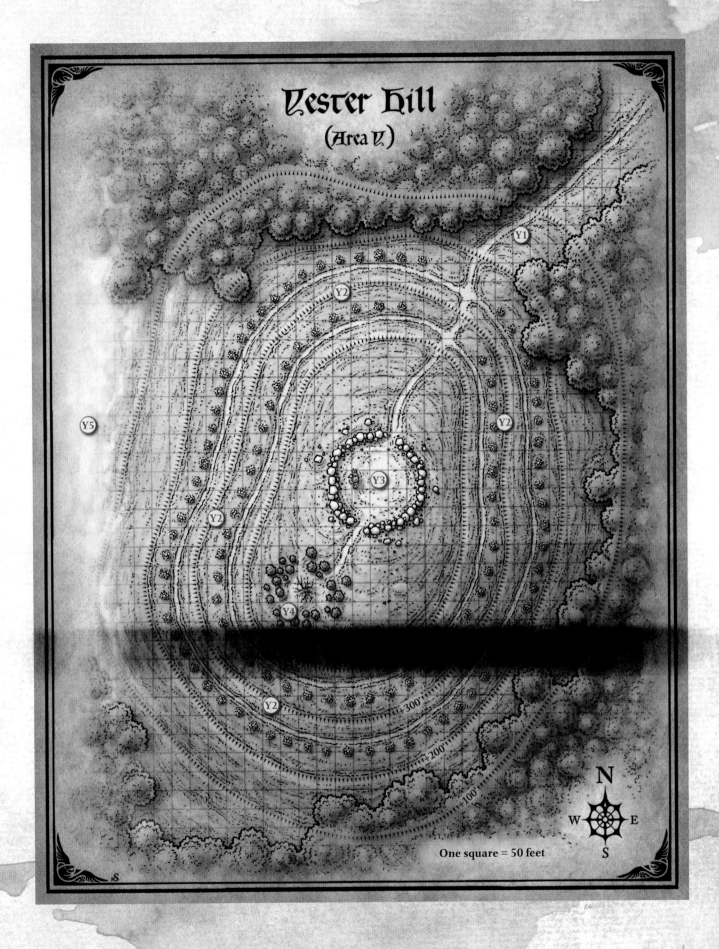

# Yester Hill
## (Area V.)

Y1

Y2

Y5

Y2

Y3

Y2

Y4

+300'

+200'

Y2

+100'

N
W E
S

One square = 50 feet

## Y5. Wall of Fog

Yester Hill gets its name from a strange phenomenon that can be observed by anyone who looks into the mists from the hilltop or the western hillside:

> As you look west into the curtain of fog, you see a white fortress on a hill above a great city. The city appears quite distant, maybe a mile away. The fog obscures all detail, but you can hear what sounds like the echo of a church bell.

The Dark Powers have created a false image of Strahd's ancestral home within the fog, just beyond reach. Strahd comes to the hill on occasion to gaze upon the city, even though he knows it can't be real. The image tantalizes him.

Any creature that enters the deadly fog is subject to its effects (see the "Mists of Ravenloft" section in chapter 2).

If the characters ask an NPC spellcaster about this part of the wall of fog, that person might relate an ancient legend about it. According to the mountain folk of Barovia, there was always a wall of mist near Yester Hill, even before the deadly mists entrapped all of Barovia. The ancient folk called the mist the Whispering Wall, for within it they could hear the whisper of voices from the past and the future. They believed that an ancient god gave up his divinity to preserve the world from destruction and that his last exhalation as a god produced this mist. Within it were all his memories of the world and all his visions of its possible futures, and with proper preparation, a seeker could go on a vision quest within it. Some students of the arcane contend that the Dark Powers took a bit of that fog and twisted it to create the mists of Barovia, and that perhaps Strahd's domain is just a dark memory in the Whispering Wall.

# Special Events

You can use one or both of the following special events while the characters explore Yester Hill.

## Druids' Ritual

You can allow this event to unfold regardless of whether the characters have visited Yester Hill. Even if the characters don't experience this event as it happens, they can still deal with the aftermath (see "Wintersplinter Attacks" in the "Special Events" section in chapter 12).

Strahd travels to Yester Hill, arriving astride his **nightmare**, Beucephalus (assuming the characters didn't kill it in the catacombs of Castle Ravenloft), or in bat form.

Strahd's arrival prompts the druids in area Y3 to rise from their "graves" and begin their ritual. When the ritual begins, the druids use their actions to chant and dance about. To complete the ritual, the druids must chant for 10 consecutive rounds, with at least one of them chanting each round. If a round goes by and none of the druids are able to chant on their turn, the ritual is ruined and must be started anew. If the Gulthias tree (area Y4) has been reduced to 0 hit points, the ritual won't work. Druids who realize that the tree has been destroyed know enough not to attempt the ritual.

Strahd observes the proceedings, defending the druids if they are attacked and retreating if outmatched.

### Development

If the characters are present when the druids complete the ritual, read:

> A thirty-foot-tall plant creature bursts out of the statue, sending twigs and earth flying. The creature resembles a dead treant with green light seeping out of it.

The creature that erupts from the wooden statue is a **tree blight** (see appendix D) that the druids call Wintersplinter. The green light comes from the magic gem embedded in its "heart." The gem can be removed only when Wintersplinter is dead.

The druids command Wintersplinter to travel north and lay waste to the Wizard of Wines vineyard (chapter 12). Although the characters might not understand what the druids are up to, they will no doubt wonder where the druids are sending the tree blight. As Wintersplinter travels north, its destination should become clear to characters who have previously visited the winery and the vineyard. Whether they try to halt its advance is up to them.

Once the tree blight departs, Strahd commands the druids and berserkers to leave the hill so that he can be alone. As they flee into the woods, he gazes longingly at the image of his ancestral homeland to the west (see area Y5).

## Blood Spear of Kavan

The spirit of Kavan, a long-dead barbarian chieftain, reaches out to one of the characters, preferably a barbarian, a druid, or a ranger. Read the following text to that character's player:

> You hear a whisper, a deep voice carried on the wind. "Long have I waited," it says, "for one who is worthy. My spear hungers for blood. Retrieve it, and rule these mountains in my stead, just like the mighty warriors from the early days of the Whispering Wall."

The character feels drawn to one of the cairns on the hillside (see area Y2). When the character approaches within 30 feet of it, the presence of Kavan's magic spear (see "Treasure" below) under the rocks is felt.

### Treasure

The rocks of the cairn are heavy but can be rolled aside, revealing a *blood spear* (see appendix C) lying amid Kavan's moldy bones. Any creature can wield the spear, but only the character chosen by Kavan to wield it gains a +2 bonus to attack and damage rolls made with this magic weapon.

# CHAPTER 15: WEREWOLF DEN

**W**EST OF LAKE BARATOK IS A CAVE complex that the werewolves of Barovia use as a den. Characters who interrogate captured werewolves can learn the den's location. Most of the werewolf pack is out hunting when the characters first arrive, including the pack's leader, Kiril Stoyanovich.

The werewolves call themselves the Children of Mother Night, because they all worship that deity. Recently, a schism formed within the pack as the result of a challenge to Kiril's leadership. The rift began when another werewolf, Emil Toranescu, questioned the treatment of children kidnapped by the pack.

Kiril would arm the children with weapons and force them to fight each other to the death until only one child was left standing. The winner would then be turned into a werewolf, ensuring what Kiril called "the strength and purity of the pack." Emil advocated keeping all the children alive and turning them into werewolves, thus increasing the pack's size. Emil believed that a larger pack would ensure the werewolves' survival, whereas Kiril saw a larger pack as too difficult to control and feed.

This ideological divide couldn't be reconciled and led to many disagreements. The other werewolves were split between the two camps, and it seemed likely that either Kiril or Emil would die before the conflict could be resolved.

Then Kiril disappeared for several days, causing the other werewolves to wonder whether he had fled or had been quietly disposed of by Emil and his allies. When Kiril returned, he was accompanied by a pack of several dozen dire wolves loyal to Strahd, and he brought word from Castle Ravenloft that Strahd was not pleased with Emil's attempt to fracture the pack. The dire wolves took Emil back to Castle Ravenloft to face punishment, and he was never seen again.

Kiril reestablished his dominance, but his ideas and tactics didn't sit well with the pack's older members, and they certainly didn't please Emil's mate, Zuleika

Toranescu. She knows she can't slay Kiril on her own, and after what happened to Emil, the rest of the pack is unwilling to challenge Kiril's authority and face Strahd's wrath. Kiril won't let Zuleika hunt, so she's more or less confined to the den.

> ### TRAVEL THROUGH THE MISTS
>
> The werewolves serve Strahd out of fear, believing that Mother Night has blessed him with godlike powers and eternal life. Although he can't leave Barovia, Strahd can allow certain creatures to come and go, such as the Vistani. He periodically allows the werewolves to slip past the misty borders as well, so that they can bring or lure others into his domain. Unlike the Vistani, however, the werewolves can't come and go as they please.

## APPROACHING THE DEN

When the characters first approach the werewolf den, read:

> Above the tree line, carved into the side of a rocky mountain spur, is a wide, torchlit cave that looks like the gaping maw of a great wolf.

One hundred feet above the cave mouth (area Z1), farther up the sloping mountainside and not visible from the cave mouth or its vicinity, is a rocky ledge (area Z8). A character can scale the slope to reach the ledge without the need for a climber's kit or ability checks.

THE WOLVES BEGAN TO HOWL.
*They knew me. All the wolves of*
*Barovia did.*

—Strahd von Zarovich
in I, *Strahd: The Memoirs of a Vampire*

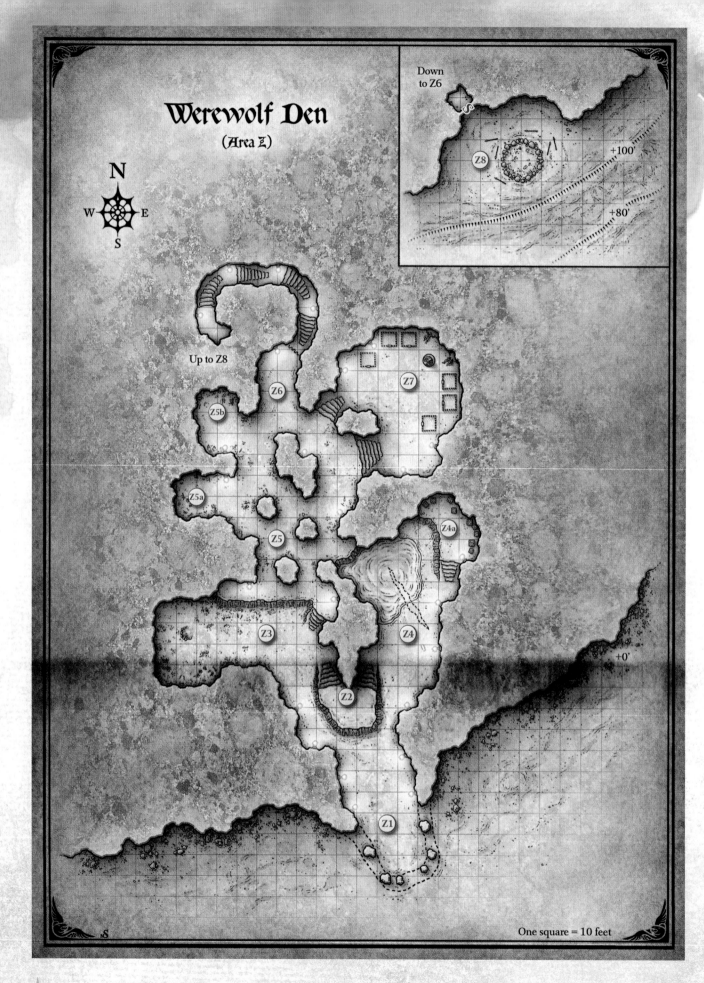

# Werewolf Den
## (Area Z)

Up to Z8

Down to Z6

Z8

+100'

+80'

Z6

Z5b

Z7

Z5a

Z4a

Z5

Z4

+0'

Z3

Z2

Z1

One square = 10 feet

# Areas of the Den

The following areas correspond to labels on the map of the werewolf den on page 202.

Mounted to the walls throughout the den are iron brackets containing lit torches. All areas are brightly lit, though shadows abound.

## Z1. Cave Mouth

> The open jaws of the wolf's head form a fifteen-foot-high canopy of rock over the cave mouth, held up by natural pillars of rock. The ceiling rises to a height of twenty feet inside the cave. Torches in iron brackets line the walls. From somewhere deep inside, you hear the echoing sounds of a flute. Some of the notes are discordant—painfully so.

The guards in area Z2 spot characters in the cave mouth who aren't hidden. Characters can track the sound of the flute to area Z3.

### Development

If the characters arrive here with Emil Toranescu (see chapter 4, area K75a) in their company or their custody, he can command the other werewolves in the den not to attack the characters as they make their way inside.

## Z2. Guard Post

> Here, the cave splits to the left and right. Standing on a five-foot-high ledge between the divide are two feral-looking women wearing shredded clothing and clutching spears.

Aziana and Davanka, two **werewolves** in human form, stand guard on the ledge. They sound the alarm when they spot intruders. Any loud noise here can be heard throughout the den, bringing quick reinforcements from areas Z3 and Z5. The werewolves fight to the death.

## Z3. Wolf Den

Nine **wolves** and a **werewolf** in human form are here. The werewolf, Skennis, has 36 hit points and is too old to hunt. Left undisturbed, he plays an electrum flute (see "Treasure" below), though not very well. The wolves are huddled behind him and go where he goes. Though well past his prime, he fights to the death to defend the den, and he takes umbrage at anyone who kills any of his wolf allies.

> A five-foot-high stone ledge overlooks this large cave, which has a smoldering campfire at the far west end. The floor is covered with gnawed bones.

If Skennis is reduced to 0 hit points, read:

> The old man cackles. "When Kiril returns," he says to you with his last breath, "he'll skin you alive."

### Treasure

Skennis's electrum flute is nonmagical and worth 250 gp. Skennis also carries a pouch containing four 50 gp gemstones.

## Z4. Underground Spring

> A gash in the rocky ceiling allows the gray light and cold drizzle of the outdoors to seep into this dank, torchlit cave, where an underground spring forms a pool of water roughly forty feet across and ten feet deep. A five-foot-high ledge to the north overlooks the pool. A similar ledge spans the eastern wall, with a rough-hewn staircase leading up to it. A few crates sit atop the eastern ledge.

The water is fresh. The ceiling is roughly 20 feet above the surface of the pool. The fissure in the ceiling is 3 feet wide at its widest point, and 6 inches at its narrowest.

The crates on the eastern ledge contain heaps of adult-sized clothing.

## Z5. Deep Caves

> A maze of torchlit tunnels and caves expands in front of you. Bones lie strewn upon the floor.

The ceiling here is 10 feet high. The bones on the floor are a warning system. They crunch loudly underfoot, and creatures have disadvantage on Dexterity (Stealth) checks made to move silently through this area.

### Z5a. South Cave

Bianca, a white-haired **werewolf** in wolf form who is Kiril Stoyanovich's mate, sleeps here. She reacts quickly to sounds of alarm, attacking any intruders she sees.

### Z5b. North Cave

Wensencia, a **werewolf** in wolf form, sleeps here with Kellen, a ten-year-old werewolf in wolf form. Kellen is a noncombatant with AC 10, 2 hit points, and a werewolf's damage immunities. He hugs a wooden doll that eerily resembles one of the characters, but is painted and dressed to look like a zombie. A tiny slogan etched into the zombie doll reads, "Is No Fun, Is No Blinsky!"

When an alarm sounds, Wensencia takes Kellen to area Z7, locks him in one of the empty cages, and tells him to take human form, which he does. She then joins her fellow werewolves in the den's defense.

Kellen was kidnapped from his home in Liam's Hold, a hamlet near the Misty Forest in the Forgotten Realms setting. He was afflicted with werewolf lycanthropy after winning one of Kiril's despicable contests. Wencensia has been tasked with training this newest member of Kiril's pack. Casting a *greater restoration* spell or a *remove curse* spell on Kellen ends his lycanthropy.

## Z6. KIRIL'S CAVE

> At the back of this cave hangs a curtain made of human skin.

When home, Kiril Stoyanovich sleeps here in wolf form.

Behind the ghastly curtain of stitched flesh is a 10-foot-high, 10-foot-wide tunnel with rough-hewn stairs leading up, interspersed with landings. The tunnel ends at a secret door, beyond which lies area Z8. The secret door is easy to spot from inside the tunnel (no ability check required).

## Z7. SHRINE OF MOTHER NIGHT

> Rough-hewn stairs lead down to a torchlit cave and a bizarre sight: wide-eyed children stand behind wooden bars and stare at you in terrified silence. The cave holds six wooden cages, their lids held shut with heavy rocks. Two of the cages are empty, and each of the others holds a pair of frightened children.
>
> A crude wooden statue stands between the cages. It bears the rough likeness of a wolf-headed woman draped in garlands of vines and night flowers. Piled around the statue's base is an incredible amount of treasure. A woman in shredded clothes kneels before the statue. Behind the statue, two maggot-ridden corpses hang from iron shackles bolted to the wall.

The ceiling here is 20 feet high. The statue is a crude depiction of Mother Night. Kneeling before it is a **werewolf** in human form named Zuleika Toranescu, who is the wife of Emil (see chapter 4, area K75a). Believing her mate to be dead by Strahd's hand, she prays to Mother Night for guidance, hoping that the goddess might hold enough sway over Strahd to persuade him to free her beloved.

Kiril has ordered Zuleika to guard the prisoners. If the characters rescue Emil and return him safely to Zuleika, she gladly releases the children. If the characters confirm that Emil is truly dead, either by their hand or Strahd's, she still might let the prisoners go if the characters help her deal with Kiril Stoyanovich, whom she blames above all. Zuleika sees the characters as the answer to her prayers and asks them to kill Kiril when he returns from his latest hunt (see "Leader of the Pack" in the "Special Events" section below).

Each of the eight children imprisoned here has AC 10, 1 hit point, and no effective attacks. To determine a child's age in years, roll 1d6 + 6. The rocks piled atop

ZULEIKA TORANESCU

each occupied cage can be knocked or lifted off, allowing the cages to be opened. The children are in shock. Those who are set free don't wander far from the characters for fear of being eaten by wolves and werewolves.

The corpses hanging on the wall behind the statue are two Barovian adults, a man and a woman, killed by the pack and presented as offerings to Mother Night. The werewolves consider the feasting maggots to be emblematic of Mother Night's "feedings." When the flesh of these corpses has been eaten away, the pack searches for new offerings to take their place.

### TREASURE

The treasure piled around the base of Mother Night's statue includes:

- 4,500 cp, 900 sp, and 250 gp (all coins of mintages foreign to Barovia)
- Thirty 50 gp gemstones and seven 100 gp gemstones
- Twelve pieces of plain gold jewelry (worth 25 gp each) and a finely wrought gold cloak-pin inlaid with shards of jet (worth 250 gp)
- An ivory drinking horn engraved with dancing dryads and satyr pipe players (worth 250 gp)
- An ornate electrum censer with platinum filigree (worth 750 gp)

Anyone who steals from Mother Night is cursed. The werewolves know this, and thus don't go out of their way to guard the hoard.

Any creature that takes treasure from this pile is haunted by horrible dreams every night lasting from dusk until dawn. The curse affects only the creature that did the pilfering and isn't passed on to anyone else who might come into possession of the item. Returning a stolen item to the treasure pile doesn't end the curse.

A creature cursed in this way gains no benefit from finishing a short or long rest at night (resting during the day works normally, since the curse is dormant from dawn to dusk). A *greater restoration* or a *remove curse* spell cast on the creature ends the curse on it. The curse on the creature also ends if it leaves Barovia.

If your card reading reveals that a treasure is here, it's lying amid the other items at the base of the statue. The curse described above applies to this treasure as well.

## Z8. RING OF STONE

> A twenty-foot-diameter ring of stones dominates a rocky ledge on the mountainside. Within the ring, you see spattered blood and small, gnawed bones. Lying on the ground outside the circle are several spears stained with dry blood.

The werewolf pack convenes here to watch their young prisoners fight with spears in the stone ring. The last child standing is bitten and turned into a werewolf; then the bodies of the dead are devoured, their bones picked clean.

Set into the mountainside is a secret door that can be pushed open to reveal a tunnel with rough-hewn stairs leading down to area Z6.

# SPECIAL EVENTS

You can use one or both of the following special events while the characters are exploring or resting in the den.

## LEADER OF THE PACK

This event doesn't occur if the characters previously encountered and defeated Kiril's hunting pack (see "Pack Attack" in the "Special Events" section in chapter 11).

Every hour the characters spend inside the werewolf den, roll a d20. On a roll of 18 or higher, the werewolf hunting party returns, dragging a dead mountain goat. It's a meager feast, at best. The party consists of Kiril Stoyanovich (a **werewolf** with 90 hit points), six normal **werewolves**, and nine **wolves**. All the werewolves arrive in wolf form.

If the wolves can see evidence of an assault on the den (such as if the guards at area Z2 are absent or dead), the werewolves assume hybrid form. Kiril sends three werewolves up the mountainside to area Z8 to enter the den from above while he and the remainder of the hunting party make their way deeper into the den.

### DEVELOPMENT

As long as Kiril lives, the characters can't negotiate with the werewolves. If Kiril dies and the characters have the upper hand, the pack is willing to negotiate with them.

If Emil Toranescu is present when Kiril returns, Emil is determined to kill his rival and become the new pack leader. If he succeeds, he allows the characters to leave the den unmolested but refuses to release the kidnapped children unless Zuleika is present to convince him otherwise (because she fears that the characters might kill her husband if he doesn't let the children go).

If both Kiril and Emil die, Zuleika becomes pack leader and cuts all ties to Strahd. The ordinary wolves leave the pack once Strahd becomes aware of this development. If the characters were drawn into Barovia

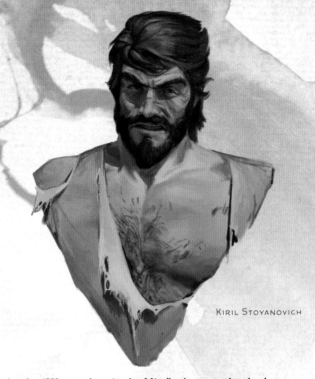

KIRIL STOYANOVICH

by the "Werewolves in the Mist" adventure hook, the werewolf attacks on the Sword Coast come to an end under Zuleika's leadership. If she is also dead, a young but fierce werewolf named Franz Groza becomes pack leader. He is vicious and treacherous, showing the characters no mercy.

## DIE KINDER

If the characters get the children away from the den while Kiril is alive, Kiril reassembles his hunting party and pursues the lost prisoners relentlessly. If Kiril is dead, the werewolf pack is too preoccupied with determining Kiril's successor to organize a hunting party.

If the characters aren't sure where to take the children, a **wereraven** (see appendix D) that has been spying on the den in raven form assumes hybrid form and suggests that they take refuge in the nearby village of Krezk (chapter 8). If the characters head that way, the wereraven scouts from overhead until the characters reach the village, whereupon it flies south to the Wizard of Wines winery (chapter 12) and reports what has happened to Davian Martikov.

The children are understandably traumatized by their imprisonment in the werewolf den. They cry and scream the whole time they're with the characters. A *calm emotions* spell quells their anguish for the duration of the spell (no saving throws required). A character can try to silence the children for a longer period of time using intimidation, or by offering them hope (real or otherwise). The character must make a DC 15 Charisma (Intimidation, Persuasion, or Deception) check, as appropriate. If the check succeeds, the children remain silent until something happens to frighten them.

If the characters take the children to Krezk, the villagers there look after the children and see that they are fed and properly clothed. If the characters take them to Vallaki instead, the Martikovs allow the children to stay at the Blue Water Inn until the characters return to collect them.

# EPILOGUE

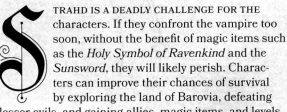

**S**TRAHD IS A DEADLY CHALLENGE FOR THE characters. If they confront the vampire too soon, without the benefit of magic items such as the *Holy Symbol of Ravenkind* and the *Sunsword*, they will likely perish. Characters can improve their chances of survival by exploring the land of Barovia, defeating lesser evils, and gaining allies, magic items, and levels of experience.

The outcome of the final showdown between Strahd and the characters determines how the adventure ends.

## STRAHD PREVAILS

Once he is done toying with the characters, Strahd sets out to defeat them utterly, having concluded that none of them is worthy to replace him as the lord of Barovia. He won't be satisfied until all the characters are dead or turned into his vampire spawn consorts.

If Strahd prevails, he seals the characters in the catacombs (chapter 4, area K84, crypt 23) and instructs his servants to hide all their magic items.

With the characters out of the way, Strahd shifts his attention back to making Ireena Kolyana his bride. If she is still alive and within his grasp, Ireena is turned into a vampire spawn and sealed in her crypt beneath Castle Ravenloft.

## STRAHD DIES

When Strahd is reduced to 0 hit points, he turns to mist and retreats to his coffin (see the Misty Escape feature in the **vampire** stat block). The vampire must be in his resting place to be utterly destroyed.

If the characters finish off Strahd in his coffin, read:

> Strahd can't hide his surprise as death takes him into the black abyss. Surprise turns to rage, and the Pillarstone of Ravenloft trembles with fury, shaking dust from the ceiling of the vampire's tomb. The shudders abate as Strahd's burning hatred melts away, replaced at last with relief. The dark orbs of his eyes wither and sink into his skull as his corpse deteriorates before you. In a matter of moments, only bones, dust, and noble garb remain. Strahd von Zarovich, the dark lord of Barovia, is dead and gone.

## RAHADIN'S REVENGE

If Strahd dies but **Rahadin** yet lives, the dusk elf chamberlain appears moments after Strahd's demise. When that occurs, read:

> "Master!" says a voice from behind you. An elf with dusky brown skin and long black hair, his face a mask of terror, looks on what you have wrought and screams.

Rahadin has served Strahd's family for hundreds of years and doesn't take his master's defeat well. The dusk elf chamberlain draws his scimitar and tries to avenge Strahd. Grief-stricken, he can't be reasoned with.

## SERGEI AND IREENA

This optional scene can be used after Strahd has been defeated. It assumes that Ireena Kolyana survived the adventure and hasn't yet been reunited with Sergei.

On the morning after Strahd's demise, the characters feel drawn to Castle Ravenloft's overlook (area K6), and there they witness the following scene.

> Thick clouds fill the sky. Through the chilly morning mists, the land of Barovia is visible far below. There is peacefulness here. Rest has come to the valley for the first time anyone can remember.
>
> A light flashes behind you. Wheeling around, you see a stately man—a being of flesh and blood—in shining armor and a flapping cape. His countenance shows great strength of will, yet the forcefulness of his presence is tempered by his calm, sad eyes. His features are those of Strahd, yet subtly different.
>
> His voice is calm and peaceful. "My name is Sergei von Zarovich." He turns to Ireena. "Tatyana, the time is at hand to rest. Come, my love and wife." He stretches forth his hand.
>
> Ireena Kolyana's questioning eyes suddenly open with recognition and knowledge. Forgotten memories rush back to her. "Sergei!" she cries, springing to him with the grace of a doe. They embrace.
>
> Ireena turns to you and says, "I am Ireena Kolyana, but in my past I was Sergei's beloved Tatyana. Through these many centuries we have played out the tragedy of our lives. Now, with our deepest gratitude to you, that tragedy is over. It is time for joy to begin again."
>
> Shimmering light surrounds Ireena and Sergei. Hand in hand, they walk east toward the edge of the overlook. Their feet do not touch the ground as they tread a path beyond this mortal world. Their invisible road takes them beyond the eastern precipice, their glow illuminating and thinning the clouds above Barovia. The clouds suddenly break open, letting shafts of glorious sunlight flood through. In the valley below, the strange fog dissolves. Barovia is free once more.

## Escape from Barovia

Strahd's death grants Barovia a reprieve. The fog that surrounds the land thins, and it no longer harms those who pass through it. The dark clouds that have loomed over the valley for centuries give way to sunshine, shocking the Barovians out of their despair.

The Barovians take the sunlight as a sign that the evil in their land has been purged. Though escape is now possible, most Barovians realize that they have nowhere to go and no reason to leave. A few depart, fearing the return of the darkness or longing to see their ancestral homelands. Those who have souls can leave the valley, while those without souls fade into nothingness as they take their first steps beyond the edge of Strahd's former domain.

## Aftermath

The bats, wolves, and dire wolves of Barovia lose their supernatural link to Strahd upon his destruction and become ordinary beasts, destined to be hunted down or driven to the farthest reaches of the Svalich Woods.

Even after Strahd's death, Castle Ravenloft remains a haunted place shunned by all Barovians. Its dark immensity and threatening countenance are enough to deter locals from plundering or reoccupying it.

### The Rise of Ismark

If he survives the adventure, Ismark Kolyanovich becomes burgomaster of the village of Barovia. He is grateful to the characters for all they have accomplished and urges them to stay in Barovia and help him rid the land of its other threats, offering his village as a safe haven.

### Vistani Exodus

Fearing that the Barovians might kill them for being spies and collaborators, the Vistani pack up their wagons and leave the valley with great haste. The Barovians are happy to see them go.

### Vampire Hunters

If he is still alive, Rudolph van Richten (see "Rictavio" in appendix D) leaves Barovia to live out his remaining days in solitude. His protégé, Ezmerelda d'Avenir (see appendix D), isn't convinced that Strahd is truly dead. She also knows that there are other evils in Barovia to be conquered, so she elects to remain in the valley.

### Consorts Unleashed

Upon his death, Strahd's vampire spawn are freed from his control, and each seeks a new destiny. Escher, in particular, leaves the realm, in search of new experiences and a way to become a vampire lord himself.

If Patrina Velikovna lives, she begins to plunder arcane knowledge from Castle Ravenloft and the Amber Temple and prepares to become Barovia's new master.

### Strahd's Return

Ezmerelda's suspicion proves justified. Strahd's destruction is temporary, for his curse can't so easily be ended. The ancient Dark Powers with which Strahd forged his pact cause the vampire to re-form after a period of months—long enough for the Barovians to discover what it feels like to live a life of hope. When Strahd is reborn, the mists surround the land of Barovia once more, and the Barovians' hope turns to horrible despair. Strahd remembers the defeat dealt to him and begins plotting his revenge.

After the mists reappear, Madam Eva and her Vistani come back to the valley, the beasts of the land once more fall under Strahd's spell, and the burgomasters fortify their settlements, hoping against all hope that someone can save them from Strahd again.

# Appendix A: Character Options

## Character Background

During character creation, players can select the following background for their characters, with your approval. It is appropriate for any character or campaign associated with eeriness or horror.

## Haunted One

You are haunted by something so terrible that you dare not speak of it. You've tried to bury it and flee from it, to no avail. This thing that haunts you can't be slain with a sword or banished with a spell. It might come to you as a shadow on the wall, a bloodcurdling nightmare, a memory that refuses to die, or a demonic whisper in the dark. The burden has taken its toll, isolating you from others and making you question your sanity. You must find a way to overcome it before it destroys you.

**Skill Proficiencies:** Choose two from among Arcana, Investigation, Religion, and Survival
**Languages:** Two of your choice, one of which is exotic (Abyssal, Celestial, Deep Speech, Draconic, Infernal, Primordial, Sylvan, or Undercommon)
**Equipment:** Monster hunter's pack (see sidebar), a set of common clothes, one trinket of special significance (choose one or roll on the Gothic Trinkets table in this appendix), and 1 sp

### Harrowing Event

| d10 | Event |
|-----|-------|
| 1 | A monster that slaughtered dozens of innocent people spared your life, and you don't know why. |
| 2 | You were born under a dark star. You can feel it watching you, coldly and distantly. Sometimes it beckons you in the dead of night. |
| 3 | An apparition that has haunted your family for generations now haunts you. You don't know what it wants, and it won't leave you alone. |
| 4 | Your family has a history of practicing the dark arts. You dabbled once and felt something horrible clutch at your soul, whereupon you fled in terror. |
| 5 | An oni took your sibling one cold, dark night, and you were unable to stop it. |
| 6 | You were cursed with lycanthropy and later cured. You are now haunted by the innocents you slaughtered. |
| 7 | A hag kidnapped and raised you. You escaped, but the hag still has a magical hold over you and fills your mind with evil thoughts. |
| 8 | You opened an eldritch tome and saw things unfit for a sane mind. You burned the book, but its words and images are burned into your psyche. |
| 9 | A fiend possessed you as a child. You were locked away but escaped. The fiend is still inside you, but now you try to keep it locked away. |
| 10 | You did terrible things to avenge the murder of someone you loved. You became a monster, and it haunts your waking dreams. |

> ### Monster Hunter's Pack
> A monster hunter's pack includes a chest, a crowbar, a hammer, three wooden stakes, a holy symbol, a flask of holy water, a set of manacles, a steel mirror, a flask of oil, a tinderbox, and three torches. Purchasing the pack costs 33 gp, which is cheaper than buying its contents individually.

### Feature: Heart of Darkness

Those who look into your eyes can see that you have faced unimaginable horror and that you are no stranger to darkness. Though they might fear you, commoners will extend you every courtesy and do their utmost to help you. Unless you have shown yourself to be a danger to them, they will even take up arms to fight alongside you, should you find yourself facing an enemy alone.

### Harrowing Event

Prior to becoming an adventurer, your path in life was defined by one dark moment, one fateful decision, or one tragedy. Now you feel a darkness threatening to consume you, and you fear there may be no hope of escape. Choose a harrowing event that haunts you, or roll one on the Harrowing Events table.

### Suggested Characteristics

You have learned to live with the terror that haunts you. You are a survivor, who can be very protective of those who bring light into your darkened life.

### Personality Traits

| d8 | Personality Trait |
|----|-------------------|
| 1 | I don't run from evil. Evil runs from me. |
| 2 | I like to read and memorize poetry. It keeps me calm and brings me fleeting moments of happiness. |
| 3 | I spend money freely and live life to the fullest, knowing that tomorrow I might die. |
| 4 | I live for the thrill of the hunt. |
| 5 | I don't talk about the thing that torments me. I'd rather not burden others with my curse. |
| 6 | I expect danger around every corner. |
| 7 | I refuse to become a victim, and I will not allow others to be victimized. |
| 8 | I put no trust in divine beings. |

### Ideals

| d6 | Ideal |
|----|-------|
| 1 | I try to help those in need, no matter what the personal cost. (Good) |
| 2 | I'll stop the spirits that haunt me or die trying. (Any) |
| 3 | I kill monsters to make the world a safer place, and to exorcise my own demons. (Good) |
| 4 | I have a dark calling that puts me above the law. (Chaotic) |
| 5 | I like to know my enemy's capabilities and weaknesses before rushing into battle. (Lawful) |
| 6 | I'm a monster that destroys other monsters, and anything else that gets in my way. (Evil) |

## Bonds

| d6 | Bond |
|----|------|
| 1 | I keep my thoughts and discoveries in a journal. My journal is my legacy. |
| 2 | I would sacrifice my life and my soul to protect the innocent. |
| 3 | My torment drove away the person I love. I strive to win back the love I've lost. |
| 4 | A terrible guilt consumes me. I hope that I can find redemption through my actions. |
| 5 | There's evil in me. I can feel it. It must never be set free. |
| 6 | I have a child to protect. I must make the world a safer place for my offspring. |

## Flaws

| d6 | Flaw |
|----|------|
| 1 | I have certain rituals that I must follow every day. I can never break them. |
| 2 | I assume the worst in people. |
| 3 | I feel no compassion for the dead. They're the lucky ones. |
| 4 | I have an addiction. |
| 5 | I am a purveyor of doom and gloom who lives in a world without hope. |
| 6 | I talk to spirits that no one else can see. |

# Gothic Trinkets

When rolling for a trinket, consider using this table, which is designed for a gothic game.

## Trinkets

| d100 | Trinket |
|------|---------|
| 01–02 | A picture you drew as a child of your imaginary friend |
| 03–04 | A lock that opens when blood is dripped in its keyhole |
| 05–06 | Clothes stolen from a scarecrow |
| 07–08 | A spinning top carved with four faces: happy, sad, wrathful, and dead |
| 09–10 | The necklace of a sibling who died on the day you were born |
| 11–12 | A wig from someone executed by beheading |
| 13–14 | The unopened letter to you from your dying father |
| 15–16 | A pocket watch that runs backward for an hour every midnight |
| 17–18 | A winter coat stolen from a dying soldier |
| 19–20 | A bottle of invisible ink that can be read only at sunset |
| 21–22 | A wineskin that refills when interred with a dead person for a night |
| 23–24 | A set of silverware used by a king for his last meal |
| 25–26 | A spyglass that always shows the world suffering a terrible storm |
| 27–28 | A cameo with the profile's face scratched away |

| d100 | Trinket |
|------|---------|
| 29–30 | A lantern with a black candle that never runs out and that burns with green flame |
| 31–32 | A teacup from a child's tea set, stained with blood |
| 33–34 | A little black book that records your dreams, and yours alone, when you sleep |
| 35–36 | A necklace formed of the interlinked holy symbols of a dozen deities |
| 37–38 | A hangman's noose that feels heavier than it should |
| 39–40 | A birdcage into which small birds fly but once inside never eat or leave |
| 41–42 | A lepidopterist's box filled dead moths with skull-like patterns on their wings |
| 43–44 | A jar of pickled ghouls' tongues |
| 45–46 | The wooden hand of a notorious pirate |
| 47–48 | A urn with the ashes of a dead relative |
| 49–50 | A hand mirror backed with a bronze depiction of a medusa |
| 51–52 | Pallid leather gloves crafted with ivory fingernails |
| 53–54 | Dice made from the knuckles of a notorious charlatan |
| 55–56 | A ring of keys for forgotten locks |
| 57–58 | Nails from the coffin of a murderer |
| 59–60 | A key to the family crypt |
| 61–62 | An bouquet of funerary flowers that always looks and smells fresh |
| 63–64 | A switch used to discipline you as a child |
| 65–66 | A music box that plays by itself whenever someone holding it dances |
| 67–68 | A walking cane with an iron ferule that strikes sparks on stone |
| 69–70 | A flag from a ship lost at sea |
| 71–72 | Porcelain doll's head that always seems to be looking at you |
| 73–74 | A wolf's head wrought in silver that is also a whistle. |
| 75–76 | A small mirror that shows a much older version of the viewer |
| 77–78 | Small, worn book of children's nursery rhymes. |
| 79–80 | A mummified raven claw |
| 81–82 | A broken pendent of a silver dragon that's always cold to the touch |
| 83–84 | A small locked box that quietly hums a lovely melody at night but you always forget it in the morning |
| 85–86 | An inkwell that makes one a little nauseous when staring at it |
| 87–88 | An old little doll made from a dark, dense wood and missing a hand and a foot |
| 89–90 | A black executioner's hood |
| 91–92 | A pouch made of flesh, with a sinew drawstring |
| 93–94 | A tiny spool of black thread that never runs out |
| 95–96 | A tiny clockwork figurine of a dancer that's missing a gear and doesn't work |
| 97–98 | A black wooden pipe that creates puffs of smoke that look like skulls |
| 99–00 | A vial of perfume, the scent of which only certain creatures can detect |

# APPENDIX B: DEATH HOUSE

You can run *Curse of Strahd* for 1st-level characters with the help of this optional mini-adventure, which is designed to advance characters to 3rd level. Players creating 1st-level characters can use the haunted one character background in appendix A, or they can pick backgrounds from the *Player's Handbook* as normal.

Before the characters can explore the haunted townhouse known as Death House, you need to guide them to the village of Barovia. The "Creeping Fog" adventure hook in chapter 1 works best, as it introduces few distractions. Once the characters arrive in Strahd's domain, steer them to the village. For the duration of this introductory adventure, any attempt by the characters to explore other locations in Strahd's domain causes the mists of Ravenloft to block their path.

---

### LEVEL ADVANCEMENT

In this mini-adventure, the characters gain levels by accomplishing specific goals, rather than by slaying monsters. These milestones are as follows:

- Characters who gain access to the secret stairs in the attic (area 21) advance to 2nd level. The stairs appear only under certain circumstances.
- Characters advance to 3rd level once they escape from the house (see the "Endings" section).

---

## HISTORY

Death House is the name given to an old row house in the village of Barovia (area E7 on the village map). The house has been burned to the ground many times, only to rise from the ashes time and again—by its own will or that of Strahd. Locals give the building a wide berth for fear of antagonizing the evil spirits believed to haunt it.

The wealthy family that built the house practiced the dark arts. Through seduction and indoctrination, they expanded their cult to include a small yet nefarious circle of friends. When word got out, the rest of the village turned a blind eye to the house and the nightly debaucheries happening within it.

The cult tried to summon malevolent extraplanar entities with no success. The cultists also preyed on visitors, sacrificed them in bizarre rituals, and hosted morbid banquets to feast on their corpses. When nothing came of these ritualized murders, the cultists' activities became thinly disguised excuses to indulge their lurid fantasies. The ranks of the cult thinned as members began to lose interest in the debacle.

Then Strahd von Zarovich arrived.

The cultists regarded Strahd as a messiah sent to them by the Dark Powers. Drawn to Strahd like moths to a flame, they pledged their devotion for a promise of immortality, but Strahd turned them away, deeming the cult and its leaders unworthy of his attention. The cultists withdrew to Death House in despair.

The cult's habit of trapping and devouring wayward visitors proved to be its downfall. On one occasion, the cult snared a band of adventurers whom Strahd had lured to his domain to be his playthings. A black carriage arrived at Death House soon thereafter, and from out of its black heart stepped the vampire himself. The cultists tried to impress Strahd. In response, he slaughtered them for slaying his playthings. Centuries later, the cultists' spirits haunt the dungeons under the house. The building itself, it seems, is unwilling to let the cult be forgotten.

## ROSE AND THORN

The characters are pulled into Strahd's domain by the mists of Ravenloft. Forced to follow a lonely road (area A), they eventually arrive at the village of Barovia (area E). Once they reach the village, read:

> The gravel road leads to a village, its tall houses dark as tombstones. Nestled among these solemn dwellings are a handful of closed-up shops. Even the tavern is shut tight.
>
> A soft whimpering draws your eye toward a pair of children standing in the middle of an otherwise lifeless street.

The children are ten-year-old Rosavalda ("Rose") and her seven-year-old brother, Thornboldt ("Thorn"). Thorn is weeping and clutching a stuffed doll. Rose is trying to hush the boy.

If the characters approach the children or call out to them, add the following:

> After shushing the boy, the girl turns to you and says, "There's a monster in our house!" She then points to a tall brick row house that has seen better days. Its windows are dark. It has a gated portico on the ground floor, and the rusty gate is slightly ajar. The houses on either side are abandoned, their windows and doors boarded up.

Characters who question the children learn the following information:

- The children don't know what the "monster" looks like, but they've heard its terrible howls.
- Their parents (Gustav and Elisabeth Durst) keep the monster trapped in the basement.
- There's a baby (Walter) in the third-floor nursery. (Untrue, but the children believe it.)

Rose and Thorn say that they won't go back in the house until they know the monster is gone. They can be convinced to wait in the portico (area 1A) while the characters search the house. Although they appear to be flesh-and-blood children, Rose and Thorn are actually illusions created by the house to lure the characters inside. The children don't know that they're illusions but vanish if attacked or forced into the house.

The children died of starvation centuries ago after their insane parents locked them in the attic and forgot about them. They were too young and innocent to understand that their parents were guilty of heinous crimes. Their parents told them stories about a monster in the basement to keep the children from going down to the dungeon level. The "terrible howls" they heard were actually the screams of the cult's victims.

THORNBOLDT
"THORN" DURST

ROSAVALDA
"ROSE" DURST

## THE MISTS

Characters who remain outside the house can see the mists close in around them, swallowing up the rest of the village. As more buildings disappear into the mists, the characters are left with little choice but to seek refuge in the house. The mists stop short of entering the house but engulf anyone outside (see chapter 2, "The Lands of Barovia," for information on the mists' effect).

# AREAS OF THE HOUSE

The following areas correspond to labels on the map of the house on page 216.

## 1. ENTRANCE

A wrought-iron gate with hinges on one side and a lock on the other fills the archway of a stone portico (area 1A). The gate is unlocked, and its rusty hinges shriek when the gate is opened. Oil lamps hang from the portico ceiling by chains, flanking a set of oaken doors that open into a grand foyer (area 1B).

Hanging on the south wall of the foyer is a shield emblazoned with a coat-of-arms (a stylized golden

### DEATH HOUSE'S FEATURES

Death House is aware of its surroundings and all creatures within it. Its goal is to continue the work of the cult by luring visitors to their doom. Various important features of the house are summarized here.

The house has four stories (including the attic), with two balconies on the third floor—one facing the front of the house, the other facing the back. The house has wooden floors throughout, and all windows have hinges that allow them to swing outward.

The rooms on the first and second floors are free of dust and signs of age. The floorboards and wall panels are well oiled, the drapes and wallpaper haven't faded, and the furniture looks new. No effort has been made to preserve the contents of the third floor or the attic. These areas are dusty and drafty, everything within them is old and draped in cobwebs, and the floorboards groan underfoot.

Ceilings vary in height by floor. The first floor has 10-foot-high ceilings, the second floor has 12-foot-high ceilings, the third floor has 8-foot-high ceilings, and the attic has 13-foot-high ceilings.

None of the rooms in the house are lit when the characters arrive, although most areas contain working oil lamps or fireplaces.

Characters can burn the house to the ground if they want, but any destruction to the house is temporary. After 1d10 days, the house begins to repair itself. Ashes sweep together to form blackened timbers, which then turn back into a sturdy wooden frame around which walls begin to materialize. Destroyed furnishings are likewise repaired. It takes 2d6 hours for the house to complete its resurrection. Items taken from the house aren't replaced, nor are undead that are destroyed. The dungeon level isn't considered part of the house and can't repair itself in this fashion.

windmill on a red field), flanked by framed portraits of stony-faced aristocrats (long-dead members of the Durst family). Mahogany-framed double doors leading from the foyer to the main hall (area 2A) are set with panes of stained glass.

## 2. MAIN HALL

A wide hall (area 2A) runs the width of the house, with a black marble fireplace at one end and a sweeping, red marble staircase at the other. Mounted on the wall above the fireplace is a longsword (nonmagical) with a windmill cameo worked into the hilt. The wood-paneled walls are ornately sculpted with images of vines, flowers, nymphs, and satyrs. Characters who search the walls for secret doors or otherwise inspect the paneling can, with a successful DC 12 Wisdom (Perception) check, see serpents and skulls inconspicuously woven into the wall designs. The decorative paneling follows the staircase as it circles upward to the second floor.

A cloakroom (area 2B) has several black cloaks hanging from hooks on the walls. A top hat sits on a high shelf.

## 3. DEN OF WOLVES

This oak-paneled room looks like a hunter's den. Mounted above the fireplace is a stag's head, and positioned around the outskirts of the room are three stuffed wolves.

Two padded chairs draped in animal furs face the hearth, with an oak table between them supporting a cask of wine, two carved wooden goblets, a pipe rack, and a candelabrum. A chandelier hangs above a cloth-covered table surrounded by four chairs.

Two cabinets stand against the walls. The east cabinet sports a lock that can be picked with thieves' tools and a successful DC 15 Dexterity check. It holds a heavy crossbow, a light crossbow, a hand crossbow, and 20 bolts for each weapon. The north cabinet is unlocked and holds a small box containing a deck of playing cards and an assortment of wine glasses.

### Trapdoor

A trapdoor is hidden in the southwest corner of the floor. It can't be detected or opened until the characters approach it from the underside (see area 32). Until then, Death House supernaturally hides the trapdoor.

## 4. Kitchen and Pantry

The kitchen (area 4A) is tidy, with dishware, cookware, and utensils neatly placed on shelves. A worktable has a cutting board and rolling pin atop it. A stone, dome-shaped oven stands near the east wall, its bent iron stovepipe connecting to a hole in the ceiling. Behind the stove and to the left is a thin door leading to a well-stocked pantry (area 4B). All the food in the pantry appears fresh but tastes bland.

### Dumbwaiter

Behind a small door in the southwest corner of the kitchen is a dumbwaiter—a 2-foot-wide stone shaft containing a wooden elevator box attached to a simple rope-and-pulley mechanism that must be operated manually. The shaft connects to areas 7A (the servants' quarters) and 12A (the master bedroom). Hanging on the wall next to the dumbwaiter is a tiny brass bell attached by wires to buttons in those other areas.

A Small character can squeeze into the elevator box with a successful DC 10 Dexterity (Acrobatics) check. The dumbwaiter's rope-and-pulley mechanism can support 200 pounds of weight before breaking.

## 5. Dining Room

The centerpiece of this wood-paneled dining room is a carved mahogany table surrounded by eight high-backed chairs with sculpted armrests and cushioned seats. A crystal chandelier hangs above the table, which is covered with resplendent silverware and crystal-ware polished to a dazzling shine. Mounted above the marble fireplace is a mahogany-framed painting of an alpine vale.

The wall paneling is carved with elegant images of deer among the trees. Characters who search the walls for secret doors or otherwise inspect the paneling can, with a successful DC 12 Wisdom (Perception) check, see twisted faces carved into the tree trunks and wolves lurking amid the carved foliage.

Red silk drapes cover the windows, and a tapestry depicting hunting dogs and horse-mounted aristocrats chasing after a wolf hangs from an iron rod bolted to the south wall.

The silverware tarnishes, the crystal cracks, the portrait fades, and the tapestry rots if removed from the house.

## 6. Upper Hall

Unlit oil lamps are mounted on the walls of this elegant hall. Hanging above the mantelpiece is a wood-framed portrait of the Durst family: Gustav and Elisabeth Durst with their two smiling children, Rose and Thorn. Cradled in the father's arms is a swaddled baby, which the mother regards with a hint of scorn.

Standing suits of armor flank wooden doors in the east and west walls. Each suit of armor clutches a spear and has a visored helm shaped like a wolf's head. The doors are carved with dancing youths, although close inspection and a successful DC 12 Wisdom (Perception) check reveals that the youths aren't really dancing but fighting off swarms of bats.

The red marble staircase that started on the first floor continues its upward spiral to area 11. A cold draft can be felt coming down the steps.

## 7. Servants' Room

An undecorated bedroom (area 7A) contains a pair of beds with straw-stuffed mattresses. At the foot of each bed is an empty footlocker. Tidy servants' uniforms hang from hooks in the adjoining closet (area 7B).

### Dumbwaiter

A dumbwaiter in the corner of the west wall has a button on the wall next to it. Pressing the button rings the tiny bell in area 4A.

## 8. Library

The master of the house used to spend many hours here before his descent into madness.

> Red velvet drapes cover the windows of this room. An exquisite mahogany desk and a matching high-back chair face the entrance and the fireplace, above which hangs a framed picture of a windmill perched atop a rocky crag. Situated in corners of the room are two overstuffed chairs. Floor-to-ceiling bookshelves line the south wall. A rolling wooden ladder allows one to more easily reach the high shelves.

The desk has several items resting atop it: an oil lamp, a jar of ink, a quill pen, a tinderbox, and a letter kit containing a red wax candle, four blank sheets of parchment, and a wooden seal bearing the Durst family's insignia (a windmill). The desk drawer is empty except for an iron key, which unlocks the door to area 20.

The bookshelves hold hundreds of tomes covering a range of topics including history, warfare, and alchemy. There are also several shelves containing first-edition collected works of poetry and fiction. The books rot and fall apart if taken from the house.

### SECRET DOOR

A secret door behind one bookshelf can be unlocked and swung open by pulling on a switch disguised to look like a red-covered book with a blank spine. A character inspecting the bookshelf spots the fake book with a successful DC 13 Wisdom (Perception) check. Unless the secret door is propped open, springs in the hinges cause it to close on its own. Beyond the secret door lies area 9.

## 9. SECRET ROOM

This secret room contains bookshelves packed with tomes describing fiend-summoning rituals and the necromantic rituals of a cult called the Priests of Osybus. The rituals are bogus, which any character can ascertain after studying the books for 1 hour and succeeding on a DC 12 Intelligence (Arcana) check.

A heavy wooden chest with clawed iron feet stands against the south wall, its lid half-closed. Sticking out of the chest is a skeleton in leather armor. Close inspection reveals that the skeleton belongs to a human who triggered a poisoned dart trap. Three darts are stuck in the dead adventurer's armor and ribcage. The dart-firing mechanism inside the chest no longer functions.

Clutched in the skeleton's left hand is a letter bearing the seal of Strahd von Zarovich, which the adventurer tried to remove from the chest. Written in flowing script, the letter reads as follows:

*My most pathetic servant,*

*I am not a messiah sent to you by the Dark Powers of this land. I have not come to lead you on a path to immortality. However many souls you have bled on your hidden altar, however many visitors you have tortured in your dungeon, know that you are not the ones who brought me to this beautiful land. You are but worms writhing in my earth.*

*You say that you are cursed, your fortunes spent. You abandoned love for madness, took solace in the bosom of another woman, and sired a stillborn son. Cursed by darkness? Of that I have no doubt. Save you from your wretchedness? I think not. I much prefer you as you are.*

*Your dread lord and master,*
*Strahd von Zarovich*

### TREASURE

The chest contains three blank books with black leather covers (worth 25 gp each), three spell scrolls (*bless, protection from poison,* and *spiritual weapon*), the deed to the house, the deed to a windmill, and a signed will. The windmill referred to in the second deed is situated in the mountains east of Vallaki (see chapter 6, "Old Bonegrinder"). The will is signed by Gustav and Elisabeth Durst and bequeathes the house, the windmill, and all other family property to Rosavalda and Thornboldt Durst in the event of their parents' deaths. The books, scrolls, deeds, and will age markedly if taken from the house but remain intact.

## 10. CONSERVATORY

Gossamer drapes cover the windows of this elegantly appointed hall, which has a brass-plated chandelier hanging from the ceiling. Upholstered chairs line the walls, and stained-glass wall hangings depict beautiful men, women, and children singing and playing instruments.

A harpsichord with a bench rests in the northwest corner. Near the fireplace is a large standing harp. Alabaster figurines of well-dressed dancers adorn the mantelpiece. Close inspection of them reveals that several are carvings of well-dressed skeletons.

## 11. BALCONY

Characters who climb the red marble staircase to its full height come to a dusty balcony with a suit of black plate armor standing against one wall, draped in cobwebs. This suit of **animated armor** attacks as soon as it takes damage or a character approaches within 5 feet of it. It fights until destroyed.

Oil lamps are mounted on the oak-paneled walls, which are carved with woodland scenes of trees, falling leaves, and tiny critters. Characters who search the walls for secret doors or otherwise inspect the paneling can, with a successful DC 12 Wisdom (Perception) check, notice tiny corpses hanging from the trees and worms bursting up from the ground.

### SECRET DOOR

A secret door in the west wall can be found with a successful DC 15 Wisdom (Perception) check. It pushes open easily to reveal a cobweb-filled wooden staircase leading up to the attic.

## 12. MASTER SUITE

The double doors to this room have dusty panes of stained glass set into them. Designs in the glass resemble windmills.

The dusty, cobweb-filled master bedroom (area 12A) has burgundy drapes covering the windows. Furnishings include a four-poster bed with embroidered curtains and tattered gossamer veils, a matching pair of empty wardrobes, a vanity with a wood-framed mirror and jewelry box (see "Treasure"), and a padded chair. A rotting tiger-skin rug lies on the floor in front of the fireplace, which has a dust-covered portrait of Gustav and Elisabeth Durst hanging above it. A web-filled parlor in the southwest corner contains a table and two chairs. Resting on the dusty tablecloth is an empty porcelain bowl and a matching jug.

A door facing the foot of the bed has a full-length mirror mounted on it. The door opens to reveal an empty, dust-choked closet (area 12B). A door in the parlor leads to an outside balcony (area 12C).

### DUMBWAITER

A dumbwaiter in the corner of the west wall has a button on the wall next to it. Pressing the button rings the tiny bell in area 4A.

### TREASURE

The jewelry box on the vanity is made of silver with gold filigree (worth 75 gp). It contains three gold rings (worth 25 gp each) and a thin platinum necklace with a topaz pendant (worth 750 gp).

## 13. Bathroom

This dark room contains a wooden tub with clawed feet, a small iron stove with a kettle resting atop it, and a barrel under a spigot in the east wall. A cistern on the roof used to collect rainwater, which was borne down a pipe to the spigot; however, the plumbing no longer works.

## 14. Storage Room

Dusty shelves line the walls of this room. A few of the shelves have folded sheets, blankets, and old bars of soap on them. A cobweb-covered **broom of animated attack** (see appendix D) leans against the far wall; it attacks any creature approaching within 5 feet of it.

## 15. Nursemaid's Suite

Dust and cobwebs shroud an elegantly appointed bedroom (area 15A) and an adjoining nursery (area 15B). Double doors set with panes of stained glass pull open to reveal a balcony (area 15C) overlooking the front of the house.

The bedroom once belonged to the family's nursemaid. The master of the house and the nursemaid had an affair, which led to the birth of a stillborn baby named Walter. The cult slew the nursemaid shortly thereafter. Unless the characters already defeated it in area 18, the nursemaid's spirit haunts the bedroom as a **specter**. The specter manifests and attacks when a character opens the door to the nursery. The specter resembles a terrified, skeletally thin young woman; it can't speak or be reasoned with.

The bedroom contains a large bed, two end tables, and an empty wardrobe. Mounted on the wall next to the wardrobe is a full-length mirror with an ornate wooden frame carved to look like ivy and berries. Characters who search the wall for secret doors or otherwise inspect the mirror can, with a successful DC 12 Wisdom (Perception) check, notice eyeballs among the berries. The wall behind the mirror has a secret door in it (see "Secret Door" below).

The nursery contains a crib covered with a hanging black shroud. When characters part the shroud, they see a tightly wrapped, baby-sized bundle lying in the crib. Characters who unwrap the blanket find nothing inside it.

### Secret Door

A secret door behind the mirror can be found with a successful DC 15 Wisdom (Perception) check. It pushes open easily to reveal a cobweb-filled wooden staircase leading up to the attic.

## 16. Attic Hall

This bare hall is choked with dust and cobwebs.

### Locked Door

The door to area 20 is held shut with a padlock. Its key is kept in the library (area 8), but the lock can also be picked with thieves' tools and a successful DC 15 Dexterity check.

## 17. Spare Bedroom

This dust-choked room contains a slender bed, a nightstand, a small iron stove, a writing desk with a stool, an empty wardrobe, and a rocking chair. A smiling doll in a lacy yellow dress sits in the northern window box, cobwebs draping it like a wedding veil.

## 18. Storage Room

This dusty chamber is packed with old furniture (chairs, coat racks, standing mirrors, dress mannequins, and the like), all draped in dusty white sheets. Near an iron stove, underneath one of the sheets, is an unlocked wooden trunk containing the skeletal remains of the family's nursemaid, wrapped in a tattered bedsheet stained with dry blood. A character inspecting the remains and succeeding on a DC 14 Wisdom (Medicine) check can verify that the woman was stabbed to death by multiple knife wounds.

If the characters disturb the remains, the nursemaid's **specter** appears and attacks unless it was previously defeated in area 15.

### Secret Door

A secret door in the east wall appears only when certain conditions are met; see area 21 for more information.

## 19. Spare Bedroom

This web-filled room contains a slender bed, a nightstand, a rocking chair, an empty wardrobe, and a small iron stove.

## 20. Children's Room

The door to this room is locked from the outside (see area 16 for details).

> This room contains a bricked-up window flanked by two dusty, wood-framed beds sized for children. Closer to the door is a toy chest with windmills painted on its sides and a dollhouse that's a perfect replica of the dreary edifice in which you stand. These furnishings are draped in cobwebs. Lying in the middle of the floor are two small skeletons wearing tattered but familiar clothing. The smaller of the two cradles a stuffed doll that you also recognize.

The Durst children, Rose and Thorn, were neglected by their parents and locked in this room until they starved to death. Their small skeletons lie in the middle of the floor, plain as day, wearing tattered clothing that the characters recognize as belonging to the children. Thorn's skeleton cradles the boy's stuffed doll.

The toy chest contains an assortment of stuffed animals and toys. Characters who search the dollhouse and succeed on a DC 15 Wisdom (Perception) check find all of the house's secret doors, including one in the attic that leads to a spiral staircase (a miniature replica of area 21).

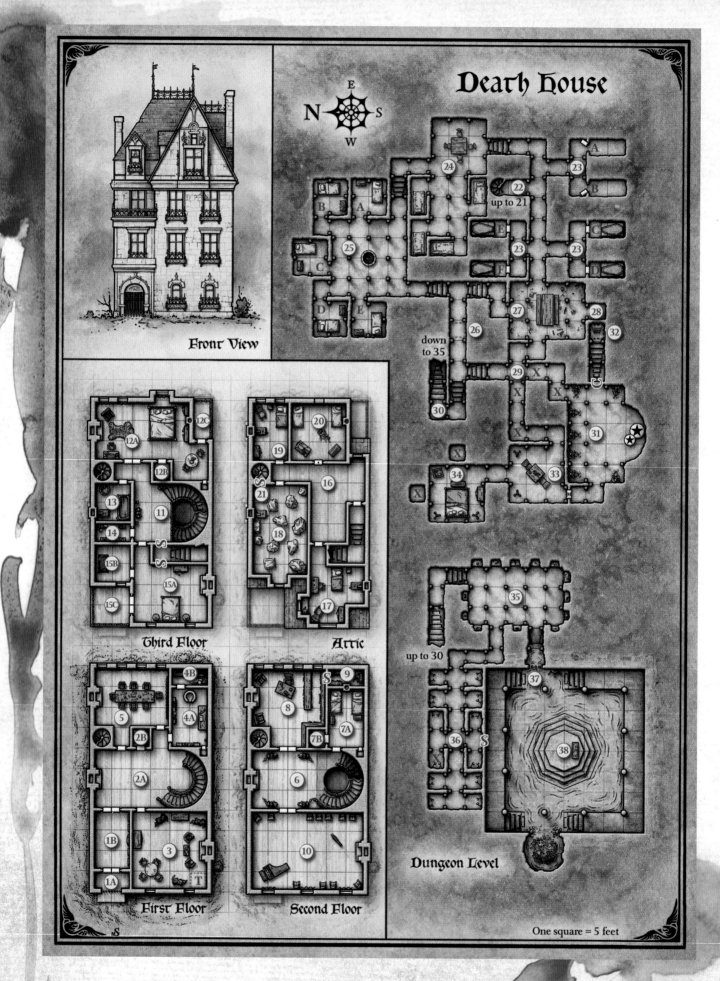

# Death House

**Front View**

N E S W

One square = 5 feet

**Third Floor**

**Attic**

**First Floor**

**Second Floor**

**Dungeon Level**

up to 21

down to 35

up to 30

## ROSE AND THORN

If either the dollhouse or the chest is disturbed, the ghosts of Rose and Thorn appear in the middle of the room. Use the **ghost** statistics in the *Monster Manual*, with the following modifications:

- The ghosts are Small and lawful good.
- They have 35 (10d6) hit points each.
- They lack the Horrifying Visage action.
- They speak Common and have a challenge rating of 3 (700 XP).

The children don't like it when the characters disturb their toys, but they fight only in self-defense. Unlike the illusions outside the house, these children know that they're dead. If asked how they died, Rose and Thorn explain that their parents locked them in the attic to protect them from "the monster in the basement," and that they died from hunger. If asked how one gets to the basement, Rose points to the dollhouse and says, "There's a secret door in the attic." Characters who then search the dollhouse for secret doors gain advantage on their Wisdom (Perception) checks to find them.

The children fear abandonment. If one or more characters try to leave, the ghost-children attempt to possess them. If one of the ghosts possesses a character, allow the player to retain control of the character, but assign the character one of the following flaws:

- A character possessed by Rose gains the following flaw: "I like being in charge and get angry when other people tell me what to do."
- A character possessed by Thorn gains the following flaw: "I'm scared of everything, including my own shadow, and weep with despair when things don't go my way."

A character possessed by the ghost of Rose or Thorn won't willingly leave Death House or the dungeon below it. Both ghosts can be intimidated into leaving their hosts with a successful DC 11 Charisma (Intimidation) check made as an action.

A ghost reduced to 0 hit points can reform at dawn the next day. The only way to put the children's spirits to rest is to put their skeletal remains in their tombs (areas 23E and 23F). The children don't know this, however.

### DEVELOPMENT

If the party lays the children's spirits to rest, each character gains inspiration (see "Inspiration" in chapter 4, "Personality and Background," of the *Player's Handbook*).

## 21. SECRET STAIRS

A narrow spiral staircase made of creaky wood is contained within a 5-foot-wide shaft of mortared stone that starts in the attic and descends 50 feet to the dungeon level, passing through the lower levels of the house as it makes its descent. Thick cobwebs fill the shaft and reduce visibility in the staircase to 5 feet.

The secret door and shaft don't exist until the house reveals them, which can happen in one of two ways:

- The characters find Strahd's letter in the secret room behind the library (area 9).

---

### DUNGEON FEATURES

The dungeon level underneath Death House is carved out of earth, clay, and rock. The tunnels are 4 feet wide by 7 feet high with timber braces at 5-foot intervals. Rooms are 8 feet tall and supported by thick wooden posts with crossbeams. The only exception is area 38, which has a 16-foot-high ceiling supported by stone pillars. Characters without darkvision must provide their own light sources, as the dungeon is unlit.

As the characters explore the dungeon, they see centuries-old human footprints in the earthen floor leading every which way.

- The characters find the replica secret door in the attic of the dollhouse (area 20).

Once the house wills the secret door into existence, characters find it automatically if they search the wall (no ability check required). Characters who descend the spiral staircase end up in area 22.

## 22. DUNGEON LEVEL ACCESS

The wooden spiral staircase from the attic ends here. A narrow tunnel stretches southward before branching east and west.

### GHOSTLY CHANTING

From the moment they arrive in the dungeon, the characters can hear an eerie, incessant chant echoing throughout. It's impossible to gauge where the sound is coming from until the characters reach area 26 or 29. They can't discern its words until they reach area 35.

## 23. FAMILY CRYPTS

Several crypts have been hewn from the earth. Each crypt is sealed with a stone slab unless noted otherwise. Removing a slab from its fitting requires a successful DC 15 Strength (Athletics) check; using a crowbar or the like grants advantage on the check.

### 23A. EMPTY CRYPT

The blank stone slab meant to seal this crypt leans against a nearby wall. The crypt is empty.

### 23B. WALTER'S CRYPT

The stone slab meant to seal this crypt leans against a nearby wall. Etched into it is the name Walter Durst. The crypt is empty.

### 23C. GUSTAV'S CRYPT

The stone slab is etched with the name Gustav Durst. The chamber beyond contains an empty coffin atop a stone bier.

### 23D. ELISABETH'S CRYPT

The stone slab is etched with the name Elisabeth Durst. The crypt contains a stone bier with an empty coffin atop it. A **swarm of insects** (centipedes) boils out of the back wall and attacks if the coffin is disturbed.

### 23E. ROSE'S CRYPT

The stone slab is etched with the name Rosavalda Durst. The chamber beyond contains an empty coffin on a stone bier.

If Rose's skeletal remains (see area 20) are placed in the coffin, the child's ghost finds peace and disappears forever. A character possessed by Rose's ghost when this occurs is no longer possessed (see also the "Development" section in area 20).

### 23F. THORN'S CRYPT

The stone slab is etched with the name Thornboldt Durst. The chamber beyond contains an empty coffin on a stone bier.

If Thorn's skeletal remains (see area 20) are placed in the coffin, the child's ghost finds peace and disappears forever. A character possessed by Thorn's ghost when this occurs is no longer possessed (see also the "Development" section in area 20).

## 24. CULT INITIATES' QUARTERS

A wooden table and four chairs stand at the east end of this room. To the west are four alcoves containing moldy straw pallets.

## 25. WELL AND CULTIST QUARTERS

A 4-foot-diameter well shaft with a 3-foot-high stone lip descends 30 feet to a water-filled cistern. A wooden bucket hangs from a rope-and-pulley mechanism bolted to the crossbeams above the well.

Five side rooms once served as quarters for senior cultists. Each contains a wood-framed bed with a moldy straw mattress and a wooden chest to hold personal belongings. Each chest is secured with a rusty iron padlock that can be picked with thieves' tools and a successful DC 15 Dexterity check.

### TREASURE

In addition to some worthless personal effects, each chest contains one or more valuable items.

**25A.** This room's chest contains 11 gp and 60 sp in a pouch made of human skin.

**25B.** This room's chest contains three moss agates (worth 10 gp each) in a folded piece of black cloth.

**25C.** This room's chest contains a black leather eyepatch with a carnelian (worth 50 gp) sewn into it.

**25D.** This room's chest contains an ivory hairbrush with silver bristles (worth 25 gp).

**25E.** This room's chest contains a silvered shortsword (worth 110 gp).

## 26. HIDDEN SPIKED PIT

The ghostly chanting heard throughout the dungeon gets discernibly louder as one heads west along this tunnel. A successful DC 15 Wisdom (Perception) check reveals an absence of footprints. Characters searching the floor for traps find a 5-foot-long, 10-foot-deep pit hidden under several rotted wooden planks, all hidden under a thin layer of dirt. The first character to step on the cover falls through, landing prone and taking 3 (1d6) bludgeoning damage from the fall plus 11 (2d10) piercing damage from the spikes.

## 27. DINING HALL

This room contains a plain wooden table flanked by long benches. Moldy humanoid bones lie strewn on the dirt floor—the remains of the cult's vile banquets.

In the middle of the south wall is a darkened alcove (area 28). Characters who approach within 5 feet of the alcove provoke the creature that lurks there.

## 28. LARDER

This alcove contains a **grick** that slithers out to attack the first character it sees within 5 feet of it. Any character with a passive Wisdom (Perception) score under 12 is surprised by it. The alcove is otherwise empty.

## 29. GHOULISH ENCOUNTER

The ghostly chanting heard throughout the dungeon is noticeably louder to the north. When one or more characters reach the midpoint of the four-way tunnel intersection, four **ghouls** (former cultists) rise up out of the ground in the spaces marked X on the map and attack. The ghouls fight until destroyed.

## 30. STAIRS DOWN

It's obvious to any character standing at the top of this 20-foot-long staircase that the ghostly chants originate from somewhere below. Characters who descend the stairs and follow the hall beyond arrive in area 35.

## 31. DARKLORD'S SHRINE

> This room is festooned with moldy skeletons that hang from rusty shackles against the walls. A wide alcove in the south wall contains a painted wooden statue carved in the likeness of a gaunt, pale-faced man wearing a voluminous black cloak, his pale left hand resting on the head of a wolf that stands next to him. In his right hand, he holds a smoky-gray crystal orb.
>
> The room has exits in the west and north walls. Chanting can be heard coming from the west.

The statue depicts Strahd, to whom the cultists made sacrifices in the vain hope that he might reveal his darkest secrets to them. If the characters touch the statue or take the crystal orb from Strahd's hand, five **shadows** form around the statue and attack them. The shadows (the spirits of former cultists) pursue those who flee beyond the room's confines.

The skeletons on the wall are harmless decor.

### CONCEALED DOOR

Characters searching the room for secret doors find a concealed door in the middle of the east wall with a successful DC 10 Wisdom (Perception) check. It's basically an ordinary (albeit rotted) wooden door hidden under a layer of clay. The door pulls open to reveal a stone staircase that climbs 10 feet to a landing (area 32).

## TREASURE

The crystal orb is worth 25 gp. It can be used as an arcane focus but is not magical.

## 32. HIDDEN TRAPDOOR

The staircase ends at a landing with a 6-foot-high ceiling of close-fitting planks with a wooden trapdoor set into it. The trapdoor is bolted shut from this side and can be pushed open to reveal the den (area 3) above.

### DEVELOPMENT

Once the trapdoor has been found and opened, it remains available to characters as a way into and out of the dungeon level.

## 33. CULT LEADERS' DEN

The door in the southwest corner is a **mimic** in disguise. Any creature that touches the door becomes adhered to the creature, whereupon the mimic attacks. The mimic also attacks if it takes any damage.

A chandelier is suspended above a table in the middle of the room. Two high-backed chairs flank the table, which has an empty clay jug and two clay flagons atop it. Iron candlesticks stand in two corners, their candles long since melted away.

## 34. CULT LEADERS' QUARTERS

This room contains a large wood-framed bed with a rotted feather mattress, a wardrobe containing several old robes, a pair of iron candlesticks, and an open crate containing thirty torches and a leather sack with fifteen candles inside it. At the foot of the bed is an unlocked wooden footlocker containing some gear and magic items (see "Treasure" below).

Two **ghasts** (Gustav and Elisabeth Durst) are hidden in cavities behind the earthen walls, marked X on the map; they burst forth and attack if someone removes one or more items from the footlocker. The ghasts wear tattered black robes.

### TREASURE

Characters searching the footlocker find a folded *cloak of protection*, a small wooden coffer (unlocked) containing four *potions of healing*, a chain shirt, a mess kit, a flask of alchemist's fire, a bullseye lantern, a set of thieves' tools, and a spellbook with a yellow leather cover containing the following wizard spells:

1st level: *disguise self, identify, mage armor, magic missile, protection from evil and good*
2nd level: *darkvision, hold person, invisibility, magic weapon*

These items were taken from adventurers who were drawn into Barovia, captured, and killed by the cult.

## 35. RELIQUARY

The ghostly chant emanating from area 38 fills this room. Characters can discern a dozen or so voices saying, over and over, "He is the Ancient. He is the Land."

The cult amassed several "relics" that it used in its rituals. These worthless items are stored in thirteen niches along the walls:

- A small, mummified, yellow hand with sharp claws (a goblin's hand) on a loop of rope
- A knife carved from a human bone
- A dagger with a rat's skull set into the pommel
- An 8-inch-diameter varnished orb made from a nothic's eye
- An aspergillum carved from bone
- A folded cloak made from stitched ghoul skin
- A desiccated frog lashed to a stick (could be mistaken for a *wand of polymorph*)
- A bag full of bat guano
- A hag's severed finger
- A 6-inch-tall wooden figurine of a mummy, its arms crossed over its chest
- An iron pendant adorned with a devil's face
- The shrunken, shriveled head of a halfling
- A small wooden coffer containing a dire wolf's withered tongue

The southernmost tunnel slopes down at a 20-degree angle into murky water and ends at a rusty portcullis (area 37).

## 36. PRISON

The cultists shackled prisoners to the back walls of alcoves here. The prisoners are long gone (their bones litter the floor in area 27), but the rusty shackles remain.

### SECRET DOOR

A secret door in the south wall can be found with a successful DC 15 Wisdom (Perception) check and pulls open to reveal area 38 beyond.

### TREASURE

Hanging on the back wall of the cell marked X on the map is a human skeleton clad in a tattered black robe. The skeleton belongs to a cult member who questioned the cult's blind devotion to Strahd. Characters who search the skeleton find a gold ring (worth 25 gp) on one of its bony fingers.

## 37. PORTCULLIS

This tunnel is blocked by a rusty iron portcullis that can be forcibly lifted with a successful DC 20 Strength (Athletics) check. Otherwise, the portcullis can be raised or lowered by turning a wooden wheel half-embedded in the east wall of area 38. (The wheel is beyond the reach of someone east of the portcullis.) The floor around the portcullis is submerged under 2 feet of murky water.

## 38. RITUAL CHAMBER

The cult used to perform rituals in this sunken room. The chanting heard throughout the dungeon originates here, yet when the characters arrive, the dungeon falls silent as the chanting mysteriously stops.

> The chanting stops as you peer into this forty-foot-square room. The smooth masonry walls provide excellent acoustics. Featureless stone pillars support the ceiling, and a breach in the west wall leads to a dark cave heaped with refuse. Murky water covers most of the floor. Stairs lead up to dry stone ledges that hug the walls. In the middle of the room, more stairs rise to form an octagonal dais that also rises above the water. Rusty chains with shackles dangle from the ceiling directly above a stone altar mounted on the dais. The altar is carved with hideous depictions of grasping ghouls and is stained with dry blood.

The water is 2 feet deep. The ledges and central dais are 5 feet high (3 feet higher than the water's surface), and the chamber's ceiling is 16 feet high (11 feet above the dais and ledges). The chains dangling from the ceiling are 8 feet long; the cultists would shackle prisoners to the chains, dangle them above the altar, cut them open with knives, and allow the altar to be bathed in blood.

Half embedded in the east wall is a wooden wheel connected to hidden chains and mechanisms. A character can use an action to turn the wheel, raising or lowering the nearby portcullis (see area 37).

The hole in the west wall leads to a naturally formed alcove. The half-submerged pile of refuse that fills it is a **shambling mound**, which the cultists dubbed Lorghoth the Decayer. It is asleep but awakens if attacked or if the characters summon the cultists but refuse to complete their ritual (see "One Must Die!" below). A character standing next to the mound can discern its true nature with a successful DC 15 Intelligence (Nature) check.

### "One Must Die!"

If any character climbs to the top of the dais, read:

> The chanting rises once more as thirteen dark apparitions appear on the ledges overlooking the room. Each one resembles a black-robed figure holding a torch, but the torch's fire is black and seems to draw light into it. Where you'd expect to see faces are voids.
>
> "One must die!" they chant, over and over. "One must die! One must die!"

The apparitions are harmless figments that can't be damaged, turned, or dispelled.

Characters on the dais when the cultists appear must sacrifice a creature on the altar or face the cult's wrath; characters can ascertain what must be done with a successful DC 11 Intelligence (Religion) or Wisdom (Insight) check. To count as a sacrifice, a creature must die on the altar. The apparitions don't care what kind of creature is sacrificed, and they aren't fooled by illusions.

If the characters make the sacrifice, the cultists fade away, but their tireless chant of "He is the Ancient. He is the Land," echoes again in the dungeon. Strahd is aware of the sacrifice, and Death House now does nothing to hinder the characters (see "Endings" below).

If the characters leave the dais without making the sacrifice, the cultists' chant changes: "Lorghoth the Decayer, we awaken thee!" This chant rouses the shambling mound and prompts it to attack. It pursues prey beyond the room but won't leave the dungeon. It can move through tunnels without squeezing and completely fills its space. At the start of the shambling mound's first turn, the chant changes again: "The end comes! Death, be praised!" If the shambling mound dies, the chanting stops and the apparitions vanish forever.

## ENDINGS

The mists of Ravenloft continue to surround Death House until the characters stand atop the dais and either appease or defy the cultists. Strahd is satisfied either way, prompting the mists to recede.

### THE CULT IS APPEASED

Death House harbors no ill will toward a party willing to sacrifice a life to appease the cult. Once the sacrifice is made, the characters are free to go. Upon emerging from the house, the characters advance to 3rd level.

### THE CULT IS DENIED

If the characters deny the cult its sacrifice and either destroy the shambling mound or escape from it, Death House attacks them as they try to leave. When they return upstairs, they must roll initiative as they discover several architectural changes:

- All the windows are bricked up; the bricked-up windows and the outer walls are impervious to the party's weapon attacks and damage-dealing spells.
- All the doors are gone, replaced by slashing scythe-blades. A character must succeed on a DC 15 Dexterity (Acrobatics) check to pass through a blade-trapped doorway unscathed. A character who spends 1 minute studying the blades in a particular doorway can try to take advantage of a momentary gap in their repeating movements and make a DC 15 Intelligence check instead. Failing either check, a character takes 2d10 slashing damage but manages to pass through the doorway. Any creature pushed through a doorway must succeed on a DC 15 Dexterity saving throw or take the damage. The blades can't be disarmed.
- Every room that contains a fireplace, an oven, or a stove is filled with poisonous black smoke. The room is heavily obscured, and any creature that starts its turn in the smoke must succeed on a DC 10 Constitution saving throw or take 1d10 poison damage.
- The interior walls become rotted and brittle. Each 5-foot-section has AC 5 and 5 hit points, and can also be destroyed with a successful DC 10 Strength (Athletics) check. Each 5-foot section of wall that's destroyed causes a **swarm of rats** to pour out and attack. The swarm won't leave the house.

Keep track of initiative as the characters make their way through the house. Once they escape, they advance to 3rd level, and the house does no more to harm them.

# Appendix C: Treasures

Scattered throughout Barovia are ancient treasures that can be brought to bear against Strahd von Zarovich and his fell servants. The locations of three of them—the *Tome of Strahd*, the *Holy Symbol of Ravenkind*, and the *Sunsword*—are determined by the results of the card reading in chapter 1. The other items can be acquired as characters discover their whereabouts during the course of the adventure.

## Tome of Strahd

The *Tome of Strahd* is an ancient work penned by Strahd, a tragic tale of how he came to his fallen state. The book is bound in a thick leather cover with steel hinges and fastenings. The pages are of parchment and very brittle. Most of the book is written in the curious shorthand that only Strahd employs. Stains and age have made most of the work illegible, but several paragraphs remain intact and readable. If the characters acquire the *Tome of Strahd* and want to read these paragraphs, show the players the "From the Tome of Strahd" section in appendix F.

If Strahd sees, or learns from a minion, that the tome has fallen into the party's possession, all of his other objectives (see chapter 1, "Into the Mists") are put on hold until the book is recovered. When Strahd attacks, his preferred target is whoever has the tome.

BLOOD SPEAR

GULTHIAS STAFF

TOME OF STRAHD

## Magic Items

The magic items described here, if they are found, can play significant roles in the adventure.

### Blood Spear

*Weapon (spear), uncommon (requires attunement)*

Kavan was a ruthless chieftain whose tribe lived in the Balinok Mountains centuries before the arrival of Strahd von Zarovich. Although he was very much alive, Kavan had some traits in common with vampires: he slept during the day and hunted at night, he drank the blood of his prey, and he lived underground. In battle, he wielded a spear stained with blood. His was the first *blood spear*, a weapon that drains life from those it kills and transfers that life to its wielder, imbuing that individual with the stamina to keep fighting.

When you hit with a melee attack using this magic spear and reduce the target to 0 hit points, you gain 2d6 temporary hit points.

### Gulthias Staff

*Staff, rare (requires attunement)*

Made from the branch of a Gulthias tree (see the blights entry in the *Monster Manual*), a *Gulthias staff* is a spongy, black length of wood. Its evil makes beasts visibly uncomfortable while within 30 feet of it. The staff has 10 charges and regains 1d6 + 4 of its expended charges daily at dusk.

If the staff is broken or burned to ashes, its wood releases a terrible, inhuman scream that can be heard out to a range of 300 feet. All blights that can hear the scream immediately wither and die.

***Vampiric Strike.*** The staff can be wielded as a magic quarterstaff. On a hit, it deals damage as a normal quarterstaff, and you can expend 1 charge to regain a number of hit points equal to the damage dealt by the weapon. Each time a charge is spent, red blood oozes from the staff's pores, and you must succeed on a DC 12 Wisdom saving throw or be afflicted with short-term madness (see "Madness" in chapter 8 of the *Dungeon Master's Guide*).

***Blight Bane.*** While you are attuned to the staff, blights and other evil plant creatures don't regard you as hostile unless you harm them.

HOLY SYMBOL
OF RAVENKIND

## ICON OF RAVENLOFT
*Wondrous item, legendary (requires attunement by a creature of good alignment)*

The *Icon of Ravenloft* is a 12-inch-tall statuette made of the purest silver, weighing 10 pounds. It depicts a cleric kneeling in supplication.

The icon was given to Strahd by the archpriest Ciril Romulich, an old family friend, to consecrate the castle and its chapel.

While within 30 feet of the icon, a creature is under the effect of a *protection from evil and good* spell against fiends and undead. Only a creature attuned to the icon can use its other properties.

***Augury.*** You can use an action to cast an *augury* spell from the icon, with no material components required. Once used, this property can't be used again until the next dawn.

***Bane of the Undead.*** You can use the icon as a holy symbol while using the Turn Undead or Turn the Unholy feature. If you do so, increase the save DC by 2.

***Cure Wounds.*** While holding the icon, you can take an action to heal one creature that you can see within 30 feet of you. The target regains 3d8 + 3 hit points, unless it is an undead, a construct, or a fiend. Once used, this property can't be used again until the next dawn.

ICON OF RAVENLOFT

## HOLY SYMBOL OF RAVENKIND
*Wondrous item, legendary (requires attunement by a cleric or paladin of good alignment)*

The *Holy Symbol of Ravenkind* is a unique holy symbol sacred to the good-hearted faithful of Barovia. It predates the establishment of any church in Barovia. According to legend, it was delivered to a paladin named Lugdana by a giant raven—or an angel in the form of a giant raven. Lugdana used the holy symbol to root out and destroy nests of vampires until her death. The high priests of Ravenloft kept and wore the holy symbol after Lugdana's passing.

The holy symbol is a platinum amulet shaped like the sun, with a large crystal embedded in its center.

The holy symbol has 10 charges for the following properties. It regains 1d6 + 4 charges daily at dawn.

***Hold Vampires.*** As an action, you can expend 1 charge and present the holy symbol to make it flare with holy power. Vampires and vampire spawn within 30 feet of the holy symbol when it flares must make a DC 15 Wisdom saving throw. On a failed save, a target is paralyzed for 1 minute. It can repeat the saving throw at the end of each of its turns to end the effect on itself.

***Turn Undead.*** If you have the Turn Undead or the Turn the Unholy feature, you can expend 3 charges when you present the holy symbol while using that feature. When you do so, undead have disadvantage on their saving throws against the effect.

***Sunlight.*** As an action, you can expend 5 charges while presenting the holy symbol to make it shed bright light in a 30-foot radius and dim light for an additional 30 feet. The light is sunlight and lasts for 10 minutes or until you end the effect (no action required).

## SAINT MARKOVIA'S THIGHBONE
*Weapon (mace), rare (requires attunement)*

*Saint Markovia's thighbone* has the properties of a *mace of disruption*. If it scores one or more hits against a vampire or a vampire spawn in the course of a single battle, the thighbone crumbles into dust once the battle concludes.

As a youth, Markovia followed her heart and became a priest of the Morninglord soon after her eighteenth birthday. She proved to be a charismatic proselytizer and, before the age of thirty, had gained a reputation for allowing no evil to stand before her.

Markovia had long considered Strahd a mad tyrant, but only after his transformation into a vampire did she dare to challenge him. As she rallied her followers and prepared to march on Castle Ravenloft, Strahd sent a group of vampire spawn to her abbey. They confronted Markovia and were destroyed to a one.

Suffused with confidence born of righteous victory, Markovia advanced on Castle Ravenloft. A great battle raged from the catacombs to the parapets. In the end, Markovia never returned to Barovia, and Strahd long afterward walked with a limp and a grimace of pain. It is said that he trapped Markovia in a crypt beneath his castle, and her remains linger there yet.

The essence of Markovia's saintliness passed partly into her bones as the rest of her body decomposed. Her remaining thighbone is imbued with power that inflicts grievous injury on the undead.

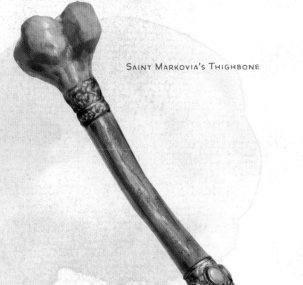

SAINT MARKOVIA'S THIGHBONE

## SUNSWORD
*Weapon (longsword), legendary (requires attunement)*

The *Sunsword* is a unique blade once possessed by Strahd's brother, Sergei von Zarovich. In its original form, it had a platinum hilt and guard, and a thin crystal blade as strong as steel.

Strahd employed a powerful wizard named Khazan to destroy the weapon after Sergei's death. The first part of the process required the hilt and the blade to be separated, which Khazan accomplished. While Khazan was busying himself destroying the blade, his apprentice stole the hilt and fled. Khazan later located his apprentice's mutilated corpse in the Svalich Woods, but the hilt was nowhere to be found. To avoid the vampire's wrath, Khazan told Strahd that the entire weapon had been destroyed.

The hilt, which is sentient, knows that it can never be reunited with its original crystal blade. It has, however, gained the properties of a *sun blade*.

**Sentience.** The *Sunsword* is a sentient chaotic good weapon with an Intelligence of 11, a Wisdom of 17, and a Charisma of 16. It has hearing and normal vision out to a range of 60 feet. The weapon communicates by transmitting emotions to the creature carrying or wielding it.

**Personality.** The *Sunsword*'s special purpose is to destroy Strahd, not so much because it wants to free the land of Barovia from evil but because it wants revenge for the loss of its crystal blade. The weapon secretly fears its own destruction.

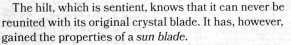

SUNSWORD

# Appendix D: Monsters and NPCs

Barovia is a land of vampires, ghosts, and werewolves. In addition, adventurers who explore this unholy realm encounter other things that go bump in the night, including creatures born out of Strahd's evil. The new monsters that appear in this adventure are described below, along with several of the vampire's allies and enemies—souls whose fates are entwined with those of the adventurers. Strahd himself appears here as well.

The monsters and NPCs are presented in alphabetical order.

## New Creatures by Challenge Rating

| Creature | CR | Creature | CR |
|---|---|---|---|
| Baba Lysaga | 11 | Pidlwick II | 1/4 |
| Baba Lysaga's creeping hut | 11 | Rahadin | 10 |
| | | Rictavio | 5 |
| Broom of animated atk. | 1/4 | Strahd's animated armor | 6 |
| Barovian witch | 1/2 | |  |
| Ezmerelda d'Avenir | 8 | Strahd von Zarovich | 15 |
| Guardian portrait | 1 | Strahd zombie | 1 |
| Izek Strazni | 5 | Tree blight | 7 |
| Madam Eva | 10 | Vladimir Horngaard | 7 |
| Mongrelfolk | 1/4 | Wereraven | 2 |
| Phantom warrior | 3 | | |

## The Abbot

No creature in Barovia is older than the master of the Abbey of Saint Markovia in Krezk. This nameless holy figure, whom others call the Abbot, was drawn to the abbey after Saint Markovia died by Strahd's hand. He sought to restore the abbey after it fell to corruption, but was himself corrupted.

***Angel in Disguise.*** The Abbot is a deva that has lived for millennia. He typically assumes the form of a strikingly handsome human priest in his late twenties or early thirties. More than a hundred years ago, the deva was sent from the Upper Planes to honor the legacy of Saint Markovia. He reopened the abbey and began tending to the physically and mentally ill. In so doing, he hoped to bring some much-needed light to Barovia. His efforts worked for a while, but then the Dark Powers began to corrupt him.

***Imperfections.*** The Abbot's fall from grace started when the Belviews—a family of sickly, inbred lepers—came to the abbey seeking salvation. The deva rid them of their diseases, an act for which they were eternally grateful, but could not cure them of certain human defects that had been present since birth. The Abbot became consumed with a prideful, obsessive desire to rid the poor Belviews of their lingering imperfections. The Belview family, however, had strange ideas of what it meant to be perfect. They didn't want to be ordinary humans. They wanted the eyes of a cat, wings to fly like a bat, the strength of a mule, and the guile of a snake. In short, they craved bestial traits, and the Abbot, taking pity on them, yielded to their mad desires.

***Enter Vasili von Holtz.*** The Abbot's early experiments proved fatal to their subjects, but the Belviews insisted that he keep trying. One day, a Barovian lord named Vasili von Holtz visited the abbey. The Abbot knew at once that the man was evil, but von Holtz stressed that he only wanted to help. He furnished the Abbot with forbidden lore plucked from the Amber Temple (chapter 13), then helped the Abbot transform the Belviews into mongrelfolk—maniacal humans with bestial deformities and traits. The Belviews were happy, albeit insane. Only then did von Holtz reveal himself to be Strahd von Zarovich. Somehow the deva realized that any attempt to slay Strahd would be futile—that the ancient curse upon the land meant that the vampire could never truly die, at least not in Barovia.

***Bride of Strahd.*** Strahd confided in the Abbot, lamenting his curse and telling the deva that he wished nothing more than to escape Barovia. His performance garnered the deva's sympathy, and the Abbot, playing into Strahd's hands, set for himself the goal of finding a cure for Strahd's "malady." The Abbot is now convinced that the cure lies in reuniting Strahd with his lost love and, in so doing, ending Barovia's curse. The Abbot has recently completed work on a flesh golem bride made from the body parts of dead women. While the Belviews languish in the abbey's madhouse, the Abbot is giving his creation lessons in etiquette and ladylike conduct so that "she" can be formally presented to Strahd and win his love.

Strahd has no interest in a flesh golem bride, but he enjoys corrupting this once angelic being and driving the Abbot to commit further acts of depravity.

***Statistics.*** Use the **deva** stat block in the *Monster Manual*, but change the Abbot's alignment to lawful evil.

## The Abbot's Traits

***Ideal.*** "I want to rid Barovia of its sickness. By giving the devil his heart's desire, I bring salvation to him and his land."

***Bond.*** "I love the creatures I create, including my beautiful golems and mongrelfolk."

***Flaw.*** "I can't be corrupted. My heart is pure, my intentions noble and good."

## Animated Objects

Animated objects are crafted with potent magic to follow the commands of their creators. When not commanded, they follow the last order they received to the best of their ability, and can act independently to fulfill simple instructions. Some animated objects might converse fluently or adopt a persona, but most are simple automatons.

***Constructed Nature.*** An animated object doesn't require air, food, drink, or sleep.

The magic that animates an object is dispelled when the construct drops to 0 hit points. An animated object reduced to 0 hit points becomes inanimate and is too damaged to be of much use or value to anyone.

# Baba Lysaga's Creeping Hut

Baba Lysaga built a hut atop the rotting stump of a giant tree that was felled long ago. It was only after she embedded a magic gemstone in the hut that the whole thing was imbued with a semblance of life. When she wills it to do so, the hut pulls its gigantic roots free of the earth and shambles around like a spidery behemoth, shaking the ground with every step. The hut attacks with its flailing and stomping roots. It can also use its roots to fling large rocks.

***Hut Interior.*** The hut is a 15-foot-square, ramshackle wooden building with a gently sloping thatch roof. Its furnishings have been bolted to the floor, since the hut lurches from side to side when it walks.

***Heart of the Hut.*** The gemstone that has given life to Baba Lysaga's hut was previously buried in the Wizard of Wines vineyard. The gem was one of three imbued with life-giving magic that made the grapevines in the vineyard healthier, guaranteeing the finest wines. Baba Lysaga stole one of the gems and perverted its magic, using it instead to animate her wooden hut.

Removing the gem from the hut renders the hut incapacitated. That task is easier said than done, however. The glowing green gem is contained in a cavity in the stump, beneath the rotted floorboards of the hut. The floorboards can be ripped up with a successful DC 14 Strength check or smashed by dealing 10 damage to them. Once the floorboards are out of the way, a creature can reach into the cavity and snatch the gem. But if someone attempts this while the hut is alive, the cavity sprouts wooden teeth, becoming a mouth that bites anything that tries to remove the gem; a creature trying to remove the gem must make a DC 20 Dexterity saving throw. On a successful save, the creature claims the stone without getting bitten. On a failed save, the creature is bitten for 10 (3d6) piercing damage and fails to obtain the gem.

# Broom of Animated Attack

A broom of animated attack is easily mistaken for a *broom of flying*. It attacks any creature that grabs it or tries to ride it.

***Flying Broom.*** Some brooms of animated attack allow their creators to ride them, in which case they behave like typical *brooms of flying*. A broom of animated attack, however, can carry only half the weight that a *broom of flying* can (see chapter 7, "Treasure," of the *Dungeon Master's Guide*).

## Baba Lysaga's Creeping Hut
*Gargantuan construct, unaligned*

**Armor Class** 16 (natural armor)
**Hit Points** 263 (17d20 + 85)
**Speed** 30 ft.

| STR | DEX | CON | INT | WIS | CHA |
|-----|-----|-----|-----|-----|-----|
| 26 (+8) | 7 (–2) | 20 (+5) | 1 (–5) | 3 (–4) | 3 (–4) |

**Saving Throws** Con +9, Wis +0, Cha +0
**Damage Immunities** poison, psychic
**Condition Immunities** blinded, charmed, deafened, exhaustion, frightened, paralyzed, petrified, prone
**Senses** blindsight 120 ft. (blind beyond this radius), passive Perception 6
**Languages** —
**Challenge** 11 (7,200 XP)

***Antimagic Susceptibility.*** The hut is incapacitated while the magic gem that animates it is in the area of an *antimagic field*. If targeted by *dispel magic*, the hut must succeed on a Constitution saving throw against the caster's spell save DC or fall unconscious for 1 minute.

***Siege Monster.*** The hut deals double damage to objects and structures.

### Actions

***Multiattack.*** The hut makes three attacks with its roots. It can replace one of these attacks with a rock attack.

***Root.*** *Melee Weapon Attack:* +12 to hit, reach 60 ft., one target. *Hit:* 30 (4d10 + 8) bludgeoning damage.

***Rock.*** *Ranged Weapon Attack:* +12 to hit, range 120 ft., one target. *Hit:* 21 (3d8 + 8) bludgeoning damage.

## Broom of Animated Attack
*Small construct, unaligned*

**Armor Class** 15 (natural armor)
**Hit Points** 17 (5d6)
**Speed** 0 ft., fly 50 ft. (hover)

| STR | DEX | CON | INT | WIS | CHA |
|-----|-----|-----|-----|-----|-----|
| 10 (+0) | 17 (+3) | 10 (+0) | 1 (–5) | 5 (–3) | 1 (–5) |

**Damage Immunities** poison, psychic
**Condition Immunities** blinded, charmed, deafened, exhaustion, frightened, paralyzed, petrified, poisoned, prone
**Senses** blindsight 30 ft. (blind beyond this radius), passive Perception 7
**Languages** —
**Challenge** 1/4 (50 XP)

***Antimagic Susceptibility.*** The broom is incapacitated while in the area of an *antimagic field*. If targeted by *dispel magic*, the broom must succeed on a Constitution saving throw against the caster's spell save DC or fall unconscious for 1 minute.

***False Appearance.*** While the broom remains motionless and isn't flying, it is indistinguishable from a normal broom.

### Actions

***Multiattack.*** The broom makes two melee attacks.

***Broomstick.*** *Melee Weapon Attack:* +5 to hit, reach 5 ft., one target. *Hit:* 5 (1d4 + 3) bludgeoning damage.

### Reactions

***Animated Attack.*** If the broom is motionless and a creature grabs hold of it, the broom makes a Dexterity check contested by the creature's Strength check. If the broom wins the contest, it flies out of the creature's grasp and makes a melee attack against it with advantage on the attack roll.

# GUARDIAN PORTRAIT

A guardian portrait looks like a finely rendered and beautifully framed work of art, usually depicting someone important in a realistic manner. The picture and its frame are bound with powerful magic and are inseparable.

***Living Image.*** The eyes of the figure depicted in the painting are imbued with darkvision, and they appear to follow creatures that move in front of them.

***Innate Spells.*** When a guardian portrait attacks, the figure in the painting animates and moves as though alive (albeit in two dimensions). The guardian portrait has no effective melee attacks, but it has a repertoire of innate spells that it can cast. When it casts a spell, the figure painted on the canvas makes all the appropriate somatic gestures and verbal incantations for the spell.

# STRAHD'S ANIMATED ARMOR

The armor that Strahd wore into battle when he was alive lives on today as a headless, animated suit of plate armor. The armor is painted burgundy and adorned with golden angelic motifs.

***Thing of Evil.*** Strahd imbued his automaton with a sliver of his being, bequeathing unto his armor a malevolence not found in most animated objects. He also fortified his armor and placed a number of permanent spell effects on it to make the armor a better castle defender.

The armor understands Common but obeys only the commands of its master.

STRAHD'S
ANIMATED ARMOR

## GUARDIAN PORTRAIT
*Medium construct, unaligned*

**Armor Class** 5 (natural armor)
**Hit Points** 22 (5d8)
**Speed** 0 ft.

| STR | DEX | CON | INT | WIS | CHA |
| --- | --- | --- | --- | --- | --- |
| 1 (−5) | 1 (−5) | 10 (+0) | 14 (+2) | 10 (+0) | 10 (+0) |

**Damage Immunities** poison
**Condition Immunities** charmed, exhaustion, frightened, grappled, paralyzed, petrified, poisoned, prone, restrained
**Senses** darkvision 60 ft., passive Perception 10
**Languages** Common, plus up to two other languages
**Challenge** 1 (200 XP)

***Antimagic Susceptibility.*** The portrait is incapacitated while in the area of an *antimagic field*. If targeted by *dispel magic*, the portrait must succeed on a Constitution saving throw against the caster's spell save DC or become unconscious for 1 minute.

***Innate Spellcasting.*** The portrait's innate spellcasting ability is Intelligence (spell save DC 12). The portrait can innately cast the following spells, requiring no material components:

3/day each: *counterspell, crown of madness, hypnotic pattern, telekinesis*

***False Appearance.*** While the figure in the portrait remains motionless, the portrait is indistinguishable from a normal painting.

## STRAHD'S ANIMATED ARMOR
*Medium construct, lawful evil*

**Armor Class** 21 (natural armor)
**Hit Points** 112 (15d8 + 45)
**Speed** 30 ft.

| STR | DEX | CON | INT | WIS | CHA |
| --- | --- | --- | --- | --- | --- |
| 17 (+3) | 13 (+1) | 16 (+3) | 9 (−1) | 10 (+0) | 9 (−1) |

**Skills** Perception +3
**Damage Resistances** cold, fire
**Damage Immunities** lightning, poison
**Condition Immunities** blinded, charmed, deafened, exhaustion, frightened, paralyzed, petrified, poisoned
**Senses** blindsight 60 ft. (blind beyond this radius), passive Perception 13
**Languages** understands Common but can't speak
**Challenge** 6 (2,300 XP)

***Antimagic Susceptibility.*** The armor is incapacitated while in the area of an *antimagic field*. If targeted by *dispel magic*, the armor must succeed on a Constitution saving throw against the caster's spell save DC or fall unconscious for 1 minute.

***False Appearance.*** While the armor remains motionless, it is indistinguishable from a normal suit of armor.

### ACTIONS

***Multiattack.*** The armor makes two melee attacks or uses Shocking Bolt twice.

***Greatsword.*** *Melee Weapon Attack:* +6 to hit, reach 5 ft., one target. *Hit:* 10 (2d6 + 3) slashing damage plus 3 (1d6) lightning damage.

***Shocking Bolt.*** *Ranged Spell Attack:* +4 to hit (with advantage on the attack roll if the target is wearing armor made of metal), range 60 ft., one target. *Hit:* 10 (3d6) lightning damage.

# BABA LYSAGA

Two women gave life to Strahd von Zarovich. The first was Queen Ravenovia van Roeyen, Strahd's biological mother. The second was the queen's midwife, a devout follower of Mother Night named Baba Lysaga. Although it was the former who raised Strahd and enabled him to follow in his father's footsteps, it was the latter who sensed a potential for greatness and darkness in Strahd surpassing that of any other mortal. Lysaga believed then, as she believes now, that she is Strahd's true mother.

**Other Mother.** When Strahd was still a baby in his crib, Baba Lysaga cast protective spells on him and crept into his nursery on stormy nights to sing magical rhymes to him. She also placed the "spark of magic" in him, ensuring that he would become a spellcaster.

Baba Lysaga's unhealthy attachment to the baby Strahd did not go unnoticed. After she received several disturbing reports, Queen Ravenovia was forced to banish the midwife from the kingdom. Lysaga never saw Strahd again, but she has succeeded in staying alive to witness the triumphs of her beloved boy, who, in her mind, is eternally blessed. Despite the horrors Strahd has wrought, Lysaga still envisions him as the perfect child she delivered into the world. Strahd is the only thing in her life that matters to her.

**Mother Nearest.** During her exile, Baba Lysaga made countless sacrifices to Mother Night, pleading with the goddess to afflict Queen Ravenovia with ill health and visit death upon her. Lysaga eventually got her wish, and after Strahd settled in the valley of Barovia, Lysaga moved as close to him as she dared to.

In the filth-ridden depths of her heart, Lysaga knows that Strahd would never accept her as his true mother, nor could she bear his rejection. As a result, she has never confronted him. She would rather exist in perpetual denial, whiling away the days, months, and years practicing fell magic and looking for ways to help her "son."

**Raven Bane.** Baba Lysaga has allies in Castle Ravenloft—a coven of witches. Through the aid of these witches, Lysaga recently uncovered a potential threat to Strahd: a secret society of wereravens called the Keepers of the Feather, a group that uses ordinary ravens as their spies.

## BABA LYSAGA

*Medium humanoid (human, shapechanger), chaotic evil*

**Armor Class** 15 (natural armor)
**Hit Points** 120 (16d8 + 48)
**Speed** 30 ft.

| STR | DEX | CON | INT | WIS | CHA |
|-----|-----|-----|-----|-----|-----|
| 18 (+4) | 10 (+0) | 16 (+3) | 20 (+5) | 17 (+3) | 13 (+1) |

**Saving Throws** Wis +7
**Skills** Arcana +13, Religion +13
**Senses** passive Perception 13
**Languages** Abyssal, Common, Draconic, Dwarvish, Giant
**Challenge** 11 (7,200 XP)

**Shapechanger.** Baba Lysaga can use an action to polymorph into a swarm of insects (flies), or back into her true form. While in swarm form, she has a walking speed of 5 feet and a flying speed of 30 feet. Anything she is wearing transforms with her, but nothing she is carrying does.

**Blessing of Mother Night.** Baba Lysaga is shielded against divination magic, as though protected by a *nondetection* spell.

**Spellcasting.** Baba Lysaga is a 16th-level spellcaster. Her spellcasting ability is Intelligence (spell save DC 17, +9 to hit with spell attacks). Baba Lysaga has the following wizard spells prepared:

Cantrips (at will): *acid splash, fire bolt, light, mage hand, prestidigitation*
1st level (4 slots): *detect magic, magic missile, sleep, witch bolt*
2nd level (3 slots): *crown of madness, enlarge/reduce, misty step*
3rd level (3 slots): *dispel magic, fireball, lightning bolt*
4th level (3 slots): *blight, Evard's black tentacles, polymorph*
5th level (2 slots): *cloudkill, geas, scrying*
6th level (1 slot): *programmed illusion, true seeing*
7th level (1 slot): *finger of death, mirage arcane*
8th level (1 slot): *power word stun*

### ACTIONS

**Multiattack.** Baba Lysaga makes three attacks with her quarterstaff.

**Quarterstaff.** *Melee Weapon Attack:* +8 to hit, reach 5 ft., one target. *Hit:* 7 (1d6 + 4) bludgeoning damage, or 8 (1d8 + 4) bludgeoning damage if wielded with two hands.

**Summon Swarms of Insects (Recharges after a Short or Long Rest).** Baba Lysaga summons 1d4 **swarms of insects**. A summoned swarm appears in an unoccupied space within 60 feet of Baba Lysaga and acts as her ally. It remains until it dies or until Baba Lysaga dismisses it as an action.

Strahd doesn't consider the wereravens a serious threat, but Lysaga has chosen to make them the bane of her existence. After much searching and scrying, she discovered a wereraven refuge at the Wizard of Wines winery (chapter 12), and she has begun to wage war against it. In addition, she has forged an alliance with the mad druids that haunt Yester Hill (chapter 14), convincing them that she gave birth to Strahd, whom the druids consider a god. With the druids on her side, she expects to rid Barovia of its wereraven menace.

**Gifts of Mother Night.** The goddess Mother Night has bestowed magical gifts on Baba Lysaga as rewards for her ceaseless devotion to Strahd. Her skin has the resilience of stone, she is resistant to harmful magic, and she is shielded against divination magic. Mother Night has also imparted to Lysaga the secret of longevity, which requires her to bathe in the blood of beasts on nights of the new moon. Failure to do so causes Lysaga to age rapidly, becoming mere dust and bones in a matter of seconds.

## BABA LYSAGA'S TRAITS

**Ideal.** "No love is greater than a mother's love for her son."

**Bond.** "I am the mother of Strahd. Anyone who disputes this fact can rot."

**Flaw.** "I will not rest until the last of my son's enemies are destroyed."

# BAROVIAN WITCH

The mad women and men known as Barovian witches forge pacts with Strahd and the Dark Powers of Ravenloft in exchange for magic and longevity. They prefer to live in the shadows and can see in the dark. When traveling in the open, they use *alter self* spells to assume less conspicuous forms. They also use these spells to grow long, sharp claws with which they can attack.

**Brothers and Sisters of Strahd.** Barovian witches have no scruples. They will deal with anyone in return for power. They will also betray anyone for the same reason. The only thing they fear is Strahd, and his wish is their command. Barovian witches sometimes refer to themselves as the brothers and sisters of Strahd, though never to Strahd's face.

**Pack Rats with Cats.** Barovian witches are obsessive collectors, each believing that almost anything found—a piece of broken bone, a dead rodent, a handful of dust, or some other worthless item or substance—could be valuable or useful as a spell component, a ritual object, or a potion ingredient.

Barovian witches use the *find familiar* spell to call forth familiars. They are particularly fond of cats, though snakes and toads are also common. These animals lurk amid the clutter of the witches' lairs, seldom wandering far from their vile masters.

BAROVIAN
WITCH

## BAROVIAN WITCH
*Medium humanoid (human), chaotic evil*

**Armor Class** 10
**Hit Points** 16 (3d8 + 3)
**Speed** 30 ft.

| STR | DEX | CON | INT | WIS | CHA |
|-----|-----|-----|-----|-----|-----|
| 7 (−2) | 11 (+0) | 13 (+1) | 14 (+2) | 11 (+0) | 12 (+1) |

**Skills** Arcana +4, Perception +2
**Senses** darkvision 60 ft., passive Perception 12
**Languages** Common
**Challenge** 1/2 (100 XP)

**Spellcasting.** The witch is a 3rd-level spellcaster. Its spellcasting ability is Intelligence (spell save DC 12, +4 to hit with spell attacks). The witch has the following wizard spells prepared:

Cantrips (at will): *mage hand, prestidigitation, ray of frost*
1st level (4 slots): *ray of sickness, sleep, Tasha's hideous laughter*
2nd level (2 slots): *alter self, invisibility*

### ACTIONS

**Claws (Requires Alter Self).** *Melee Weapon Attack:* +3 to hit, reach 5 ft., one target. *Hit:* 4 (1d6 + 1) slashing damage. This attack is magical.

**Dagger.** *Melee or Ranged Weapon Attack:* +2 to hit, reach 5 ft. or range 20/60 ft., one target. *Hit:* 2 (1d4) piercing damage.

# BLIGHT, TREE

Blights (as described in the *Monster Manual*) are evil, ambulatory plant creatures, and a tree blight is a particularly enormous variety. It looks like a dead tree or treant, 30 feet tall, with spongy wooden flesh, thorny branches, and rubbery roots that trail behind it. It has blood for sap and is so saturated with blood that it doesn't catch fire easily.

***Vicious Carnivore.*** A tree blight feeds on warm-blooded prey and takes perverse delight in causing carnage. It strikes with its heavy branches and crushes prey to death with its roots. It can open its gaping, tooth-filled mouth and bite a creature caught in its roots. The roots of a tree blight can be severed, though cutting them causes the blight no harm.

***Blight Animosity.*** A tree blight will often fight along-side other kinds of blights, but it hates other tree blights and will attack them given the chance. Tree blights also hate treants, and the feeling is mutual.

---

## TREE BLIGHT

*Huge plant, neutral evil*

---

**Armor Class** 15 (natural armor)
**Hit Points** 149 (13d12 + 65)
**Speed** 30 ft.

---

| STR | DEX | CON | INT | WIS | CHA |
|-----|-----|-----|-----|-----|-----|
| 23 (+6) | 10 (+0) | 20 (+5) | 6 (−2) | 10 (+0) | 3 (−4) |

---

**Condition Immunities** blinded, deafened
**Senses** blindsight 60 ft. (blind beyond this radius), passive Perception 10
**Languages** understands Common and Druidic but doesn't speak
**Challenge** 7 (2,900 XP)

---

***False Appearance.*** While the blight remains motionless, it is indistinguishable from a dead tree.

***Siege Monster.*** The blight deals double damage to objects and structures.

### ACTIONS

***Multiattack.*** The blight makes four attacks: two with its branches and two with its grasping roots. If it has a target grappled, the blight can also make a bite attack against that target as a bonus action.

***Bite.*** *Melee Weapon Attack:* +9 to hit, reach 5 ft., one target. *Hit:* 19 (3d8 + 6) piercing damage.

***Branch.*** *Melee Weapon Attack:* +9 to hit, reach 15 ft., one target. *Hit:* 16 (3d6 + 6) bludgeoning damage.

***Grasping Root.*** *Melee Weapon Attack:* +9 to hit, reach 15 ft., one creature not grappled by the blight. *Hit:* The target is grappled (escape DC 15). Until the grapple ends, the target takes 9 (1d6 + 6) bludgeoning damage at the start of each of its turns. The root has AC 15 and can be severed by dealing 6 slashing damage or more to it at once. Cutting the root doesn't hurt the blight but ends the grapple.

EZMERELDA
D'AVENIR

## EZMERELDA D'AVENIR

Ezmerelda d'Avenir, a Vistana, is the protégé of Rudolph van Richten—despite the fact that her first encounter with the vampire hunter was anything but pleasant.

***Witness to Tragedy.*** When Ezmerelda was a little girl, her family kidnapped van Richten's teenage son, Erasmus, and delivered him into the clutches of a vampire. Even today, years later, she can still hear Erasmus's pleas for mercy. That event haunted her childhood.

Van Richten tracked down Ezmerelda's family soon after the kidnapping, but not before the Vistani had sold the boy. Though van Richten could have done them harm, he instead interrogated Ezmerelda's mother and father on the whereabouts of his missing son. Satisfied with their answers, he spared their lives before departing with the information they had given him. Ezmerelda witnessed van Richten's act of mercy and was deeply moved by it.

***Van Richten's Tragic Tale.*** At the age of fifteen, Ezmerelda, still troubled by what her family had done to van Richten, ran away from home. After many harrowing adventures, she tracked down van Richten two years later. Thinking she was a Vistana assassin, he put a sword to her throat and threatened to spill her blood. Ezmerelda convinced him that she genuinely wanted to help him find his missing son, whereupon van Richten told her the saddest of tales. He had found his son, who had been transformed into a vampire spawn. When Erasmus pleaded to his father for salvation, van Richten granted his request by ending his existence.

***Farewell.*** Ezmerelda remained by van Richten's side for two years, helping him track down and slay many creatures of the night. But because van Richten could never bring himself to fully trust a Vistana, he kept

# Ezmerelda d'Avenir

Medium humanoid (human), chaotic good

**Armor Class** 17 (+1 *studded leather armor*)
**Hit Points** 82 (11d8 + 33)
**Speed** 30 ft.

| STR | DEX | CON | INT | WIS | CHA |
|-----|-----|-----|-----|-----|-----|
| 14 (+2) | 19 (+4) | 16 (+3) | 16 (+3) | 11 (+0) | 17 (+3) |

**Saving Throws** Wis +3
**Skills** Acrobatics +7, Arcana +6, Deception +9, Insight +3, Medicine +3, Perception +6, Performance +6, Sleight of Hand +7, Stealth +7, Survival +6
**Senses** passive Perception 16
**Languages** Common, Elvish
**Challenge** 8 (3,900 XP)

**Special Equipment.** In addition to her magic armor and weapons, Ezmerelda has two *potions of greater healing*, six vials of holy water, and three wooden stakes.

**Spellcasting.** Ezmerelda is a 7th-level spellcaster. Her spellcasting ability is Intelligence (spell save DC 14, +6 to hit with spell attacks). Ezmerelda has the following wizard spells prepared:

Cantrips (at will): *fire bolt, light, mage hand, prestidigitation*
1st level (4 slots): *protection from evil and good, magic missile, shield*
2nd level (3 slots): *darkvision, knock, mirror image*
3rd level (3 slots): *clairvoyance, lightning bolt, magic circle*
4th level (1 slot): *greater invisibility*

## Actions

**Multiattack.** Ezmerelda makes three attacks: two with her *+1 rapier* and one with her *+1 handaxe* or her silvered shortsword.

**+1 Rapier.** *Melee Weapon Attack:* +8 to hit, reach 5 ft., one target. *Hit:* 9 (1d8 + 5) piercing damage.

**+1 Handaxe.** *Melee or Ranged Weapon Attack:* +6 to hit, reach 5 ft. or range 20/60 ft., one target. *Hit:* 6 (1d6 + 3) slashing damage.

**Silvered Shortsword.** *Melee Weapon Attack:* +7 to hit, reach 5 ft., one target. *Hit:* 7 (1d6 + 4) piercing damage.

**Curse (Recharges after a Long Rest).** Ezmerelda targets one creature that she can see within 30 feet of her. The target must succeed on a DC 14 Wisdom saving throw or be cursed. While cursed, the target has vulnerability to one type of damage of Ezmerelda's choice. The curse lasts until ended with a *greater restoration* spell, a *remove curse* spell, or similar magic. When the curse ends, Ezmerelda takes 3d6 psychic damage.

**Evil Eye (Recharges after a Short or Long Rest).** Ezmerelda targets one creature that she can see within 10 feet of her and casts one of the following spells on the target (save DC 14), requiring neither somatic nor material components to do so: *animal friendship, charm person,* or *hold person*. If the target succeeds on the initial saving throw, Ezmerelda is blinded until the end of her next turn. Once a target succeeds on a saving throw against this effect, it is immune to the Evil Eye power of all Vistani for 24 hours.

secrets from her. The two vampire hunters got on each other's nerves, and their arguments became more frequent. At last, Ezmerelda suggested that they part company with some shred of their friendship still intact, and van Richten agreed.

**Ezmerelda's Secret.** Since bidding farewell to van Richten, Ezmerelda has amassed a sizable personal fortune, some of which she used to buy a wagon to carry her vampire-slaying paraphernalia. On one of her less successful adventures, a werewolf bit off her right leg below the knee, and although she avoided being afflicted with lycanthropy, Ezmerelda was sidelined for months. She commissioned a master artisan to craft a prosthetic lower leg and foot. After several tries, he delivered a prosthesis that restored her mobility. She has since adapted well to the false appendage and takes care to hide it from view.

**The Great Vampire Hunt.** While in the company of a Vistani caravan, Ezmerelda heard a rumor that Rudolph van Richten had gone to Barovia to slay the most powerful vampire of them all. She decided that he might need help and traveled for months to reach Strahd's domain. She rode her wagon to Vallaki and learned about an old tower that seemed the sort of place van Richten would use as a base. When she arrived there, she found some of van Richten's belongings, but of the vampire hunter there was no sign. Although she is anxious to learn the whereabouts of her mentor, she is also eager to earn his trust and respect. To that end, she has been poring over van Richten's research and learning about Strahd and

Castle Ravenloft, with every intention of dispatching the vampire herself.

**Tarokka Deck.** Ezmerelda keeps a deck of tarokka cards in her wagon (chapter 11, area V1). Although the cards aren't magical, Ezmerelda can use them to perform a card reading for the characters (see chapter 1), like the one that can be performed by Madam Eva.

## Ezmerelda d'Avenir's Traits

**Ideal.** "Evil that feeds on the innocent is the worst of all evils and must be destroyed."

**Bond.** "My mentor and teacher, Dr. Rudolph van Richten, is like a father to me."

**Flaw.** "I go where angels fear to tread."

# Izek Strazni

Izek and his sister were born in Vallaki. One morning, their father and their uncle took them fishing on Lake Zarovich. On the way back to town, a dire wolf attacked Izek and bit off his right arm. His father carried Izek back to town while his uncle distracted the beast. His sister ran and hid in the woods and was never seen again.

Unlike his sister, Izek was born without a soul. As time wore on, he forgot his lost sister and learned to cope with his disability.

**Orphaned Killer.** Izek's parents succumbed to their grief, leaving him an orphan. He became a sociopath. Other children ruthlessly mocked him because of his dead family and his missing arm, but he was a large boy and had no trouble killing them and disposing of their bodies. He was eventually caught in the act and brought to the burgomaster. Instead of punishing the boy for his crimes, Baron Vallakovich pardoned Izek and took him into his home. Izek has been loyal to the burgomaster ever since, enjoying the power of his position and the comforts of his master's mansion. When he isn't enforcing the burgomaster's will, Izek drinks copious amounts of wine.

***Fiendish Gift.*** After years of doing Baron Vallakovich's dirty work, Izek awakened from a drunken stupor one morning to find that he had grown a new arm to replace the one he had lost.

The new appendage has barbed spines, elongated fingers, and long nails. He can create fire with the snap of his fiendish fingers and has used the flames to put the fear of the devil in every Vallakian.

***Doll Collector.*** Perhaps more disturbing than his fiendish arm and his murderous nature is Izek's collection of dolls, which he keeps in his bedroom in the burgomaster's mansion. Izek often has dreams of a beautiful young woman, and for years he has forced a local toymaker named Gadof Blinsky to craft dolls in her likeness. The woman is Ireena Kolyana, although Izek doesn't know her name.

***Family Is Forever.*** Izek has dreams of Ireena. If he spots her, he tries to take her by force to the burgomaster's mansion. If he succeeds, he holds her captive in his bedroom (chapter 5, area N3j). Unknown to Izek and Ireena, they are brother and sister. Ireena fled after Izek was attacked by the dire wolf and became lost in the woods. She wandered for days in shock until she was

found and adopted by Kolyan Indirovich in the village of Barovia. Izek covets her in an unwholesome way and won't allow anyone or anything to come between them.

## IZEK STRAZNI'S TRAITS

***Ideal.*** "Fear is a powerful weapon. I use it to get what I want."

***Bond.*** "I am loyal to my master, Baron Vallakovich, for he brought me into his home. I owe him my life, but he isn't family."

***Flaw.*** "I would do anything, kill anything, to find my sister."

# KASIMIR VELIKOV

Kasimir, a mutilated and grief-stricken dusk elf, has been trapped in Barovia for centuries. His people were on the verge of being annihilated by Strahd's armies when they surrendered. Strahd left the few survivors to the mercy of the Vistani, who bore them to the valley of Barovia, where they have lived ever since.

***Old Friends.*** Kasimir's allegiance to the Vistani is so strong that he adopted the name of the Vistana who welcomed him into his clan, a man named Velikov. Although Velikov passed away more than a century ago, Kasimir continues to live among Velikov's descendants. Unfortunately, in his view, these modern Vistani are neither as noble nor as enlightened as their forebears. Not one to press the issue, Kasimir hopes to outlive the present leadership and see a return to the old ways.

***Dreams of the Damned.*** Kasimir's sister, Patrina Velikovna, is sealed in the catacombs below Castle Ravenloft. Convinced that she was the concubine of the devil Strahd, Kasimir and his fellow dusk elves stoned Patrina to death. As punishment for depriving him of his bride, Strahd butchered all the women in the dusk elf tribe, and Kasimir's ears were cut off to punish him for

---

## IZEK STRAZNI
*Medium humanoid (human), neutral evil*

**Armor Class** 14 (studded leather armor)
**Hit Points** 112 (15d8 + 45)
**Speed** 30 ft.

| STR | DEX | CON | INT | WIS | CHA |
|-----|-----|-----|-----|-----|-----|
| 18 (+4) | 15 (+2) | 16 (+3) | 10 (+0) | 9 (−1) | 15 (+2) |

**Skills** Intimidation +8, Perception +2
**Senses** passive Perception 12
**Languages** Common
**Challenge** 5 (1,800 XP)

**Brute.** A melee weapon deals one extra die of its damage when Izek hits with it (included in the attack).

### ACTIONS

**Multiattack.** Izek makes two attacks with his battleaxe.

**Battleaxe.** *Melee Weapon Attack:* +7 to hit, reach 5 ft., one target. *Hit:* 13 (2d8 + 4) slashing damage, or 15 (2d10 + 4) when used with two hands.

**Hurl Flame.** *Ranged Spell Attack:* +5 to hit, range 60 ft., one target. *Hit:* 10 (3d6) fire damage. If the target is a flammable object that isn't being worn or carried, it catches fire.

instigating the stoning. He wears a cowl to conceal his mutilation.

Kasimir's feeling of loss is tinged with simmering rage. Patrina now speaks to her brother in dreams, telling him how years of guilt and regret have dispelled all evil thoughts from her mind and cleansed her tortured soul. But Kasimir remains unconvinced by her assertions, because he knows that Strahd has corrupted Patrina and led her down a path of evil and deceit. For that reason, Kasimir wants to see the vampire destroyed so that his sister can be rescued from her eternal damnation.

**Secrets of the Amber Temple.** Patrina has told Kasimir that the Amber Temple, an ancient vault hidden in the Barovian mountains, is where Strahd forged his pact with evil powers and discovered how to become a vampire. Kasimir has been spying on the temple for years, but he needs adventurers to help him survive its perils. He thinks that the secret to breaking Strahd's pact and freeing Barovia from its curse might be hidden there, but more important, he believes that the Amber Temple holds the secret to bringing the ancient dead back to life.

With the characters' help, Kasimir thinks he might be able to find out how to restore Patrina to flesh and blood, whereupon he can travel to Castle Ravenloft and end his sister's torment. Kasimir has no inkling that Patrina is using him for exactly that purpose, and that her ultimate goal is to become as powerful a vampire as Strahd.

**Statistics.** Use the **mage** stat block in the *Monster Manual*, with the following adjustments:

- Kasimir's alignment is neutral.
- Kasimir has darkvision out to a range of 60 feet.
- Kasimir has the Fey Ancestry feature, which means he has advantage on saving throws against being charmed, and magic can't put him to sleep.
- Kasimir wears a *ring of warmth* and carries a spellbook (see chapter 5, area N9a, for a list of the spells it holds in addition to his prepared spells).

## KASIMIR VELIKOV'S TRAITS

**Ideal.** "I failed my people and my sister, and now I must atone or be damned."

**Bond.** "I seek to return my long-dead sister, Patrina, to life—even at the cost of my own life."

**Flaw.** "I believe my sister can be redeemed."

# MADAM EVA

The fortune-teller Madam Eva lives among the Vistani but isn't truly one of them. She appears to be in her seventies, but she is, in fact, much older.

**Royal Blood.** Madam Eva is Strahd's half-sister, though Strahd is unaware of this fact. Her real name is Katarina, and she is the daughter of a Vistani woman whom King Barov, Strahd's father, took to his bed during one of his many crusades. Madam Eva knows she is Strahd's half-sister but has told no one of the royal blood flowing through her veins.

**Mother Night.** Over four hundred years ago, Katarina came to Barovia and insinuated herself into Strahd's court, working as a maid in Castle Ravenloft. She came to know the castle like the back of her hand, and she

## MADAM EVA
*Medium humanoid (human), chaotic neutral*

**Armor Class** 10
**Hit Points** 88 (16d8 + 16)
**Speed** 20 ft.

| STR | DEX | CON | INT | WIS | CHA |
|-----|-----|-----|-----|-----|-----|
| 8 (-1) | 11 (+0) | 12 (+1) | 17 (+3) | 20 (+5) | 18 (+4) |

**Saving Throws** Con +5
**Skills** Arcana +7, Deception +8, Insight +13, Intimidation +8, Perception +9, Religion +7
**Senses** passive Perception 19
**Languages** Abyssal, Common, Elvish, Infernal
**Challenge** 10 (5,900 XP)

**Spellcasting.** Madam Eva is a 16th-level spellcaster. Her spellcasting ability is Wisdom (spell save DC 17, +9 to hit with spell attacks). Madam Eva has the following cleric spells prepared:

Cantrips (at will): *light, mending, sacred flame, thaumaturgy*
1st level (4 slots): *bane, command, detect evil and good, protection from evil and good*
2nd level (3 slots): *lesser restoration, protection from poison, spiritual weapon*
3rd level (3 slots): *create food and water, speak with dead, spirit guardians*
4th level (3 slots): *divination, freedom of movement, guardian of faith*
5th level (2 slots): *greater restoration, raise dead*
6th level (1 slot): *find the path, harm, true seeing*
7th level (1 slot): *fire storm, regenerate*
8th level (1 slot): *earthquake*

## ACTIONS

**Dagger.** *Melee Weapon Attack:* +4 to hit, reach 5 ft., one target. *Hit:* 2 (1d4) piercing damage.

**Curse (Recharges after a Long Rest).** Madam Eva targets one creature that she can see within 30 feet of her. The target must succeed on a DC 17 Wisdom saving throw or be cursed. While cursed, the target is blinded and deafened. The curse lasts until ended with a *greater restoration* spell, a *remove curse* spell, or similar magic. When the curse ends, Madam Eva takes 5d6 psychic damage.

**Evil Eye (Recharges after a Short or Long Rest).** Madam Eva targets one creature that she can see within 10 feet of her and casts one of the following spells on the target (save DC 17), requiring neither somatic nor material components to do so: *animal friendship, charm person,* or *hold person*. If the target succeeds on the initial saving throw, Madam Eva is blinded until the end of her next turn. Once a target succeeds on a saving throw against this effect, it is immune to the Evil Eye power of all Vistani for 24 hours.

was present for the wedding of Sergei and Tatyana. After Strahd went mad and murdered his brother, she fled the castle and took refuge with the Vistani. Later, she forged a pact with the goddess Mother Night, trading her youth for the power to undo the evil that Strahd had wrought. Mother Night transformed Katarina into an ageless crone gifted with the power of magical foresight. In the guise of Madam Eva, she uses this ability to help

Strahd. She can send her Vistani out in their wagons to visit other worlds and bring adventurers to Strahd's domain, in hopes that they will find a way to destroy the vampire or set Strahd free.

**For the Love of Strahd.** The Dark Powers of Ravenloft would consider Madam Eva a worthy choice to replace Strahd as the master of Ravenloft, but she has all the power she desires and doesn't seek to supplant him. She would rather help Strahd find someone else to succeed him, although she has grave doubts about her ability to locate such an individual.

None of Madam Eva's Vistani kin know her true identity or purpose. They puzzle over her desire to remain in Barovia.

## MADAM EVA'S TRAITS

**Ideal.** "I wish Strahd to be free of his curse."
**Bond.** "The Vistani are my people now."
**Flaw.** "The people whose fates I divine aren't important. They are but the means to an end."

# MONGRELFOLK

Mongrelfolk are humanoids that have undergone, or whose ancestors underwent, horrific magical transformations, to the extent that they retain only a fraction of their original being. Their humanoid bodies incorporate the features of various beasts. For example, one mongrelfolk might have the basic body shape of a dwarf with a head that combines the features of a cat and a lizard, one arm that ends in a crab's pincer, and one leg that ends in a cloven hoof. Another might have the skin and horns of a cow, the eyes of a spider, frog's legs, and a scaly lizard's tail. Each mongrelfolk's mad combination of humanoid and animal forms results in its having a slow, awkward gait.

**Sound Mimicry.** Mongrelfolk have misshapen mouths and vocal cords. They speak fragmented Common mixed with various animal cries and nonsense. They can effectively imitate sounds made by beasts and humanoids that they've heard. Mongrelfolk aren't sophisticated enough to use these sounds as a covert form of communication, but they can use the sounds to lure enemies into a trap or otherwise distract them.

**Outcasts.** Mongrelfolk are seldom welcome in other humanoid societies, where they are abused, enslaved, or shunned. They typically live on the fringes of civilization in ruins, deserted buildings, or other places that other humanoid races once lived in or built. They tend to be timid and skittish outside their homes and fiercely territorial within their lairs.

**Camouflage Experts.** Mongrelfolk often hide their deformities under cloaks and cowls. In this way, they can sometimes pass as stout humans or thin dwarves. They are fond of camouflage, attaching leaves and twigs to their cloaks, making brown paint to cover their skin, and weaving grass nets under which they can hide. They use such camouflage while hunting in the wild or while standing guard outside their lairs. Until it is seen, a camouflaged mongrelfolk has advantage on Stealth checks made to hide.

---

## MONGRELFOLK
*Medium humanoid (mongrelfolk), any alignment*

**Armor Class** 11 (natural armor)
**Hit Points** 26 (4d8 + 8)
**Speed** 20 ft.

| STR | DEX | CON | INT | WIS | CHA |
|-----|-----|-----|-----|-----|-----|
| 12 (+1) | 9 (−1) | 15 (+2) | 9 (−1) | 10 (+0) | 6 (−2) |

**Skills** Deception +2, Perception +2, Stealth +3
**Senses** passive Perception 12
**Languages** Common
**Challenge** 1/4 (50 XP)

**Extraordinary Feature.** The mongrelfolk has one of the following extraordinary features, determined randomly by rolling a d20 or chosen by the DM:

**1–3: Amphibious.** The mongrelfolk can breathe air and water.
**4–9: Darkvision.** The mongrelfolk has darkvision out to a range of 60 feet.
**10: Flight.** The mongrelfolk has leathery wings and a flying speed of 40 feet.
**11–15: Keen Hearing and Smell.** The mongrelfolk has advantage on Wisdom (Perception) checks that rely on hearing or smell.
**16–17: Spider Climb.** The mongrelfolk can climb difficult surfaces, including upside down on ceilings, without needing to make an ability check.
**18–19: Standing Leap.** The mongrelfolk's long jump is up to 20 feet and its high jump is up to 10 feet, with or without a running start.
**20: Two-Headed.** The mongrelfolk has advantage on Wisdom (Perception) checks and on saving throws against being blinded, charmed, deafened, frightened, stunned, or knocked unconscious.

**Mimicry.** The mongrelfolk can mimic any sounds it has heard, including voices. A creature that hears the sounds can tell they are imitations with a successful DC 12 Wisdom (Insight) check.

### ACTIONS

**Multiattack.** The mongrelfolk makes two attacks: one with its bite and one with its claw or dagger.

**Bite.** *Melee Weapon Attack:* +3 to hit, reach 5 ft., one target. *Hit:* 3 (1d4 + 1) piercing damage.

**Claw.** *Melee Weapon Attack:* +3 to hit, reach 5 ft., one target. *Hit:* 3 (1d4 + 1) slashing damage.

**Dagger.** *Melee or Ranged Weapon Attack:* +3 to hit, reach 5 ft. or range 20/60 ft., one target. *Hit:* 3 (1d4 + 1) piercing damage.

---

**Horrific Offspring.** It's possible to restore a mongrelfolk to its original form using a *greater restoration* spell, but the same can't be said for a mongrelfolk's offspring. Only mongrelfolk that are made by magic can be restored to their original forms. Mongrelfolk that are born are true mongrelfolk and not the subjects of a spell or an effect that can be undone.

Mongrelfolk can breed with other humanoids, but nearly all children born to such parents are mongrelfolk. (About one child in every hundred is born looking like its non-mongrelfolk parent.)

PHANTOM
WARRIOR

# PHANTOM WARRIOR

A phantom warrior is the spectral remnant of a willful soldier or knight who perished on the battlefield or died performing its sworn duty. It appears like a translucent version of its living self.

**Task Driven.** Although one is often mistaken for a ghost, a phantom warrior isn't bound by a yearning to complete some unresolved goal. It can choose to end its undead existence at any time. Its spirit lingers willingly, either out of loyalty to its former master or because it believes it must perform a task to satisfy its honor or sense of duty. For example, a guard who dies defending a wall might return as a phantom warrior and continue guarding the wall, then disappear forever once a new guard assumes its post or the wall is destroyed. The period between the time it died and the time it rises as a phantom warrior is usually 24 hours.

**Faded Memories.** A phantom warrior retains the alignment and personality it had before it died, and it remembers how it died. Memories of its life from shortly before it died are hazy, and older memories are forgotten. A phantom warrior can usually remember the last 1d10 + 10 days of its life; everything that happened before that is an impenetrable fog.

**Forceful Presence.** Although they are incorporeal, phantom warriors can harness the energy around them to deflect incoming attacks and strike with great force. An invisible sheath of energy surrounds a phantom warrior's ghostly armor, shields, and weapons, which become as hard as steel yet don't impede the warrior's ability to move through walls and other solid objects.

**Undead Nature.** A phantom warrior doesn't require air, food, drink, or sleep.

---

## PHANTOM WARRIOR
*Medium undead, any alignment*

**Armor Class** 16
**Hit Points** 45 (6d8 + 18)
**Speed** 30 ft.

| STR | DEX | CON | INT | WIS | CHA |
|-----|-----|-----|-----|-----|-----|
| 16 (+3) | 11 (+0) | 16 (+3) | 8 (−1) | 10 (+0) | 15 (+2) |

**Skills** Perception +2, Stealth +4
**Damage Resistances** bludgeoning, piercing, and slashing from nonmagical attacks
**Damage Immunities** cold, necrotic, poison
**Condition Immunities** charmed, exhaustion, frightened, grappled, paralyzed, petrified, poisoned, prone, restrained
**Senses** darkvision 60 ft., passive Perception 12
**Languages** any languages it knew in life
**Challenge** 3 (700 XP)

**Ethereal Sight.** The phantom warrior can see 60 feet into the Ethereal Plane when it is on the Material Plane, and vice versa.

**Incorporeal Movement.** The phantom warrior can move through other creatures and objects as if they were difficult terrain. It takes 5 (1d10) force damage if it ends its turn inside an object.

**Spectral Armor and Shield.** The phantom warrior's AC accounts for its spectral armor and shield.

### ACTIONS

**Multiattack.** The phantom warrior makes two attacks with its spectral longsword.

**Spectral Longsword.** *Melee Weapon Attack:* +5 to hit, reach 5 ft., one target. *Hit:* 7 (1d8 + 3) force damage.

**Etherealness.** The phantom warrior enters the Ethereal Plane from the Material Plane, or vice versa. It is visible on the Material Plane while it is in the Border Ethereal, and vice versa, yet it can't affect or be affected by anything on the other plane.

---

# PIDLWICK II

After her husband died in battle, Duchess Dorfniya Dilisnya set her sights on becoming Count Strahd von Zarovich's bride, but she failed to win his love. Her visits to the castle were nonetheless frequent, and she never traveled without her fool, the delightful Pidlwick. The little man was like a ray of sunshine in Castle Ravenloft, and though he failed to amuse Strahd, he delighted Tatyana and Sergei with his jokes and gambols. As a result, Strahd didn't object whenever Pidlwick and the duchess came to visit.

Eager to please and desiring to return the courtesy, the duchess commissioned the legendary toymaker Fritz von Weerg to build a clockwork effigy of Pidlwick as a gift for Strahd's family. Although the duchess's heart was in the right place, the effigy didn't have Pidlwick's abilities, and it failed to entertain anyone. Even though Pidlwick himself had spent months training it, the effigy couldn't speak, and its movements were more awkward than amusing.

PIDLWICK II

## PIDLWICK II

*Small construct, neutral evil*

**Armor Class** 14 (natural armor)
**Hit Points** 10 (3d6)
**Speed** 30 ft.

| STR | DEX | CON | INT | WIS | CHA |
|-----|-----|-----|-----|-----|-----|
| 10 (+0) | 14 (+2) | 11 (+0) | 8 (−1) | 13 (+1) | 10 (+0) |

**Skills** Performance +2
**Damage Immunities** poison
**Condition Immunities** paralyzed, petrified, poisoned
**Senses** passive Perception 11
**Languages** understands Common but doesn't speak and can't read or write
**Challenge** 1/4 (50 XP)

**Ambusher.** During the first round of combat, Pidlwick II has advantage on attack rolls against any creature that hasn't had a turn yet.

### ACTIONS

**Club.** *Melee Weapon Attack:* +2 to hit, reach 5 ft., one target. *Hit:* 2 (1d4) bludgeoning damage.

**Dart.** *Ranged Weapon Attack:* +4 to hit, range 20/60 ft., one target. *Hit:* 4 (1d4 + 2) piercing damage.

A harsh winter trapped the duchess, her fool, and her fool's effigy in Castle Ravenloft for several months. The duchess subsequently succumbed to illness, after which Tatyana asked Pidlwick to remain at Castle Ravenloft.

***One Pidlwick Too Many.*** Von Weerg was no ordinary toymaker, and he put a little of himself into all his creations, which is to say his works had a touch of their creator's madness. Pidlwick II knew that it had no purpose as long as Pidlwick remained in Castle Ravenloft, so it pushed Pidlwick down a long flight of stairs, killing him. Everyone else thought it was an accident. In the days that followed, Pidlwick II tried its best to fill its name-

sake's shoes, but the effigy's mere presence was upsetting to Tatyana, and it was never called on to perform. Eventually, it was shut away like a discarded toy.

***Evil Toy.*** Pidlwick II was kept in a small closet adjacent to one of the guest bedrooms. On rare occasions when someone stayed there, Pidlwick would sneak out of the closet in the middle of the night, smother the guest with a pillow, and then retreat back to the closet. The castle staff never considered that the effigy might be responsible, instead assuming that the guests had died in their sleep.

But Strahd was not fooled. He came to realize fairly quickly that the clockwork effigy had begun to display a murderous nature. Rather than have Pidlwick II destroyed, Strahd kept the fool around to dispose of irksome guests from time to time.

After the deaths of Sergei and Tatyana, the castle became virtually abandoned, and there were no more guests for Pidlwick II to "entertain." The clockwork effigy emerged from its closet and found new places to hide. It fears Strahd and eagerly follows anyone who gives it the attention it craves.

Pidlwick II is basically an oversized toy—a 4-foot-tall mechanism stuffed with gears, springs, and other components expertly fitted together to impart a semblance of life to it. Its skin is made of stitched leather pulled taut over an articulated wooden frame. Pidlwick II has rubbed soot around its eyes and mouth, giving it the triangular eyes and jagged grin of a jack-o'-lantern.

## PIDLWICK II'S TRAITS

***Ideal.*** "I wish I could make people happy."
***Bond.*** "I would like to find someone—anyone—who isn't afraid of me and who enjoys my company."
***Flaw.*** "When I'm upset, I do bad things."

# RAHADIN

Rahadin, the dusk elf chamberlain of Castle Ravenloft, has served Strahd's family faithfully for nearly five hundred years. He is Strahd's eternal servant, a longtime comrade-in-arms, and a ruthless warrior who has killed thousands in his lifetime.

***Exile.*** Rahadin was exiled for refusing to bow down to a dusk elf prince whom he considered weak and corrupt. When the dusk elves later declined to pay fealty to King Barov, Rahadin helped Barov conquer them. The elf kingdom's royal line was obliterated, the dusk elves hunted like rabbits. The few that survived were either subjugated or forced to live among the Vistani. So pleased was Barov with Rahadin that the king made the dusk elf an honorary member of his family.

***Chamberlain.*** After Barov died, Rahadin continued to fight as one of Strahd's generals. When the wars ended and Strahd turned his attention to building Castle Ravenloft, Rahadin saw to it that wizards and artisans were brought to Barovia. Years later, Strahd appointed Rahadin his castle chamberlain. Rahadin was pleased to do whatever Strahd asked of him, and he instilled terror in the castle staff by routinely flogging those who didn't perform their duties to his exacting standards.

When a dusk elf named Patrina Velikovna came knocking on Strahd's door, Rahadin could see that she intrigued Strahd, but Rahadin was suspicious of her motives. Patrina tried to seduce Strahd with the prospect of immortality—something Strahd desired above all. She told him of a vault of forbidden lore called the Amber Temple, where the secret of gaining immortality was hidden. While Strahd was off exploring the temple, Rahadin handled all of his master's affairs and began searching for a woman who could tear Strahd away from Patrina Velikovna. In this task, he failed. His goal was fulfilled, however, when Sergei, Strahd's brother, found Tatyana.

Tatyana was Strahd's type—a woman of exquisite beauty and gentle manner. When Strahd returned to Ravenloft, the young woman instantly caught his eye, and Rahadin had the pleasure of informing Patrina that her presence at the castle was no longer desired.

Rahadin's loyalty didn't waver after Tatyana died and Strahd became a vampire. Rahadin continued to do his master's bidding. Eager to put Tatyana out of his mind, Strahd lured more women to the castle, taking several of them as brides before draining their lives and turning them into vampire spawn. Rahadin would see to it that these women were lavished with jewels and fine clothes, and made comfortable during their stay in Ravenloft.

**Executioner.** Patrina Velikovna and her people were living among the Vistani when they heard of Tatyana's death and Strahd's curse. The ageless Patrina returned to Ravenloft in the hope of winning Strahd's love. This time, it was clear that Patrina craved Strahd's power and that Strahd would never love her. Rahadin assumed that Patrina would suffer the same fate as those women who had come before her. He was proven wrong when Patrina's own people stoned her to death to keep Strahd from claiming her as his wife.

Strahd was upset that the dusk elves had taken Patrina from him. After securing her body and entombing it in the catacombs of Ravenloft, Strahd sent Rahadin to punish the dusk elves. Rahadin slew the female elves so that the males couldn't breed. He also sliced off the ears of Patrina's brother, Kasimir, who had orchestrated the stoning.

**Screams of the Dead.** So dreadful a creature is Rahadin that anyone who stands within 10 feet of him can hear the howling screams of the countless men and women he has killed in his lifetime. Rahadin can't hear them, nor would he be haunted by them if he could. The only thing he cares about is Strahd von Zarovich, for whom he would gladly give his life.

## RAHADIN'S TRAITS

**Ideal.** "Loyalty is everything."

**Bond.** "I am a son of King Barov von Zarovich, and I will serve his son—my brother and lord—forever."

**Flaw.** "I have slain thousands of men. I will slaughter thousands more to preserve the von Zarovich legacy."

## RAHADIN
*Medium humanoid (elf), lawful evil*

**Armor Class** 18 (studded leather)
**Hit Points** 135 (18d8 + 54)
**Speed** 35 ft.

| STR | DEX | CON | INT | WIS | CHA |
|-----|-----|-----|-----|-----|-----|
| 14 (+2) | 22 (+6) | 17 (+3) | 15 (+2) | 16 (+3) | 18 (+4) |

**Saving Throws** Con +7, Wis +7
**Skills** Deception +8, Insight +7, Intimidation +12, Perception +11, Stealth +14
**Senses** darkvision 60 ft., passive Perception 21
**Languages** Common, Elvish
**Challenge** 10 (5,900 XP)

**Deathly Choir.** Any creature within 10 feet of Rahadin that isn't protected by a *mind blank* spell hears in its mind the screams of the thousands of people Rahadin has killed. As a bonus action, Rahadin can force all creatures that can hear the screams to make a DC 16 Wisdom saving throw. Each creature takes 16 (3d10) psychic damage on a failed save, or half as much damage on a successful one.

**Fey Ancestry.** Rahadin has advantage on saving throws against being charmed, and magic can't put him to sleep.

**Innate Spellcasting.** Rahadin's innate spellcasting ability is Intelligence. He can innately cast the following spells, requiring no components:

3/day: *misty step, phantom steed*
1/day: *magic weapon, nondetection*

**Mask of the Wild.** Rahadin can attempt to hide even when he is only lightly obscured by foliage, heavy rain, falling snow, mist, and other natural phenomena.

## ACTIONS

**Multiattack.** Rahadin attacks three times with his scimitar, or twice with his poisoned darts.

**Scimitar.** *Melee Weapon Attack:* +10 to hit, reach 5 ft., one target. *Hit:* 9 (1d6 + 6) slashing damage.

**Poisoned Dart.** *Ranged Weapon Attack:* +10 to hit, ranged 20/60 ft., one target. *Hit:* 8 (1d4 + 6) piercing damage plus 5 (2d4) poison damage.

# RICTAVIO

*Medium humanoid (human), lawful good*

**Armor Class** 12 (leather armor)
**Hit Points** 77 (14d8 + 14)
**Speed** 30 ft.

| STR | DEX | CON | INT | WIS | CHA |
|-----|-----|-----|-----|-----|-----|
| 9 (−1) | 12 (+1) | 13 (+1) | 16 (+3) | 18 (+4) | 16 (+3) |

**Saving Throws** Con +4, Wis +7
**Skills** Arcana +9, Insight +7, Medicine +7, Perception +7, Religion +6, Sleight of Hand +4
**Senses** passive Perception 17
**Languages** Abyssal, Common, Elvish, Infernal
**Challenge** 5 (1,800 XP)

**Special Equipment.** In addition to his sword cane, Rictavio wears a *hat of disguise* and a *ring of mind shielding*, and he carries a *spell scroll* of raise dead.

**Spellcasting.** Rictavio is a 9th-level spellcaster. His spellcasting ability is Wisdom (spell save DC 15, +7 to hit with spell attacks). Rictavio has the following cleric spells prepared:

Cantrips (at will): *guidance, light, mending, thaumaturgy*
1st level (4 slots): *cure wounds, detect evil and good, protection from evil and good, sanctuary*
2nd level (3 slots): *augury, lesser restoration, protection from poison*
3rd level (3 slots): *magic circle, remove curse, speak with dead*
4th level (3 slots): *death ward, freedom of movement*
5th level (1 slot): *dispel evil and good*

**Undead Slayer.** When Rictavio hits an undead with a weapon attack, the undead takes an extra 10 (3d6) damage of the weapon's type.

## ACTIONS

**Multiattack.** Rictavio makes two attacks with his sword cane.

**Sword Cane.** *Melee Weapon Attack:* +4 to hit, reach 5 ft., one target. *Hit:* 4 (1d6 + 1) bludgeoning damage (wooden cane) or piercing damage (silvered sword).

RICTAVIO

# RICTAVIO

Several months ago, a colorfully dressed half-elf bard came to Barovia in a carnival wagon, with a pet monkey on his shoulder. He took over an abandoned tower on Lake Baratok before rolling into the town of Vallaki several months later. Claiming to be a carnival ringmaster in search of new actors, he began regaling locals with tales of distant lands.

**Monster Hunter.** The half-elf ringmaster is, in fact, a legendary human vampire hunter named Rudolph van Richten. Van Richten's tale is a sad one. A scholar and doctor from a land called Darkon, he married his childhood sweetheart, Ingrid, and together they had a son, Erasmus. When he was fourteen, Erasmus was stolen away by Vistani and sold to a vampire named Baron Metus to be used as a companion. By the time van Richten found his son, it was too late: the baron had already transformed Erasmus into a vampire spawn. Erasmus begged his father to end his suffering, which van Richten

did by pounding a wooden stake through his son's chest. Baron Metus avenged that deed by killing van Richten's wife, and van Richten has lived with the horror of his family's destruction ever since. After destroying Baron Metus in turn, van Richten sought revenge against the Vistani and took up a life of hunting evil monsters.

**The Waiting Game.** Van Richten isn't a young man anymore. He knows his road is coming to an end, but his work isn't done. He has come to Barovia to kill Strahd von Zarovich, the greatest vampire of them all. Van Richten has studied Strahd for years and knows he can't hope to best the vampire in a straight-up confrontation: he must wait for the right moment to strike. He has good evidence to suggest that Strahd periodically hibernates in his coffin, sometimes for years, when all is quiet in the realm. While he bides his time, van Richten hides in plain sight with the aid of a *hat of disguise*, his thoughts protected by a *ring of mind shielding*. He is trying to learn more about the Keepers of the Feather—a society of wereravens that oppose Strahd—while trying not to expose the secret society to their mutual enemy. He thinks the wereravens might prove helpful when the time comes. Van Richten also wants to take out as many of Strahd's spies as he can, starting with evil Vistani.

**Man with a Plan.** Van Richten doesn't know that his former protégé, a good-aligned Vistana named Ezmerelda d'Avenir, has come to Barovia looking for him. He taught her many of his monster-hunting techniques, but she doesn't know all of his tricks and disguises. So far, their paths haven't crossed. In the event that van Richten becomes aware of Ezmerelda's presence, he does his utmost to protect her without putting his own plans in jeopardy. If he can manipulate a party of adventurers into keeping an eye on her, he will do so.

Van Richten works alone. A curse placed on him long ago by a Vistani seer brings doom to those he befriends. Furthermore, he believes too much is at stake to risk exposure. Consequently, if he thinks he's in danger of being unmasked, he retreats to his tower (see chapter 11) or some other quiet corner of Strahd's domain.

## RICTAVIO'S TRAITS

**Ideal.** "Evil cannot go unchallenged."
**Bond.** "To protect those I love, I must keep them distant and hidden from my enemies."
**Flaw.** "I am cursed. Thus, I will never have peace."

# Strahd von Zarovich

With his mind sharp and his heart dark, Strahd von Zarovich is a formidable foe. Courage and lives beyond measure have been lost to him. Reread chapter 1, "Into the Mists," to understand his personality and goals.

Although Strahd can be encountered almost anywhere in his domain, the vampire is always encountered in the place indicated by the card reading in chapter 1, unless he has been forced into his tomb in the catacombs of Castle Ravenloft.

## Strahd's Tactics

Because the entire adventure revolves around Strahd, you must play him intelligently and do everything you can to make him a terrifying and cunning adversary for the player characters.

When you run an encounter with Strahd, keep the following facts in mind:

- Strahd attacks at the most advantageous moment and from the most advantageous position.
- Strahd knows when he's in over his head. If he begins taking more damage than he can regenerate, he moves beyond the reach of melee combatants and spellcasters, or he flies away (using summoned wolves or swarms of bats or rats to guard his retreat).
- Strahd observes the characters to see who among them are most easily swayed, then tries to charm characters who have low Wisdom scores and use them as thralls. At the very least, he can order a charmed character to guard him against other members of the adventuring party.

## The Vampire's Minions

Whenever Strahd appears in a location other than his tomb or the place indicated by the card reading, roll a d20 and consult the Strahd's Minions table to determine what creatures he brings with him, if any.

### Strahd's Minions

| d20 | Creatures |
| --- | --- |
| 1–3 | 1d4 + 2 **dire wolves** |
| 4–6 | 1d6 + 3 **ghouls** |
| 7–9 | 1d4 + 2 **Strahd zombies** (in this appendix) |
| 10–12 | 2d4 **swarms of bats** |
| 13–15 | 1d4 + 1 **vampire spawn** |
| 16–18 | 3d6 **wolves** |
| 19–20 | None |

If the characters are in a residence, Strahd's creatures break through doors and windows to reach them, or crawl up through the earth, or swoop down the chimney. The vampire spawn (all that's left of a party of adventurers that Strahd defeated long ago) can't enter the characters' location unless invited.

## Heart of Sorrow

Strahd can afford to be bold in his tactics, for he has additional protection in the form of a giant crystal heart hidden inside Castle Ravenloft.

Any damage that Strahd takes is transferred to the Heart of Sorrow (see chapter 4, area K20). If the heart absorbs damage that reduces it to 0 hit points, it is destroyed, and Strahd takes any leftover damage. The Heart of Sorrow has 50 hit points and is restored to that number of hit points each dawn, provided it has at least 1 hit point remaining. Strahd can, as a bonus action on his turn, break his link to the Heart of Sorrow so that it no longer absorbs damage dealt to him. Strahd can reestablish his link to the Heart of Sorrow as a bonus action on his turn, but only while in Castle Ravenloft.

The effect of the protection afforded by the Heart of Sorrow can be chilling to behold, as damage to Strahd is quickly undone. For example, a critical hit might dislocate Strahd's jaw, but only for a moment; then the vampire's jaw quickly resets itself.

The ability of the Heart of Sorrow to absorb damage is suppressed if it or Strahd is fully within an *antimagic field*.

## Lair Actions

While Strahd is in Castle Ravenloft, he can take lair actions as long as he isn't incapacitated.

On initiative count 20 (losing initiative ties), Strahd can take one of the following lair action options, or forgo using any of them in that round:

- Until initiative count 20 of the next round, Strahd can pass through solid walls, doors, ceilings, and floors as if they weren't there.
- Strahd targets any number of doors and windows that he can see, causing each one to either open or close as he wishes. Closed doors can be magically locked (needing a successful DC 20 Strength check to force open) until Strahd chooses to end the effect, or until Strahd uses this lair action again.
- Strahd summons the angry spirit of one who has died in the castle. The apparition appears next to a hostile creature that Strahd can see, makes an attack against that creature, and then disappears. The apparition has the statistics of a **specter**.
- Strahd targets one Medium or smaller creature that casts a shadow. The target's shadow must be visible to Strahd and within 30 feet of him. If the target fails a DC 17 Charisma saving throw, its shadow detaches from it and becomes a **shadow** that obeys Strahd's commands, acting on initiative count 20. A *greater restoration spell* or a *remove curse* spell cast on the target restores its natural shadow, but only if its undead shadow has been destroyed.

STRAHD'S CREST

# Strahd von Zarovich

*Medium undead (shapechanger), lawful evil*

---

**Armor Class** 16 (natural armor)
**Hit Points** 144 (17d8 + 68)
**Speed** 30 ft.

---

| STR | DEX | CON | INT | WIS | CHA |
|-----|-----|-----|-----|-----|-----|
| 18 (+4) | 18 (+4) | 18 (+4) | 20 (+5) | 15 (+2) | 18 (+4) |

---

**Saving Throws** Dex +9, Wis +7, Cha +9
**Skills** Arcana +15, Perception +12, Religion +10, Stealth +14
**Damage Resistances** necrotic; bludgeoning, piercing, and slashing from nonmagical attacks
**Senses** darkvision 120 ft., passive Perception 22
**Languages** Abyssal, Common, Draconic, Elvish, Giant, Infernal
**Challenge** 15 (13,000 XP)

---

***Shapechanger.*** If Strahd isn't in running water or sunlight, he can use his action to polymorph into a Tiny bat, a Medium wolf, or a Medium cloud of mist, or back into his true form.

While in bat or wolf form, Strahd can't speak. In bat form, his walking speed is 5 feet, and he has a flying speed of 30 feet. In wolf form, his walking speed is 40 feet. His statistics, other than his size and speed, are unchanged. Anything he is wearing transforms with him, but nothing he is carrying does. He reverts to his true form if he dies.

While in mist form, Strahd can't take any actions, speak, or manipulate objects. He is weightless, has a flying speed of 20 feet, can hover, and can enter a hostile creature's space and stop there. In addition, if air can pass through a space, the mist can do so without squeezing, and he can't pass through water. He has advantage on Strength, Dexterity, and Constitution saving throws, and he is immune to all nonmagical damage, except the damage he takes from sunlight.

***Legendary Resistance (3/Day).*** If Strahd fails a saving throw, he can choose to succeed instead.

***Misty Escape.*** When Strahd drops to 0 hit points outside his coffin, he transforms into a cloud of mist (as in the Shapechanger trait) instead of falling unconscious, provided that he isn't in running water or sunlight. If he can't transform, he is destroyed.

While he has 0 hit points in mist form, he can't revert to his vampire form, and he must reach his coffin within 2 hours or be destroyed. Once in his coffin, he reverts to his vampire form. He is then paralyzed until he regains at least 1 hit point. After 1 hour in his coffin with 0 hit points, he regains 1 hit point.

***Regeneration.*** Strahd regains 20 hit points at the start of his turn if he has at least 1 hit point and isn't in running water or sunlight. If he takes radiant damage or damage from holy water, this trait doesn't function at the start of his next turn.

***Spellcasting.*** Strahd is a 9th-level spellcaster. His spellcasting ability is Intelligence (spell save DC 18, +10 to hit with spell attacks). He has the following wizard spells prepared:

Cantrips (at will): *mage hand, prestidigitation, ray of frost*
1st level (4 slots): *comprehend languages, fog cloud, sleep*
2nd level (3 slots): *detect thoughts, gust of wind, mirror image*
3rd level (3 slots): *animate dead, fireball, nondetection*
4th level (3 slots): *blight, greater invisibility, polymorph*
5th level (1 slot): *animate objects, scrying*

***Spider Climb.*** Strahd can climb difficult surfaces, including upside down on ceilings, without having to make an ability check.

***Vampire Weaknesses.*** Strahd has the following flaws:

*Forbiddance.* He can't enter a residence without an invitation from one of the occupants.

*Harmed by Running Water.* He takes 20 acid damage if he ends his turn in running water.

*Stake to the Heart.* If a piercing weapon made of wood is driven into his heart while he is incapacitated in his coffin, he is paralyzed until the stake is removed.

*Sunlight Hypersensitivity.* While in sunlight, Strahd takes 20 radiant damage at the start of his turn, and he has disadvantage on attack rolls and ability checks.

## Actions

***Multiattack (Vampire Form Only).*** Strahd makes two attacks, only one of which can be a bite attack.

***Unarmed Strike (Vampire or Wolf Form Only).*** *Melee Weapon Attack:* +9 to hit, reach 5 ft., one target. *Hit:* 8 (1d8 + 4) slashing damage plus 14 (4d6) necrotic damage. If the target is a creature, Strahd can grapple it (escape DC 18) instead of dealing the bludgeoning damage.

***Bite.*** *Melee Weapon Attack:* +9 to hit, reach 5 ft., one willing creature, or a creature that is grappled by Strahd, incapacitated, or restrained. *Hit:* 7 (1d6 + 4) piercing damage plus 10 (3d6) necrotic damage. The target's hit point maximum is reduced by an amount equal to the necrotic damage taken, and Strahd regains hit points equal to that amount. The reduction lasts until the target finishes a long rest. The target dies if its hit point maximum is reduced to 0. A humanoid slain in this way and then buried in the ground rises the following night as a vampire spawn under Strahd's control.

***Charm.*** Strahd targets one humanoid he can see within 30 feet of him. If the target can see Strahd, the target must succeed on a DC 17 Wisdom saving throw against this magic or be charmed. The charmed target regards Strahd as a trusted friend to be heeded and protected. The target isn't under Strahd's control, but it takes Strahd's requests and actions in the most favorable way and lets Strahd bite it.

Each time Strahd or his companions do anything harmful to the target, it can repeat the saving throw, ending the effect on itself on a success. Otherwise, the effect lasts 24 hours or until Strahd is destroyed, is on a different plane of existence than the target, or takes a bonus action to end the effect.

***Children of the Night (1/Day).*** Strahd magically calls 2d4 **swarms of bats** or **swarms of rats**, provided that the sun isn't up. While outdoors, Strahd can call 3d6 **wolves** instead. The called creatures arrive in 1d4 rounds, acting as allies of Strahd and obeying his spoken commands. The beasts remain for 1 hour, until Strahd dies, or until he dismisses them as a bonus action.

## Legendary Actions

Strahd can take 3 legendary actions, choosing from the options below. Only one legendary action option can be used at a time and only at the end of another creature's turn. Strahd regains spent legendary actions at the start of his turn.

**Move.** Strahd moves up to his speed without provoking opportunity attacks.

**Unarmed Strike.** Strahd makes one unarmed strike.

**Bite (Costs 2 Actions).** Strahd makes one bite attack.

# STRAHD ZOMBIE

Strahd zombies are undead that serve the vampire Strahd von Zarovich. Created from the long-dead guards of Castle Ravenloft, they were called into being through dark magic by Strahd himself.

***Loathsome Limbs.*** A Strahd zombie's gray-green flesh looks soft, and its bones seem brittle. Any good hit from a bludgeoning or slashing weapon severs part of the zombie's body. Strahd zombies are suffused with horrible necromantic magic that allows their severed body parts to continue to attack. All parts of a Strahd zombie are considered one and the same creature, so damage to any part damages the whole creature.

***Undead Nature.*** A Strahd zombie doesn't require air or sleep.

## STRAHD ZOMBIE

*Medium undead, unaligned*

**Armor Class** 8
**Hit Points** 30 (4d8 + 12)
**Speed** 20 ft.

| STR | DEX | CON | INT | WIS | CHA |
|-----|-----|-----|-----|-----|-----|
| 13 (+1) | 6 (−2) | 16 (+3) | 3 (−4) | 6 (−2) | 5 (−3) |

**Saving Throws** Wis +0
**Damage Immunities** poison
**Condition Immunities** poisoned
**Senses** darkvision 60 ft., passive Perception 8
**Languages** understands the languages it knew in life but can't speak
**Challenge** 1 (200 XP)

***Loathsome Limbs.*** Whenever the zombie takes at least 5 bludgeoning or slashing damage at one time, roll a d20 to determine what else happens to it:

**1–8:** One leg is severed from the zombie if it has any legs left.
**9–16:** One arm is severed from the zombie if it has any arms left.
**17–20:** The zombie is decapitated.

If the zombie is reduced to 0 hit points, all parts of it die. Until then, a severed part acts on the zombie's initiative and has its own action and movement. A severed part has AC 8. Any damage it takes is subtracted from the zombie's hit points.

A severed leg is unable to attack and has a speed of 5 feet.

A severed arm has a speed of 5 feet and can make one claw attack on its turn, with disadvantage on the attack roll. Each time the zombie loses an arm, it loses a claw attack.

If its head is severed, the zombie loses its bite attack and its body is blinded unless the head can see it. The severed head has a speed of 0 feet. It can make a bite attack, but only against a target in its space.

The zombie's speed is halved if it's missing a leg. If it loses both legs, it falls prone. If it has both arms, it can crawl. With only one arm, it can still crawl, but its speed is halved. With no arms or legs, its speed is 0 feet, and it can't benefit from bonuses to speed.

## ACTIONS

***Multiattack.*** The zombie makes three attacks: one with its bite and two with its claws.

***Bite.*** *Melee Weapon Attack:* +3 to hit, reach 5 ft., one target. *Hit:* 3 (1d4 + 1) piercing damage.

***Claw.*** *Melee Weapon Attack:* +3 to hit, reach 5 ft., one target. *Hit:* 4 (1d6 + 1) slashing damage.

# VLADIMIR HORNGAARD

Vladimir Horngaard joined the Order of the Silver Dragon at a young age and quickly earned the friendship of its founder, the silver dragon Argynvost. When he became a knight of the order, he traveled to distant lands to wage war against the forces of evil. The dragon stayed home and, in the guise of a human noble named Lord Argynvost, brought new initiates into the order.

***Enemies of Strahd.*** Vladimir found himself fighting Strahd's armies time and again as they swept across the land. When it became clear that Strahd couldn't be stopped, the knights of the order led hundreds of refugees to Argynvost's valley, but Strahd tracked them to their sanctuary and overwhelmed them with a vast force. Vladimir, whom Argynvost had made a field commander, couldn't hold back the evil tide and was killed, only after the heartbreak of witnessing Strahd himself slay Vladimir's beloved, his fellow knight Sir Godfrey Gwilym. With the battle won, Strahd surrounded Argynvostholt. Rather than cower in his lair, Argynvost emerged and battled Strahd's armies to the bitter end.

***Deadly Vengeance.*** Unwilling to accept his failure, Vladimir returned as a revenant. So great was his hatred of Strahd and his thirst for vengeance that those feelings fueled the spirits of many of his fellow knights—including Godfrey—to come back as revenants as well. Vladimir continued to wage the hopeless war, even as Strahd tightened his grip on the valley.

VLADIMIR HORNGAARD

When Strahd became a vampire, Vladimir and his revenants should have gone to their eternal rest. But Strahd's deeds were so heinous that Barovia and the knight's spirits became trapped behind curtains of mist.

**Blinded by Hatred.** Vladimir hates Strahd but doesn't want to see the vampire given his final rest. Vladimir wants Strahd to suffer forever for the deaths of Godfrey and Argynvost, the destruction of their order, and all the other crimes of which the vampire is guilty. Vladimir believes that all of Barovia has been swept into hell, and he wants to make sure that Strahd stays trapped in it forever. It angers Vladimir that he and his fellow knights are also trapped, but in Vladimir's mind, such is the price of keeping the vampire confined. Even his love for Godfrey is now just a dim memory shrouded by his hate.

Were Vladimir to let go of his hatred, his spirit would find peace and could remember the warmth of love. Were Strahd to be defeated, even temporarily, the mists surrounding Barovia would fade, allowing the spirits of Vladimir and his knights to enter the afterlife. Nevertheless, Vladimir would rather savor Strahd's torment than bring peace to his fallen order or peace to the land of Barovia. Gone are the days of honor and valor.

**Statistics.** Vladimir Horngaard has the statistics of a **revenant** with the following modifications:

- Vladimir's alignment is lawful evil.
- His Armor Class is 17 (half plate).
- He has 192 hit points.
- He speaks Common and Draconic.
- Vladimir wields a *+2 greatsword* with a hilt sculpted to resemble silver dragon wings and a pommel shaped like a silver dragon's head clutching a black opal between its teeth. As an action, he can make two attacks with the sword (+9 to hit). It deals 20 (4d6 + 6) slashing damage on a hit. Against Strahd, Vladimir deals an extra 14 (4d6) slashing damage with the weapon.
- Vladimir has a challenge rating of 7 (2,900 XP).

## VLADIMIR HORNGAARD'S TRAITS

**Ideal.** "Vengeance is all I have left."

**Bond.** "I have sworn oaths of allegiance to the Order of the Silver Dragon. Broken though the order may be, my allegiance never dies."

**Flaw.** "Destroying Strahd would end the vampire's torment, and that is something I will never allow."

# WERERAVEN

Wereravens are secretive and extraordinarily cautious lycanthropes that trust one another but are wary of just about everyone else. Although skilled at blending into society, they keep mostly to themselves, respect local laws, and strive to do good whenever possible.

In their human and hybrid forms, wereravens favor light weapons. They are reluctant to make bite attacks in raven form for fear of spreading their curse to those who don't deserve it or who would abuse it.

**A Kindness of Wereravens.** Wereravens refer to their tightly knit groups as kindnesses. A kindness of wereravens usually numbers between seven and twelve individuals. Not surprisingly, wereravens get along well with ravens and often hide in plain sight among them.

**Charitable Collectors.** Wereravens like to collect shiny trinkets and precious baubles. They are fond of sharing their wealth with those in need and, in their humanoid forms, modestly give money to charity. They take steps to keep magic items out of evil hands by stashing them in secret hiding places.

**Characters as Wereravens.** The *Monster Manual* has rules for characters afflicted with lycanthropy. The following text applies to wereraven characters specifically.

A character cursed with wereraven lycanthropy gains a Dexterity of 15 if his or her score isn't already higher. Attack and damage rolls for the wereraven's bite are based on whichever is higher of the character's Strength and Dexterity. The bite of a wereraven in raven form deals 1 piercing damage (no ability modifier applies to this damage) and carries the curse of lycanthropy; see the "Player Characters as Lycanthropes" sidebar in the lycanthropes entry in the *Monster Manual* for details.

---

## WERERAVEN
*Medium humanoid (human, shapechanger), lawful good*

---

**Armor Class** 12
**Hit Points** 31 (7d8)
**Speed** 30 ft. (fly 50 ft. in raven and hybrid forms)

---

| STR | DEX | CON | INT | WIS | CHA |
|-----|-----|-----|-----|-----|-----|
| 10 (+0) | 15 (+2) | 11 (+0) | 13 (+1) | 15 (+2) | 14 (+2) |

---

**Skills** Insight +4, Perception +6
**Damage Immunities** bludgeoning, piercing, and slashing from nonmagical attacks not made with silvered weapons
**Senses** passive Perception 16
**Languages** Common (can't speak in raven form)
**Challenge** 2 (450 XP)

---

**Shapechanger.** The wereraven can use its action to polymorph into a raven-humanoid hybrid or into a raven, or back into its human form. Its statistics, other than its size, are the same in each form. Any equipment it is wearing or carrying isn't transformed. It reverts to its human form if it dies.

**Mimicry.** The wereraven can mimic simple sounds it has heard, such as a person whispering, a baby crying, or an animal chittering. A creature that hears the sounds can tell they are imitations with a successful DC 10 Wisdom (Insight) check.

### ACTIONS

**Multiattack (Human or Hybrid Form Only).** The wereraven makes two weapon attacks, one of which can be with its hand crossbow.

**Beak (Raven or Hybrid Form Only).** *Melee Weapon Attack:* +4 to hit, reach 5 ft., one target. *Hit:* 1 piercing damage in raven form, or 4 (1d4 + 2) piercing damage in hybrid form. If the target is a humanoid, it must succeed on a DC 10 Constitution saving throw or be cursed with wereraven lycanthropy.

**Shortsword (Humanoid or Hybrid Form Only).** *Melee Weapon Attack:* +4 to hit, reach 5 ft., one target. *Hit:* 5 (1d6 + 2) piercing damage.

**Hand Crossbow (Humanoid or Hybrid Form Only).** *Ranged Weapon Attack:* +4 to hit, range 30/120 ft., one target. *Hit:* 5 (1d6 + 2) piercing damage.

# APPENDIX E: THE TAROKKA DECK

The Vistani have long been masters of fortune-telling. In the hands of a Vistani seer, a deck of tarokka cards can tell tales of the future and provide answers to many a dark and mysterious question.

Although the workmanship and artistic quality of the cards can vary from deck to deck, the ability of the cards to call forth information about the future is far more valuable than the monetary worth of a deck.

Anyone can craft a deck of tarokka cards, but only someone of Vistani blood can imbue the cards with the gift of prophecy. Once they are crafted and empowered, they must be stored in accordance with ancient tradition, or they lose their efficacy. When not in use, tarokka cards must be wrapped in silk and stored in a wooden box.

## COMPOSITION

A tarokka deck has fifty-four cards, each of which has its own name. Forty of them comprise the common deck, which is divided into four suits: swords, coins, stars, and glyphs.

Each suit contains cards numbered one through nine, plus a tenth card that is called the master of that suit. A card can be referred to by its suit designation or by its name. For instance, the three of glyphs is also known as the healer, and the wizard card is also known as the master of stars.

The remaining fourteen cards make up the high deck, which symbolizes the natural forces of the multiverse. These cards are represented by a crown symbol and are the most powerful cards in the deck.

## HIGH DECK

The cards that compose the high deck aren't considered to be one suit, although they are often denoted with a crown icon to mark their importance. Rather, each card is an important power in its own right. If one of these cards comes out in a casting and seems to contradict the prediction of an earlier card, the Vistani always assume that this card takes precedence.

## COMMON DECK

The four suits and their respective cards are described in more detail below.

### SWORDS

This suit symbolizes aggression and violence. It is the suit of warriors, be they paladins, soldiers, mercenaries, or gladiators. It also symbolizes the power of governments and leaders, whether noble or corrupt.

### STARS

This suit symbolizes the desire for personal power and control over things beyond the ken of mortals. It is the suit of arcane mages, sages, and intellectuals. It also represents the triumph of magic, science, and reason over religion, mysticism, and superstition.

### COINS

This suit symbolizes avarice and the desire for personal and material gain. It is also symbolic of gluttony, lust, and obsession. On the side of good, this suit can suggest the accumulation of wealth for the benefit of a charity or a just cause. On the side of evil, it embodies the worst aspects of greed. It speaks to the power of gold, and how that power can build or destroy nations.

### GLYPHS

This suit symbolizes faith, spirituality, and inner strength. It is the suit of priests and those who devote themselves to the service of a deity, a higher power, or a heightened philosophy. On the side of good, it represents willpower and dedication. On the side of evil, the suit signifies weakness of character, self-doubt, and betrayal of one's ideals or beliefs. It symbolizes health and healing, as well as illness and disease.

## HIGH DECK

| Name | Represents |
|------|-----------|
| Artifact | The importance of some physical object that must be obtained, protected, or destroyed at all costs |
| Beast | Great rage or passion; something bestial or malevolent hiding in plain sight or lurking just below the surface |
| Broken One | Defeat, failure, and despair; the loss of something or someone important, without which one feels incomplete |
| Darklord | A single, powerful individual of an evil nature, one whose goals have enormous and far-reaching consequences |
| Donjon | Isolation and imprisonment; being so conservative in thinking as to be a prisoner of one's own beliefs |
| Ghost | The looming past; the return of an old enemy or the discovery of a secret buried long ago |
| Executioner | The imminent death of one rightly or wrongly convicted of a crime; false accusations and unjust prosecution |
| Horseman | Death; disaster in the form of the loss of wealth or property, a horrible defeat, or the end of a bloodline |
| Innocent | A being of great importance whose life is in danger (who might be helpless or simply unaware of the peril) |
| Marionette | The presence of a spy or a minion of some greater power; an encounter with a puppet or an underling |
| Mists | Something unexpected or mysterious that can't be avoided; a great quest or journey that will try one's spirit |
| Raven | A hidden source of information; a fortunate turn of events; a secret potential for good |
| Seer | Inspiration and keen intellect; a future event, the outcome of which will hinge on a clever mind |
| Tempter | One who has been compromised or led astray by temptation or foolishness; one who tempts others for evil ends |

## Swords

| Card | Name | Represents |
| --- | --- | --- |
| Master of swords | Warrior | Strength and force personified; violence; those who use force to accomplish their goals |
| One of swords | Avenger | Justice and revenge for great wrongs; those on a quest to rid the world of great evil |
| Two of swords | Paladin | Just and noble warriors; those who live by a code of honor and integrity |
| Three of swords | Soldier | War and sacrifice; the stamina to endure great hardship |
| Four of swords | Mercenary | Inner strength and fortitude; those who fight for power or wealth |
| Five of swords | Myrmidon | Great heroes; a sudden reversal of fate; the triumph of the underdog over a mighty enemy |
| Six of swords | Berserker | The brutal and barbaric side of warfare; bloodlust; those with a bestial nature |
| Seven of swords | Hooded One | Bigotry, intolerance, and xenophobia; a mysterious presence or newcomer |
| Eight of swords | Dictator | All that is wrong with government and leadership; those who rule through fear and violence |
| Nine of swords | Torturer | The coming of suffering or merciless cruelty; one who is irredeemably evil or sadistic |

## Stars

| Card | Name | Represents |
| --- | --- | --- |
| Master of stars | Wizard | Mystery and riddles; the unknown; those who crave magical power and great knowledge |
| One of stars | Transmuter | A new discovery; the coming of unexpected things; unforeseen consequences and chaos |
| Two of stars | Diviner | The pursuit of knowledge tempered by wisdom; truth and honesty; sages and prophecy |
| Three of stars | Enchanter | Inner turmoil that comes from confusion, fear of failure, or false information |
| Four of stars | Abjurer | Those guided by logic and reasoning; warns of an overlooked clue or piece of information |
| Five of stars | Elementalist | The triumph of nature over civilization; natural disasters and bountiful harvests |
| Six of stars | Evoker | Magical or supernatural power that can't be controlled; magic for destructive ends |
| Seven of stars | Illusionist | Lies and deceit; grand conspiracies; secret societies; the presence of a dupe or a saboteur |
| Eight of stars | Necromancer | Unnatural events and unhealthy obsessions; those who follow a destructive path |
| Nine of stars | Conjurer | The coming of an unexpected supernatural threat; those who think of themselves as gods |

## Coins

| Card | Name | Represents |
| --- | --- | --- |
| Master of coins | Rogue | Anyone for whom money is important; those who believe money is the key to their success |
| One of coins | Swashbuckler | Those who like money yet give it up freely; likable rogues and rapscallions |
| Two of coins | Philanthropist | Charity and giving on a grand scale; those who use wealth to fight evil and sickness |
| Three of coins | Trader | Commerce; smuggling and black markets; fair and equitable trades |
| Four of coins | Merchant | A rare commodity or business opportunity; deceitful or dangerous business transactions |
| Five of coins | Guild Member | Like-minded individuals joined together in a common goal; pride in one's work |
| Six of coins | Beggar | Sudden change in economic status or fortune |
| Seven of coins | Thief | Those who steal or burgle; a loss of property, beauty, innocence, friendship, or reputation |
| Eight of coins | Tax Collector | Corruption; honesty in an otherwise corrupt government or organization |
| Nine of coins | Miser | Hoarded wealth; those who are irreversibly unhappy or who think money is meaningless |

## Glyphs

| Card | Name | Represents |
| --- | --- | --- |
| Master of glyphs | Priest | Enlightenment; those who follow a deity, a system of values, or a higher purpose |
| One of glyphs | Monk | Serenity; inner strength and self-reliance; supreme confidence bereft of arrogance |
| Two of glyphs | Missionary | Those who spread wisdom and faith to others; warnings of the spread of fear and ignorance |
| Three of glyphs | Healer | Healing; a contagious illness, disease, or curse; those who practice the healing arts |
| Four of glyphs | Shepherd | Those who protect others; one who bears a burden far too great to be shouldered alone |
| Five of glyphs | Druid | The ambivalence and cruelty of nature and those who feel drawn to it; inner turmoil |
| Six of glyphs | Anarchist | A fundamental change brought on by one whose beliefs are being put to the test |
| Seven of glyphs | Charlatan | Liars; those who profess to believe one thing but actually believe another |
| Eight of glyphs | Bishop | Strict adherence to a code or a belief; those who plot, plan, and scheme |
| Nine of glyphs | Traitor | Betrayal by someone close and trusted; a weakening or loss of faith |

| ARTIFACT | BEAST | BROKEN ONE |
|---|---|---|
| 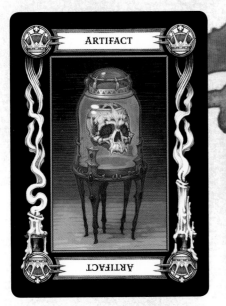 |  |  |
| ARTIFACT | BEAST | BROKEN ONE |

| DARKLORD | DONJON | GHOST |
|---|---|---|
|  |  |  |
| DARKLORD | DONJON | GHOST |

| EXECUTIONER | HORSEMAN | INNOCENT |
|---|---|---|
|  |  |  |
| EXECUTIONER | HORSEMAN | INNOCENT |

MARIONETTE

MISTS

RAVEN

SEER

TEMPTER

WARRIOR

1 AVENGER

2 PALADIN

3 SOLDIER

**4 · MERCENARY**

**5 · MYRMIDON**

**6 · BERSERKER**

**7 · HOODED ONE**

**8 · DICTATOR**

**9 · TORTURER**

**WIZARD**

**1 · TRANSMUTER**

**2 · DIVINER**

**3** ENCHANTER

**4** ABJURER

**5** ELEMENTALIST

**6** EVOKER

**7** ILLUSIONIST

**8** NECROMANCER

**9** CONJURER

ROGUE

**1** SWASHBUCKLER

2 PHILANTHROPIST

3 TRADER

4 MERCHANT

5 GUILD MEMBER

6 BEGGAR

7 THIEF

8 TAX COLLECTOR

9 MISER

PRIEST

APPENDIX E | THE TAROKKA DECK

# Appendix F: Handouts

## Kolyan Indirovich's Letter (Version 1)

Hail to thee of might and valor.

I, a lowly servant of Barovia, send honor to thee. We plead for thy so desperately needed assistance.

The love of my life, Ireena Kolyana, has been afflicted by an evil so deadly that even the good people of our village cannot protect her. She languishes from her wound, and I would have her saved from this menace.

There is much wealth in this community. I offer all that might be had to thee and thy fellows if thou shalt but answer my desperate plea.

Come quickly, for her time is at hand! All that I have shall be thine!

Kolyan Indirovich
Burgomaster

## Strahd's Invitation

My friends,

Know that it is I who have brought you to this land, my home, and know that I alone can release you from it. I bid you dine at my castle so that we can meet in civilized surroundings. Your passage here will be a safe one. I await your arrival.

Your host,
Strahd von Zarovich

I am the Ancient. I am the Land. My beginnings are lost in the darkness of the past. I was the warrior, I was good and just. I thundered across the land like the wrath of a just god, but the war years and the killing years wore down my soul as the wind wears stone into sand.

All goodness slipped from my life. I found my youth and strength gone, and all I had left was death. My army settled in the valley of Barovia and took power over the people in the name of a just god, but with none of a god's grace or justice.

I called for my family, long unseated from their ancient thrones, and brought them here to settle in the castle Ravenloft. They came with a younger brother of mine, Sergei. He was handsome and youthful. I hated him for both.

From the families of the valley, one spirit shone above all others. A rare beauty, who was called "perfection," "joy," and "treasure." Her name was Tatyana, and I longed for her to be mine.

I loved her with all my heart. I loved her for her youth. I loved her for her joy. But she spurned me! "Old One" was my name to her—"elder" and "brother" also. Her heart went to Sergei. They were betrothed. The date was set.

With words she called me "brother," but when I looked into her eyes they reflected another name: "death." It was the death of the aged that she saw in me. She loved her youth and enjoyed it. But I had squandered mine.

The death she saw in me turned her from me. And so I came to hate death—my death. My hate is very strong. I would not be called "death" so soon. I made a pact with death, a pact of blood. On the day of the wedding, I killed Sergei, my brother. My pact was sealed with his blood.

I found Tatyana weeping in the garden east of the chapel. She fled from me. She would not let me explain, and a great anger swelled within me. She had to understand the pact I made for her. I pursued her. finally, in despair, she flung herself from the walls of Ravenloft, and I watched everything I ever wanted fall from my grasp forever.

It was a thousand feet through the mists. No trace of her was ever found. Not even I know her final fate.

Arrows from the castle guards pierced me to my soul, but I did not die. Nor did I live. I became undead, forever.

I have studied much since then. "Vampyr" is my new name. I still lust for life and youth, and I curse the living that took them from me. Even the sun is against me. It is the sun and it's light I fear the most, but little else can harm me now. Even a stake through my heart does not kill me, though it holds me from movement. But the sword, that cursed sword that Sergei brought! I must dispose of that awful tool! I fear and hate it as much as the sun.

I have often hunted for Tatyana. I have even felt her within my grasp, but she escapes. She taunts me! She taunts me! What will it take to bend her love to me?

I now reside far below Ravenloft. I live among the dead and sleep beneath the very stones of this hollow castle of despair. I shall seal shut the walls of the stairs that none may disturb me.

For more than three decades now, I have undertaken to investigate and expose creatures of darkness to the purifying light of truth and knowledge. "Hero" I am named in some circles; "sage" and "master hunter" I am called in others. That I have survived countless supernatural assaults is seen as a marvel among my peers; my name is spoken with fear and loathing among my foes.

In truth, this "virtuous" calling began as an obsessive effort to destroy a vampire that murdered my child, and it has become for me a tedious and bleak career. Even as my life of hunting monsters began, I felt the weight of time on my weary shoulders. Today I am a man who has simply lived too long. Like a regretful lich, I find myself inexorably bound to an existence I sought out of madness and, seemingly, must now endure for all eternity. Of course I shall die, but whether I shall ever rest in my grave haunts my idle thoughts, and torments me in my dreams.

I expect that those who think me a hero will change their minds when they know the whole truth about my life as a hunter of the unnatural. Nevertheless, I must reveal, here and now, that I have been the indirect yet certain cause of many deaths, and the loss of many good friends. Mistake me not! I do not merely feel sorry for myself. Rather, I come to grips with a devastating realization: I now see that I am the object of a baleful Vistani curse. More tragically, the nature of this hex is such that I have not borne the brunt of it; instead, far worse, those who surround me have fallen victim to it!

I have related the tragic story of how my only child Erasmus was taken by Vistani and sold to a vampire. I explained how Erasmus was made a minion of the night stalker, and how it was my miserable part to free him from that fate at the point of a stake. What I have neglected to illuminate before is how I tracked Erasmus's kidnappers across the land, or how I "extracted" Erasmus's whereabouts from them.

In fact, the Vistani took Erasmus with my own, unwitting permission. They had brought an extremely ill member of their tribe to me one evening and insisted that I treat him, but I was unable to save the young man's life. In fear of their retribution, I begged the Vistani to take anything of mine if only they would withhold their terrifying powers, of which I knew nothing. To my lasting astonishment, they chose to surreptitiously take my son in exchange for their loss! By the time I realized what had occurred, they were already an hour gone.

Incensed beyond reason, I strapped the body of the dead young man to my horse and doggedly followed the Vistani caravan through the woods, naively allowing the sun to set before me without seeking shelter from the night. Shortly after darkness fell, I was beset by undead that would have slain me, had not their master—a lich—intervened and spared my life, for reasons that I do not completely understand. He somehow detected me and, with his powerful magic, took control of a pack of zombies that wandered in the forest. He spoke to me through the mouths of the dead things and placed a magic ward against undead on me, then animated the dead Vistana and bade it tell me where I could find its people. Unfortunately (I say in hindsight), the plan worked. I found the child-stealers, and my unwelcome entourage included a growing horde of voracious undead that could not touch me, thanks to the lich's ward.

When I found the caravan, I threatened to set the zombies on the Vistani unless they returned my dear boy. They replied that he had been sold to the vampire, Baron Metus. Something inside me snapped. I released the zombies, and the entire tribe was eaten alive.

Yet the story has not ended. Before she died, the leader cursed me, saying, "Live you always among monsters, and see everyone you love die beneath their claws!" Even now, so many years later, I can hear her words with painful clarity. A short time later, I found my dear Erasmus made into a vampire. He begged me to end his curse, which I did with a heavy heart. The darkness had torn him from my loving arms forever, and I foolishly believed that the curse had exacted its deadly toll. I wept until an insatiate desire for vengeance filled the bottomless rift in my heart.

# Kolyan Indirovich's Letter (Version 2)

Hail thee of might and valor:

I, the Burgomaster of Barovia, send you honor—with despair.

My adopted daughter, the fair Ireena Kolyana, has been these past nights bitten by a vampyr. For over four hundred years, this creature has drained the life blood of my people. Now, my dear Ireena languishes and dies from an unholy wound caused by this vile beast. He has become too powerful to conquer.

So I say to you, give us up for dead and encircle this land with the symbols of good. Let holy men call upon their power that the devil may be contained within the walls of weeping Barovia. Leave our sorrows to our graves, and save the world from this evil fate of ours.

There is much wealth entrapped in this community. Return for your reward after we are all departed for a better life.

Kolyan Indirovich
Burgomaster

# Journal of Argynvost

My knights have fallen, and this land is lost. The armies of my enemy will not be stopped by sword or spell, claw or fang. Today I will die, not avenging those who have fallen, but defending that which I love—this valley, this home, and the ideals of the Order of the Silver Dragon.

The evil surrounds me. The time has come to throw off this guise and show these heathens my true fearsome form. Let it spark terror in their hearts! Let them tell their stories of dark triumph against the protector of the Balinok Mountains! Let Argynvost be remembered as a dragon of honor and valor. My one regret is that my remains will not lie in their rightful place, in the hallowed mausoleum of Argynvostholt. No doubt my bones will be scattered among my enemies like the coins of a plundered hoard, trophies of a hard-won victory.

I do not fear death. Though my body will die, my spirit will live on. Let it serve as a beacon of light against the darkness. Let it bring hope to a land wrought with despair.

Now, to battle!

A